DONNE'S *ANNIVERSARIES* AND THE
POETRY OF PRAISE

Donne's
Anniversaries

AND THE POETRY OF PRAISE

THE CREATION

OF A SYMBOLIC MODE

BARBARA KIEFER LEWALSKI

PRINCETON UNIVERSITY
PRESS

For Ken and David

THE starting-point for this book was the experience of teaching the *Anniversary* poems in several graduate seminars, and the sense most of us had that these poems have not yielded very fully to the customary approaches. Another stimulus has been my long-term concern with various aspects of "Biblical Poetics"—the ways in which sixteenth- and seventeenth-century Protestant theory regarding the literary elements of scripture (genre, figurative language, symbolic mode) affected contemporary English poetry and poetics, especially religious poetry. Once under way, however, the book took on a scope larger than that of the *Anniversary* poems and only partly intersecting with the central issues of Biblical Poetics: its subject came to be the development of a special symbolic mode in seventeenth-century poetry of praise and compliment—a mode in large measure created by Donne's occasional poems of compliment and especially the *Anniversaries*. This book attempts to identify and analyze some of the traditions and habits of thought in sixteenth- and seventeenth-century epideixis, in Protestant meditation, in biblical hermeneutics, in funeral sermons (and especially in Donne's own practice of these arts) which gave rise to the *Anniversary* poems and their distinctive symbolic mode.

Throughout the several stages of its making, this study has received invaluable assistance from more sources than I can now mention or perhaps even remember—not least among them the seminal scholarship of H.J.C. Grierson, Helen Gardner, Wesley Milgate, Frank Manley, R. C. Bald, E. R. Curtius, Louis Martz, and O. B. Hardison. From colleagues and friends I have had the kind of generous, unstinting help that reaffirms one's sometimes faltering belief in the community of scholars. Some portions of this study were first presented as lectures at the Central Renaissance Conference in Boulder, Colorado, and at the Brown Renaissance Colloquium; the final formulation has benefited greatly from the penetrating questions and comments of participants in these conferences as well as other colleagues near and far—Andrew Sabol, John Major, John Murphy, Arthur Kinney, Sacvan Bercovitch, Katherine Van Eerde, Jane Ruby, and Harold Fisch. Former and present graduate students working in related areas have also helped by perceptive questions and a lively interchange of ideas, especially Winfried Schleiner, Steven Zwicker, James Scanlon, Yvonne Sandströem, Helen Marlborough, Jeannie Duffy, and Elizabeth Jefferis. My deepest thanks, together with apologies for the faults which still remain after all their efforts, go to several friends who read and criticized all or part of the manuscript. Sears Jayne and Irene Samuel raised important substantive issues and made helpful stylistic suggestions. Edward Cranz brought his prodigious learning in the classics, in medieval and reformation theology, and in theories of allegoresis to bear upon the complex problems of chapters four and five. Earl Miner, from the vantage point of his own impressive overview of Metaphysical and Cavalier poetry, forced me to draw out the specific literary significance of several of the arguments developed here. Above all I am indebted to Rosalie Colie who cannot now receive these thanks for the priceless boon of our stimulating discussions of these matters during three rich years of colleagueship at Brown, as well as for her incisive and judicious comments as the writing progressed.

The basic research for this study was made possible by a Guggenheim Fellowship in 1967-1968, supplemented by summer research grants from Brown University in 1968 and 1970, and a summer fellowship grant from the Henry E. Huntington Library in 1971. For their skillful and cheerful assistance with research materials I am grateful to the library staffs of the British Museum, the Bodleian, the Bibliothèque Nationale, the Houghton Library of Harvard University, the Huntington Library, and the Rockefeller and John Hay Libraries of Brown University. I am indebted also to the University of California Press for permission to include in chapter two of this study the substance of an article first published in a collection of critical essays edited by Earl Miner, *Seventeenth-Century Imagery* (Berkeley and Los Angeles, 1971). In addition, this book has been fortunate far beyond the usual hap in its interested and highly knowledgeable editors, George Robinson and Mrs. Arthur Sherwood of Princeton University Press. Leslie Fetner typed the manuscript with intelligent care.

This book is dedicated to my husband and my young son, who have assisted its making by their (respective) knowledge and forbearance—but chiefly by their gift to its author of a secular version of that "essentiall Joye" which Donne writes about in the *Anniversaries*.

Barbara Kiefer Lewalski
Brown University

TABLE OF CONTENTS

DONNE'S *ANNIVERSARIES* AND THE
POETRY OF PRAISE

D ONNE'S TWO *Anniversaries*, panegyrical and elegiac poems written to commemorate the death of a fifteen-year-old girl, Elizabeth Drury, are at once the longest and most ambitious poems Donne wrote, as well as being among the very few poems he published during his lifetime. *The First Anniversarie* appeared in 1611, with the title, *"An Anatomy of the World. Wherein, By Occasion of the untimely death of Mistris Elizabeth Drury the frailty and the decay of this whole world is represented."* In 1612 this work was reprinted, together with a companion poem entitled, *"The Second Anniversarie. Of the Progres of the Soule. Wherein: By Occasion of the Religious Death of Mistris Elizabeth Drury, the incommodities of the Soule in this life and her exaltation in the next, are Contemplated."* These poems have fascinated and irritated generations of readers, with their powerful vision of cosmic and microcosmic disintegration and wretchedness, their *sui generis* conflation of *contemptus mundi* meditations with epideictic praise, their extravagantly hyperbolic language. In particular, from Donne's time to our own, critical controversy has raged over the apparent disparity between the ostensible object of the hyperbolic praise, an insignificant young girl whom Donne admittedly knew only by report as the daughter of an acquaintance and patron-to-be, Sir Robert Drury, and the profound religious meanings and significances of which the girl is made, in some way, a symbol. The predominant critical attitude was established early by Ben Jonson who pronounced *The First Anniversarie* "profane and full of Blasphemies," and said that "he told Mr. Donne, if it had been written of ye Virgin Marie it had been something." To which Donne reportedly answered, "that he described the Idea of a Woman, not as she was."[1]

[1] "Conversations with Drummond of Hawthornden," *Ben Jonson*, ed. C. H. Herford and Percy and Evelyn Simpson, xi vols. (Oxford, 1925-1952), I, 133.

The difficulty of ascertaining how the link is forged between Elizabeth Drury and the profound meanings indicated in the titles is intensified by the pervasive Christian theological language of the poems, which seems to guarantee the validity and sincerity of the extravagant figures. As William Empson noted, the *Anniversaries* seem to make the girl a kind of Logos-figure.[2] The *Anatomy* affirms that she is the vital principle, or the essential creative principle of the world itself: the speaker undertakes to teach the world that "thou [the world] wast/ Nothing but she" (ll. 31-32); that "Her name defin'd thee, gave thee forme and frame" (l. 37); that she was "Thy'ntrinsique Balme, and thy preservative" (l. 57); that the ancients "who thought soules made/ Of Harmony" would have concluded "That Harmony was shee, and thence infer,/ That soules were but Resultances from her,/ And did from her into our bodies go" (ll. 311-316); that her death caused the decay and death of the world, and that her very ghost is capable of creating a "new" world (ll. 70-78). Also, the *Anatomy* declares her to be the source of whatever was of worth or value in the world: she had "all Magnetique force alone,/ To draw, and fasten sundred parts in one" (ll. 221-222); she was an "unvext Paradise" (l. 363), and the "first originall/ Of all faire copies" (ll. 227-228). The *Progres* continues this language: she was "both this lower worlds, and the Sunnes Sunne,/ The Lustre, and the vigor of this All" (ll. 4-5); and she was "the forme, that made it [the world] live" (l. 72). If the poems are to be taken seriously—and their tone testifies that they are—then the "shee" whose death brought the world to its moribund condition must be a cause adequate to the impressive effects described. And unless Donne is utterly irresponsible and sycophantic, the connection between Elizabeth Drury and the complex of meanings pointed to by the lady of the poems must be more than simply arbitrary. In fact, these remarkable poems

[2] William Empson, *Some Versions of Pastoral* (New York, 1935), p. 84.

transform conventional praise into a symbolic mode: how they do so, what ideas and materials they draw upon in the process, and how they influence subsequent poems of praise are questions central to this study.

Poems such as these, which are by definition occasional poems, and problems such as these, which concern the meaning of poetic symbols, the appropriateness of language to subject, and the poetic portrayal of the conditions of human life, cannot be approached exclusively in terms of formal literary analysis: we are obliged to seek the proper literary and intellectual contexts to illuminate them. But more than this, we have to recognize the important role played by writers like Donne in defining and reshaping contemporary formulas. This book is concerned therefore not only with discovering contexts for and influences upon the *Anniversary* poems, but also with the effect of those poems—as well as of other portions of Donne's writing in related kinds —upon contemporary developments in poetry and upon the literature of English Protestantism. The argument looks in two directions—Janus-like, though I hope not schizophrenically. It endeavors to show how Donne responds to, and how he promotes, certain literary and intellectual trends, recognizing the *Anniversary* poems as a focus for this interaction.

The basic problems of symbol and language in the *Anniversary* poems must be addressed in more fundamental terms than those afforded by specific genres such as funeral elegy, verse epistle, and the like: the generic conventions relevant to these questions pertain to the broad category of occasional poetry of praise. Therefore this study begins with a survey of theoretical formulations about rhetorical and poetic praise and of characteristic poems of praise and compliment written by Donne's immediate predecessors and contemporaries, so as to identify the generic données he inherited and the new directions he marks out in the *Anniversaries*. An examination of Donne's own Epicedes and Obsequies and Verse Letters follows, since this puzzling and seldom studied body of poetry is closely related to the *Anniversary* poems and poses many of the same problems. The unique Donnean emphases evident in this entire range of poetry afford an insight into the assumptions which lie behind his creation of poetic praise. These assumptions themselves ask clarification through investigation of certain theological conceptions and materials.

The literature of contemporary English Protestantism constitutes a second large body of concepts and materials at once influential for the *Anniversary* poems and itself influenced by Donne's works. The proposition that many of Donne's writings, in particular the theologically grounded *Anniversary* poems, might profitably be studied in relation to the contemporary Protestant movement with which he was so directly concerned seems a likely hypothesis, but the almost exclusive scholarly emphasis upon Donne's Roman Catholic alignments, together with an uncritical acceptance of the idea that Protestantism is inherently anti-literary, has kept the obvious from being seriously attempted. My investigation reveals, for one thing, an emerging Protestant meditative tradition whose assumptions and method diverge markedly from the Ignatian and other Counter-Reformation meditative works often assumed to be Donne's poetic models; this material has relevance for the *Anniversary* poems and, in the other direction, Donne's sermons and *Devotions upon Emergent Occasions* were themselves important to the theory and method of English Protestant meditation. In another area, a study of the various ramifications of the Protestant theology of man as image of God, and also of the extensive discussions about figurative language, allegory, and typological symbolism in Protestant biblical commentary and other such materials, mines an important source of contemporary attitudes about poetic language and symbolic meaning which illuminate the symbolic method of the *Anniversaries*. Donne himself contributed impressively to this developing Protestant poetics through many comments in his Sermons and *Devotions* about the poetic dimension of scripture. In yet another vein, a study of contemporary Protestant funeral sermons identifies thematic and structural elements as well as specific *topoi* which are important for the *Anniversaries* as funeral and memorial celebrations, even as, conversely, Donne's own funeral sermons proved to be among the most remarkable and innovative works in that kind.

My reading of the *Anniversary* poems does not pretend to be exhaustive. It recognizes them as complex, mixed-genre works which weld together formal, thematic, and structural elements from various sources—the occasional poem of praise, the funeral elegy, the funeral sermon, the hymn, the anatomy, the Protestant meditation, to mention only the most important. In bringing these various materials to bear upon the *Anniversaries*, I have concentrated upon theme and structure, in an effort to demonstrate the poems' coherent symbolic meaning and method as well as their careful logical articulation, both as individual poems and as companion-pieces. As a result of this focus the pyrotechnics of wit and language-play in these brilliant works may receive somewhat short shrift, not from any denial of their importance, but only because of my emphasis upon a perhaps more significant though seldom explored aspect of these poems—the profound metaphysical basis in them for the pyrotechnics.

In using the vexed term "metaphysical" my intention is not to produce yet another definition of metaphysical poetry, or even of Donnean metaphysical poetry considered as a whole. Yet these investigations of Donne's theological speculations about the nature of man as well as about figurative language and symbolic meaning may give some specificity to that much misused term. Though Donne does not write as a systematic philosopher, the appropriateness of designating him a metaphysical poet is not simply a matter of style or of his penchant for the conceit. With regard to the *Anniversary* poems, that name properly signifies Donne's attempt to explore with thoroughness and precision, albeit through the poetic means of figure and symbol, the essence of man's nature and the conditions of human life. Louis Martz's proposed substitution of the category of "meditative" poetry for that of "metaphysical" poetry does less than justice to the prominence of these concerns. The final segment of this study traces the influence of Donne's symbolic conceptions and innovative poetic strategies upon the development of a "metaphysical" strain in seventeenth-century poetry of praise, the most remarkable of such creations in the Donnean symbolic mode being Marvell's *Upon Appleton House*.

The approaches here suggested should have important implications for Donne's divine poems, as well as for the religious lyrics of other so-called metaphysical poets of the period—but that is matter for another study.

PART I

LITERARY CONTEXTS AND
DONNEAN INNOVATIONS

CHAPTER I

Contemporary Epideictic Poetry:
The Speaker's Stance and the
Topoi of Praise

Although their oddity and complexity make Donne's *Anniversaries* appear to be *sui generis*, a large number of generic alignments have been proposed for one or both of them: funeral elegy, epideictic lyric, Menippean satire, Ignatian meditation, epistomological poetry, medieval complaint, hymn.[1] This startling diversity of opinion as to the poems' kind gives much force to Rosalie Colie's view of them as impressive examples of *genera mixta*, creating a new coherence out of the elements of several generic traditions.[2] Nonetheless, it seems evident that the poems are in some basic sense epideictic or panegyric works; at all events this is the element in the mixture which has caused difficulties for readers and critics from Donne's time to our own.

Considered as epideictic works, the most obvious generic classification for these poems is the funeral elegy. George Williamson has placed them in the broad category of

[1] See, e.g., O. B. Hardison, Jr., *The Enduring Monument: A Study of the Idea of Praise in Renaissance Literary Theory and Practice* (Chapel Hill, N.C., 1962); Northrop Frye, *Anatomy of Criticism* (Princeton, 1969), pp. 298, 308-314; Louis L. Martz, *The Poetry of Meditation*, rev. ed. (New Haven, 1962), pp. 211-248; Rosalie Colie, *Paradoxia Epidemica* (Princeton, 1969), pp. 396-429; John Peter, *Complaint and Satire in Early English Literature* (Oxford, 1956), esp. pp. 60-80; Dennis Quinn, "Donne's *Anniversaries* as Celebration," *Studies in English Literature*, 9 (1969), 97-105.

[2] Rosalie Colie, "'All in Peeces:' Problems of Interpretation in Donne's *Anniversary Poems*," in *Just So Much Honor*, ed. Amadeus P. Fiore (University Park, Pa., 1971).

praises for the dead, which includes the classical *epicedium*, the funeral oration, and the Christian funeral sermon.[3] Refining upon this classification in his masterful account of the centrality of praise in poetic theory from antiquity through the Renaissance, O. B. Hardison identifies the *First Anniversarie* with the typical funeral elegy, which is composed of praise, lament, and consolation, and the *Second Anniversarie* with the so-called anniversary poem, which according to Scaliger differs from funeral elegy chiefly in omitting the lament: "no one continues to lament a man who has been dead for one or two years."[4] On the basis of these identifications, Hardison explains the constituent elements of Donne's poems by reference to conventions and common tropes in the funeral elegy: e.g., he reads the lengthy passages about the decay of the world as a version of the conventional "nature reversed" trope, which the elegist often employs in lamenting that for him the world and all its good is dead.[5] Moreover, because of their exaggerated language of compliment and their idealization of a woman, the *Anniversary* poems are often related to the Petrarchan tradition. Seeking to define that relationship precisely, Hardison suggests that the poems' closest generic affinity is with Petrarchan elegy, whose conventions were established by the second part of the *Canzoniere*, written after Laura's death. Those conventions were: the poet-lover's focus upon the lady's soul as the subject of his praise; his attempt to understand her soul's pure spiritual essence as image both of the Platonic idea of virtue and of the Christian divine; and his gradual progress in spiritual understanding as he comes to perceive the lady's death to be both cause and symbol of his own mystic death to the

---

[3] George Williamson, "The Design of Donne's *Anniversaries*," *MP*, 60 (1963), 183-191, reprinted in *Milton and Others* (London, 1965), pp. 150-164.

[4] Hardison, *Enduring Monument*, p. 163.

[5] *Ibid.*, pp. 170-176.

world.[6] Obviously, these conventions have relevance for Donne's poems.

Yet recognition of the poems' likeness to these generic kinds has not helped greatly with those matters which have caused the greatest difficulties for readers of the *Anniversaries* and which have aroused the most intense furor from critics—the extravagance of the hyperbole, and the apparently inexplicable symbolic weight attaching to the dead girl. For neither the conventional funeral elegy nor Petrarch's *Canzoniere* seem to provide a basis for the kind of praise Donne's speaker accords Elizabeth Drury. Williamson, who takes the subjects of the poems to be, respectively, the consequences of original sin and the potential destiny of the soul, can explain Elizabeth only as a blank counter arbitrarily made a synonym for the world—a "personification of virtue" in relation to the microcosm, and the "form or soul of the world" in relation to the macrocosm. It is not clear on what grounds she personifies or points to these meanings, or whether Williamson intends to adduce a serious flaw when he observes that the "ideological connections between Elizabeth Drury and both of these worlds turn into extreme hyperbole on the elegiac side of the poems."[7] On the other hand, Hardison's view that Elizabeth Drury herself is the subject of the *Anniversary* poems[8] leaves out of account the subject matter pointed to in both titles (*The Anatomy of the World, The Progres of the Soul*), and the testimony of both subtitles that Elizabeth Drury is "occasion" rather than subject—the problem being how and why extravagant praises of Elizabeth Drury should be linked to these weighty subjects. Moreover, the assimilation of the *Anniversaries* to Petrarchan elegy ignores the all-important matter of the speaker's stance. In Petrarch the dramatic situation of the speaker as lover qualifies the hyperbole: it is

[6] *Ibid.*, pp. 142-155, 166-186.
[7] Williamson, "The Design of Donne's *Anniversaries*," p. 158.
[8] Hardison, *Enduring Monument*, pp. 167-168.

the speaker's world (not the real world) that has been de-
stroyed by Laura's death; it is to and for him that she is a
donna angelicata, a sun, a phoenix, a miracle, the cause and
symbol of spiritual transformation, the image of the divine.
Donne adopts such a Petrarchan stance in *Twickenham
Garden*, where the speaker is a lamenting lover whose
world is blasted by the death of his lady, but in the *Anni-
versaries* the speaker is not a lover: he professes to speak
of the real world and for us all.[9] Hardison finds "disappoint-
ing" Donne's failure to advance from Elizabeth Drury to a
more adequate image of the Divine or to the vision of God
as Petrarch (and Dante) do,[10] but this very difference sug-
gests that the Petrarchan reading of the *Anniversary* poems
somehow misses their essence.

It seems important then to seek other literary contexts
which may illuminate Donne's conception of poetic praise.
An obvious starting point is the theory and practice of oc-
casional epideictic poetry in England during the period
contemporaneous with Donne's *Anniversaries* and his other
poems of compliment—i.e., 1595-1616.[11] Such an investiga-
tion may highlight what is commonplace and what is unique
about the *Anniversary* poems, what traditional assumptions
and poetic conventions they call upon, and what strikingly
new directions they define.

[9] Hardison argues that the "world" referred to is only the "world"
of her acquaintance, that the speaker only seems to complain of the
real decay of the world because the expected eulogy-lament se-
quence is reversed in Donne's poem. But this seems tenuous—an effort
to find the expected generic traits operative in poems which seem
concerned instead to modify them profoundly. The point is dis-
cussed in detail in chap. 7 below.

[10] Hardison, *Enduring Monument*, p. 185.

[11] This period is bounded by the publication date of *Astrophel*
(1595), the collection of elegies for Sir Philip Sidney, and the pub-
lication date of Ben Jonson's folio (1616), which includes numerous
poems of compliment addressed to a variety of persons and occasions.
Jonson's collections entitled *Epigrammes* and *The Forrest*, included in
the folio, were in fact completed by 1613.

Some norms deriving from Renaissance rhetorical theory and from contemporary funeral elegies, especially those for Queen Elizabeth and Prince Henry, may be briefly summarized, for these materials have been studied extensively by O. B. Hardison, E. C. Wilson, Marjorie Hope Nicolson, Ruth Wallerstein, and several others.[12] For the purposes of the present study, special attention must be given to poetic praises addressed to members of the nobility and gentry—often to individuals whom Donne also praised—for we need to know how such poems customarily differed from the praises of princes. My primary focus here is upon those elements in Renaissance epideictic theory and practice which bear directly upon the problems critics have had with the *Anniversaries*. Such elements are: the stance the speaker takes toward his subject (which is not of course to be equated with the actual relationship obtaining between the poet and the person praised), and the image which the poem projects of the person praised—a matter which can be approached with some rigor through an examination of the basic *topoi* of praise out of which specific tropes and images are developed. The fundamental question is, does Donne depart radically in the *Anniversary* poems from the conventions of praise acceptable in his own age, and, if so, in what particular areas and to what effect.

A. Some Norms for Renaissance Praise and Compliment

Occasional poems of compliment in the Renaissance are based upon classical and Renaissance rhetorical theory. From Aristotle onward it had been customary to distinguish

---

[12] See Hardison, *Enduring Monument*; Elkin Calhoun Wilson, *England's Eliza* (Cambridge, Mass., 1939); Wilson, *Prince Henry and English Literature* (Ithaca, New York, 1946); Nicolson, *The Breaking of the Circle*, rev. ed. (New York, 1960), pp. 81-122. Some important theoretical and stylistic aspects of the Prince Henry elegies have been examined by Ruth Wallerstein in *Studies in Seventeenth-Century Poetic* (Madison, Wis., 1965).

three principal kinds of oratory—judicial (argument in the law courts), deliberative (the oratory of political assemblies), and demonstrative or epideictic (the oratory of ceremonial occasions such as patriotic festivals, commemorations, funerals, and the like) where the purpose is praise or blame. Theoretical precepts concerning poems of praise and compliment were derived from treatises on and examples of demonstrative rhetoric, and also from reading classical hymns to the gods and heroes in the light of the formulas for demonstrative rhetoric.[13]

From Plato onward there was common agreement that the proper object of praise is virtue, and that praise of virtue serves a didactic purpose—to delineate outstanding moral qualities and to inspire the hearer to emulate them.[14] The seminal discussion of the sources and methods of praise occurs in Aristotle's *Rhetoric* (I.ix); later, the various topics of praise were codified by Menander and the author of the *Ad Herennium*[15] as the goods of nature, fortune, and character. Almost all Renaissance theorists agreed with Cicero and Quintilian that the goods of nature or fortune are not properly objects of praise in themselves, but should be treated chiefly as means of displaying the subject's virtue in using them rightly.[16] Moreover, the speaker's stance or

[13] See Donald Lemen Clark, *Rhetoric and Poetic in the Renaissance* (New York, 1922), pp. 131-161. Among the chief theorists who adapted rhetorical theory to poetry are Scaliger, Minturno, and Puttenham.

[14] Plato, *Republic* III.386-392, ed. Paul Shorey, 2 vols. (Loeb, London, 1930), I, 201-225; Julius-Caesar Scaliger, *Poetices libri septem* ([Heidelberg], 1581), p. 408. See Hardison, *Enduring Monument*, pp. 26-27.

[15] In *The Basic Works of Aristotle*, ed. Richard McKeon (New York, 1941), p. 1357. Cf. Hardison, *Enduring Monument*, p. 30.

[16] Cicero, *De Oratore* II.lxxxiv.342, ed. H. Rackham, 2 vols. (Loeb, London, 1942), I, 459; Quintilian, *Institutes of Oratory* III.vii.12-15, trans. H. E. Butler (Loeb, London, 1907), I, 469-471. Cf. Thomas Wilson, *The Arte of Rhetorique* (1553), facsim. ed. by Robert H. Bowers (Gainesville, Fla., 1962), pp. 24-30. See Hardison, *Enduring Monument*, pp. 24-58.

16

self-characterization was understood to affect significantly the credibility of his praises. For Aristotle this was a matter of rhetorical art: the speaker is to offer "ethical proof" by presenting himself as a judicious and trustworthy judge of virtue.[17] For Cicero and Quintilian, on the other hand, it is a matter of the orator's nature: only one who has knowledge of all the virtues (Cicero) or who is himself a good man (Quintilian) can properly praise goodness.[18]

In regard to method and style, Aristotle, Quintilian, and the Renaissance rhetorical handbooks identified many varieties of amplification and embellishment as suited to the accepted function of demonstrative rhetoric, to give pleasure; they also recommended the use of tropes which augment the subject's good qualities and compare him to paragons of virtue, as well as the organization of the whole according to such schemes as the six stages of man's life or the four cardinal virtues.[19] Also, since most theorists also viewed praise as a persuasion to virtue, they frequently found appropriate some techniques of deliberative rhetoric which create the semblance of argument and proof. Stylistic devices deriving from the actual literary tradition include the topics E. R. Curtius has found to be characteristic of both classical and medieval praises: inexpressibility, according to which the speaker proclaims his inability to do justice to his superlative subject; outdoing, whereby the subject is said to surpass any with whom he can be compared; and universal renown, whereby "all" mankind is said to honor and praise the person in question.[20]

[17] Aristotle, *Rhetoric* I.9, *Basic Works*, pp. 1353-1354.

[18] Cicero, *De Oratore* II.lxxxv.348-349, *Rackham*, I, 463; Quintilian, *Institutes* III.vii.25, *Butler*, I, 477.

[19] See, e.g., Aristotle I.9, *Basic Works*, pp. 1357-1359; Quintilian III.vii.28, VIII.iii.11-13, VIII.iv; *Butler*, I, 479, III, 217-218, 263-281. A. L. Bennett, "The Principal Rhetorical Conventions in the Renaissance Personal Elegy," *SP*, 51 (1954), 107-126, has found that several Elizabethan funeral elegies make significant use of these recommended schemes of organization.

[20] Curtius, *European Literature and the Latin Middle Ages*, trans. Willard R. Trask (New York, 1963), pp. 154-164.

He who praises has Aristotle's warrant to heighten and idealize the qualities of his subject by "drawing on the virtues akin to his actual qualities," so that "rashness will be called courage and extravagance generosity."[21] This raises the ethical issue of flattery and excessive hyperbole, which classical and Renaissance theorists usually dealt with by asserting that the actual character of the man should be subordinated to the didactic motive of providing fit images of virtue for emulation, or of inciting the person praised to live up to his ideal self, thus projected.[22] Erasmus, for example, declared, "No other way of correcting a prince is so efficacious as presenting, in the guise of flattery, the pattern of a really good prince."[23] There was, however, a decorum governing hyperbole. Quintilian permitted it when the subject was truly exceptional, and the Renaissance rhetorician Henry Peacham concurred, allowing hyperbole when the matter is somehow consonant with such exaggeration.[24] Most agreed with Puttenham in counselling discretion: "although a prayse or other report may be allowed beyond credit, it may not be beyond all measure."[25] Another principle of decorum provided for the suiting of the genre, style, and subject matter of an encomiastic poem to the social position of the person praised. This idea was implicit in Menander's definitions of epideictic kinds in the *Peri Epideiktikon*, but it received explicit and emphatic formulation by Renaissance theorists such as Scaliger and Puttenham.[26] Ap-

---

[21] *Rhetoric* I.ix, *Basic Works*, p. 1356.

[22] Hardison, *Enduring Monument*, p. 31, cites Pliny's defence of his flattery of Trajan on the ground that in it "good princes might recognize what they had done; bad, what they ought to have done."

[23] Cited by Lester K. Born, in "The Perfect Prince According to the Latin Panegyrists," *American Journal of Philology*, 55 (1934), 35; *Opus Epistolarum Erasmi*, ed. P. S. Allen (Oxford, 1906), I, 397.

[24] Quintilian, *Institutes of Oratory* VIII.vi.67-76, in *Butler*, III, 339-345; Peacham, *The Garden of Eloquence* (1593), facsim. ed. by William G. Crane (Gainesville, Fla., 1954), p. 31.

[25] Puttenham, *The Arte of English Poesie*, p. 160.

[26] See Hardison, *Enduring Monument*, pp. 194-198. See also the discussions of state panegyric in Ruth Nevo, *The Dial of Virtue*

plying the classical discriminations specifically to English poetry, Puttenham identified hymns praising the gods as the "highest and the stateliest" kind of epideictic lyric, followed by "ballades of praise called *Encomia*" and also historical poems, which were appropriate especially to princes and great men who "most resembled the gods by excellencie of function, and . . . by more then humane and ordinarie vertues."[27] These kinds are to be written in the high style— lofty, eloquent, highly embellished. For inferior or private persons a lower genre and style is appropriate, because their virtues are necessarily of a less heroic order, less "exemplarie" and of less moment: "Wherefore the Poet in praising the manner of life or death of anie meane person, did it by some litle dittie or Epigram or Epitaph in fewe verses & meane stile conformable to his subject."[28]

Some indication of the implications of these principles for the poetry of praise in the English Renaissance, as well as some measure of the changing fashions in such poetry in the decade preceding the writing of the *Anniversaries*, can be derived from two large collections of contemporary epideictic poetry: the praises and elegies for Queen Elizabeth (d. 1603), and those for young Prince Henry (d. 1613). For one thing, these praises and elegies provide examples of most of the stances available to the speaker of an epideictic poem, though modified in accordance with the particular social decorum appropriate to princes. The speaker might focus upon his own personal responses (admiration, wonder, grief), or he might present himself as spokesman for a group, a community, an entire nation, or nature herself: usually, the speaker of royal praises combined the two.

Within these general categories the speaker could adopt a more specific self-characterization. One posture, not

---

(Princeton, N. J., 1963), and in Warren L. Chernaik, *The Poetry of Limitation: A Study of Edmund Waller* (New Haven, 1968) pp. 115-171.

[27] Puttenham, *Arte of English Poesie*, pp. 23, 35, 38.

[28] *Ibid.*, p. 35.

usually available to the praiser of princes, presented the speaker as intimate friend and associate of the person complimented and thus able to observe and attest to his worthiness. The pastoral stance (the speaker as shepherd celebrating or mourning the loss of another shepherd or shepherdess) was extremely common in the praises of Elizabeth but declined markedly in the Prince Henry elegies. For both princes, not surprisingly, the most common stance was that of an inferior in status and merit—a distant admirer, dependent, or subject—giving reverent testimony to his subject's superlative merit. Common also in the praises of Queen Elizabeth, though obviously inappropriate for Henry, was a modified Petrarchan stance, modified in that the traditional amorous basis for the speaker's praise or grief is set aside, and the Petrarchan conceits and attitudes of devotion, dependence, quasi-religious adoration, dolor, and despair are adopted for courtly and political purposes, without the warrant of a deep love relationship.[29] Nevertheless these poems preserve something of a dramatic relationship between speaker and lady, in that the speaker adopts one aspect of the traditional Petrarchan poet's role, that of the humble, devoted servant worshipping his exalted lady from afar. Yet another option for the speaker, evident in the elegies for both princes but especially in the praises of Queen Elizabeth (*vide* Spenser) is the posture of the Neoplatonic lover who celebrates the Ideas of Beauty and Virtue reflected in the particular person, and who attempts, by ascending the Neoplatonic ladder of love, to embrace those Ideas and the God who is their source.[30] By redefining the

[29] For these permutations of Petrarchism see Donald Guss, *John Donne Petrarchist* (Detroit, Michigan, 1966), pp. 21-33. Leonard Forster in *The Icy Fire: Five Studies in European Petrarchism* (Cambridge, 1969), pp. 122-147, argues that Queen Elizabeth quite deliberately, as a matter of policy and politics, cast herself as the ideal Petrarchan lady, and elicited from her courtiers and subjects responses to that role.

[30] See Marsilio Ficino, "Commentary on Plato's Symposium," trans. Sears R. Jayne, *University of Missouri Studies*, 19, 1 (Columbia, Mo., 1944); Baldassare Castiglione, *The Book of the Courtier*, trans. Sir.

personal love, which is the traditional basis for this stance, as devoted admiration—not difficult since Neoplatonic love is in any case a matter of the mind and spirit—the poetic speaker could address in Neoplatonic terms persons of either sex or even persons unknown to him.

One special means of developing the speaker's stance in the funeral elegy was through the classical and Petrarchan topic of "nature reversed" or "society dissolved."[31] In pastoral funeral elegies the speaker conventionally describes, as a true observation of reality, nature mourning, disrupted, moribund, or itself dead in sympathy with the lost shepherd, but in the nonpastoral forms this topos is usually subjective, referring to the speaker's distraught, grief-stricken state of mind. Joseph Hall's poem on Queen Elizabeth's death affords an illustration of the latter use: he invokes the nature-reversed topic—"I fear'd to finde the frowning skie/ Clothed in dismall black, and dreadful red"—but then, with ironic awareness of the distance between his expectations and detached nature, notes his surprise that the heavens still give light and "that the worlds course with her cours was not ended."[32] On the other hand, these speakers describe as objective, observable fact the disruption of society and the overturning of its values, noting that arts, learning, virtues, sciences, and especially religion are maimed and endangered by the loss of Queen Elizabeth's or Prince Henry's protective care. Perhaps the most moving formulation of the "society disordered" topos in relation to Elizabeth is John Lane's typological presentation of the nation as a lost Eden, a destroyed Jerusalem, a Canaan turned wilderness:

Thomas Hoby [1561] (London, 1928). See also John S. Harrison, *Platonism in English Poetry* (New York, 1903); Sears Jayne, "Ficino and the Platonism of the English Renaissance," *Comparative Literature*, 4 (1952), 214-238; and Guss, *John Donne, Petrarchist*, pp. 124-138.

[31] See Hardison, *Enduring Monument*, pp. 116-117.

[32] Hall, *The Kings Prophacie: Or, Weeping Joy* (London, 1603), ll. 43-44, 76-78. See also Christopher Brooke, "A Funerall Elegie on the Prince," in *Two Elegies, Consecrated to the Never-dying Memorie of . . . Henry* (London, 1613), sig. C 3ᵛ.

Let *Israel* weepe, the house of *Jacob* mourne,
Syon is fallne, and *Judah* left forlorne,
The Hill of *Hermon* drops no precious oyle,
Nor fruitfull *Bashan*, from his fattest soile,
But *Davids* throne has all his beautie lost,
So farre admir'd through every forreigne coast,
The Paradice and *Eden* of our Land
Planted and kept by GODS almightie Hand:
With milke and honie *Canaan*-like did flow,
And Flowers of peace, and fruites of plentie grow;
Where Vines and Olives, ever more were seene,
Vines ever Fresh, and Olives ever greene:
With Brambles now and Briers over-cast,
And like a desert desolate and wast.[33]

In the Prince Henry elegies, on the other hand, the most remarkable development of this topic presents the death of the Prince as wounding or destroying the heart of the nation, a figure probably suggested by Donne's *Anniversaries*. In Henry Holland's elegy the speaker finds that because of grief for Henry the nation's heart "is broke, or hugely wounded,"[34] and John Davies' speaker elaborates the same figure:

So, HEAD [King James] and *Members* die with
    this our HEART!
We die, though yet we move, with griefe conceav'd
For this his death; whose Life gave all our Parts
Their lively motion; which they had receav'd
From his rare vertue, *Life* of all our *Hearts*.[35]

[33] J. L. [John Lane], *An Elegie upon the Death of the High and Renowned Princesse, Our Late Soveraigne Elizabeth* (London, 1603), in *Fugitive Tracts, 2nd Series, 1600-1700* (London, 1875), no. 2.

[34] Holland, "Elegie on the Untimely Death of the Incomparable Prince, Henry," in *Sundry Funeral Elegies, on the Untimely Death of the Most Excellent Prince, Henry* ([London], 1613).

[35] John Davies, *The Muses-Teares for the Losse of their Hope* (London, 1613), sig. B 3ᵛ.

The untimely death of Prince Henry gave rise to a special formulation of the "society-disordered" topic, whereby the speaker castigates himself, as spokesman for the nation, for those sins which called down the death as a divine punishment. So, Joshua Sylvester enumerates and identifies himself with the particular sins of every occupation and class, concluding,

> *Wee* were the *Mooving Cause*
> That sweet *Prince* HENRY breath no longer drawes,
> *Wee* All (alas!) have had our hands herein:
> And each of us hath, by some *cord* of *Sinne*,
> Hal'd down from Heaven, from *Justice* awfull Seat,
> This *heavy Judgement* (which yet more doth threat).
>
> . . . .
>
> For, for the *Peoples* Sinnes, for *Subjects* crymes
> God takes-away good *Princes* oftentimes.[36]

The epideictic poems on Queen Elizabeth and Prince Henry also provide a lexicon of the *topoi* of praise, of the various possibilities for their development, and of significant changes in their use from 1603 to 1613. The topics are distinguished for analysis here, but the poets tended to conflate them, setting forth one after another as well-understood counters or social gestures which did not have to be developed in detail. By far the most common topic is the praise of the subject as an exemplar of virtues—often of the particular virtues appropriate to his station and role. As woman, Queen Elizabeth is a "Merrour of Chastitie," exhibiting "Prudence, and Constancie . . . / A rare memoriall for all women-kinde."[37] As sovereign, "Her *Bountie, Grace,*

[36] Joshua Sylvester, *Lachrymae Lachrymarum* ([London, 1612]), revised and reissued with *Sundry Funeral Elegies*, sigs. B-B 3. See also Richard Niccols, *The Three Sisters Teares, Shed at the Late Solemne Funeralls of the Royall Deceased Henry* (London, 1613), sig. F 2; Thomas Heywood, "A Funerall Elegie," in *Three Elegies on the Most Lamented Death of Prince Henrie* (London, 1613), sig. B 3.

[37] T. W., *The Lamentation of Melpomene, for the Death of Belphœbe our late Queene* (London, 1603), sig. A 3ᵛ.

23

and *Magnanimitie,/* Her princely minde did plainely signi-
fie."[38] Praise of virtue might be allegorized in terms of clas-
sical mythology—Elizabeth is chaste as Diana, wise as
Athena—and it could be hyperbolically extended to assert
that Elizabeth is the perfection of certain virtues, or indeed
of all virtues.[39] The praises of Henry also dwelt upon the
virtues which accord with his role and situation, e.g., zeal,
justice, prudence, bravery, and learning; he also was de-
scribed as the perfection of virtue: "Nature's masterpiece,"
"Virtues Pattern," *"Panaretus."*[40] Yet another topic praised
the subject as the "image" or "pattern" of virtue in the Neo-
platonic sense. As E. C. Wilson observed, Elizabeth was
constantly celebrated in mythological terms as the perfect
copy or image of the heavenly "Ideas" of particular virtues
—she was Diana or Cynthia the pattern of Chastity, Juno
the pattern of Sovereignty, Astraea the pattern of Justice,
or she was the image of perfect Virtue itself: the "heavenly
image of perfection."[41] The topic was used much less fre-
quently in the Prince Henry poems, but yet like several
other princes before him Henry enacted an Astraea-like
role in regard to the glories anticipated from his forthcom-
ing reign: with him "The golden Age, Star-like, shot
through our Skye."[42] A related topic celebrated these
Princes' attainment of the Platonic harmony of body and
soul. According to Sir John Davies, Elizabeth's fair soul
gave to her body "such lively life, such quickening power,/
Such sweet celestial influences to it/ As keeps it still in

---

[38] [Anthony Nixon?], *Elizaes Memoriall, King James his Arrivall,
and Romes Downefall* (London, 1603), sig. A 3ᵛ.

[39] E.g., Richard Barnfield, "Cynthia" quoted in M. C. Bradbrook,
ed., *The Queen's Garland* (London, 1953), p. 14.

[40] See, e.g., Davies, *Muses-Teares*, sig. B; Joshua Sylvester, *Lachry-
mae Lachrymarum*, sigs. A 2, B.

[41] Wilson, *England's Eliza*, pp. 360-361; cf. Spenser, *Faerie Queene*
IV.vi.24, in J. C. Smith and E. De Selincourt, eds., *The Poetical Works
of Edmund Spenser* (Oxford, 1950), p. 242.

[42] George Chapman, "Epitaphium," in *An Epicede or Funerall Song*
(London, 1612), sig. C 3ᵛ.

youth's immortal flower."[43] Prince Henry's uncorrupted youth made the topic more apt for and rather more frequently employed in, his praises: William Cornwallis observed that "no Vice could e'r infuse/ Her poison into His well ordered Minde," and many elegists registered surprise that such entire perfection could be subject to death and dissolution.[44] The *topos* of Neoplatonic virtue was sometimes given hyperbolic extension in Queen Elizabeth's praises, so that the Queen was celebrated as Astraea herself, the very Platonic Idea incarnate, not merely a pattern or image of it: she is "Earth's true Astraea," the very Maid (Virgo) who "Hath brought againe the golden dayes."[45] On the other hand, although Cyril Tourneur calls Prince Henry the "President of virtu," and Davies says that virtue and Henry "are still Corelatives,"[46] Henry is never (and scarcely could be) identified with Astraea as the very Idea of Virtue or Justice.

Another *topos* important in the praises of Queen Elizabeth presents her as a celestial being, the *donna angelicata* of *stilnovisti* and Petrarchan convention. Though for Dante, and to a lesser extent for Petrarch, the beloved lady after her death became a manifestation of God to the lover and a way to that highest love, in this occasional poetry of praise the Petrarchist conceits are constantly employed without

[43] Davies, "To my most gracious dread sovereign," Dedication to *Nosce Teipsum*, in Gerald Bullett, ed., *Silver Poets of the Sixteenth Century* (London, 1962), p. 343.

[44] Brookes, "A Funerall Elegie," sig. B 3v; Sir William Cornwallis, "Elegie on the Untimely Death of the Incomparable Prince, Henry," in *Sundry Funeral Elegies*, sig. E 4v. See also, e.g., Heywood, "A Funerall Elegie," sig. B 3.

[45] [Henry A. Chettle], *Englandes Mourning-Garment* (London, 1603), sig. F; Sir John Davies, "Hymne I," *Hymnes of Astraea* (London, 1599), p. 1; see also *Histrio-mastix* ([London], 1610), facsimile ed., John S. Farmer, Tudor Facsimile Texts, 1912, Act VI, final song. See Frances Yates, "Queen Elizabeth as Astraea," *Journal of the Warburg and Courtauld Institute*, x (1947), 27-82.

[46] Tourneur, "A Griefe on the Death of Prince Henrie," in *Three Elegies*, l. 11; Davies, *Muses-Teares*, sig. C 3v.

this romantic basis and with only very general Christian significance.[47] Using the Petrarchan conceits, the poets often praise Queen Elizabeth as "divine," that is, celestial, heavenly, an inhabitant with God and the Angels: "O deare, deare Saint, I could have worship thee;/ And still I would, but for idolatry."[48] She is also a sun or star: for Davies a "Rich Sun-beame of th'æternall light"; for John Lane her "starry eyes" give light to the world and to the Sun itself; and for many poets she is the phoenix of the world.[49]

Other common topics, deriving from scripture and Christian theology, make a more serious claim to be taken as unvarnished truth, for the recognized sanctity of these materials, especially among Protestants, invites the expectation that they will not be used falsely, irresponsibly, or merely conventionally. The most common topic praises the individual as regenerate soul, saint, heir to the scripture promises. Queen Elizabeth is the "floure of grace," the "prime of Gods elect," and she now dwells "amongst the blessed Sainctes" dressed in "milke-white Robes."[50] The Prince Henry elegies make still greater use of the topic of Christian sainthood, reflecting, no doubt, the growing earnestness about religion which characterized the earlier seventeenth century as well as the staunch Protestantism associated with Henry. Henry

[47] See Guss, *John Donne, Petrarchist*, pp. 124-138.

[48] Henry Petowe, *Eliza's Funerall, A Few Aprill Drops, Shoured on the Hearse of Dear Eliza* (London, 1603), sig. B; Thomas Cecill, in *Sorrowes Joy; or a Lamentation for our Late Deceased Soveraigne Elizabeth* (Cambridge, 1603), p. 16.

[49] See, e.g., Davies, "Hymne XIII," *Hymnes of Astraea*, p. 13; Lane, *An Elegie*, n.p. The Petrarchan topic of the celestial lady was obviously not available for the praises of Prince Henry, but the poets frequently applied some of the traditional Petrarchan conceits to him: he is a star, a sun, and very often a phoenix. See, e.g., Davies, *Muses-Teares*, sig. A 2; Cornwallis, *Elegie*, sigs. E 3, E 4ᵛ; G. G. [George Gerrard], "An Elegie on the Untimely Death of the Incomparable Prince, Henry," in *Sundry Funeral Elegies*, sig. D.

[50] "Pageant at Norwich," quoted in Wilson, *England's Eliza*, p. 81. Richard Johnson, *Anglorum Lacrimae* (London, 1603), in *Fugitive Tracts, 2nd Series, 1600-1700*, n.p.; Lane, *An Elegie*, n.p.

is "spot-les without Sinn," a regenerate soul graced "with Justice, Goodnes, and integrity."[51] Davies emphasized his religious meditations upon eternal things, and many elegists celebrated his triumph in heaven, "Imbrightned into that celestiall light."[52]

Another Christian topic relates the person praised to Christ or to some other biblical personage on the basis of Christian typology, a mode of historical symbolism whereby a real historical person or event figures forth, foreshadows, or recapitulates Christ. In the political sphere, and especially among Protestants, the Christocentric thrust of traditional typology was somewhat muted and often implicit, and the emphasis was laid upon the present age as an extension of sacred history, recapitulating and repeating Old Testament events as correlative types within a total providential order. What God accomplished with one chosen people (the Jews), prefiguring Christ's redemption, he might repeat with another chosen people (the English), recapitulating and extending the application of that redemption and perhaps foreshadowing Christ's perfect millennial Kingdom.[53] As correlative type Queen Elizabeth was a "Judith just" defeating the Spanish Holofernes, a "Debora that judged Israell," an Esther who preserved her people from the Spanish Haman in 1588.[54] For Francis Sabie she was "That *Moses*" who delivered her people "From Romish *Pharoahs* tyrannous bondage," led them through the Red Sea of difficulties, and fed them "With *manna, nectar*, manie

[51] Cornwallis, "Elegie," in *Sundry Funeral Elegies*, sigs. E 3ᵛ, F.

[52] Davies, *Muses-Teares*, sig. A 2v-A 3; Giles Fletcher, "Upon the Most Lamented Departure of . . . Prince Henrie," in *Epicedium Cantabrigiense* (Cambridge, 1612).

[53] See the discussion of the point in Lewalski, "*Samson Agonistes* and the 'Tragedy' of the Apocalypse," *PMLA*, 85 (1970), 1050-1062.

[54] See, e.g., "A godlie Dittie to be Song for the Preservation of the Queene's most Excelent Majestie's Raigne" (broadside, London, 1586), quoted in Wilson, *Eliza*, p. 36. [Anon.], *Ave Caesar, God Save the King . . . With an Epitaph upon the Death of her Majestie* (London, 1603), n.p.; Lane *Elegie*, n.p.

yeares."[55] She was also a Joshua defending her people in the promised land, another Canaan which "Did plentiously with milke and honey flow."[56] Prince Henry, by contrast, was related to only one Old Testament type, but that constantly—Josiah, a king of Judah who also died young; whose death was identified by many exegetes as the occasion for Jeremiah's dirge or funeral elegy, The Book of Lamentations; and who had sought to eradicate idolatry from the land, restoring the full ceremony of the Law. Joshua Sylvester's formula is typical: "So good JOSIAH (HENRY'S *parallel*)/ Was (soon) bereft from Sinfull *Israel*."[57] In addition, both princes were occasionally presented as types (recapitulations) of Christ the King and Savior—as *Christomimētēs*, to use Kantorowicz' suggestive phrase.[58] Elizabeth was most often associated with traditional emblematic figures of Christ: she is a phoenix, established emblem of Christ's death and resurrection, or else a pelican, emblem of Christ's sacrifice—"that Royall maide, that Pellican, who for her people's good/ . . . Stickt not to spill, alas! her owne deare blood."[59] Prince Henry was more often and more explicitly presented as type of Christ through descriptions of him as a "young Saviour" who died because of our sins; in this vein Heywood observed, "Let after ages of this Prince record,/ Hee freely gave a life, a land to save."[60]

Both princes were sometimes described as images of God.

[55] Sabie, *Pans pipe, Three pastoral Eglogues*, quoted in Wilson, *Eliza*, p. 148.

[56] [Nixon?], *Elizas Memoriall*, sig. B 3ᵛ.

[57] Sylvester, *Lachrymae Lachrymarum*, sig. B 4. The aptness of this typological relation inheres in the fact that Prince Henry was heir apparent to the crown, cut off by death in his hopeful youth; as heir apparent he was the focus for Protestant hopes of continued reformation in the English Church and increased opposition to the Pope and the Spaniard.

[58] Ernst H. Kantorowicz, *The King's Two Bodies* (Princeton, N.J., 1957), p. 47.

[59] Henry Campion, "Elegy," in *Sorrowes Joy*, p. 11.

[60] Heywood, "A Funerall Elegie," in *Three Elegies*, sig. B 4. See also Sylvester, *Lachrymae Lachrymarum*, sigs. C-C 2ᵛ.

This *topos* was most often applied to Queen Elizabeth, on the basis of the monarch's recognized status as vicegerent of God, invested with God's own authority: she was, as Thomas Holland put it in a funeral sermon, "by birth, vocation, descent a Queene, by consequente thereof . . . a living Image of God."[61] George Chapman called upon her to imitate the Creator: "let your breath/ Goe foorth upon the waters, and create/ A golden worlde in this our yron age." Others described her reign as an image of the divine rule: "Her *Government* seem'd perfect blessednes,/ Her *Mercie* with her *Justice* ever swaie'd."[62] Though Henry was never an anointed king the *topos* was occasionally applied to him, not so much in relation to his potential royal office as for his goodness. Chapman called him "God-like," "True Image" of God, and "nothing-lesse-then-mortall Deitie," primarily because of his "matchlesse vertues."[63] Davies declared that he was "A *Prince*, like *God* for State,/ Stile, Vertue, and Effect," but elsewhere Davies praised him as Godlike by reason of the created natural goodness which he preserved or refurbished by grace; so formulated, this *topos* is applicable to all mankind, as Davies observes:

> The *Simile* twixt *God* and *Man* is such,
> That *God* is said to be *immortall Man*;
> And *Man* a mortall *God*: He was so much.[64]

B. Renaissance Praises of the Nobility and Gentry

When the subject is not queen or prince but some lesser lord or lady, patron or patroness, the poetic praises were

---

[61] Holland, *Panegyris D. Elizabethae . . . A Sermon Preached at Paul's in London the 17. of Nov. Ann. Dom. 1599* (Oxford, 1601), sig. A 2ᵛ.

[62] Chapman, "De Guiana, Carmen Epicum," in *Works*, ed. Phyllis Brooks Bartlett (London, 1941), p. 254; [Nixon?], *Elizaes Memoriall*, sig. A 3ᵛ.

[63] Chapman, *An Epicede or Funerall Song* (London, 1612).

[64] Davies, *Muses-Teares*, sigs. C, A 4ᵛ, A 3, A 3ᵛ.

more circumspect and the hyperbole much muted, in accordance with the social decorum recommended by the rhetorics. In such poems the speaker could adopt various stances, as suited his assumed relationship to the person praised, but he normally combined the expression of his own feeling with a public role as spokesman for some community. In contrast to the Prince Henry poems, however, the speaker of these lesser praises only very occasionally expresses the community's guilty responsibility for the death in question.[65] In these poems also the "nature reversed" *topos* is employed with more circumspection than in the elegies for princes. It occurs commonly in pastoral elegies such as Spenser's *Daphnaïda* and *Astrophel*,[66] but in these works the topic is to be understood as part of the all-embracing pastoral convention of nature's empathy with man. Elsewhere its force is explicitly qualified. In Thomas Churchyard's poem for Sir Francis Knowles (1596) the harshness of the winter season and the natural evidences of God's wrath are presented as fact, but they are said to attend the demise of a long list of notable churchmen and statesmen dead in a single year, not only Knowles.[67] And when Michael Drayton invokes the topic in his "Elegie upon the Death of the Lady Penelope Clifton" (1613), it is qualified by the speaker's ironic sense that what he describes is not fact but the projection of his own feelings upon nature, his sense that if heaven had responded appropriately it "would have show'd,"

[65] Such an exceptional case was an epitaph for John Whitgift, Archbishop of Canterbury, whose death (along with the death of Queen Elizabeth and the plague) was attributed to "our great sinnes," by I. R., *An Epitaph on the Death of the Late . . . John . . . Arch-Byshop of Canterburie* (London, 1604), sig. A 2.

[66] Spenser, *Daphnaïda*, and *Astrophel*, in *Poetical Works*, pp. 528-534, 547-550.

[67] Thomas Churchyard, *A Sad and Solemne Funerall, of the Right Honorable Sir Francis Knowles* (London, 1596), n.p.

That change of Kingdomes to her death it ow'd;
And that the world still of her end might thinke,
It would have let some Neighbouring mountaine sinke,
Or the vast Sea it in on us to cast,
As *Severne* did about some five yeares past.[68]

In these poems also, as might be expected, the most common topic of praise is the subject's virtue—usually the virtues appropriate to his station, sometimes (hyperbolically) his distinction as paragon of virtue, often his privileges as regenerate soul. In general, as decorum dictated, the praises addressed to the nobility and gentry make only occasional use of the more extravagant *topoi* so generously employed in the praises of princes, such as the conception of the person as Neoplatonic image or embodiment of virtue itself, as type of Christ or correlative type with Old or New Testament personages, or as image and manifestation of God. An illustration of the characteristic restraint in the use of such tropes is afforded by Thomas Rogers' *Celestiall Elegies* for Lady Frances Beauchamp, Countess of Hertford. In these poems, various classical goddesses and muses lament the great loss Lady Beauchamp's death will bring to the specific quality or virtue each represents, but no attempt is made, as so often it was with Queen Elizabeth, to identify the lady with these goddesses or to make her the incarnation of these abstractions.[69]

Most of the praises of great ladies are characterized by the speaker's quasi-Petrarchan stance, the *topos* of the celestial lady, and many of the familiar Petrarchan conceits. In Spenser's *Daphnaïda* (1591) the lover-husband of Daphne describes her as Petrarchan beauty and *donna angelicata*: "Shee did excell, and seem'd of Angels race,/

[68] In J. W. Hebel, ed., *The Works of Michael Drayton*, 5 vols. (Oxford, 1931-1941), III, 219-222, ll. 102-106.

[69] Thomas Rogers, *Celestiall Elegies of the Goddesses and the Muses, Deploring the Death of . . . the Ladie Fraunces Countesse of Hertford* (London, 1598).

Living on earth like Angell new divinde,/ Adorn'd with
wisedome and with chastitie"; she was "my faire Starre,"
"my love that was, my Saint that is."[70] In Michael Drayton's
elegy for Penelope Clifton the Petrarchan speaker praises
the lady's beauty and her "Godlike features" which put him
in danger of idolatry.[71] Some of Ben Jonson's early epigrams
to ladies also employ the Petrarchan stance, but they inter-
mix neoclassical mythological allegory with Petrarchan con-
ceits. Jonson acclaims Lucy Bedford by means of a verbal
play on her name, "LUCY, you brightnesse of our spheare,
who are/ Life of the *Muses* day, their morning-starre."[72]
And he praises Cecelia Boulstred as one who might have
been a fourth grace, who might have "taught Pallas lan-
guage; Cynthia modesty"; who was so perfect that she was
"As fit to have encreas'd the harmony/ Of Spheares, as light
of Starres"; who was "earthes Eye."[73] This last figure is a
formulation of the Petrarchan conceit of the lady as sun, but
it also implies that she was the means by which the earth
sees (understands).

These praises of lesser personages often employ topics
from the Christian order, the most common being the cele-
bration of the individual praised as regenerate soul, made
what he is by the grace of God. Samuel Daniel praises Mar-
garet, Countess of Cumberland, by defining her goodness
in terms of grace and innocence: her mind cannot be cast
"Out of her forme of goodness"; she enjoys a "cleere con-
science that without all staine/ Rises in peace, in innocencie
rests"; in her the (Platonic) harmony of parts, the "concord
. . . of a well-tun'd mind," is effected by the "all-working

---

[70] *Daphnaïda, Poetical Works*, ll. 213-215, 379, 480.

[71] Drayton, *Works*, III, 220, ll. 61-82.

[72] "XCIV. To Lucy, Countesse of Bedford," *Epigrammes*, in *Ben
Jonson*, ed. Herford and Simpson, VIII, 60, ll. 1-2.

[73] "Epitaph," in "Ungathered Verse," *ibid.*, VIII, 371-372, ll. 6-9.
Compare the very different satiric account Jonson published in her
lifetime, "XLIX. An Epigram on the Court Pucell," *Under-wood*,
ibid., VIII, 222-223.

hand/ Of heaven."[74] Similarly, Daniel praises Lady Anne Clifford's sanctity and innocence. In her,

> ... there is left no room at all t'invest
> Figures of other forme but sanctitie:
> Whilst yet those cleare-created thoughts, within
> The Garden of your innocencies rest.[75]

But yet this sanctity derives from grace rather than from herself, "for in our strongest parts we are but weake." The Calvinist Henry Lok directs his praises yet more explicitly to the regenerate soul. Declaring that the pure conscience and seemly behavior of Lady Anne Russell, Countess of Warwick, "No doubt a hart regenerate doth bewray," he observes that all her gifts of birth, marriage, and nature "With gift of grace herein may not compare." He praises Lady Rich (Sidney's Stella) for her perfect beauty, wisdom, and bright virtue, concluding that "These gifts of nature, since they meet with grace,/ In you, have powre more then faire Venus face." In the sonnet to Lady Carey the speaker presents himself as one led to meditations on heaven through her agency—not as Petrarchan or Neoplatonic lover or admirer but strictly as a Christian concerned for his salvation: "By view of your rare vertues I was bent,/ To meditate of heaven and heavenly thing."[76]

A tendency evident in the praises of nobles and gentlemen (who unlike the ladies performed public deeds and carried out particular vocations) is toward greater specificity in suiting the topics of praise to the conditions of the person's life. This is accompanied by some modification of the idealizing, worshipful tone customarily adopted toward

[74] Daniel, "To the Ladie Margaret, Countesse of Cumberland," in A. B. Grosart, ed., *The Complete Works in Verse and Prose of Samuel Daniel*, I (London, 1885), 205-207.

[75] Daniel, "To the Ladie Anne Clifford," *ibid.*, p. 213.

[76] Lok, "Sonnets of the Author to Divers," in *Ecclesiastes*, etc. (London, 1597), sigs. Y 1ᵛ, Y 2ᵛ, Y 4ᵛ. See James Scanlon, ed., "Sundry Christian Passions," unpublished Ph.D. dissertation, Brown University, 1970, "Introduction."

princes and great ladies, in favor of a more forthright stance. The elegies for Sir Philip Sidney in the volume *Astrophel* (1595), titled from Spenser's contribution, use for the most part the conventional hyperboles praising Sidney as a paragon among men, the perfection of virtue, a phoenix, but the two nonpastoral poems also take note of the special circumstances of his life and his death on the battlefield. In Sir Walter Raleigh's "Epitaph" the speaker is direct and terse: he laments but is not overcome by grief. He praises Sidney in general but simple terms as one who, in life and death, "Vertue exprest, and honor truly taught." But then he specifies, alluding to Sidney's notable achievements by comparing him with certain ancient worthies: Sidney was the *"Scipio, Cicero,* and *Petrarch* of our time," whom only heaven can properly praise.[77] The speaker in Sir Edward Dyer's elegy for Sidney also adopts a simple and direct stance. He is a close friend expressing heartfelt but controlled grief and pain, and also a sense of the whole world's loss: "dead is my friend, dead is the worlds delight." The praises are straightforward and apt: Sidney is "a spotless friend, a matchles man, whose vertue ever shined," and with his death, "Knowledge her light hath lost."[78]

For all this, the special mystique and the ideality which Sidney's life and death held for contemporaries set him apart from most other noblemen and gentry, whose praises were much more frequently characterized by the stance of forthright honesty and the development of the *topos* of virtue in terms of specific qualities and actions. An epitaph for Sir Edward Stanhope of the Court of Chancery honors him with precise appropriateness as "the *Cato* of our Nation," the "sonne of Justice dropt from heaven hye."[79] In his funeral poem for Sir Francis Vere (1609) Cyril Tourneur

[77] Raleigh, "An Epitaph upon the Right Honourable Sir Phillip Sidney," in Spenser, *Poetical Works*, pp. 558-560.

[78] Dyer, "Another of the Same," *ibid.*, pp. 559-560.

[79] [Anon.], "An Epitaph upon the death of . . . Sir Edward Stanhope," in *A Century of Broadside Elegies*, ed. John W. Draper (London, 1928), p. 5.

is perfectly direct in his claim to present an honest and factual account: "All that I speake, is *unexacted, true* and *free;*/ Drawne clearely from *unalter'd* certaintee"; and the poem analyzes in detail the "goods" of Vere's mind and character as well as his distinguished deeds on the battlefield and in the Councils of Princes.[80] Even more remarkable for its speaker's judicious directness is Samuel Daniel's funeral poem for Charles Mountjoy, Earl of Devonshire (1606). In a lengthy apologia Daniel disclaims all flattery or exaggeration now that his patron is dead; he sets forth the usual justifications for hyperbole and fictionalized praise while renouncing all such practices in the present case; and he affords a suggestive analogue for Donne in that he labels his detailed poetic description of Devonshire's qualities of mind and heart, an "anatomy":

> Let those be vassals to such services
> Who have their hopes, or whose desires are hye,
> For me, I have my ends, and know it is
> For Free-men to speake truth, for slaves to lye.
> And if mistaken by the Paralax
> And distance of my standing too farre off
> I heretofore might erre, and men might tax
> My being to free of prayses, without proofe.
> But here it is not so . . .
>
> .   .   .   .
>
> True prayses doe adorne, the false obrayd:
> And oftentimes to greatness we are glad
> To attribute those parts we wish they had.
> But *Devonshire* I here stand cleere with thee
> I have a manumission to be free,
> I owe thee nothing, and I may be bold
> To speake the certaine truth of what I know,
>
> .   .   .   .

---

[80] [Tourneur], *A Funerall Poeme, Upon the Death of the Most Worthie and True Souldier, Sir Francis Vere, Knight* (London, 1609), sig. [A 4ᵛ].

35

And now being dead I may anatomise,
And open here all that thou wert within,
Shew how thy minde was built, and in what wise
All the contexture of thy heart had been:
Which was so nobly fram'd, so well compos'd,
As vertue never had a fairer seat.[81]

The poem proceeds with an account of Mountjoy's notable deeds as soldier and statesman and of his deathbed piety. Another long elegy about him, by John Forde, incorporates even more details of his life and deeds.[82]

Ben Jonson elevated to new poetic heights this conception of praise as involving a stance of forthright, judicious honesty and a precise definition of the topic of virtue in terms of specific qualities and actions.[83] Moreover, his poems are tightly organized in relation to a single unified topic, thereby giving the primary impetus to the trend, observable also in some of the Prince Henry elegies,[84] toward more orderly structure and more analytic development in the poem of compliment. Among his early poems, Jonson's epigram "To Thomas [Egerton] Lord Chancelor" concentrates on Egerton's integrity and conscience, concluding that Astraea (Justice) "T'our times return'd, hath made her heaven in thee." Yet more specifically, the epigram on Henry Saville praises him for his excellent translation of Tacitus and for his learned and critical judgments of past

[81] [Daniel], *A Funerall Poeme uppon the Death of the Late Noble Earle of Devonshire* ([London], 1606), sigs. A 1v-A 2.

[82] John Forde, *Fames Memoriall, or The Earle of Devonshire Deceased* (London, 1606).

[83] These points are discussed at length by Helen Marlborough in "Ben Jonson and the Poetry of Praise," Ph.D. dissertation in process, Brown University. See also Richard S. Peterson, "The Praise of Virtue: Ben Jonson's Poems," unpub. Ph.D. dissertation, University of California at Berkeley, 1969.

[84] Especially, Tourneur, "A Griefe"; Goodyere, "Elegie on the Untimely Death of the Incomparable Prince Henry," in *Sundry Funeral Elegies*, sigs. F 3-F 4.

and present times, of which the translation in question is a notable example.[85]

As a yet more radical innovation, Ben Jonson departed from the customary practice of his contemporaries when he adapted the poetic manner just defined to the praises of ladies, eschewing the usual quasi-Petrarchan stance and *topoi*. One epigram to the Countess of Bedford appears to have a Petrarchan speaker describing the lady he would wish to serve "as *Poets* use." He proceeds, however, not to devotion but to precise and straightforward analysis of the qualities he requires in such a lady, discovering them all in Lady Bedford: she is "faire, and free, and wise,/ . . . curteous, facile, sweet," but the speaker values especially her strength of mind and her "learned, and . . . manly soul."[86] An epigram to Elizabeth, Countess of Rutland, praises quite specifically her strength of mind and her discretion: while her husband travels she shows such a virtue, "As makes *Penelopes* old fable true," but she improves on Penelope by surrounding herself with good company and good books which she studies, "Searching for knowledge." Jonson especially commends her for this effort "to keepe your mind/ The same it was inspir'd, rich, and refin'd."[87] This poetic stance is more fully developed in the verse letter to Lady Aubigny: its ordering principle is the speaker's declared intention to "speake true" of her "good minde," despite the fact that the age has few such speakers or such minds. Jonson's poem is to be her true glass, showing not her physical beauty but the "beauties of the mind" manifested in her choice of a retired life, her careful maintenance of her husband's estate, her love of and devotion to him, and the faithful issue she has raised to him. The concluding praise asserts her constancy: the poem will always be her true glass,

[85] "LXXIV. To Thomas Lord Chancelor" and "XCV. To Sir Henrie Savile," in *Ben Jonson*, VIII, 51-52, 61-62.

[86] "LXXVI. On Lucy Countesse of Bedford," *ibid.*, VIII, 52.

[87] "52. An Epigram. To the Honour'd _____ Countesse of _____," *Under-wood, ibid.*, VIII, 224-225. This was obviously an early poem, as the Countess died in 1612.

"Because nor it can change, nor such a minde."[88] Jonson is also original in addressing to a woman (the Countess of Rutland) one of his early experiments with the Horatian epistle, in which a subject is developed for its own sake and praise is tendered primarily by the expectation that the recipient will understand and value the communication. Here the subject—the worth and value of poetry as giver of the greatest gift, fame—is developed by closely reasoned argument and specific example.[89]

It is evident that the poetry of praise written by Donne's contemporaries for the most part follows established classical and Renaissance precepts governing poetic and rhetorical praises. These poems assume the didactic function of praise, they identify moral virtue as the proper object of praise, and they portray their subjects as ideal types rather than as peccable individuals. From the rhetorical tracts these poems derive their major topics—the goods of nature, fortune, and especially of character; the stages of man's life; the particular virtues appropriate to the individual's status and role. Obviously, hyperbolic praises are the rule rather than the exception: certain stances and certain tropes recur constantly as generic conventions and social gestures without inviting literal belief. However, these poems generally adhere to the principle of decorum defined in the rhetorics, which calls for prudent regulation of hyperbole according to the greatness of the matter and the rank of the person praised. Accordingly, extraordinary deeds and great monarchs are praised much more fulsomely than other actions or persons. Moreover, the stances assumed by the speakers in some measure qualify the hyperbole, since the praises are based in part upon an assumed personal relationship between speaker and subject portrayed in the poems.

[88] "XIII. Epistle. To Katherine, Lady Aubigny," *The Forrest, ibid.* VIII, 116-120.

[89] "XII. Epistle. To Elizabeth Countesse of Rutland," *The Forrest, ibid.,* VIII, 113-116.

Donne's *Anniversaries* resemble in several respects the contemporary poetry of compliment. First, they clearly assume that the chief function of praise is didactic, proposing Elizabeth Drury as in some sense a model for us. Second, the speaker of the *Anniversaries* expresses both public griefs and fears and his own sorrow, resembling most closely perhaps those speakers in the Prince Henry elegies who bewail the general sinfulness held to be responsible for the Prince's death but also associate themselves with it. Third, the *Anniversary* poems employ the full range of available topics, including those chiefly used of princes;[90] but they reflect the trend (evident when we compare the elegies for Prince Henry with those for Elizabeth) toward the Christianization of the poetry of praise by deriving its topics from the Christian order. Finally, these poems are in the vanguard of a trend in the poetry of compliment toward greater unity and analytic rigor, often achieved by extended exploration of a particular issue or topic.

However, the differences between Donne's *Anniversaries* and such contemporary analogues are much more remarkable than the similarities. For one thing, none of the usual dramatic stances adopted by the speaker toward his subject

---

[90] This exploration casts doubt upon Marjorie Hope Nicolson's hypothesis (*The Breaking of the Circle*, pp. 81-122) that Queen Elizabeth is the true subject of the poems. Most readers have been skeptical of the orthographic evidence cited for this identification—that the form "she" in the poem refers to Elizabeth Drury and the form "Shee" to the Queen—since such variation is, if not accidental, the common contemporary means of differentiating unemphatic and emphatic vowels. But also, the present examination of tropes indicates that several of the passages Miss Nicolson cites as referring to a monarch (e.g., *Anatomy*, ll. 7-17, and *Progres*, ll. 361-380) are in fact statements of common Neoplatonic and Christian topics celebrating the soul's spiritual and political governance over itself. It shows also, that although the Queen received more fulsome praise than any other figure in Donne's lifetime, the specific topics employed to praise her could be and were used about others: Egerton was an Astraea figure for Ben Jonson, as Prince Henry was for George Chapman. Such allusions need not, then, signify a reference to the Queen.

—intimate friend, respectful subordinate, Petrarchan or Neoplatonic lover or devoted admirer—is employed by Donne's speaker: he does not claim any kind of personal relationship to the lady. For another, in contrast to the usual presentation of the "nature reversed" *topos* as manifestation of the speaker's distraught state, Donne's speaker eschews all ironic qualification of the topic, professing instead to see and describe the real world as dead and decaying. Again, though Donne's poems undertake to celebrate the lady's goodness, it quickly becomes evident that they do not deal with virtue in the expected senses: the *Anniversary* poems provide no analysis of the four cardinal virtues, or of the goods of character, or of the special virtues appropriate to Elizabeth Drury as well-born young virgin, or of the virtuous use she made of the goods of nature and fortune. And obviously nothing in the *Anniversaries* reflects the trend toward forthrightness and specificity in presenting the individual's character and deeds, the manner Ben Jonson was employing for praises of ladies as well as men. Finally, though Donne uses all the expected, conventional tropes of praise, he does so with a difference. For one thing, he ignores the social decorum which would reserve such profuse, elaborate hyperbole to monarchs or to truly extraordinary actions. And for another, he does not present these praises in the usual offhand manner as the polite small change of social intercourse, but rather as sober, literal truth.

The context we have been examining, the theory and practice of poetic compliment at the time Donne wrote his *Anniversaries*, quite obviously offers some insights into those remarkable poems. Yet the striking differences noted reveal that in just the most fundamental matters, and notably in regard to the conception of praise itself, Donne seems to be marking out a new direction. What Donne's special conception of poetic praise involves should become clearer from an investigation of his other poetry of compliment, the Epicedes and Obsequies and those Verse Letters whose chief object is personal praise. These works provide a still more immediate context for the *Anniversary* poems, but they also provide a record of Donne's continuing effort during a period of several years to transform the conventional mode of occasional complimentary verse into a fit vehicle for symbolic subjects, bringing into being a recognizably "metaphysical" poetry of praise.

CHAPTER II

Donne's Poetry of Compliment:
Meditative Speaker and
Symbolic Subject

T HOUGH Donne's several occasional poems of praise and
compliment provide what is in some respects the most
obvious context for the *Anniversaries*, they have, curiously
enough, been virtually ignored by critics.[1] In this category
I include the Epicedes and Obsequies and several verse let-
ters, especially those written to patronesses; excluded are
the Epithalamia, which celebrate marriages rather than in-
dividuals, and those verse letters which give advice on
moral conduct in the forthright terms of manly friendship
and thereby differ from the others in tone and intention.[2]

[1] All quotations from the verse letters are from Wesley Milgate's
standard edition, *The Satires, Epigrams, and Verse Letters of John
Donne* (Oxford, 1967); unless otherwise indicated, quotations from
the Epicedes and Obsequies are from H.J.C. Grierson, *The Poems of
John Donne*, 2 vols. (Oxford, 1966). Milgate's introduction to the
edition cited considers Donne's verse letters seriously, though all too
briefly, and Laurence Stapleton's article, "The Theme of Virtue in
Donne's Verse Epistles" *SP*, 55 (1958), 187-200, highlights an im-
portant aspect of them. Ruth Wallerstein's study of Donne's elegy for
Prince Henry in *Studies in Seventeenth-Century Poetic*, pp. 67-95, is
of great significance for that poem and for stylistic developments in
seventeenth century elegy. The substance of the present chapter first
appeared in *Seventeenth-Century Imagery: Essays on Uses of Figura-
tive Language from Donne to Farquhar*, ed. Earl Miner (Berkeley, Los
Angeles, and London, 1971), pp. 45-67.

[2] I also exclude the verse letter "To Mrs. M. H." (Magdalen Her-
bert) which begins "Mad paper stay" (1608), as it is much more famil-
iar in tone than the poems to the other great ladies. It is less a poem
of compliment as such than a genial, witty tribute in quasi-Petrarchan
terms to a good friend on the occasion of her impending marriage. See
H. W. Garrod, "Donne and Mrs. Herbert," *ELH*, 21 (1945), 161-173.

The remaining poems can properly be considered together as a body of poetry whose intention is compliment and praise. The fact that, when read at all, these poems, like the *Anniversaries*, have provoked vehement critical denunciation for their outrageous flattery suggests that a study of them may well help to clarify Donne's idea of Elizabeth Drury. More broadly, an effort to define the kind of praise Donne characteristically accords his subjects, whoever they are, can help us identify just what is significantly new in Donne's conception and practice of poetic praise.

Donne's occasional poetry of praise impresses the reader as radically different from the epideictic poetry of his contemporaries, and the impression is not a mistaken one. The Epicedes and Obsequies and the verse letters in question—almost all written in the period 1605-1614[3]—are very similar in style, regardless of subject or genre or occasion. In writing them Donne clearly did not respect the precise distinctions of the rhetoricians and writers of *artes poeticae* prescribing the form and decorum of a poem of praise—encomium, epigram, panegyric, epitaph, epicede, elegy —according to the specific occasion and social status of the person praised.[4] These poems are all analytic epistles of a sort, and those for funeral occasions, no less than the others, are audaciously witty and hyperbolic. Besides constituting an illuminating approach to Donne's *Anniversaries*, many

[3] The dates for the poems cited are based upon evidence supplied in Milgate's edition of the *Satires, Epigrams, and Verse Letters*, in Grierson's edition of the *Poems*, in John T. Shawcross, *The Complete Poetry of John Donne* (Garden City, N.Y., 1967), in Edmund Gosse, *The Life and Letters of John Donne*, 2 vols. (New York, 1899), and especially in R. C. Bald's biography, *John Donne: A Life* (Oxford, 1970), revised and completed by Wesley Milgate. Only one poem of the type with which I am concerned falls outside the dates indicated, the "Hymn to the Saints, and to the Marquesse Hamylton" (1625).

[4] See J. C. Scaliger, *Poetices libri septem*, pp. 405-438; Puttenham, *Arte of English Poesie*, pp. 18-47; see also Hardison, *Enduring Monument*, pp. 62-122.

of these poems are significant in their own right, richly deserving of rescue from critical oblivion.

The difference we sense between Donne's poetry of compliment and that of his contemporaries does not result from his radical departure from contemporary poetic forms. Donne uses in these occasional poems precisely the topics of praise we have identified as conventional, and he promotes many of the current trends—the Horatian verse letter which explores a subject, the growing Christian emphasis upon grace and regeneration, the tighter logical organization of poems. Nor are the actual occasions and motivations for this verse significantly different from those which give rise to the verse of his contemporaries. R. C. Bald's comprehensive biography describes how some of these poems figured in Donne's efforts to secure patronage through fashionable quasi-Petrarchan addresses to various ladies, and quotes a few uneasy letters in which Donne offered tenuous explanations for the extravagance or promiscuity of his praises.[5] What distinguishes Donne from a host of poets seeking patronage by their craft, in addition of course to his prodigious talent, is his transformation of these occasions into poetic explorations of the question of praise itself. Specifically, the unique elements of Donne's poetry of compliment are the speaker's meditative stance and the symbolic value he discovers in the person addressed—both of which have profound implications for the way in which the conventional *topoi* are developed. In Donne's practice the poem of praise undergoes a sea-change, becoming, for all its audacious wit, a metaphysical inquiry into the bases of human worth.

The characteristic stance of Donne's speaker is one of "studying" or "meditating upon" or "contemplating" the person he addresses or elegizes. The meditation may be presented as peculiarly the speaker's, or, more commonly, he may involve "us"—the sympathetic audience—in the experience. As we have seen, this "meditational" stance was

---

[5] See Bald, *John Donne*, pp. 155-277.

taken occasionally in Henry Lok's poems, but no contemporary poet approaches Donne's consistent use of it; moreover, this stance differs significantly from the more or less logical analysis of a person or a concept which occurs in some of Jonson's poems and in certain of the elegies on Prince Henry.[6] In Donne's poems, the speaker is in the position of seeking to discover or understand something about the nature of reality by means of—through—the person praised. Accordingly, he proposes to study the Countess of Bedford through her friends in an effort to reach the divinity in her; elsewhere he declares that he finds in her "all record, all prophecie."[7] He finds Edward Herbert to be "All worthy bookes," and offers on different occasions to tell the Countesses of Salisbury and Huntington what he has learned "by daring to contemplate" them.[8] In the elegy on Prince Henry he recounts how we can understand the near relation of Reason and Faith by "contemplation of that Prince."[9] In his "Obsequies to the Lord Harrington" he rejoices that he has grown good enough "that I can studie thee,/ And, by these meditations refin'd,/ Can unapparell and enlarge my minde."[10] And, by a nice reversal, in an "Epitaph on Himselfe" he offers his (dead) self as an object of meditation to everybody (*Omnibus*), so that each of his readers can "in my graves inside see what thou art now," and by contemplation of the changes wrought in the speaker's soul and body by death can "mend thy selfe."[11]

This meditational stance does not involve use of the Ignatian or any other method of meditation. It means simply

---

[6] See above, chap. 1, pp. 33, 36-37.

[7] "Reason is our Soules left hand," ll. 9-10, *Milgate*, p. 90; "You have refin'd mee," l. 52, *ibid.*, p. 93.

[8] "To Sir Edward Herbert, at Julyers," l. 48, *ibid.*, p. 81; "Man to Gods Image," l. 46, *ibid.*, p. 87; "Faire, great, and good," l. 32, *ibid.*, p. 108.

[9] "Elegie upon the Untimely Death of the Incomparable Prince Henry," l. 18, in *Sundry Funeral Elegies*, sigs. E-E 2ᵛ.

[10] ll. 10-12, Grierson, *Poems*, I, 271.

[11] ll. 10, 21, Milgate, *Satires, etc.*, p. 103.

that the speaker—often explicitly and always in practice—undertakes to explore religious or philosophical truth by writing the praises of an individual. Therefore, the conventional topics of praise are not used as counters, but are subjected to intensive analysis to force them to yield their essential meanings. Also, the speakers constantly employ the theological language and imagery appropriate to conventional religious meditation, thereby evoking in the reader expectations of seriousness and sincerity. As a result, Donne's poems of compliment have created a critical furor most other epideictic poems escape, precisely because Donne's are neither praises of moral virtue in the time-honored classical fashion, nor yet simply the conventional small change of polite social intercourse, but are presented as a means of arriving at profound spiritual truths.

The second major difference is in the symbolic conception of the person praised, which permits Donne consistently to apply to any individual those extreme formulations of the conventional *topoi* most contemporary poets invoked (and then with circumspection) only for praises of royalty. Donne's topics are framed so as to insist that virtue, or goodness, or divinity is incarnate in the individual praised or mourned: the "All" is persistently epitomized in the particular example. Robert Ellrodt has rightly observed that this is a contra-Platonic impulse:

> This [unity] is not, one can see, an ideal, mathematical, intelligible unity of the Platonic or Plotinian One, the One beyond Being. The effort of Donne to seize the totality of being in the individual being is oriented on the contrary according to the Christian perspective of the Incarnation. This is easily done when the All means precisely Christ, the Man God. . . . More remarkable is the instance which shows the author of the Anniversaries and the Epicedes "incarnating" the All in the person who is the object of his praises.[12]

[12] Ellrodt, *L'Inspiration Personnelle et L'Esprit du Temps chez les Poètes Metaphysiques Anglais*, vol. i (Paris, 1960), p. 137: "Ce n'est

The human individual is symbolic in a particular way for Donne—not as image or reflection of an ideal Platonic Form or Idea, but, more precisely, as image of God; on that ground the individual can be said to embody, restate, or incarnate divine reality or the entire Book of the Creatures in himself. This symbolic perspective is not casually assumed by Donne, and, though it is applied to one patron or patroness after another, it is not meaningless hyperbole. Of course these propositions are developed with a good deal of wit, and part of that wit inheres in the social manner which exalts the particular subject at hand over all other persons, some of whom Donne may have praised in quite the same terms in other poems. This is apt to strike us as the shallowest social posturing. But behind these gestures of witty compliment is a conception of the source of human worth which is hinted at in many of the poems and made explicit in one of the most hyperbolic of them, the verse letter "To the Countesse of Salisbury:" "Faire, great, and good, since seeing you, wee see/ What Heaven can doe, 'and what any Earth can be."[13] These are not praises judiciously evaluating the specific virtues and characteristics of the individual, as Ben Jonson's often are,[14] but metaphysical praises of the possibilities of the human spirit acted upon by God. Yet these possibilities are never treated abstractly, but only as they may inhere in a particular person. And they may inhere in any particular individual whom Donne wishes or needs to praise at any given time. The patrons and patronesses can be substituted one for another since the

---

pas, on le voit, l'unité idéale, mathématique, intelligible, de l'Un platonicien, ou plotinien, l'Un au-delà de l'Etre. L'effort de Donne pour saisir la totalité de l'Etre dans l'être individuel s'oriente au contraire selon la perspective chrétienne de l'Incarnation. Ceci s'admet aisément lorsque le Tout désigne précisément le Christ, l'Homme-Dieu. Plus remarquable est l'insistance que met l'auteur des *Anniversaires* et des *Epicedes* à 'incarner' le Tout en la personne qui est l'objet des ses louanges."

[13] Milgate, *Satires, etc.*, p. 107.

[14] See above, chap. I, pp. 36-37.

47

hyperbolic *topoi* do not belong to any individual as such: they are recognitions of what heaven can make of any piece of human clay, of what we can study and discern through any good Christian's life, of the "God" *in* the Countess of Bedford—or any other.

A. Methods of Development

Certain of Donne's verse letters and funeral elegies resemble Jonson's verse letters in that the subject is a general proposition relating to virtue, or religion, or death, or sorrow, and the poem takes the form of an analytical argument demonstrating the proposition or exploring its implications. In these poems Donne takes the occasion of a verse letter to explore a subject whose ramifications extend far beyond the particular occasion, yet the individual addressed or elegized is organic to the development of the argument. The nonpersonal but incarnational focus means that the person praised is not an allegory or exemplum, or merely the recipient of the poetic argument, but is precisely *the* individual in whom (for the purposes at hand) the "All" may be said to inhere.

The epistle "To Sir Edward Herbert, at Julyers" (1610) develops the argument that man is capable of producing all things, good and evil, out of himself. Taking the posture of one of Herbert's "good friends" and speaking for that select group, the speaker argues in objective, analytic terms, that "Man is a lumpe" which produces all beasts (passions); that he is happy only when wisdom controls those beasts, but that normally (like the devils who inhabited the Gadarene swine) he incites them and makes them worse; and that he himself adds corrosiveness to the curses of God and the punishments God sends for his good.[15] The next point is that, because our business is "to rectifie/ Nature, to what she was" (ll. 33-34), we do wrong to conceive of man as a microcosm since he is greater than all: "Man into himselfe

[15] Milgate, *Satires, etc.*, pp. 80-81.

can draw/ All; All his faith can swallow, 'or reason chaw./
. . . All the round world, to man is but a pill"—variously
"Poysonous, or purgative, or cordiall" depending upon who
takes it (ll. 37-42). In conclusion the speaker addresses
Herbert directly, as the embodiment of all that has been
said: Herbert bravely and truly claims to know man and
therefore knows all the world. In him (and thereby for his
friends who contemplate him) this universal knowledge is
cordial:

> As brave as true, is that profession than
> Which you doe use to make; that you know man.
> This makes it credible; you'have dwelt upon
> All worthy bookes, and now are such a one.
> Actions are authors, and of those in you
> Your friends finde every day a mart of new.
>
> (ll. 45-50)

Also of this kind is the epistle "To the Countesse of Hun-
tington" beginning "That unripe side of earth" (1605?).[16]
Here the central issue of the poem is the right definition
and conduct of a worthy love. The speaker's stance is per-
sonal: he analyzes his own problem, but then expands the
terms so that at the end of the poem he speaks for all "able
men, blest with a vertuous Love" (l. 121). The situation—
the great distance the speaker observes between himself
and the exalted lady whose friendship he enjoys—might
seem to invite Petrarchan adoration, but the speaker, con-
cerned to prove himself an "able" lover, satirizes and repu-
diates that stance: no calf-eyed Petrarchan devotion for
him. Either he will win love in return, or he will cease lov-
ing: "I cannot feele the tempest of a frowne,/ I may
be rais'd by love, but not throwne down" (ll. 27-28); "The
honesties of love with ease I doe,/ But am no porter for a
tedious woo" (ll. 75-76). The problem of how to love
worthily one so elevated in rank and merit is resolved by

---

[16] *Ibid.*, pp. 81-85. The Countess addressed is the Lady Elizabeth
Hastings.

the transformation of the terms from Petrarchan amorous devotion to Neoplatonic admiration of perfection. The speaker affirms that when we reach our height of goodness she is still the Sun above, so that her love has the bounty of light, "That gives to all, and yet hath infinite" (l. 102). Such perfection evokes men's love, but the impure soul cannot reach this height " 'Till slow accesse hath made it wholy pure" (l. 105). Passion is mere profanity to this Neoplatonic love which—whether the object is near or far—is all delight, the epitome of all virtues. The general problem of identifying worthy love is hereby resolved by means of the solution of the personal difficulty—how the lowly but self-respecting poet is to "love" the great lady.

Some of the funeral elegies are also epistles of this kind. They pose and explore, on the occasion of a particular death, some general problem—usually the power (or paradoxical lack of power) which death or sorrow is able to exercise over mankind when the counterpoise is a regenerate Christian soul. To be sure, this problem is addressed in one way or another in most Christian funeral elegy: it is a donnée of the genre. But, characteristically, Donne embodies the problem and its resolution in the particulars of the occasion, and he bases the traditional consolation of elegy less upon the departed person's happy condition in heaven than upon the full recognition of his worth and privileges as regenerate soul.

The "Elegie on the Lady Marckham" (d. 1609) queries the extent and limitations of death's power in that constant, perpetual conflict between death and mankind.[17] The speaker, addressing a generalized audience assumed to be concerned about this death, notes that God has set bounds between man (the microcosm) and death, as between land and sea at the creation: "Man is the World, and death th' Ocean,/ To which God gives the lower parts of man" (ll. 1-2). Yet death "breaks our bankes, when ere it takes

[17] Grierson, *Poems*, I, 279-281. Lady Bridget Markham was a cousin of Lucy, Countess of Bedford.

a friend" (l. 6) and our grief makes us, like Noah, drown our world again. But these tears of passion prevent us from seeing what we are, and what she is. The problem posed by her death is resolved by the revelation of her nature as a regenerate soul. Death has no true power over that soul, now freed by corporal death from the spiritual death of sin, or over her flesh which in the grave will be refined as in an alembic, becoming at the last day "th'Elixar of this All" (l. 28). Her worth, and its power to resolve the problem, pertains to her as regenerate soul:

> Grace was in her extremely diligent,
> That kept her from sinne, yet made her repent.
> Of what small spots pure white complaines! Alas,
> How little poyson cracks a christall glasse!
> She sinn'd, but just enough to let us see
> That God's word must be true, All, sinners be.
>
> (ll. 39-44)

She wept for her imperfections (as common natures do) and seemed to climb to heaven by repentance though in fact she was already there. At length the speaker, having resolved in general terms the problem of death's power, composes his elegy so that it is itself a force in man's ongoing conflict with death. He affirms his willingness to testify "How fit she was for God" so that Death may repent his vain haste, but declares his unwillingness to show "How fit for us . . . How Morall, how Divine," lest this add to Death's triumphs (ll. 53-62).

The "Elegie on Mistress Boulstred" (d. 1609) also analyzes the power of death and its paradoxical defeat in taking the souls of the just.[18] As several critics have recognized, the poem begins with a recantation of the "Death Be Not Proud" sonnet, the speaker throughout addressing Death in personal terms but also as spokesman for "us," her

---

[18] *Ibid.*, pp. 282-284. Cecelia Boulstred was also related to Lucy Bedford. Cf. Jonson's "Epitaph" on her death, chap. 1, p. 32, and note 73.

friends: "Death I recant, and say, unsaid by mee/ What ere hath slip'd, that might diminish thee" (ll. 1-2). The speaker then describes vividly—by means of a "nature reversed" *topos* taken as actual fact, rather than in the more usual sense as the speaker's grief-induced aberration—the whole world as a universe of death: all life is devoured by Death and served up to his table, not only creatures of the earth but also the fishes of the sea and the birds of the air. In this perspective the countervailing power of the regenerate soul looks slight at first: Death must indeed lay all he kills at God's feet, but God reserves only a few, leaving most to Death. Yet meditation on Boulstred as one of those regenerate few reveals that Death has achieved no triumph here: her soul is in heaven, her body only waits to go there where it will be "almost another soule," for this is her privilege as one of the elect, secure in grace: "Death gets 'twixt soules and bodies such a place/ As sinne insinuates 'twixt just men and grace,/ Both work a separation, no divorce" (ll. 43-45). By his haste Death has lost what chance he might have had of winning her by the vices of age—ambition, covetousness, spiritual pride—or of winning others to sin by thinking evil of her or desiring her wrongfully. Death still has the opportunity to provoke others to sin through immoderate grief for her, but the speaker proposes that her "knot of friends" counter that by weeping only because we are not so good as she is.

The elegy "Death" which begins "Language thou art too narrow" (also assumed to have been occasioned by the death of Cecelia Boulstred)[19] analyzes the problem of sorrow in relation to the death of the just. The speaker, as "our" spokesman, begins with a conventional *topos* of inexpressibility (he is so grief-stricken that he cannot express it) and then undertakes a tirade against Sorrow, the chief addressee of the poem, for attempting to extend his empire over all mankind by taking Mistress Boulstred. Paradoxically, however, Sorrow fails in that effort, for if we

[19] Grierson, *Poems*, 1, pp. 284-286.

52

pine and die in sorrowing for her death, that is no misery after she has left us. The resolution of this problem also comes from her status as regenerate soul, the embodiment of all worth:

> For of all morall vertues she was all,
>   The Ethicks speake of vertues Cardinall.
> Her soule was Paradise; the Cherubin
>   Set to keepe it was grace.
>
> (ll. 33-36)

The point is reinforced by several biblical images: since she was Paradise, God took her lest (like Adam and Eve) we love her above him and his laws; her heart was a Moses' bush burning with religious fires but not consumed; she prefigured here her life in heaven; she was of seraphical order on earth and now dwells with the seraphim next to God. Then the speaker, by means of a lovely image, conveys how her body and soul together will be transformed through death: "the tree/ That wraps that christall in a wooden Tombe,/ Shall be tooke up spruce, fill'd with diamond" (ll. 58-60). Through her status as a regenerate soul, heir to the promises, the general problem of the ambiguities of Christian sorrow for death is resolved and the specific "we" of the poem can be appropriately, if paradoxically, termed her "sad glad friends" (l. 61).

A second category of verse letters comprises poems primarily concerned with exploring that most common of the conventional topics of praise, the virtuous lady, in its characteristic Donnean formulation whereby the lady is regarded as the very embodiment or incarnation of virtue. Usually the poems state explicitly that God has made her so. In these tightly unified poems, the *topos* is analyzed logically and seriously, and in the course of such analysis some important philosophical issue is posed and resolved—notably, how can complete virtue exist in, act in, or manifest itself to an essentially wicked world. The speaker's stance in these poems is superficially one of Petrarchan admiration, and the particular addressee is of course expected to be pleased by it, but by means of the analytic method and meditational posture the poems probe much deeper levels of significance. They suggest that by meditating upon the lady in terms of the conventional *topos* of virtue, taken as truth, the speaker himself and also the larger audience influenced by the lady can come to understand the weighty philosophical and religious issues raised.

One such poem, particularly interesting in relation to the theological basis of the symbolism invested in the person praised, is the letter "To the Countesse of Huntingdon" (1608-1609) which begins, "Man to Gods image."[20] It poses the question as to why virtue has embodied itself in woman's weak form; the answer is, to reveal perfect virtue to weak souls. The speaker first calls attention to the traditional theological strictures against women: Eve was made to man's image, not God's; there is some doubt whether she was given a soul; women may not hold ecclesiastical or civil offices; in woman mild innocence might sometimes appear (as a "seldome comet") but active goodness is a miracle. The Countess is a miracle like the star that led the Magi, revealing virtue both to "apt soules, and the worst." The Countess, like all the others, is virtue incarnate: virtue exiled by men has "fled to heaven, that's heavenly things, that's you" (l. 22). Virtue which gilded others has turned her to gold and transubstantiated her into virtue itself. But she retains the lowly roles of wife and mother to manifest herself and virtue, "Else, being alike pure, wee should neither see" (l. 33). The references to the star and Magi, and to the revelation of heavenly things in low, fleshly form, invite us to connect her as incarnation of virtue with the Incarnation: continuing the analogy, the speaker finds her a far-off "revelation" to himself, and concludes that he shows some virtue in daring to contemplate her. But he insists that he does not flatter in saying these things: he had prophesied them before and now merely records them (as

[20] Milgate, *Satires, etc.*, pp. 85-88.

a prophet or an apostle telling of an incarnation). And he makes explicit what he praises, the source of her virtue— "God in you":

> Now that my prophesies are all fulfill'd,
>   Rather then God should not be honour'd too,
> And all these gifts confess'd, which hee instill'd,
>   Your selfe were bound to say that which I doe.
>
> So I, but your Recorder am in this,
>   Or mouth, and Speaker of the universe,
> A ministeriall Notary, for 'tis
>   Not I, but you and fame, that make this verse;
>
> I was your Prophet in your yonger dayes,
> And now your Chaplaine, God in you to praise.
>
> (ll. 61-70)

The epistle "To the Countesse of Bedford" which begins "T'have written then" (1609)[21] identifies her as perfect virtue and, in analyzing this *topos*, addresses the problem of true virtue in the world from another point of view. The speaker identifies himself as a "nothing," but one which might produce something (as mines in barren ground yield coal or stone) since her virtue acting on him has hallowed a pagan muse. She is "the worlds best part, or all It" (l. 20); she is the home of virtue (which fled from courtiers); or she is virtue itself which preserves one court and ransoms one sex. But since she does not understand her own worth, he invites her to meditate with him on the ills of others—chiefly, that our bodies taint our minds and souls, that our bodies which are able to produce all things out of themselves produce only vicious things, and that we grudge to make ourselves fit for heaven. In such a world her complete virtue poses a problem: can it exist as unalloyed virtue or is there some perverseness or tincture of vice in the fact that she is unaware (and hence unbelieving) of her own worth, and that her ignorance of vice may lessen her compassion

---

[21] *Ibid.*, pp. 95-98.

for others. But the conclusion is that virtue can remain un-alloyed in her: in others the aspersion of vice or vice itself may play a role in counteracting another vice, but in her it has no such office. Cordial virtue is appropriately her sole nourishment.

Another epistle to Lady Bedford beginning, "Honour is so sublime perfection" (1608-1612)[22] queries how her per-fect virtue can be properly manifested to, or praised by, the unworthy. The first argument relating to this issue is that all honor, even to God himself, comes from inferiors. The second is that radiation from her can subdue the clouds of the speaker's darkness and give him light to contemplate her. A hyperbolic figure provides the terms for resolving the problem: she teaches the speaker (and his audience) "the use of specular stone,/ Through which all things within without were shown" (ll. 29-30)—that is, her external be-havior fully reveals her inner state:

> You, for whose body God made better clay,
> Or tooke Soules stuffe such as shall late decay,
> Or such as needs small change at the last day.
>
> This, as an Amber drop enwraps a Bee,
> Covering discovers your quicke Soule; that we
> May in your through-shine front your hearts
>   thoughts see.
>
> (ll. 22-27)

In her, therefore, virtue can be revealed or manifested, since she gives equal care to being and seeming, to religion (the internal state) and to wit or discretion (external ac-tions). Not content to make wit and religion colleagues, she transmutes wit into religion, thereby resolving the problem of the revelation of virtue in the wicked world. According-ly, the speaker urges her to continue in this path, "great and innocent" (l. 54).

Still another verse letter, "To the Countesse of Bedford.

[22] "To the Countesse of Bedford," *ibid.*, pp. 100-102.

At New-yeares Tide" (1610),[23] explores the topic celebrating her as the embodiment of perfect virtue by focusing upon a problem personal to the speaker: how is he as poet to praise her in such a way as to gain credence from his audience. He desires, "since these times shew'd mee you," to "show future times/ What you were" (ll. 10-12), for it is appropriate that verse embalm virtue. One problem is his own nothingness, but another is that she, as embodiment of virtue, is a miracle: the audience may not believe in her now that faith is so scarce, or at least not believe that so low a thing as he could truly express her. Here the resolution of the problem is left to God, who will teach her appropriate discretion in manners so that her virtue will be apparent to all, and will so exercise her with doubts, temporary absences of his comfort, and involvement with others' weaknesses that she will become comprehensible to weaker mortals. Finally, the speaker declares that her merit is the result of God's grace proclaiming the "private Ghospell" of her enrollment among the elect:

> From need of teares he will defend your soule,
>   Or make a rebaptizing of one teare;
> Hee cannot, (that's, he will not) dis-inroule
>   Your name; and when with active joy we heare
>   This private Ghospell, then 'tis our New Yeare.
>
> (ll. 61-65)

Yet another verse letter of this kind to Lady Bedford beginning "You have refin'd mee, and to worthyest things" (1608?)[24] develops from the *topos* defining the lady as the embodiment or essence of both beauty and virtue. Her virtue manifests itself chiefly at court, where this quality is rare, and her beauty chiefly in the country, where beauty is similarly rare. Since she is now in the country, the speak-

---

[23] Milgate's dating; pp. 98-100. In *Life*, Bald suggests (p. 173) the possibility that this was the poem referred to and enclosed in a letter to the Countess on Dec. 31, 1607.

[24] Bald's dating, *Life*, p. 175; Milgate, *Satires, etc.*, pp. 91-94.

er determines to praise her beauty, which is a light produc-
ing in the country a new world and new creatures. The
problem is simply whether, and how, it is appropriate to
praise beauty instead of virtue, given the consensus of clas-
sical and Renaissance rhetoricians that praises ought to be
directed primarily to virtue. The resolution of the problem
begins with the praise of her beauty as "vertues temple":

> Yet to that Deity which dwels in you,
>   Your vertuous Soule, I now not sacrifice;
> These are Petitions, and not Hymnes; they sue
>   But that I may survay the edifice.
>
> (ll. 31-34)

The speaker therefore seeks to go on a "pilgrimage" to a
temple (to behold her beauty), praising her "not as conse-
crate, but merely'as faire" (l. 49). There is a further justi-
fication of this procedure in that Platonic identity of beauty
and goodness somehow realized in her:

> If good and lovely were not one, of both
>   You were the transcript, and originall,
> The Elements, the Parent, and the Growth,
>   And every peece of you, is both their All:
> So'intire are all your deeds, and you, that you
> Must do the same thing still: you cannot two.
>
> (ll. 55-60)

But the speaker then discounts this argument as logic-
chopping school divinity: the testimony of the senses them-
selves lead to the Neoplatonic intuition. "Senses decree"
confirms her estate and herself "The Mine, the Magazine, the
Commonweale,/ The story'of beauty," and to the speaker it
is evident that whoever has seen that beauty would also wish
to see her beauty-and-virtue, "As, who had bin/ In Paradise,
would seeke the Cherubin" (ll. 69-72).

A third category includes poems centering upon a con-
ventional *topos* but one more hyperbolic than the topic of
virtue. Instead of posing and resolving a problem, these

poems analyse the terms of the topic (as pertaining to the person praised) to arrive at a precise and complete definition. Given Donne's incarnational focus, the assumption in poems of this kind is that meditation upon a particular person in the terms of such a topic, defined precisely and taken as truth, will reveal something about the nature of things— to the speaker in the first instance, but also to the audience joining him in the analysis/meditation.

Of this kind is the verse epistle or elegy addressed to the Countess of Bedford, probably on the occasion of the death of Lady Markham (1609), beginning, "You that are she and you, that's double shee."[25] The central *topos* is the commonplace on friendship which Plato originated, "they doe/ Which build them friendships, become one of two" (ll. 3-4); both ladies are praised by means of an analysis of this figure.[26] At first the praise seems to center upon the departed: Lady Bedford is defined as "double shee," and the topic "one of two" is first explained by analogy to the unity of soul and body, with Lady Markham as the heavenly soul and the Countess (because of her grief) as the "dead" body to whom the mourners pay tribute *as if* to the whole person: "She like the Soule is gone, and you here stay,/ Not a live friend; but th'other halfe of clay" (ll. 13-14). But then the terms are pressed further, so that they take on meanings very suggestive for the metaphysical significances incorporated in Elizabeth Drury. The particular unity of the two friends is defined as an entity subject to decay in some parts but not in its elements (virtues), which being pure cannot decay. The speaker accordingly observes to the Countess that although Lady Markham's soul is fled to heaven and her flesh to death, her virtues "as to their proper spheare,/ Returne to dwell with you, of whom they

[25] "To the Lady Bedford," Milgate, pp. 94-95. The friend is probably Lady Markham, though possibly Cecelia Boulstred. These ladies died at Twickenham within three months of each other in 1609.

[26] See Laurens J. Mills, *One Soul in Bodies Twain* (Bloomington, Indiana, 1937).

were" (ll. 29-30). This deft turn associates the Countess of Bedford with God as source and end of all good: all Lady Markham's virtues are said to be contracted in the Countess who (again like God) cannot by taking additions of this sort be diminished or changed in any way. Lady Bedford is advised, finally, that she cannot replace Lady Markham with another friend; only a faithful book, indeed only the Book of Judith, can be such a "book of virtues" as she. In this poem, analysis of the topic "one of two" in regard to this particular friendship leads, although the conclusion is not stated explicitly, to a metaphysical intuition about the "conservation of good" in the world, which operates through the interrelationships of faithful friendship to prevent the loss of any dram of virtue.

The "Letter to the Lady Carey, and Mrs. Essex Riche, From Amyens," was written in 1611-1612, when Donne was abroad with Sir Robert Drury;[27] it is nearly contemporaneous with *The Second Anniversarie* and was evidently occasioned by a suggestion from their brother, Sir Robert Rich, when he visited Donne in Amiens. Like Elizabeth Drury, these ladies were not personally known to Donne:[28] the poem claims knowledge of them solely by "faith and ecstasy." Here a conventional Petrarchan *topos* affords the focus—Lady Carey is a "saint"; but the precise definition of the term "saint" is worked out in serious Christian terms, albeit with whimsical wit. The speaker, located in idolatrous France where all saints are invoked, refuses to become a schismatic by separating himself from the common practice, nor yet a heretic by addressing any saint other than Lady Carey. Moreover, to redress the "low degree" of faith in that place he undertakes to tell what he has understood of her sainthood by the only means able to produce such understanding—by faith: "I thought it some Apostleship in mee/ To speake things which by faith alone I see" (ll. 11-12). By this means he sees that her "sainthood" is not a collection of individual virtues as papist devotees of

<hr>

[27] Milgate, pp. 105-107. [28] Bald, pp. 248-249.

saints might think, or as obtains with those whose virtues are "But in their humours, and at seasons show" (l. 18). Rather, true virtue is a unity, is "our Soules complexion" (l. 32), or, yet more precisely, "True vertue'is *Soule,* Alwaies in all deeds *All*" (l. 36). Virtue, so defined, could not work upon her soul, "For, your soule was as good Vertue, as shee" (l. 39), and therefore it wrought upon her beauty, transforming that beauty to virtue also, so that her beauty moves others to virtue. Her sister is identified as worthy of praise in the same terms, being virtue and beauty of the same stuff. At length the speaker reaffirms his stance as one rendering "true devotion" to true saints, declaring that he has written what "in this my Extasie/ And revelation of you both I see" (l. 54). However whimsically, the poem intimates the metaphysical insight that true goodness (sanctity) is not a balance-sheet of virtues but the total transformation of the self: the pervasive language (apostleship, faith alone, extasie, revelation) indicates that the cause of the tranformation (and the object of the speaker's devotion) is the indwelling presence of God.

The letter to the Countess of Bedford beginning "Reason is our Soules left hand, Faith her right/ By these wee reach divinity, that's you" (1608-1612)[29] is in some ways the most outrageously hyperbolic of all these poems. It focuses upon the conventional Petrarchan topic, the celestial (or divine) lady, and in analyzing that topic with theological precision appears (for a while at least) to conflate Lady Bedford with God himself. The speaker declares his concern to "reach" (that is, to love) divinity— identified as Lady Bedford—and he proceeds by the theologically recognized means of reaching God: reason and faith. Those "who have the blessing of your sight" (like those who dwell with God) love her by reason. The speaker (being distant) loves by faith, and so presumably is heir to the biblical promises

---

[29] "To the Countesse of Bedford," Milgate, pp. 90-91. Bald locates the poem in the early stages of Donne's relationship with the Countess, probably 1608.

here echoed: "Blessed are they that have not seen, and yet have believed"; "faith is the ... evidence of things not seen."[30]

Nevertheless, reason plays a role in relation to faith, not "to'encrease, but to expresse" it, that is, to clarify it to the understanding. Accordingly, the speaker undertakes rationally to seek the traces, evidences, and effects of her divinity in the world: "Therefore I study you first in your Saints,/ Those friends, whom your election glorifies,/ Then in your deeds. . ." (ll. 9-11). Finally, as the reasons for loving her grow infinite (as God is infinite) he is thrown back upon "implicite faith" in that overarching attribute of divinity acknowledged by all, "That you are good" (l. 17). At this point the *topos* of divinity begins to be restricted and further clarified: her goodness is said to be preserved because her birth and beauty is as a balm (inborn preservative) to keep it fresh, and also because she makes of learning and religion and virtue a mithridate (curative against poisons) to keep off or cure ills—her share in the mortal condition being acknowledged by the need of such medicine. She is praised as the "first good Angell" to appear in woman's shape, and as "Gods masterpeece, and so/ His Factor for our loves" (ll. 31-34). At this point the topic is revealed as something other than witty blasphemy. The Countess is divine because, being good, she preserves and manifests the image of God, and in doing so she becomes God's "Factor" —that is, his agent or deputy—attracting our loves to that divinity in herself. The final lines return to the issue of the speaker's reaching (loving) divinity. The speaker urges Lady Bedford to concern herself before all else (even before benefiting him by being the object of his contemplation or his patroness) with her "returne home" to heaven, and with making that return "gracious," that is, fraught with grace for others (in imitation of Christ, the primary Factor for God in that role). For the worst that can happen to a man

[30] "To the Countesse of Bedford," ll. 3-4. Cf. John 20:29, Heb. 21:1.

62

is to "miss" the Divine in heaven: "For so God helpe mee, 'I would not misse you there/ For all the good which you can do me here" (ll. 35-38). Meditation on the *topos* of the divine lady, in relation to Lucy, Countess of Bedford, yields the insight that her divine soul—as image and therefore manifestation of God—can lead the meditator to God. In such a poem we are very close both to the kind of hyperbole found in the *Anniversary* poems, and to their fundamental assumptions.

B. POEMS ABOUT PRAISING

The poems in the final category—the longest and most complex of the verse letters and funeral poems—fuse the various methods of development we have noted: a problem is posed and resolved as the poet studies its embodiment in the person praised; and a conventional topic is closely analysed for whatever problems or metaphysical insights it may yield. But the focus shifts: in these poems it is squarely upon the person praised as an object of contemplation, and upon the speaker's concern with the analytic and meditative process itself. These poems directly address the issue of what the speaker can understand by meditating upon a human being, and what it is that he praises in such an exercise. In a sense, then, these are poems about themselves, and about Donne's conception of the poetry of praise. It is no accident, surely, that all these poems were composed within two years of the *Anniversaries*—reflecting, perhaps, Donne's wish to explain more clearly what he had attempted in those complex, much misunderstood poems, but more probably indicating that the challenge of writing the *Anniversaries* had markedly increased his capacity to articulate the premises of his poetry of praise.

The letter "To the Countesse of Salisbury," dated August, 1614,[31] undertakes to determine exactly what the speaker (and we sharing the exercise with him) can come to know

[31] Milgate, pp. 107-110. The addressee is Lady Catherine Howard.

and understand by meditating upon the Countess—"daring to contemplate you" (l. 32). First, she manifests what "Faire, great, and good" really are, given their absence from the decaying world; she becomes, indeed, the embodiment of those qualities, which have the force of Platonic ideas. Now that the sun is grown stale and little valued, she comes "to repaire/ Gods booke of creatures, teaching what is faire" (ll. 7-8). Also, now that all is "wither'd, shrunke, and dri'd"; now that the world's frame is "crumbled into sand"; now that "Integritie, friendship, and confidence,/ (Ciments of greatnes)" are vaporized; and now that men by love of littleness seek to "draw to lesse,/ Even that nothing, which at first we were"; the speaker by contemplating her greatness learns that one must be great in order to get "Towards him that's infinite" (ll. 9-24). Also, in an age so evil that all are guilty of crimes, and a good person seems a monster, she manifests what goodness is. He learns further that he and others also can have some share in these qualities that she embodies and manifests as absolutes. This principle affords the speaker an excuse for having praised others (Elizabeth Drury?) in similar terms. One justification is that, like one who would praise God's works of creation as they occurred, day by day, the speaker's praises of each person are true when given, although the next day may reveal something better to him. More important, he insists that he has praised the same qualities in all these persons:

> I adore
> The same things now, which I ador'd before,
> The subject chang'd, and measure; the same thing
> In a low constable, and in the King
> I reverence; His power to worke on mee:
> So did I humbly reverence each degree
> Of faire, great, good; but more, now I am come
> From having found their *walkes*, to finde their *home*.
>
> (ll. 57-64)

Lesser manifestations of fair, great, and good in other women have enabled him now to "read" these Platonic absolutes in her, and he can do so despite residing in Plato's "darke Cave" or in the "Grave" of human mortality, because she is able to "illustrate" those who study her. Despite his blindness and unworthiness (deprived as he is of physical means to see her at court), he believes that by contemplating her with his inner vision, "I shall . . . all goodnesse have discern'd,/ And though I burne my librarie, be learn'd" (ll. 83-84). Since the Countess is the present subject she is taken as the embodiment, the incarnation of these Platonic absolutes, and other ladies are images or imitations to lead the speaker to her. But this hyperbole is placed in perspective by the opening couplet, "Faire, great, and good, since seeing you, wee see/ What Heaven can doe, 'and what any Earth can be." This statement reveals that the praise is directed primarily to the qualities themselves, wherever resident, and that the speaker celebrates what Heaven can make of any human clay, any good Christian.

Central to Donne's elegy on Prince Henry (d. November 6, 1612)[32] is the contemporary commonplace identifying Henry as a type (recapitulation) of Christ. The problem of the poem, developed by means of a nature-reversed *topos* taken as fact, is the dislocation of reason and faith in the world caused by the death of the expected savior. Again the chief focus is upon the speaker as meditator, seeking to discover what contemplation of this prince may mean. As Ruth Wallerstein has noted, analytic meditation fuses with devotion as the speaker begins with a plea for the preservation of his faith—"Look to Me, *Faith*, and look to my *Faith*, God"—and ends by imagining himself an "Angel singing."[33]

The speaker begins by defining for himself, but also for "us," the respective roles of reason and faith as the two centers of man. Reason is concerned with "All that this naturall

---

[32] In *Sundry Funeral Elegies*, sigs. E-E 2ᵛ.
[33] Wallerstein, *Seventeenth-Century Poetic*, pp. 70-71.

World doth comprehend" (l. 6), faith with the enormous greatnesses (divine things) that are beyond the world. Yet (in scholastic terms) reason and faith almost meet, and contemplation of Prince Henry offered "us" our best opportunity to experience their congruence: "For, All that *Faith* could credit Mankinde *could,/ Reason* still seconded that This PRINCE would" (ll. 19-29). Now that he is gone, "Wee see not what to beleeve or know" (l. 24). It was believed that he would fulfill the Christ-type/ savior role: he "Was His great *Father's* greatest Instrument,/ And activ'st spirit to convey and tye/ This soule of *peace* through CHRISTIANITIE" (ll. 32-34), and his peace, an emblem of the millennial peace, was expected to last until the end of the world. But now this faith is heresy: God's curse on us is not death but a life which is "As but so manie *Mandrakes* on his Grave" sustained by "his putrification" (ll. 54-56), and the soul of our world is now grief. Moreover, as a Logos figure he was also the object of reason, the "only *Subject* REASON wrought upon" (l. 70); now that reason is gone "Wee/ May safelier say, that Wee are dead, then *Hee*" (ll. 79-80). At this point Henry's value as object of the meditation is stated precisely: as a type of Christ he is "Our Sowle's best Bayting and Mid-*period/* In her long *Journey* of *Considering* God" (ll. 85-86). As a type of the *Logos*, the object of reason and faith, his absence causes the dislocation of both these centers in macrocosm and microcosm. Just as God cannot be understood in his essence, so the speaker despairs of contemplating Henry in himself—"as *Hee* is HEE" (l. 84)—but concludes that if he cannot "reach" him by reason and faith he may do so through love, "As *Hee* embrac't the *Fires* of *Love* with us" (l. 88). The speaker might do this by contemplating that "shee-Intelligence that moved this sphere." The allusion may be to his devoted sister Princess Elizabeth who was often mentioned in contemporary elegies as chief mourner for him, but the identification is deliberately vague: "Who-e'r thou bee/ Which hast the noble *Con*-

science, Thou art *Shee*" (ll. 91-92). "Conscience" here
surely carries the Latin sense of sharing knowledge with
another.[34] The speaker accordingly pleads that whoever
had such a relationship of love and fidelity and communion
of souls with Henry will let the speaker know their his-
tories, their oaths, their souls, so that thereby he can "reach"
Henry. This understanding achieved through love will
make him an angel: "So, much as *You Two mutual Heavens*
were *here,*/ I were an *Angel singing* what *You* were" (ll.
97-98). As Miss Wallerstein observed, the poem itself is a
testimony that the speaker has attained his wish. In this
poem the individual praised is a recognized type of Christ
whom the speaker takes as an appropriate "mid-point" in
the "long *Journey* of *Considering* God." The object of the
meditation is clearly designated as the Divine manifested
in the individual.

The "Obsequies to the Lord Harrington," brother to Lady
Bedford (d. February 27, 1614),[35] is the longest of these
poems of compliment. The praise of Harrington is con-
ducted in terms both of the Platonic *topos* of the soul
as harmony, and the *topos* of virtue; his death poses
the problem of the uses of good men to the world and its
loss by their death. The speaker focuses directly upon his
own meditative purposes and his endeavor to see God in
the good person praised, but "we"—the audience—are per-
mitted to share in this very personal formal meditation, con-
ducted at the wholly appropriate hour of midnight. Invok-
ing Lord Harrington, as he might invoke God in another
kind of meditation, the speaker observes that Harrington
has retained his soul's infused harmony and, accordingly,
is now a part of God's cosmic organ. He invites Harrington
to rejoice that the speaker himself has,

[34] *Conscientia,* "a knowing of a thing together with another person
. . . a being privy to," *A Latin Dictionary,* ed. Charlton T. Lewis and
Charles Short (Oxford, 1958).

[35] "Obsequies to the Lord Harrington, brother to the Lady Lucy,
Countesse of Bedford," in Grierson, *Poems,* I, 271-279.

> to that good degree
> Of goodnesse growne, that I can studie thee,
> And, by these meditations refin'd,
> Can unapparell and enlarge my minde,
> And so can make by this soft extasie,
> This place a map of heav'n, my selfe of thee.
>
> (ll. 9-14)

As he pursues his meditation, the speaker sees Harrington as a sun illuminating him so that he is enabled to see all things in and through Harrington: "I see/ Through all, both Church and State, in seeing thee;/ And I discerne by favour of this light,/ My selfe, the hardest object of the sight" (ll. 27-30). This is so because in Harrington he sees the "All" that God manifests to us, by reason of Harrington's goodness:

> God is the glasse; as thou when thou dost see
> Him who sees all, seest all concerning thee,
> So, yet unglorified, I comprehend
> All, in these mirrors of thy wayes, and end.
> Though God be our true glasse, through which we see
> All, since the beeing of all things is hee,
> Yet are the trunkes which doe to us derive
> Things, in proportion fit, by perspective,
> Deeds of good men; for by their living here,
> Vertues, indeed remote, seeme to be neare.
>
> (ll. 31-40)

Next, by meditating on Harrington he comes to understand more about virtue—that it cannot be divided into separate virtues but grows "one intirenesse" (l. 62), one compound, instantly discerned. This is especially obvious in short-lived good men like Harrington, forced "to bee/ For lack of time, his owne epitome" (ll. 77-78). Then the problem posed by his death is engaged directly. He has set an example of living virtuously in youth, and of a pious death, but the world also needs examples relating to other ages and cases. Since

68

Harrington was like a true clock constantly controlled by God, he ought to have stayed here as "a generall/ And great Sun-dyall, to have set us All" (ll. 153-154). Now that he has died, Death, "else a desert," is "growne a Court," and the churchyard is the suburb of the New Jerusalem, the place from which Harrington begins his triumph. The speaker then claims a right, analogous to the prerogative of the Roman citizen, to chide the person accorded a triumph. Since by Roman custom triumphs were given only to those who had enlarged a kingdom, and since Harrington by conquering himself only rendered back his own soul and body "as intire/ As he, who takes endeavours, doth require" (ll. 211-212), his triumph is premature. He should have stayed to enlarge God's kingdom "By making others, what thou didst, to doe" (l. 214). He had such a charge, for "the Diocis/ Of ev'ry exemplar man, the whole world is" (ll. 225-226). Yet the speaker cannot chide the sovereign, God, for permitting the early triumph, and he must agree that "It was more fit,/ That all men should lacke thee, then thou lack it" (ll. 245-246). Indeed, the speaker by implication has undercut his complaint, for he has testified to his own advance in goodness through contemplating Harrington, who thereby is shown to be able after death to enlarge God's kingdom. To the world he is an exemplary man; to the meditator he is more—a glass in which to see God and all else besides. He is this because he is a regenerate soul whose perfections arise not of himself but of God "who takes endeavours" as perfected actions.

What has been said should not obscure the fact that witty praise is of the essence of Donne's poetry of compliment, or that the addressee and the broader audience are expected to enjoy the witty figures, the deft turns of phrase and thought, the extravagant postures, for their own sake. And yet this wit is compatible with—indeed, is the very vehicle for—serious "metaphysical" explorations of the bases of human worth. As so often with Donne in these extravagantly hyberbolic poems of compliment, wit and high seriousness have fused so completely as to become indistinguishable. Indeed, the praise one of these poems accords to the Countess of Bedford's way of life—in which the term "wit" carries the rich multiplicity of senses common in the age —seems to define with precision Donne's own method in the poetry of compliment: "Nor must wit/ Be colleague to religion, but be it."[36]

An important perspective upon the *Anniversary* poems is afforded by this demonstration that Donne's speaker characteristically assumes a meditative stance toward the person praised, and that the praises are not directed to the specific moral qualities of particular individuals (as were Ben Jonson's) but rather to the potentialities of the human soul as image of God. Moreover, the fact that these distinctive characteristics recur in poem after poem indicates that the *Anniversary* poems are not quite *sui generis*, but are only the longest and most complex of the poems of praise couched in the new symbolic mode Donne was creating—if not quite from nothing then at least from elements not customarily used in making poems of compliment and praise. The identification of these novel elements, and the specific sources of them in traditions of meditation, theological speculation, biblical exegesis, and funeral sermons, should next engage us. Study of these traditions shows them to be important contexts for Donne's *Anniversary* poems, but also reveals Donne's own formative influence upon these traditions themselves and the several proto-literary forms deriving from them in the early seventeenth century. In these areas also Donne must be regarded as an important influence upon the immediate intellectual and literary milieu, which itself so profoundly affected and was so largely manifested in his complex and ambitious *Anniversary* poems.

[36] "Honour is so sublime perfection," ll. 44-45, Milgate, *Satires, etc.*, p. 102. See George Williamson, *The Proper Wit of Poetry* (Chicago, 1961).

PART II

THEOLOGICAL CONTEXTS AND DONNEAN DEVELOPMENTS

Chapter III

Protestant Meditation and the Protestant Sermon

THE MEDITATIVE stance Donne characteristically employs in his poetry of compliment might seem to invite consideration in terms of the traditions of meditation which Louis L. Martz has explored in his important study, *The Poetry of Meditation*.[1] Martz has traced the widespread seventeenth-century fascination with meditation to Counter-Reformation influences, asserting that the failure of English Protestants to produce methodical treatises of their own on private devotion and meditation led them to adopt and make constant use of the continental Jesuit and Salesian manuals. Asserting the relevance of the Ignatian or Jesuit method of meditation for Donne's *Holy Sonnets* and especially for the *Anniversary* poems, Martz has pointed out structural and thematic similarities between the *Anniversaries* and certain five-part and seven-part meditative sequences in which meditations on the worthlessness of the world alternate with eulogies of an ideal pattern of virtue.[2] Approaching the poems through the continental meditative treatises, Martz considers Elizabeth Drury's death simply as the point of departure for poems whose true subject is the age-old meditative concern, the *contemptus mundi* and the true end of man.

Yet useful as they are for establishing general attitudes about meditation and suggesting typical structural patterns, the analogues Martz cites do not, as he himself admits, resolve the central problem of the *Anniversary* poems. For in the traditional meditations the ideal pattern of virtue eulo-

[1] Martz, *The Poetry of Meditation* (New Haven, 1954).
[2] *Ibid.*, pp. 218-248.

gized is Christ or the Virgin, and Martz does not find an adequate explanation for Donne's substitution of this unknown girl as the object of the eulogies. This fact leads him to conclude that the Petrarchan hyperbole of the eulogies mars both poems but especially blurs the focus of the *Anatomy*, since the eulogies of the dead girl are largely unrelated to the subject developed in the powerfully moving "meditative" sections of that poem, the decay of man and the world from the beginning because of original sin.[3] A more promising approach is indicated, I would suggest, by the evidence that Donne's poems of compliment are informed by a conception of meditation strikingly different from the Ignatian method. As we have seen, in Donne's occasional poems of praise even as in the *Anniversaries* the speaker customarily insists that meditation upon and praise of a particular person upon a specific occasion is the means to discovery of the highest spiritual truth.[4] "Occasion" in this usage does not seem to mean an adventitious circumstance, but rather an event infused with profound spiritual meaning and significance.

To illuminate the conception of meditation relevant for Donne's poetry of compliment and for the *Anniversaries*, I propose to attend to another immediate context—contemporary English Protestant theory and practice of meditation. This emphasis, and the general focus upon Protestant theology which informs this portion of the study, is not intended as a rejection but rather as a counterpoise to the several important studies which have emphasized Roman Catholic influences upon Donne.[5] The need for greater attention to Donne's Protestantism has been urged by Charles

[3] *Ibid.*, pp. 238-239.   [4] See above, Chapter II.

[5] See, e.g., M. P. Ramsay, *Les Doctrines médiévales chez Donne* (Oxford, 1916); Dennis Quinn, "Donne's Christian Eloquence" *ELH*, 27 (1960), 276-297; Winfried Schleiner, *The Imagery of John Donne's Sermons* (Providence, 1970); Malcolm Ross, *Poetry and Dogma: The Transfiguration of Eucharistic Symbols in Seventeenth-Century English Poetry* (New Brunswick, N. J., 1954); Thomas F. Van Laan, "John Donne's *Devotions* and the Jesuit Spiritual Exercises," *SP*, 60 (1963), 191-202.

and Katherine George in their useful study, *The Protestant Mind of the English Reformation*. Underscoring a point we are sometimes in danger of forgetting—the dominance of Calvinist theology throughout the English Church in the late sixteenth and early seventeenth centuries—the Georges suggest that Donne's own highly original theology aligns him more closely in thought and feeling with contemporary English Protestantism than with his Roman Catholic ancestors. In their view, "he is not a Catholic; for his revolt from the Church of Aquinas is in some ways the most absolute of that of any English divine; none is as impatient as Donne with synthetic theological science and facile rationality."[6] In this vein also, William Halewood has recently emphasized the importance of Augustinian and reformation theology for the religious lyrics of Donne, Herbert, Vaughan, and Marvell.[7]

This Protestant milieu, I am suggesting, promoted an approach to the theory and practice of meditation which had important ramifications for poetry, and notably for Donne's *Anniversaries*. I suggest further that the emerging Protestant tradition of meditation influenced Donne's divine poems, complimentary verse, and especially his *Anniversary* poems, as regards both form and conception of the subject. In the other direction, Donne's comments about meditation in his sermons, together with his own meditative sequence, the *Devotions upon Emergent Occasions*, contributed to the development of distinctive English Protestant forms of this ancient devotional practice.

A. Toward a Theory of Protestant Meditation

Helen C. White's wide-ranging studies of English devotional literature and Louis Martz' studies of the meditative tradition have demonstrated that English Protestants in the

[6] Charles H. George and Katherine George, *The Protestant Mind of the English Reformation*, *1570-1640* (Princeton, 1961), p. 69.

[7] William H. Halewood, *The Poetry of Grace: Reformation Themes and Structures in English Seventeenth-Century Poetry* (New Haven and London, 1970).

late sixteenth and early seventeenth centuries were indebted in important ways to Roman Catholic devotional and meditative works.[8] To begin with, Catholic manuals of meditation circulated widely in England. Especially popular were the *Imitatio Christi* and the works of Ignatius Loyola, Luis de Granada, and Gaspar Loarte in the originals and in English translations, as well as the *Christian Directory* of the Jesuit Robert Parsons.[9] Also, English Protestants sometimes produced recensions or epitomes of the Catholic materials without attribution or essential change. Yet for all this the dependence was far from absolute. William Halewood sought an explanation for the English Protestant acceptance of the Ignatian manuals in their common concern with individual religious experience and with the conversion event,[10] but he did not take account of the various signs of a developing Protestant tradition in meditation. Terence Cave, however, working with French devotional literature during the period 1570-1613 has provided a most suggestive comparative analysis of Catholic and Calvinist devotional treatises and poems, observing a marked similarity in their themes and styles, but identifying certain distinctive features of the Calvinist works—a dominant concern with psalm meditations and penitential themes, and a tendency

[8] Helen C. White, *English Devotional Literature [Prose] 1600-1640*, University of Wisconsin Studies in Language and Literature, No. 29 (Madison, 1931), and *Tudor Books of Private Devotion* (Madison, 1951).

[9] See, among many other issues and translations, [Thomas à Kempis], *The Folowing of Christ* [trans. Richard Whitford] ([Rouen?], 1585); Thomas de Villa-castin, *A Manuall of Devout Meditations and Exercises . . . Drawn for the most part, out of the Spirituall Exercises of B. F. Ignatius*, trans. [Henry More], ([St. Omer], 1618); Luis de Granada *Granados Spirituall and Heavenlie Exercises*, trans. Francis Meres (London, 1598); G[aspar] L[oarte], *The Exercise of a Christian Life*, trans. [Stephen Brinkley] ([Rheims?], 1584); another edition, (London, 1594); Robert Parsons, *The Christian Directory Guiding Men to Eternal Salvation* ([Douai?], 1607). See also R. S. [Richard Southwell], *A Foure-Fould Meditation, of the Foure Last Things* (London, 1606).

[10] Halewood, *Poetry of Grace*, pp. 71-87.

to promote simple meditations arising out of particular occasions in place of the elaborate procedures recommended in the Catholic manuals.[11]

Despite the importance of the Catholic treatises on meditation, there is evidence that English Protestants at the turn of the century were making a serious, self-conscious, and not unsuccessful attempt to develop a distinctively Protestant meditative theory and literature. The first stage of this undertaking involved the extensive revision and "reformation" of some of the famous Catholic treatises by wholesale alteration of their theological content and meditative focus, provision of explanatory annotations on controversial points, and large additions of biblical language. In this spirit Thomas Rogers, chaplain to Archbishop Bancroft and author of an influential exposition of the Thirty-nine Articles,[12] reworked the *Soliloquia animae ad Deum* and other meditative works which had been erroneously attributed to St. Augustine. He altered or omitted whole chapters or passages redolent in his view of Catholic doctrinal error, he added biblical language and quotations in great profusion, and he reinforced the impression of the biblical foundation of these works by dividing the prose text of the *Soliloquia* into segments resembling biblical verses.[13] In so doing, as a contemporary Roman Catholic translator of

[11] Terence C. Cave, *Devotional Poetry in France, c. 1570-1613* (Cambridge, 1969), pp. 39, 77.

[12] *DNB*. See Thomas Rogers, *The Faith, Doctrine, and Religion, Professed and Protected in the Realme of England . . . Expressed in 39 Articles* (Cambridge, 1607). Donne is known to have had a copy of this volume in his library.

[13] *A Pretious Booke of Heavenlie Meditations; called, A private talke of the soule with God* (London, 1612); published with *A Right Christian Treatise, Entituled, S. Augustines Praiers* (London, 1612); and *Saint Augustines Manuel: Containing Speciall and picked Meditations, and godlie Prayers* (London, 1612). Rogers' versions of all these works were first published in 1581, and enjoyed several reissues. For texts and discussion of the provenance of these pseudo-Augustinian works, see *Patrologiae Cursus Completus, Series Latina*, ed. J-P. Migne, 221 vols. (Paris, 1844-1864), XL (Appendix), cols. 863-942, 950-968.

these pseudo-Augustinian works complained, Rogers quite obliterated their original meditative and devotional focus upon Christ's passion: "And where S. Augustin, in the fervour of his devotion, with most eloquent, and wary termes, representeth unto his soule, and the readers thoughts, the dolefull spectacle of our Saviours passion, this impious heretick leaveth all that out, or els wickedlie transformeth it, censuring it as escapes, and oversights."[14]

Rogers gave similar treatment to Diego de Stella's *Methode unto Mortification*,[15] and to the *Imitatio Christi*, very generally ascribed to Thomas à Kempis; in the latter case he omitted the treatise on the Eucharist which constitutes the fourth book of the *Imitatio*, substituting for this another treatise by Thomas à Kempis which he found more congenial to Protestant theology, the *Soliloquium Animae. The Sole-Talke of the Soule*.[16] In the preface to his version of the *Imitatio*, as elsewhere, Rogers defended his editorial procedures on the ground that they would promote Christian truth and sound devotion:

[14] *A Heavenly Treasure of Comfortable Meditations and Prayers Written by S. Augustine, Bishop of Hyppon. In three several treatises of his Meditations, Soliloquies, and Manual*, trans. Antony Batt (St. Omers, 1624), p. 12.

[15] Diego de Stella, *A Methode unto Mortification, Called Heretofore, The Contempt of the World, and the Vanitie thereof*, trans. Thomas Rogers (London, 1586).

[16] Thomas à Kempis' claims to authorship of the *Imitatio* have been challenged from time to time, but are generally accepted; he is the recognized author of the *Soliloquium Animae*, which went through several Latin editions but received its first English translation and publication by Thomas Rogers in 1592, replacing the fourth book of the *Imitatio Christi*. Interestingly enough, the Protestant Edward Hake in his own earlier translation of the *Imitatio* (1568) also appended a substitute treatise (anonymous) to take the place of the eucharistic fourth book, as his title indicates: *The Imitation or Following of Christ, and the contemning of worldly vanities: Whereunto, as springing out of the same roote, we have adjoyned another pretie treatise, entituled, The perpetuall rejoyce of the Godly, even in this life.* For discussion of the provenance of the *Imitatio Christi* in England, and of the various Catholic and Protestant versions, see White, *English Devotional Literature*, pp. 81-86.

In which my translation, I have rather followed the sence of the Author then his very wordes, in some places, the which also I have studied, as nigh as I could, to expresse by the phrase of the holie Scripture, supposing it to be a commendation as to Ciceronians to use the phrase of Cicero: so to Christians most familiarly, to have the wordes of the holy Scripture in their mouthes and bookes.

Now touching my correction, I trust no good man will mistake the same. For I have left out nothing but what might bee offensive to the godlie. . . . For my part, I had rather come into the displeasure of man, then displease God, and rather move the obstinate hereticke, then offend the weake and simple Christian.[17]

Along the same lines, Edmund Bunny perpetrated a bowdlerized version of Robert Parson's *Christian Directory*,[18] with wholesale omissions and substitutions, and such pervasive alterations of style that Parsons later complained of being made to sound throughout like an English Protestant. Commenting upon the widespread Protestant activity in this kind, Parsons drew a wryly satiric conclusion: "This made me to muse . . . how poore, and barren these new Doctors are of all spirituall doctrine tending to good life, and reformation of manners; seing they are content to use, and pervert our Bookes for some shew therof: wherin I was the more confirmed by many other examples, in like manner."[19]

[17] *Of the Imitation of Christ. Three, both for wisedome and godlinesse, most excellent Bookes, made 170 yeeres since by one Thomas of Kempis . . . now newly corrected*, trans. Thomas Rogers (London, 1607), sigs. A 9-A 12; first published, 1580. To which is added, *Soliloquium Animae. The sole-talke of the Soule, or, A Spirituall and heavenly Dialogue, betwixt the Soule of Man and God* (London, 1608).

[18] Edmund Bunny, *A Booke of Christian Exercise Appertaining to Resolution, that is, shewing how that we should resolve our selves to become Christians indeede*. By R. P. (London, 1585). Bunny was a fellow of Magdalen and Merton Colleges, and chaplain to Archbishop Grindal of York.

[19] Robert Parsons, *The Christian Directory Guiding Men to Eternal Salvation* ([Douai?], 1607), Preface, [sig. *v].

Though clever, the riposte was not wholly justified. For, in addition to these exercises in recasting Catholic materials for Protestant uses, by the turn of the century Protestants were producing devotional and meditative tracts of their own in some numbers. Documenting this point, Norman Grabo compiled a suggestive list of Anglo-Catholic and Puritan-minded Anglicans who wrote in this vein—among them Richard Day, Henry Bull, Abraham Fleming, Samuel Hieron, Lewis Bayly, Paul Bayne, Michael Sparke, John Cosin, Daniel Featley, George Downame, Richard Sibbes, John Preston, and William Perkins.[20] Without discussing these works in detail, Grabo notes that they constituted a steady stream of "collections of prayers and meditations, instructions in meditation, treatises, guides to the good life and instructions for rectifying crooked and fallen souls, road maps to heaven," and on this evidence he challenged Martz' designation of Richard Baxter's *The Saints Everlasting Rest* (1650) as the first Puritan treatise "in the art of methodical meditation."[21] Several of the early Protestant tracts virtually conflate prayer and meditation, often alluding to St. Bernard's dictum that meditation is a preparative to prayer and prayer (colloquy) is the end of meditation.[22]

[20] Norman S. Grabo, "The Art of Puritan Meditation," *Seventeenth-Century News*, 26 (1968), 7-9. See especially Abraham Fleming, *The Diamond of Devotion, cut and squared into six severall points* (London, 1608); Daniel Featley, *Ancilla Pietatis, or The Hand-Maid to Private Devotion*, 3rd ed. (London, 1628); Henry Bull, ed., *Christian Prayers and Holy Meditations* (1566, 1570), in Parker Society Reprints (Cambridge, Eng., 1842). See also Helen White's bibliography of such works in *English Devotional Literature*, pp. 271-291.

[21] Grabo, "The Art of Puritan Meditation," p. 8; Martz, *Poetry of Meditation*, p. 154; Richard Baxter, *The Saints Everlasting Rest* (London, 1650).

[22] See especially Thomas Rogers, ed. *S. Augustines Manual* (London, 1581), preface, sig. a 3; Leonard Wright, *The Pilgrimage to Paradise* (London, 1608), pp. 55-56; I. Alliston, *The Exercise of True Spirituall Devotion. Consisting of holy Meditations and Prayers* (London, 1610), sigs. 9-9ᵛ.

Still more often, these tracts take meditation to mean "considerations" or general reflections upon doctrinal or devotional topics in the form of short, informal essays or soliloquies.[23] Such works are certainly not methodical in the Jesuit way, but they do testify to an emerging Protestant meditative literature. In these works can be found the beginnings of the three varieties of meditation which U. Milo Kaufmann finds to be prominent in Puritan literature after 1650—meditations on doctrine, on the creatures and events of the natural world, and on one's own spiritual experience.[24]

Of particular interest for Donne because of their widespread influence and their early date of publication are two long treatises which undertake to define and develop in detail a specifically Protestant mode of meditation. In his *Seven Treatises, Containing . . . the practice of Christianity* (1603) Richard Rogers challenged Parson's assertion that the Protestants had produced no materials for the daily direction of the Christian life, declaring that "both in catechismes, sermons, and other treatises, there is set forth by

[23] See Alliston, *Exercise*; John Carpenter, *The Plaine Mans Spirituall Plough* (London, 1607); Christopher Sutton, *Holy Meditations upon the Most Holy Sacrament of the Lordes Supper* (London, 1601); Robert Hill, *The Pathway to Prayer, and Pietie* (London, 1610); Anthony Stafford, *Meditations and Resolutions, Moral, Divine, Politicall* (London, 1612). The most significant work exemplifying this concept of meditation is Joseph Hall's *Meditations and Vowes, Divine and Morall* (London, 1605); the first part, or "Centurie," was dedicated to Sir Robert Drury, the second Century to Lady Drury. These meditations, and also Hall's *Holy Observations* (London, 1607), were short, largely aphoristic reflections upon aspects of doctrine or of the moral life. Though her emphasis in general is upon traditional survivals in devotional literature, Helen White also observes that the Protestant reformers had a quite different conception of the book of devotion from that of the Roman Catholics, assimilating it in fact to the theological or moral treatise (*English Devotional Literature*, p. 68).

[24] U. Milo Kaufmann, *The Pilgrim's Progress and Traditions in Puritan Meditation* (New Haven, 1966), pp. 118-150, 175-216.

us that which may cleerly direct Christians, and stir up godly devotion in them."[25] For good measure, however, he offered his own work, which includes a lengthy chapter on meditation, as a full-scale Protestant counterpart to Parson's *Christian Directory* and Loarte's recently reissued *Exercise* (1596 or 1597). Rogers' critique of the Roman Catholic handbooks points up some differences in the Protestant approach. He denounces Parsons' work as theologically unsound and morally lax, tending "rather to persuade men to resolve with themselves to leave some grosse evils, then to shew them soundly how to attaine pardon, or teaching how to live christianly." And he derides Loarte's handbook of devotion and meditation for its reliance upon humanly devised and mechanical methods to produce devotion, a "ridiculous tying men to a daily taske of reading some part of the storie of Christs passion, and saying certaine prayers throughout the weeke."[26] By contrast, Rogers described his own directory as one which would not bind the Christian to useless forms, but would rather encourage the purification of the heart: his program calls for the public exercise of attendance at sermons and sacraments, supplemented by various private exercises—meditation upon a great variety of religious topics grounded in scripture, watchfulness over one's own heart, and the reducing of all the precepts of scripture to experimental knowledge within the self.

The second important Protestant treatise, Joseph Hall's *Arte of Divine Meditation* (1606), was recognized by Kaufmann as seminal for later Puritan meditation.[27] In contrast to the Christocentric focus of the Jesuit tracts, Hall's treatise defines and exemplifies two distinct varieties of Prot-

---

[25] Rogers, *Seven Treatises, Containing Such Direction as is gathered out of the Holie Scriptures, leading and guiding to true happines, both in this life, and the life to come; and may be called the Practice of Christianity* (London, 1603), sigs. A 5ᵛ-B.

[26] *Ibid.*, sigs. A 6-A 6ᵛ.

[27] Joseph Hall, *Arte of Divine Meditation* (London, 1607); cf. Kaufmann, pp. 120-135.

estant meditation: "deliberate" meditation upon doctrines and religious topics, and "extemporall" meditation upon the occasions offered by the natural world. That Donne was aware of, and perhaps directly influenced by, Hall's theories of meditation at the time of writing the *Anniversaries* is a strong possibility, given the terms of their personal association. As R. C. Bald has shown, their relationship evidently began sometime in the period 1601-1607, when Hall was rector at Sir Robert Drury's establishment at Hawstead. Hall wrote the long, perceptive, prefatory poem to Donne's *Second Anniversarie*, and almost certainly that for the *First Anniversarie* as well. In addition, he very probably saw the 1612 edition of the *Anniversaries* through the press in Donne's absence, Donne's printer Samuel Macham having already published several of Hall's works, including his *Arte of Divine Meditation*.[28]

Three characteristics of these Protestant discourses on meditation distinguish them sharply from the Roman Catholic treatises. One is the near-identification of sermon and meditation in terms of methods and purposes: so widespread is this conflation that it goes far to explain the paucity of specific Protestant "methods" of meditation, the assumption being that the sermon itself offered an appropriate model and one in no way compromised by involvement with suspect Roman Catholic devotions. The second characteristic is an insistence, like that typical of the Protestant sermons of the period, upon detailed and forceful "application to the self" of the materials meditated (or preached) upon. The third is the widespread use of the two kinds of meditation described by Hall: instead of the classic Jesuit subjects, the Passion of Christ and the four last things, the Protestants essayed meditations upon a large number of doctrines or religious topics, often abstractly formulated, and also upon the occasions offered by the natural world and the events of daily life. Donne's conception of meditation, as evidenced by his sermons and by his own

[28] Bald, *Life*, pp. 238-46.

meditative exercise, the *Devotions upon Emergent Occasions*, appears to have been shaped by these Protestant emphases. I suggest that this is also the conception of meditation whose poetic analogue is to be found in Donne's poetry of compliment and in the *Anniversary* poems.

Since for Protestants generally the characteristic and predominant form of religious expression and activity was the sermon, it is hardly surprising that other forms of religious exercise were assimilated to this mode. Terence Cave has observed a similar interrelationship between French meditative treatises and sermons in this period: Catholics such as Luis de Granada afforded a basis for this conflation by such comments as, ". . . il n'y a autre différence entre le predication et contemplation, que entre la lecture et consideration de ce qu'on lit: ou qu'entre la viande mise en un plat, et la mesme cuite, et digeree en nostre estomach, . . ."[29] but the fusion was especially notable among the Calvinists.[30] For example, Theodore Beza and Jean de Sponde established a paradigm for French Protestant meditation by adopting certain features of the sermon method—statement of text, analysis, apostrophe, and prayer—to private devotion, and by conjoining a reflective, meditative tone with an aggressive, urgently persuasive, hortatory tone, interrogating or apostrophizing the reader or the self.[31] Of particular interest for Donne's *Anniversary* poems is Cave's suggestion that some French Protestant poems in the tradition of the *Vanitas* or *Memento Mori* may be indebted to sermon literature for certain stylistic features—their aggressive, demonstrative, argumentative tone, and their use of the rhetoric of the second person, implying an audience.[32]

[29] Luis de Granada, *Le Vray Chemin*, trans. F. de Belleforest (Paris, 1579), fol. 1, cited in Cave, *Devotional Poetry in France*, p. 36.

[30] Cave, *Devotional Poetry in France*, pp. 36-39.

[31] Theodore de Bèze, *Chrestiennes méditationes*, ed. M. Richter (Geneva, 1964), p. 53; Jean de Sponde, *Meditations avec un essai de poèmes chrétiens*, ed. A. Boase (Paris, 1954).

[32] Cave, *Devotional Poetry in France*, pp. 146-183.

The basis in Protestant theory for the near-fusion of the sermon and the meditation was the supposed identity of their purposes and their parts. According to numerous Protestant *artes predicandi*, the fundamental elements of the Protestant sermon were the presentation and explication of a biblical text; the exposition of doctrine derived from it, together with their proofs; and the forceful urging of the "uses" or "applications" of these materials.[33] The sermon's purposes were twofold: instruction (carried on by means of an analysis of the text and doctrines), and stimulation of the affections and the heart (achieved through the searching application of text and doctrines to the particular audience). As William Haller noted, the Puritan sermon typically emphasized the uses as opposed to the fine points of textual explication: the Puritan preacher John Dod was described by a contemporary as one who preached "most largely and very home in application, mightily convincing and diving into mens hearts and consciences," and his admirer and imitator Richard Harris complained about those preachers who spend too much time on doctrinal points and too little upon applications "wherein . . . a Sermons excellency doth consist."[34] The particular emphasis upon "application" among English Protestants of Puritan tendencies supports Frazer Mitchell's alignment of Donne with contemporary Puritan rather than Anglican preachers in this important respect, for Donne characteristically probed the spiritual state of his congregation with great psychological insight, vividness, and directness.[35]

Like the sermon, meditation as the Protestants conceived

[33] E.g., William Perkins, *The Arte of Prophecying. Or, A Treatise Concerning the Sacred and Onely True Manner and Method of Preaching*, trans. Thomas Tuke, in *Workes*, II (London, 1613), pp. 646-673; Richard Bernard, *The Faithfull Shepheard* (London, 1607), pp. 1-80; Joannis Hepinus, *De sacris concionibus formandis* (London, 1570).

[34] Haller, *The Rise of Puritanism* (New York, 1938), pp. 134-135.

[35] W. Frazer Mitchell, *English Pulpit Oratory from Andrewes to Tillotson* (London, 1932), p. 198.

it involves argument and persuasion, illustration and analysis; it may also begin with and be based upon a biblical text, and it customarily interrogates and apostrophizes an audience—the self or God. Joseph Hall's *Arte of Divine Meditation* identified as pertaining to exercises of meditation precisely the same purposes and elements which Protestant *artes concionandi* defined for the sermon—the analysis of a religious doctrine or topic by the understanding, and the stimulation of the affections and the heart. Looking beyond Ignatius to a method outlined by the monk Mauburnus (who himself had borrowed it from the crypto-Protestant Johan Wessel Gansfort),[36] Hall eliminated the Ignatian appeal to the imagination and the senses in the preliminary stage of meditation, setting forth instead a two-stage process beginning with the analysis of the subject by the understanding. Meditation, he declared "begins in the understanding, ends in the affections; It begins in the braine, descends to the heart; Begins on earth, ascends to heaven."[37] But in place of Mauburnus' rather complex directions for the analytic stage, Hall substituted a simple analysis according to some of the places of logic, such as often occurred in sermons. Moreover, he permitted great flexibility in the analytic stage, asking only for a "deep and firme *Consideration* of the thing propounded," and declaring any method of analysis acceptable which can "worke in our hearts so deepe an apprehension of the matter meditated, as it may duely stirre the affections."[38] Hall asserted that the primary end of meditation, like that of the sermon, is the stirring of the affections: "That . . . is the verie soule of Meditation, whereto all that is past [of analysis] serveth but as an instrument."[39]

Given this identity of elements and purposes, the terms *sermon* and *meditation* became well-nigh interchangeable in Protestant theory. The sermon was frequently described

[36] See Martz, *Poetry of Meditation*, pp. 331-333.
[37] Hall, *Arte*, p. 85. [38] *Ibid.*, p. 91. [39] *Ibid.*, p. 150.

as a meditation shared with the auditory, or as the fruit of
the preacher's meditation which the auditory should con-
tinue to meditate upon, thereby "preaching" the sermon
over again with specific and rigorous application to the self.
Richard Greenham declared that meditation differs from
the sermon chiefly in that the meditator can apply the mat-
ter more closely to himself than the preacher can: "If we
meditate of those generall rules which we have heard out
of the word, wee shall many times see more cleerly into the
trueth of it, than he that preacheth, or at least more then he
expressed unto us. For by the Spirit of God wee shall be
taught to applie it more particularly to our selves, than hee
did or could doe, because wee are most privie to our owne
estate."[40] Along with Lewis Bayly, Joseph Hall, and many
others,[41] Richard Rogers also envisaged meditation as de-
riving from the sermon, and argued the special suitability
of such exercises for Sunday, "the word preached giving so
gratious occasions."[42] Samuel Hieron was yet more explicit
about the connection between the two forms: "When you
are departed from the Sermon, forget not to finde a time as
soone as is possible, whilest things heard are most fresh, in
which to *commune with your own heart*, and to ponder,
and scanne, and *search diligently* those things which were
delivered. This is that which wee call meditation, an exer-
cise which *David* exceedingly delighted in: it is the same

[40] Richard Greenham, *Workes*, ed. H. Hammond, 3rd ed. (London,
1601), p. 22.

[41] Lewis Bayly in *The Practice of Pietie* (London, 1616), p. 379,
urged meditation while hearing the sermon—"in hearing, apply every
speech as spoken to *thy selfe*"—and suggested further meditation
after returning home "upon those things, which thou hast heard." Hall
also (*Arte*, pp. 58-59) found the sabbath especially conducive to
meditation, in that the sermon "stirres thee up to this action, and filles
thee with matter" and also in that meditation serves as an extension
of the sermon wherein the devout person brings "all he hears home to
his heart, by a self-reflecting application."

[42] Rogers, *Seven Treatises*, pp. 236, 233, 259.

to the minde, that digestion is to the bodie: that which we heare is by it made our own, so that the soule receiveth nourishment thereby."[43]

From the other standpoint, Richard Rogers discussed meditation as the minister's necessary preparation for his sermon, as his method of exploring the matter he intended to present to his congregation: "*Paul* willed *Timothy to meditate and throughly exercise and season his minde with the doctrine* which he delivered to the people, even to be taken up of it, that both he himself might be throughly seasoned with the doctrine for every part of his life; & that he might feede his hearers the more plentifully."[44] In his advice to ministers in *The Faithfull Shepheard* (1607) Richard Bernard also urged that the minister "use meditation seriously" upon the matter he proposed to speak about, since "to make Application to his hearers, to doe it profitably, he must *First*, preach to them from knowledge out of himself."[45] The eloquent Puritan preacher Thomas Adams provides a striking illustration of such a meditation-sermon on a topic closely related to the themes of the *First Anniversarie*, the sickness and death of the world as a result of sin; he also assumes that sermons express "the meditations of their [the ministers'] hearts," and concludes by voicing the hope that the congregation will "judge this that hath beene spoken, worthy your meditation, laying it affectionately to your hearts."[46]

That the Protestant conflation of sermon and meditation was both thoroughgoing and widely accepted is perhaps most clearly indicated by the several published sermons of Thomas Gataker subtitled "A Meditation"—for example, *True Contentment in the Gaine of Godliness . . . A Meditation on I. Timoth. 6.6* (London, 1620), and *Davids Remem-*

---

[43] Samuel Hieron, "The Preachers Plea," in *All the Sermons of Samuel Hieron* (London, 1614), p. 550.

[44] Rogers, *Seven Treatises*, p. 258.

[45] Bernard, *Faithfull Shepheard*, pp. 84, 332.

[46] Thomas Adams, *The Sinners Passing-Bell* (London, 1614), pp. 216, 333.

brancer. *A Meditation on Psalm 13.1* (London, 1623).[47] All this evidence indicates that when Richard Baxter in 1650 discussed the sermon at length as a model for meditation, he was making no new departure but merely elaborating upon what had been for half a century a Protestant commonplace:

> Because meer Cogitation if it be not prest home, will not so pierce and affect the heart, Therefore we must here proceed to a second step, which is called Soliloquy, which is nothing but a pleading the case with our own souls. . . . As every good Master and Father of a Family, is a good Preacher to his own Family; so every good Christian, is a good Preacher to his own soul. Soliloquy is a Preaching to ones self. Therefore the very same Method which a Minister should use in his Preaching to others, should a Christian use in speaking to himself. . . . Dost thou know the right parts and order of a Sermon? and which is the most effectual way of application? why then I need to lay it open no further: thou understandest the Method and partes of this soliloquy. Mark the most affecting, heart-melting Minister; observe his course both for matter and manner; set him up as a patern before thee for thy imitation; and the same way that he takes with the hearts of his people, do thou also take with thy own heart.[48]

[47] See also, e.g., Thomas Gataker, *Jacobs Thankfulnesse to God for Gods Goodnesse to Jacob. A Meditation on Genesis 32:10* (London, 1624); *A Mariage Praier, or Succinct Meditations: Delivered in a Sermon on the Praier of Eleazer the Servant of Abraham, Gen. 24:12, 13, 14* (London, 1624); *Noah His Obedience, With the Ground of it: Or, His Faith, Feare, and Care. A Meditation on Hebrewes 11.7* (London, 1623); *A Sparke Toward the Kindling of Sorrow for Sion. A Meditation on Amos 6.6* (London, 1621); *The Spirituall Watch, or Christ's Generall Watch-word. A Meditation on Mark 13.37* (London, 1619).

[48] Baxter, *The Saints Everlasting Rest* (4th part), pp. 749-751. Martz, *Poetry of Meditation*, p. 174, argues, on the contrary, that this position is novel, and that it is developed primarily for rhetorical reasons, to render meditative practice more acceptable to Protestants.

Donne also merged the genres of *sermon* and *meditation* in the characteristic Protestant fashion. In his sermons he constantly refers to the ideas he is developing as "meditations": "We cannot take into our Meditation, a better Rule, then that of the Stoick. . . . There is no such unhappiness to a sinner, as to be happy." Or again, "But this is not the object of our speculation, the subject of our meditation, now."[49] For Donne also, the parts and the purposes of sermon and meditation are identical, with application to the self (or audience) as the most important element of both exercises. He urges his congregation to "apply" the sermons they hear through meditation: "You are of this *quorum* [the Elect], if you preach over the Sermons which you heare, to your owne soules in your meditation."[50] And again:

They that come to heare Sermons, and would make benefit by them, by a subsequent meditation, must not think themselves frustrated of their purposes, if they do not understand all, or not remember all the Sermon. . . . For the refreshing of . . . one span of ground, God lets fall a whole showre of rain; for the rectifying of . . . one soul, God poures out the Meditations of the Preacher, into such a subject, as perchance doth little concern the rest of the Congregation. . . . If thou remember that which concerned thy sin, and thy soul, if thou meditate upon that, apply that, thou hast brought away all the Sermon, all that was intended by the Holy Ghost to be preached to thee.[51]

On the other hand, Donne describes his own sermons as the direct outgrowth of, the public rendering of, his meditations:

[49] Donne, *Sermons*, ed. G. F. Potter and Evelyn Simpson, 10 vols. (Berkeley, 1953-62), I, 168. Sermon on Eccles. 8:11, at Whitehall, April, 1616; VI, 278. Sermon on John 5:28-29, at St. Paul's, Easter, 1625.

[50] *Sermons*, VI, 347-348. Sermon on Gal. 4:4-5, at St. Paul's, Christmas, 1625.

[51] *Sermons*, VII, 327-329. Sermon on Matt. 5:8, on Candlemas [1626/7?].

I acknowledge, that my spirituall appetite carries me still, upon the *Psalms of David*, for a first course, for the Scriptures of the Old Testament, and upon the *Epistles of Saint Paul*, for a second course, for the New; and my meditations even for these *publike exercises* to Gods Church, returne oftnest to those two. For, as a hearty entertainer offers to others, the meat which he loves best himself, so doe I oftnest present to Gods people, in these Congregations, the meditations which I feed upon at home, in these two Scriptures.[52]

Or again, he declares: "If he [God] aske me an Idea of my Sermons, shall I not be able to say, It is that which the Analogy of Faith, the edification of the Congregation, the zeale of thy worke, the meditations of my heart, have imprinted in me? . . . To Beleeve according to ancient beliefes, to pray according to ancient formes, to preach according to former meditations."[53]

In this Protestant—and Donnean—identification of sermon and meditation we have one basis for the "public" voice of meditation in Donne's poetry of compliment. Though presented as "meditations," these exercises are not those of a solitary meditating in his chamber but are set forth as public exercises. Typically, Donne's speaker explores what "we" learn by meditation or contemplation of the person in question, or else he proposes to "teach" others what he has learned by such meditation. This stance suggests a basis for accommodating the diverse modes to which critics have related the *Anniversaries*: Louis Martz, Carol Sicherman, and Richard Hughes insist that the poems are private meditations; Dennis Quinn, George Williamson, and O. B. Hardison urge as vehemently that their mode is public instruction and communal celebration.[54] In fact, in

[52] *Sermons*, II, 49. Sermon on Psalm 38:2, at Lincoln's Inn, 1618.

[53] *Sermons*, VII, 61. Sermon on Psalm 63:7, at St. Paul's, January, 1625/6.

[54] Carol Sicherman, "Donne's Timeless Anniversaries," *UTQ* 39 (1970), 127-143; Richard E. Hughes, *The Progress of the Soul* (New

both *Anniversaries*, and especially in the *Anatomy of the World*, we find something approximating the typical Protestant identification of sermon and meditation. The speaker at once addresses his own soul and "us," undertaking both to describe his own feelings and to teach the world "remaining still" what his meditations have revealed: "Shee, Shee is dead, she's dead; when thou knowst this/ Thou knowst . . . / And learnst" (ll. 325-327). And in keeping with Protestant theory regarding both meditation and sermons, the speaker of the *Anatomy* not only develops an analysis of the topics in question but also undertakes to move the affections—his own and ours—so that we realize "who it is that's gone" (ll. 42), and so feel our condition.

B. Occasional Meditation and Deliberate Meditation

In regard to subjects and kinds of meditation, the Protestant treatises also were suggestive for Donne. The early Protestant manuals recognized a wide variety of kinds, and their openness in this regard is provided for by Hall's definition, "Divine Meditation is nothing else but a bending of the minde upon some spirituall object."[55] Several of these manuals imply a distinction between two broad categories of meditation: formal meditations upon such standard religious topics as Christ's passion, or death's commodites, or heaven's joys, and also short, prayer-like reflections upon the common occurrences of the daily round—waking, eating, saying the Lord's prayer, going on a journey, retiring.[56] In

---

York, 1968), pp. 196-255; Dennis Quinn, "Donne's Anniversaries as Celebration," *SEL*, 9 (1969), 97-105; George Williamson, "The Design of Donne's *Anniversaries*" (1963), in *Milton and Others*, pp. 150-164; O. B. Hardison, *Enduring Monument*, pp. 163-186.

[55] Hall, *Arte*, pp. 6-7.

[56] See especially Henry Bull, ed., *Christian Prayers and Holy Meditations, as well for Private as Public Exercise* (1566, 1570), Parker Society (Cambridge, 1842). See also Richard Rogers, William Perkins, et al., *A Garden of Spiritual Flowers* (London, 1616), sig. G 2; John Bradford, *Holy Meditations* (London, 1622).

his influential treatise Joseph Hall gives precise definition to these kinds, classifying as "Deliberate" meditations those "wrought out of our owne heart" and practised according to a set method, and as "Occasional or Extemporall" meditations those "occasioned by outward occurences offered to the minde."[57]

Hall's category of extemporal or occasional meditation incorporates the ancient tradition of meditation upon the creatures which Calvin had recommended to Protestants, urging them to contemplate the creatures as mirrors of God's wisdom, justice, goodness, and power.[58] It also incorporates meditations upon events or situations presented by daily life. Henry Bull offers several examples of meditations on such occasions as the lighting of candles:

> Think that the knowledge and understanding which God hath given unto us by the candlelight (whereby we see those things in this night of our bodies which are expedient for us), maketh us to wish much more for this doctrine of God, and when we get it, the more to esteem it and diligently embrace it. Again, that as all would be horror without candles, so there is nothing but mere confusion where God's word taketh not place.[59]

Joseph Hall expands this category to include the whole range of subjects which the natural world offers to us as occasions. The *Arte of Divine Meditation* declares, "Wherefore as travellers in a forraine countrey make everie sight a lesson; so ought wee, in this our pilgrimage." Or again, "God hath not straited us for matter, having given us the scope of the whole world; so that there is no creature,

[57] Hall, *Arte*, p. 7. At the end of the century, Edmund Calamy's *Art of Divine Meditation* (London, 1680) virtually recapitulates Hall's theory, especially in regard to the conception of, and the appropriate method for, occasional and deliberate meditation.

[58] Calvin, *Institutes* I.xiv.20-21, ed. John T. McNeill, "Library of Christian Classics," xx (Philadelphia, 1960), pp. 180-181.

[59] Bull, *Holy Meditations*, pp. 74-75.

event, action, speech, which may not afford us new matter of Meditation."[60] "Occasion" in this usage has genuine symbolic import: God provides us with occasions invested with spiritual meaning, in order that by meditation we may discover and apply that meaning to our own lives.

Hall's book of examples in this kind, *Occasionall Meditations*, was not published until 1630, though according to his son, who identified himself as its collector and publisher, its contents had been written according to the formula laid down in the *Arte* over a period of some years.[61] The meditations include such topics as: "Upon the Sight of a Marriage"; "Upon the Araignment of a Felon"; "Upon Gnats in the Sun"; "Upon the Crowing of a Cocke"; "Upon the Tolling of a passing-Bell"; "Upon the Beginning of a Sickness"; "Upon a quartan Ague." The last two topics, meditations upon the occasion of an illness, resemble Donne's own meditative sequence, the *Devotions upon Emergent Occasions* (1624), in their exploration of the relations between sin and physical illness: "It was my owne fault, if I look't not for this. . . . Could I have done well, without any mixtures of sin; I might have hoped for entire health; But, since I have interspersed my obedience with many sinfull faylings, and enormities, why doe I thinke much, to interchange health with sickenesse? . . . . I have sinned and must smart; It is the glory of thy mercy to beat my body for the safety of my soule."[62]

Unquestionably, such exercises have some traditional roots. As Jonathan Goldberg has shown, devotional literature for centuries had traced the relation between sin and sickness on the one hand, and sickness and salvation on the other, in manuals of prayers designed for use in the various

---

[60] Hall, *Arte*, pp. 19-20.

[61] *Occasionall Meditations* (London, 1633). I have used this edition because it is enlarged to include forty-nine meditations in addition to those in the 1630 volume.

[62] *Ibid.*, pp. 253-255.

crises of the Christian life.[63] In Donne's period Lewis Bayly wrote general meditations of this kind for the time of sickness: developing an analogy between the state of the body and the condition of the soul, he traced in a lengthy exercise the course of an illness from its inception to its conclusion in recovery (emergence into a new life) or death.[64] Yet another sequence in this kind occurs in *A Garden of Spiritual Flowers*, which incorporates meditations upon sin as the cause of illness, and upon God as the only true physician of soul and body.[65] But the special significance of the Occasional Meditations written by Hall and Donne is the fact that they made their own experiences with illness the specific ground for the meditative exercise. The persistence of this special Protestant conception of occasional meditation is evidenced by Robert Boyle's *Occasional Reflections upon Several Subjects* (1665), which incorporates a theoretical defense of this kind of meditation, identifies as its subjects "the most Obvious Works of Nature, and the most Familiar Occurences of humane Life," and conflates the mode with the sermon through the suggestion that such meditation makes "every Creature turn a Preacher, and almost every Accident suggest an Use of Instruction, Reproof, or Exhortation." Among Boyle's several examples, ostensibly based upon his own experiences, is an extended series of reflections "Upon the Accidents of an Ague."[66]

---

[63] Goldberg, "The Understanding of Sickness in Donne's *Devotions*," *Renaissance Quarterly*, 24 (1971), 507-517. See Schleiner, *The Imagery of John Donne's Sermons*, pp. 68-85, for an examination of the patristic and medieval background of the *topos*, "Sin as a Sickness."

[64] Bayly, *The Practice of Pietie*, pp. 578-675.

[65] Rogers, et al., *Garden of Spiritual Flowers*, sigs. E 2ᵛ-F 2.

[66] Robert Boyle, *Occasional Reflections upon Several Subjects. Whereto is premis'd a Discourse about such kind of Thoughts* (London, 1665), sig. B 1ᵛ, pp. 79, 187-240. Boyle's sequence on his ague obviously owes something to Hall's and much to Donne's *Devotions*; like the latter, it also follows the emergent stages of the illness, deriv-

Donne's *Devotions* may be seen as a special variety of occasional meditation. As is usual in that kind, they begin with the offered occasion of a personal illness, but then they proceed to develop the subject at great length and with method and order according to the stages of the sickness, rather than in the customary brief, extemporal fashion. Each stage is considered in three parts: A *Meditation* exploring the illness in relation to the conditions of the natural world; an *Exposition* presenting the illness as an image and effect of the sickness of the soul caused by sin; and a *Prayer* addressing God as giver of the grace which can heal the body and especially the soul. This meditative exercise in its general conception provides an analogue to the *Anniversary* poems in that a particular occasion (an illness) together with the subsequent "emergent occasions" presented by the course of the illness, constitute the basis for an extended, sequential meditation. The *Devotions* further resemble the *Anniversaries* in that they assert the spiritual, symbolic significance of an occasion, and regard that occasion as affording a challenge to the meditator to discern and apply its meanings rightly: "Let me think no degree of this thy correction, *casuall*, or without signification; but yet when I have read it in that language, as it is a *correction*, let me translate it into another, and read it as a *mercy*. . . . Whether thy *Mercy*, or thy *Correction*, were the primary, and original intention in this sicknes, I cannot conclude."[67]

Of course the specific occasion for the *Anniversary* poems —a death or funeral—was constantly proposed by Protestants as a basis for meditation. Rogers had urged "That we observe the departure of men of this life, their mortalitie, the vanitie and alteration of things below, the more to contemne the world, and to continue our longing after the

---

ing moral and spiritual meaning from them, though its method is analogical rather than symbolic, as Donne's is.

[67] *Devotions upon Emergent Occasions, and severall steps in my Sicknes* (London, 1624), pp. 173-174.

life to come. And that we meditate and muse often of our own death, and going out of this life, how we must lie in the grave, all our glory put off; which will serve to beate downe the pride of life that is in us."[68] Hall's "occasional" meditation "On the tolling of a passing bell" exemplifies how we are to find in such an occasion the summons to our own death, and how the death of another should become an occasion for our spiritual growth: "How doleful and heavy is this summons of Death? This sound is not for our eares, but for our hearts; it calls us not onely to our prayers, but to our preparation . . . for our own departing. . . . And for me, let no man dye without mee, as I dye dayly, so teach mee to dye once; acquaint mee before hand with that messenger, which I must trust too."[69] But the most suggestive analogue for the *Anniversary* poems considered as occasional meditations is from Donne's own meditative exercise, the *Devotions* (XVI-XVIII)—notably the long sequence on the passing-bell:

> In that Contemplation I make account that I heare this dead brother of ours, who is now carried out to his *buriall*, to speake to mee, and to *preach* my *funerall Sermon*, in the voice of these *Bells*. . . .
>
> The *death* of others, should *catechise* us to *death*. . . . I am a *younger brother* . . . to this Man, who *died now*, and to every man whom I see, or heare to die before *mee*, and all they are *ushers* to mee in this *schoole* of *death*. . . . Thou hast sent *him* in this *bell* to mee . . . that in this weaknes of *body*, I might receive spiritual strength, by these occasions. . . .
>
> O Eternall and most gracious *God*, I have a new occasion of *thanks*, and a new occasion of *prayer* to *thee*, from the *ringing* of this bell. Thou toldst me in the other *voice*, that I was *mortall* and approaching to *death;* In this I may heare thee say, that I am *dead*, in an *irremediable*,

[68] Rogers, *Seven Treatises*, pp. 256-257.
[69] Hall, *Occasionall Meditations*, pp. 193-195.

in an *irrecoverable* state. . . . *I am dead*, I was *borne dead*, and from the first laying of these *mud-walls* in my *conception*, they have *moldred* away, and the whole course of *life* is but an *active death*.[70]

This sequence illuminates some of the meanings the occasion of Elizabeth Drury's death has for Donne's meditative speaker, and reveals some part of the significance investing the term "occasion" in the subtitles to the *Anniversary* poems: "Wherein, by occasion of the untimely death of Mistris Elizabeth Drury the frailty and the decay of this whole world is represented"; "Wherein: By occasion of the religious death of Mistris Elizabeth Drury the incommodities of the soule in this life and her exaltation in the next, are contemplated."

But Donne's *Devotions*, and the *Anniversary* poems as well, partake of the nature of deliberate as well as occasional meditation. The subject matter of this second category of meditation, deliberate meditation, was also various, embracing the whole range of scripture and of religious precept. We have noted the characteristic Protestant suspicion of formal Jesuit meditative sequences on the Passion, the Eucharist, or the four last things; as Kaufmann observes, this suspicion was grounded in part upon the fear that contemplation of religious images, symbols, and stories, especially with the generous aid of such faulty instruments as the senses and the imagination, would lead to error and idolatry.[71] Protestants preferred instead to begin from an abstract doctrinal formulation or a biblical text such as a preacher might set forth at the beginning of his sermon, and from this authoritative base to proceed to logical analysis and the all-important "application to the self." Indicating that possible topics for this kind of meditation might come from "any part of Gods Word," Paul Bayne especially recommended contemplation "of God himselfe, on his workes

[70] Donne, *Devotions*, pp. 408-464.
[71] Kaufmann, *Traditions in Puritan Meditation*, pp. 41-60.

of mercy and judgement, of our owne estate, of the vanity and misery of this world, and of the manifold privileges which wee with the rest of God's children enjoy."[72] In similar terms Richard Rogers suggested that the Christian meditate upon "love, humilitie, meekenes, peace of conscience, the glorie of Gods kingdom, his love, and the contrarie," stimulating his mind to fruitful meditation by reading from the doctrinal and devotional parts of scripture—the psalms, the epistles, and Christ's sermons.[73]

To illustrate the category of deliberate meditation, Hall presented a sample meditation upon the condition of the Saints in heaven which has relevance for both the subject and the method of the *Anniversary* poems insofar as they are concerned with the striking contrasts between Elizabeth Drury's state and ours. Urging meditation upon the life to come, Hall declared: "Whereon shouldest thou rather meditate than of the life and glory of Gods Saints? A worthier employment thou canst never finde, than to thinke upon that estate, thou shalt once possesse, and now desirest. . . . Who are the Saints, but those which having beene weakely holy upon earth, are perfectly holy above? which even on earth were perfectly holy in their Saviour, now are so in themselves."[74] After analyzing the saints' bliss and holiness according to the places of logic—causes, fruits, effects, etc.—Hall proceeds to the "place" of contraries, thereby providing an example of the alternation of positive and negative descriptions so fundamental to the method of the *Anniversaries*. The contrary estate to that of the Saints is this world:

Looke round about thee, and see whether thine eyes can meet with any thing but either sinnes or miseries. Those few and short pleasures thou seest, end ever sorrowfully; and in the mean time are intermingled with many griev-

[72] Bayne, *Brief Directions unto a Godly Life* (London, 1637), p. 129.
[73] Rogers, *Seven Treatises*, p. 245.
[74] Hall, *Arte*, pp. 84, 95-96.

ances. Here thou hearest one crie out of a sicke bodie, whereof there is no part which affords not choice of diseases. . . . But, that which is yet more irksome, thy one eare is beaten with cursings and blasphemies; thy other with scornefull, or wanton, or murdering speeches; thine eyes see nothing but pride, filthines, profanenesse, blood, excesse . . . and if all the world besides were innocent, thou findest enough within thy selfe, to make thy selfe weary, and thy life loathsome.[75]

The place of contraries serves also to begin the second stage of the meditation, the stimulation of the affections. The first exercise is to experience a feeling, a taste of the blessed condition: "Oh blessed estate of the Saints! O glory not to bee expressed, even by those which are glorified." This is to be followed by a complaint, bewailing our wants and untowardness, "where-in the hart bewayleth to it selfe his owne poverty, dulnesse, and imperfection; chiding and abasing it selfe, in respect of his wants and indisposition."[76] Conceived and constructed on much the same lines are Lewis Bayly's contrasting meditative sequences. The first concerns "the Miserie of a man, not reconciled to God" in his life, death, and condition after death, with particular emphasis upon the corruptions and vileness of the mortal condition. The second concerns the estate of a Christian reconciled to God in life, death, and after death, with special focus upon his privileges in life in that "all the righteousnes of Christ . . . [is] freely and fully imputed to him"; upon his peaceful death and swift ascent to heaven; and upon the delights and fullness of knowledge he there enjoys.[77]

Donne's *Devotions upon Emergent Occasions* is innovative in that it fuses the methods of occasional and deliberate meditation. This work takes a particular event—Donne's own illness—as an occasion fraught with spiritual significance to be discerned by the speaker and applied to himself

[75] *Ibid.*, pp. 121, 124.   [76] *Ibid.*, pp. 152, 154.
[77] Bayly, *Practice of Pietie*, pp. 59-120.

and his auditors. But in the *Devotions* the development of this central topic is "deliberate" in that it involves an ordered, sequential exploration of the complex relationship of sin and sickness, much as a preacher might develop the topic in a sermon. Indeed, as Janel Mueller has persuasively argued. Donne's *Devotions* fuse devotional and homiletic methods, in that they comment upon the exigencies of his own condition by means of an exegesis of numerous apt biblical texts.[78] The point is reinforced by Mrs. Mueller's comparison of Donne's *Devotions* and his sermons on Psalm VI about seven months later, on the subject of David's sin and sickness: she calls attention to a great number of similarities in the handling of scripture texts as well as to many thematic and verbal links. In thus conflating the theory and method of deliberate meditation and the sermon Donne is, as has been shown, quite in accord with contemporary Protestant practice. Yet in his *Devotions* the "deliberate" development of the topic is carried forward in relation to successive "emergent occasions" which arise as the illness proceeds. Donne's *Devotions* may well be the first significant example of the fusion of these two forms of Protestant meditation, and of both with sermon techniques, as it may also be the most elaborate contemporary presentation—the great precedent of course is Augustine's *Confessions*—of a personal experience as the symbolic center for such meditation.

The fusion of the two kinds of meditation is developed yet more elaborately in the *Anniversary* poems. In those poems also a particular event—Elizabeth Drury's death—is approached as an occasion fraught with significance, challenging interpretation from speaker and audience alike.

[78] Janel M. Mueller, "The Exegesis of Experience: Dean Donne's *Devotions upon Emergent Occasions*," *JEGP*, 67 (1968), 1-9. The analogue of the sermon affords a much more significant insight into Donne's meditative method than does Van Lann's Procrustean effort to fit Donne's sequence to the Ignatian pattern, "John Donne's *Devotions*," pp. 191-202.

Moreover, in those poems the occasion of the death leads to a full-scale "deliberate" meditation or sermon upon two religious topics: first, "the frailty and the decay of this whole world," and second, "the incommodities of the soule in this life and her exaltation in the next." But the death of Elizabeth Drury is not merely a point of departure for these "deliberate" meditations: rather, like Donne's illness in the *Devotions*, that death is made the symbolic center to which everything in the two poems relates, since the topics explored are embodied in the particular individual and occasion.

C. Meditative and Poetic "Application to the Self"

In occasional meditation the starting-point is some occasion or event in the Protestant meditator's personal experience, and his purpose is to interpret that event in terms of God's providential plan and Word. In "deliberate" meditation and in most sermons the starting-point is usually a biblical text or event or a theological doctrine, and in these forms the constant emphasis of the Protestant is upon "application to the self." Exploration of just what is meant by such "application" yields the insight that whether the starting-point is a text or an occasion, the Protestant concern in meditation and sermon alike is to trace the interrelation between the biblical message and the pattern of events in the Christian's own experience, so that the one is seen to be the reflection or manifestation of the other. The Christian's experience comments upon the biblical text, and the text upon his experience. This interrelationship precisely distinguishes the Protestant emphasis in meditative and poetic practice, as it contrasts with the Roman Catholic tradition. The meditative element in Donne's divine poems, as well as in the *Anniversary* poems, asks for discussion in terms of this distinction.

As Martz has observed, concern with the interior life is

basic to all kinds of meditative practice, Catholic and Protestant. Yet there is a difference in focus between Protestant "application," and the Ignatian or Salesian modes of meditation. In these modes the meditator typically seeks to apply himself to the subject, so that he participates in it. He imagines vividly, as if it were taking place in or displayed in his presence, some scene in the life of Christ or the Virgin, or some aspect of the four last things or the sacraments, or the desperate condition of his sinful soul; he analyzes the subject in detail so as to understand it fully; and he stirs up his affections so as to produce emotions appropriate to the scene or event or symbol or personal spiritual condition. Crashaw's poems upon the Holy Name of Jesus, upon the Nativity, upon the Epiphany, and upon St. Teresa, exemplify this procedure:[79] the speaker's powers of imagination and analysis are brought to focus upon a scene or personage or symbol until the affections are moved to appropriate response and active participation. Donne's poetic "meditations" in this kind include "Good Friday, 1613. Riding Westward" and the *La Corona* sonnet sequence.

The typical Protestant procedure is very nearly the reverse. Instead of the application of the self to the subject, the Protestant theory in regard to both sermons and deliberate meditation calls for the application of the subject to the self, indeed for the location of the subject in the self. W. R. Haller develops this point with regard to Puritan sermons and devotions, but the emphases if not always the rejections he describes are evident in seventeenth-century English Protestant works generally:

[79] See, e.g., "To the Name above Every Name, the Name of Jesus. A Hymn"; "In the Holy Nativity of Our Lord God. A Hymn Sung as by the Shepheards"; "In the Glorious Epiphanie of our Lord God, A Hymn. Sung as by the Three Kings"; "A hymn to the Name and Honor of the Admirable Sainte Teresa"; "The Flaming Heart, Upon the Book and Picture of the Seraphicall Saint Teresa," in L. C. Martin, ed., *The Poems, English, Latin, and Greek of Richard Crashaw*, 2nd ed. (Oxford, 1957), pp. 239-262, 317-327.

103

The symbolism of the nativity and the passion came to mean little to the Puritan saints. . . . The Puritan saga did not cherish the memory of Christ in the manger or on the cross, that is, of the lamb of God sacrificed in vicarious atonement for the sins of man. The mystic birth was the birth of the new man in men. The mystic passion was the crucifixion of the new man by the old, and the true propitiation was the sacrifice of the old to the new.[80]

In his sermons Donne constantly urges this kind of application: "Draw the Scripture to thine own heart, and to thine own actions, and thou shalt finde it made for that: all the promises of the Old Testament made, and all accomplished in the New Testament, for the salvation of thy soule hereafter, and for thy consolation in the present application of them."[81] Meditation thus involved finding the whole of salvation history traced in one's own soul: "all that God sayes is spoken to me, and all that Christ suffered was suffered for me. . . . Postdate the whole Bible, and whatsoever thou hearest spoken of such, as thou art, before, beleeve all that to be spoken but now, and spoken to thee."[82]

In relation to this, Haller notes that in the earlier seventeenth century the constantly repeated topic for Puritan sermons was "the course of the godly soul out of hardness and indifference to the consciousness of its lost condition, and so . . . to faith in God, to active perseverence, and confident expectation of victory and glory," and he observed also the disposition to locate that formula in particular individuals.[83] Often the preacher presented himself as illustration: "the preacher saw, and generally recorded, his own life as an image of the truth."[84] But the formula might also

[80] Haller, *Rise of Puritanism*, p. 151.

[81] Donne, *Sermons*, II, 308. Sermon on Matt. 4:18-20, at The Hague, Dec., 1619.

[82] Donne, *Sermons*, VI, 219-220. Sermon on Acts 9:4, at St. Paul's, 1624/5.

[83] Haller, *Rise of Puritanism*, p. 141.

[84] *Ibid.*, p. 143.

be discovered in other good Christians who, according to Edward Topsell, may be seen as "the starres [that] give light in the night . . . the soules that shield others from danger."[85] This topic and these methods were by no means the special province of Puritans: seventeenth-century Protestants generally, and Donne in particular, employed them constantly. Donne characteristically urged every member of his auditory to trace the paradigm of salvation in his own soul:

> We must . . . anatomize our soule . . . and find every sinnewe, and fiber, every lineament and ligament of this body of sinne, and then every breath of that newe spirit, every drop of that newe blood that must restore and repayre us. Study all the history, and write all the progres of the Holy Ghost in thy selfe. . . .thou wilt find an infinite comfort in this particular tracinge of the Holy Ghost, and his workinge in thy soule.[86]

Also, citing David and Solomon as authority, Donne recommended that the preacher "preach out of our owne history . . . to declare . . . what God hath done for my soule."[87] Such passages invite some reconsideration of Joan Webber's conclusions regarding the very different uses of the "I" in Anglican and Puritan autobiographical writing;[88] they indicate that in his sermons at least Donne accommodated himself to a general Protestant norm regarding the use of the self as paradigm. He constantly spoke to his auditory in the first person, creating a typical or symbolic "I" to whom all

[85] Edward Topsell, *Times Lamentation: Or an Exposition on the Prophet Joel* (London, 1599), p. 391.

[86] Donne, *Sermons*, II, 159. Sermon on Psalm 38:9, at Lincoln's Inn, 1618.

[87] Donne, *Sermons*, IX, 279. Sermon on Psalm 32:3-4, at St. Paul's.

[88] Webber, *The Eloquent I: Style and Self in Seventeenth-Century Prose* (Madison, 1968), pp. 3-52. The foregoing discussion has suggested that, though the focus in the *Devotions*, as occasional meditations, necessarily differs from that of the sermons, they are not essentially different in this use of the self as paradigm.

105

the biblical texts could be applied in the first instance, and in whom the pattern of salvation was manifested.

Appreciation of what is involved in this kind of "application" forces a modification, for the earlier seventeenth century at least, of Kaufmann's view that the Calvinist emphasis upon Doctrine (*Logos*) in meditation was a force making for abstraction and against poetic imagination.[89] To be sure, in Protestant meditation the senses were not stimulated to recreate and imagine biblical scenes in vivid detail; this kind of meditation would not encourage poetry based upon visual imagery and sensuous immediacy. But Protestant meditation did engage the mind in the effort to penetrate deeply into the motives and motions of the psyche, and also to realize and represent the self (or another person) as the very embodiment of the subject meditated upon. The Word was still to be made flesh, though now in the self of the meditator (or of the preacher and his audience). This new emphasis could certainly contribute to the creation of poetry having a new depth and sophistication of psychological insight and a new focus upon the symbolic significance of the human individual. It is not an accident that critics often characterize Donne's poetry in just such terms.

Donne's *Holy Sonnets* are meditations more nearly in the Protestant spirit than in the Ignatian. The topics are persistently applied to, located within, the self. "Spit in my face you Jewes" presents the speaker (not Christ) as the proper subject of the crucifixion, and explores why he deserves such treatment. "Death be not Proud" presents the speaker (not Christ) engaged upon a conquest over Death as he apprehends the meaning of Christ's victory over that enemy. "What if this present were the world's last night" bypasses the expectations aroused by the opening line for a traditional meditation upon the terrors of the last day, and instead analyzes the speaker's experience of the crucified

[89] Kaufmann, *Traditions in Puritan Meditation*, pp. 49-55.

Christ's countenance "in my heart" as an earnest of his mercy and pity on that day. "Batter my Heart" conceives of God as exercising the whole of his redemptive activity solely and directly upon the speaker's heart.

Donne's poems of compliment—and especially the *Anniversaries*—present, I would suggest, a variation of this kind of "application." In them the subject is located, embodied, in the person who is praised in the poem, and then it is apprehended by the speaker (and his auditory) through meditation on that person. If the preacher of sermons may find the spiritual truths conveyed by his text illustrated by, embodied within, himself, or if, alternatively, the meditator may discover that the occasions of his own life enact the paradigm of God's redemptive activity (as Donne found to be the case with his own illness), so the poet engaged upon complimentary poetry may find profound spiritual significances embodied in some particular individual offered on some specific occasion to his praises.

The theoretical and theological bases for Donne's characteristic transformations of particular individuals into all-encompassing symbols must be examined next, through an analysis of just how Donne understood and used the classic Christian idea that a man—or a woman—is the image of God.

CHAPTER IV

The Ordering Symbol: The Restored
Image of God in Man

IF THE SPEAKER in Donne's poems of compliment, including the *Anniversaries*, proposes to meditate upon a particular individual as the embodiment of the poetic subject at hand, it is important to discover just what symbolic meanings attach to the personage celebrated, and on what basis. In criticism of the *Anniversaries*, the significance of Elizabeth Drury has been approached from four principal directions. One approach takes her as simply a point of departure for a poem about some other identifiable person or persons: for Marjorie Nicolson "shee" is Queen Elizabeth primarily, with archetypal overtones of Astraea and the Blessed Virgin; for William Empson, she is Christ, the indwelling *Logos*; for Patrick J. Mahony, an eclectic mix of Miss Nicolson's figures and such allegorical personifications as Lady Virtue, Lady Wisdom, Lady Justice; for Richard Hughes, St. Lucy conceived as a pattern of Christian regeneration, wisdom, and illumination.[1] The problem with this approach is its arbitrariness: whatever case can be made for Donne's general interest in the personages mentioned, there is little or nothing in the poems themselves that points unambiguously to any of these identifications. Consequently, they have not found wide acceptance.

A second position assumes that Donne's object of praise is an ambiguous symbol arbitrarily or paradoxically in-

---

[1] Marjorie Hope Nicolson, *The Breaking of the Circle* (New York, 1960), pp. 81-122; William Empson, *Some Versions of Pastoral* (New York, 1935), p. 84; Patrick Joseph Mahony, "A Study of Donne's *Anniversaries*" (unpublished Ph.D. dissertation, New York University, 1963); Richard E. Hughes, *The Progress of the Soul* (New York, 1968), pp. 196-255.

vested with profound significances and transcendent values. Harold Love understands the poem's "shee" to be at once the Soul of the World and its corporal (and therefore vulnerable) Heart. Carol Sicherman finds that Elizabeth Drury is at first simply the stimulus for Donne's inquiry into values (the *Anniversary* poems being essentially about Donne himself), and that she subsequently represents Donne's achieved vision of spiritual perfection. For Eric LaGuardia the imprecise "shee" of the poem is by the "arts of equiparation" made into a "deity of symbolic wholeness," in an aesthetic universe where the symbol or trope need have no meaning or referent outside itself.[2] The problem with this general position is its nebulousness: the symbolic center of the poems is understood to be capable of bearing whatever meanings the poet wishes to attach to her, but we are not shown what connection exists between this amorphous figure and Elizabeth Drury, or how the poems develop connections between the dead girl and those meanings.

Beginning from Donne's reported answer to Ben Jonson's criticism of the hyperbole of the *First Anniversarie*—"that he described the Idea of a Woman, not as she was"—[3] Frank Manley has developed a third position, describing the symbolic "shee" in terms of Christian Neoplatonic thought about wisdom.[4] He presents Elizabeth initially as a genuine symbol—that is, as a particular reality pointing to a universal meaning and participating in that universal—but his discussion of that symbol finally becomes both nebulous and arbitrary. At the outset, his approach to the symbolic dimension of the poem associates the lady with

---

[2] Love, "The Argument of Donne's *First Anniversary*," *MP*, 63 (1966), 125-131; Sicherman, "Donne's Timeless Anniversaries," *UTQ*, 39 (1970), 127-143; Eric LaGuardia, "Aesthetics of Analogy," *Diogenes*, 62 (1968), 49-61.

[3] "Conversations with Drummond of Hawthornden," *Ben Jonson*, 1, 133.

[4] Frank Manley, "Introduction," *The Anniversaries*, pp. 10-50. For some background to this tradition, see Jon A. Quitslund, "Spenser's Image of Sapience," *Studies in the Renaissance*, 16 (1969), 181-213.

literary and archetypal identifications of woman as Edenic Garden and as Jungian Anima (the "Idea of a Woman" in man which presents his own deepest reality to him); soon, however, these free-floating associations harden into a personification allegory identifying the lady as *Sapientia Creata*—that wisdom which is the knowledge of this world and the next, given to man through faith—on little basis other than that *Sapientia* was customarily female in Neoplatonic thought, and was associated with the figure of wisdom of Proverbs 8. Moreover, Manley's suggestion that Beatrice of the *Commedia* was a prototype for Elizabeth Drury in embodying such meanings[5] discounts the degree to which Beatrice's symbolic meaning is defined by a dramatic context: she is made the manifestation of wisdom and heavenly grace only for Dante the speaker, whereas Elizabeth Drury's symbolic role is formally and constantly extended to the world at large.

O. B. Hardison is the most persuasive exponent of a fourth position: that the poems are about Elizabeth Drury herself, "a virtuous young woman concerning whom Donne had received 'good report' "—or, more precisely, about the "soul" of Elizabeth Drury, celebrated by means of recognized *stilnovisti* and Petrarchan concepts and tropes. Hardison's reading is in some ways reductive in that by identifying the subject of the poems simply as the praise of Elizabeth Drury it scants the evidence in titles, subtitles, and text designating profound metaphysical issues as subject matter. Like Manley, Hardison also disregards Donne's failure to supply anything like the customary Petrarchan dramatic context: Donne's speaker, as we have noted, refrains from asserting any kind of personal, dramatic relationship to the lady he celebrates. Accordingly, Hardison's assertion that the speaker's lament for the dead and decaying world and praise of Elizabeth Drury's transcendent merit have significance only for the "world" of her acquaintance seems a tenuous effort to import the dramatic context of Petrarchan elegy by appealing to generic expectations

[5] *Ibid.*, pp. 36-38.

which in fact are deliberately frustrated in this poem.[6] Accepting Hardison's view of Elizabeth Drury, P. G. Stanwood has argued perceptively that Donne uses this particular girl "to describe the life of grace in its fullness and in its withdrawal." But the Roman Catholic conception of "sanctifying" grace upon which Stanwood's perception is grounded —"an 'accident,' something added to a man who is already a completely constituted being and inhering in him . . . a divine quality, a supernatural and additional abundance"[7]— runs counter to Donne's own theological principles, as will be seen below, and does not provide adequate terms to account for the utter decay and death of the natural world which the *Anniversary* poems describe. Nevertheless, this focus upon grace, together with Hardison's proposition that Elizabeth's "soul" is the subject of the poem and that "there is nothing startling about the assertion that the virtuous Christian cultivates the image of God in his soul"[8] points us toward a symbolic dimension which is neither nebulous nor arbitrary, and which can relate Elizabeth Drury to all that is discussed in both poems.

Analysis of Donne's occasional poetry of compliment in relation to contemporary exercises in the kind has revealed that his characteristic approach to the poetry of praise is in a strict sense metaphysical—that his praises are directed not to the particular qualities of individuals, but to the image of God which they severally may bear. The *Anniversary* poems are governed by this concern to an even greater degree, since the death of Elizabeth Drury appears to have offered Donne an occasion he found nowhere else for an elaborate poetic analysis of the Divine image in man and its implications for the human condition here and hereafter. That this symbolic dimension is of central importance to the *Anniversary* poems is intimated in the description of Elizabeth Drury as one who "kept, by diligent devotion,/ Gods

---

[6] Hardison, *Enduring Monument*, pp. 186, 173-179.
[7] P. G. Stanwood, "'Essentiall Joye' in Donne's *Anniversaries*," *Texas Studies in Literature and Language*, 13 (1971), 227, 229, 234.
[8] Hardison, *Enduring Monument*, p. 170.

Image, in such reparation,/ Within her heart, that what decay was growen,/ Was her first Parents fault, and not her own" (II *Ann.* 455-458).

To explore this range of significance we may begin, as everyone does, with Donne's observation that his *First Anniversarie* described "the Idea of a Woman and not as she was." The comment appears to demand, and has usually received, explication in generalized Neoplatonic terms, but in fact Donne's sermons provide a precise, consistent, and clearly relevant gloss upon the term "Idea" used in such a context. His sermon on Genesis 1:26, "And God said, let us make man, in our Image, after our likenesse," clearly indicates that for Donne the *Idea* of any human being is the image of God designated by God himself as the pattern by which humankind was produced: "God had deposited, and laid up in himselfe certaine formes, patternes, *Ideas* of every thing that he made. . . . And when he had made any thing, he saw it was good; good because it answered the pattern, the Image; good, because it was like to that. . . . But . . . thou hast . . . a Meridionall heighth, by which thou seest thine Image, thy pattern, to be no copy; no other man, but the originall it selfe, God himselfe: *Faciamus ad nostram, Let us make man in our Image, after our likenesse.*"[9] Elsewhere Donne is yet more explicit in identifying the Idea of mankind as the image of God: "Whatsoever is made, in time, was alive in God, before it was made, that is, in that eternall Idea, and patterne which was in him. . . . Of all things in Heaven, and earth, but of himselfe, God had an Idea, a patterne in himselfe, before he made it. . . . If, I aske God, by what Idea he made me, God produces his *Faciamus hominem ad Imaginem nostram,* That there was a concurrence of the whole Trinity, to make me in *Adam,* according to that Image which they were, and according to that Idea, which they had pre-determined."[10]

[9] Donne, *Sermons,* IX, 73-76. Sermon preached to the king at court in April, 1629.

[10] *Sermons,* VII, 60-61. Sermon on Psalms 63:7, preached at St. Paul's, January 29, 1625/6.

Donne's sermons also use the term "Idea" in regard to the restoration of the image of God in man through grace. Characteristically, he describes the process of man's regeneration in terms of the defaced image being conformed anew to Christ, the true Image of God, as its Platonic Idæa: "If thou wilt be a new Creature . . . then Christ is thy *Idæa*, thy Pattern, thine Original. . . . To be produc'd by this *Idæa*, built up by this Model, copied by this Original, is truely, is onely to be a new Creature."[11] It is evident then that for Donne the Idea of a man, or of a woman, is—quite precisely—the image of God, since that is the pattern by which God created mankind, and Christ the true Image of God is the pattern by which he restores mankind. Moreover, as has been seen, Donne's constant focus both in poems of compliment and in meditation is upon the manifestation or embodiment of abstractions in particular individuals or in the self.[12] If, then, Donne declared his intention to praise Elizabeth Drury not as she was but rather as the Idea of a Woman, we may suppose that he undertook to praise the image of God created and restored in her. This characteristic Donnean focus helps to explain the curious praise of the "Shee" of the poem as at once image (of God) and Platonic archetype—"The best and first originall/ Of all faire copies" (I *Ann.* 227-228).[13]

Recognition of the fact that the phrase "the image of God"

[11] *Ibid.*, IV, 99. Sermon on II Cor. 4:6, preached at Spital Cross, in the Churchyard of St. Mary's without Bishopsgate, Easter Monday, 1622.

[12] See above, pp. 44-47, 100-107. Robert Ellrodt, *Neoplatonism in the Poetry of Spenser* (Geneva, 1960), pp. 141-151, has called attention to a somewhat similar focus in Spenser upon the manifestations of beauty and virtue in particular individuals rather than upon the transcendent Ideas.

[13] A fairly close poetic analogue to this view of the soul as both Platonic Idea and image of God is to be found in Abraham Jackson's elegy for Lord Harrington, *Sorrowes Lenitive* (London, 1614):

> O had I all forgone what so is mine
> Within the compass of this massie round;
> Except that part of me that is divine,
> Wherein th'Idea of my God is found. (sig. A 5v)

alludes to God's comment in Genesis regarding man's creation and nature does not advance our understanding of it very far, or our sense of how the concept may function in Donne's poems. To discover the precise symbolic force it carries there, we need to examine how Donne related himself to, and how he contributed to, the complex theological debate over what constituted the image of God infused in man at the creation, and what was the restored image recreated in him after the Fall.[14] In his discussion of *The Second Anniversarie*, Professor Martz has also referred to Elizabeth Drury as image of God, noting that Donne "consistently attempts to transmute the girl into a symbol of virtue that may fitly represent the Image and Likeness of God in man."[15] But this conception of the restored image and likeness of God in man as being grounded in human virtue is a Catholic idea, whose substantive meaning is at a very far remove, I shall argue here, from Donne's understanding of these terms. Indeed, as the Georges and William Halewood have intimated, Donne's understanding of the nature of man is grounded in Reformation Protestantism;[16] moreover, his characteristic uses of the Genesis formula are couched not in ethical but in metaphysical terms. Accordingly, I suggest that the various symbolic personages in Donne's poetry of compliment, and most notably Elizabeth Drury, are to be understood in terms of these Protestant and metaphysical significations. Yet despite the fact

[14] For some background in these matters see, e.g., G.W.H. Lampe, *The Seal of the Spirit: A Study in the Doctrine of Baptism and Confirmation in the New Testament and the Fathers* (London, 1951); Robert Javelet, *Image et Ressemblance au Douzième Siècle*, 2 vols. (Paris, 1967); Charles Trinkaus, *In our Image and Likeness: Humanity and Divinity in Italian Humanist Thought*, 2 vols. (Chicago, 1970). See also Winfried Schleiner, *The Imagery of John Donne's Sermons* (Providence, R. I., 1970).

[15] Martz, *Poetry of Meditation*, pp. 238-48.

[16] See Charles and Katherine George, *The Protestant Mind of the English Reformation*, pp. 68-71; Halewood, *The Poetry of Grace*, pp. 33-70.

114

that the conception of the image of God in man must some-how suggest manifestation of the Divine, Donne's primary emphasis in these poems is not upon God but upon man: the symbol is for him a means of exploring human nature, of presenting a vision of what man once was, and what his regeneration can mean.

A. The Original Image of God in Man, and its Corruption

The Church Fathers and the medieval schoolmen usually located the image of God in the powers or faculties of the mind or soul. Though some of the Greek Fathers found the image and the likeness to be virtually indistinguishable, emphasizing as they did the likeness that must always obtain between an image and its archetype,[17] the Latin Fathers normally understood the image to be in the powers or faculties themselves, and the likeness to be the excellence and perfection of those powers and the virtues arising from them.

In his *De Genesi ad literam* Augustine at times conflates these terms, explaining that God made man according to his image and likeness, giving him a soul whereby in reason and understanding he excelled all other creatures; but in *De Trinitate* he refines the distinction, locating the image in man's mind (*mens*) which in its trinity of memory, understanding, and will reflects the Divine Trinity.[18] After the Fall, Augustine declared, this image was wretchedly defaced: "the whole mass of the human race was under condemnation, was lying steeped and wallowing in misery, and

[17] See, e.g., Gregory of Nyssa, "On the Making of Man" xi.1-3, ed. and trans. Henry Wace, "A Select Library of Nicene and Post-Nicene Fathers of the Christian Church," v (New York, 1917), 306-307.

[18] Augustine, *De Genesi ad literam* iii.20 (#30), *Patrologiae Cursus Completus, Series Latina*, ed. J.-P. Migne, 221 vols. (Paris, 1844-1864), xxxiv, 292-293; *De Trinitate* X.xi-xii (#17-19) in *The Works of Aurelius Augustine*, ed. Marcus Dods, 15 vols. (Edinburgh, 1871-1876), vii, 381-383.

was being tossed from one evil to another." Especially was the will in bondage, so that man could perform nothing good "whether in thought, or will and affection, or in action," any more than a man who has killed himself can restore himself to life.[19] Yet, though defaced, the image is not utterly lost: some ungodly persons do actions worthy of praise (though if their motives were carefully examined those actions would hardly seem righteous), and this is because the "meerest lineaments" of God's image, and the rational soul itself, are not wholly erased.[20]

Bernard of Clairvaux understood the image of God in the soul to inhere chiefly in the soul's greatness, i.e., in its capacity and desire for eternal existence and eternal excellences —truth, wisdom, righteousness; this greatness of capacity he defines as "the soul's form which it cannot lose."[21] But he takes the distinction between image and likeness to be in some respects arbitrary, since "it is of necessity that he who is in a certain image should be in conformity with that image, and not merely share in the empty name of the image": on this understanding he defines the chief elements of likeness between the soul and God to be simplicity of substance, immortality of existence, and freedom of will.[22] Bernard argues that these attributes constituting the image and likeness of God cannot be totally obliterated: indeed, he affirms that even in hell the image persists, *"Imago siquidem in gehenna ipsa uri poterit, non exuri; ardere, sed non deleri."*[23] The soul after the Fall "has . . . not put off its original form, but has put on over it one which is foreign to it": the intellectual faculties in themselves are essentially un-

[19] *Enchiridion* viii (#24), *Works*, IX, 195; *A Treatise on Rebuke and Grace* i (#1), *Works*, XV, 71.

[20] *On the Spirit and the Letter* xxviii (#48), *Works*, IV, 205-206.

[21] Bernard of Clairvaux, *Sermons on the Song of Songs*, in *Life and Works of Saint Bernard*, ed. John Mabillon, trans. S. J. Eales, 4 vols. (London, 1889-1896), IV, 487-491.

[22] *Ibid.*, IV, 488, 494-501.

[23] Bernard, "In festo annuntiationis, i.7," *Sermone de Tempore*, *Pat. Lat.*, 183, col. 386 c.

changed and even liberty remains inherent in the will itself although that will now unwillingly obeys the law of sin. But the likeness is wholly obscured if not destroyed, for original sin is as a mantle or cloak of unlikeness laid over the soul, making it unlike to God and unlike even to its own nature.[24]

Thomas Aquinas, whose definitions of these concepts became normative for post-Tridentine Roman Catholic thought, alters some of these emphases. He located the image especially in the reason and free will—through which faculties the soul possesses a natural aptitude for understanding and loving God.[25] The likeness is the perfection of the image—an analogy of power with God insofar as this is possible to man, a love of virtue, and an original justice which involves the supernatural gifts of integrity, bodily immortality, holiness, righteousness, wisdom, charity, and dominion.[26] For Thomas the effects of original sin are much less severe than they are in the Augustinian-Bernardine formulation. What is lost in the Fall are the supernatural gifts superadded to man's nature which perfect the image of God in him and which constitute his likeness to God.[27] The constituents of the image itself, the intellectual faculties, are corrupted, but rather by being disordered than destroyed or defaced: "when the bond of original justice, which held together all the powers of the soul in a certain order, is broken, each power . . . tends to its own proper movement."[28] Especially do the senses rebel against reason. The will retains its liberty, though it can no longer by its natural power love God above all else, as it ought to do. But

[24] *Sermons on the Song of Songs, Works*, IV, 502-505.

[25] Aquinas, *Summa Theologica* I, Q. xciii, Art. 6-7, ed. Anton C. Pegis, *Basic Writings of Saint Thomas Aquinas*, 2 vols. (New York, 1945), I, 893-879; cf. Robert Bellarmine, *A Most Learned and Pious Treatise . . . forming a ladder whereby our Mindes may ascend to God, by the Steppes of his Creatures* (Douay, 1616), pp. 19-20.

[26] *Summa Theologica* I, Q. xciii, Art. 9; Q. xciv, Art. 1-4; Q. xcv, Art. 1-4, *Basic Works*, I, 899-922.

[27] *Ibid.*, S.T. I, Q. xcv, Art. 1, *Basic Works*, I, 911.

[28] *Ibid.*, S.T. I-II, Q. lxxxii, Art. 4, *Basic Works*, II, 677-678.

the intellect is much less affected: it is still, by its own pow-
ers, able to attain to knowledge of natural things, and even
to some knowledge of God.[29]

The Protestant reformers usually located the image of
God in man's soul,[30] but defined it as man's entire spiritual
endowment rather than as the soul's powers or faculties.
They ignored or explicitly denied any real distinction be-
tween the image and the likeness, defining both as the soul's
perfect state of original righteousness. For the reformers
generally, original sin meant the almost total destruction of
both image and likeness, the depravity—not merely the dis-
ordering—of the highest intellectual powers as well as of
the sensual appetites.

Luther quarrelled sharply with the traditional distinction
between image and likeness, since in his view it helped pro-
mote the belief that fallen man's natural endowments would
permit him to cooperate in his own salvation. On the con-
trary, Luther asserted that the loss of the divine image in us
is so complete that we cannot now understand what it once
was.[31] His tentative definition of it identifies as proper to
man's nature at his creation the following elements, some
of which had been incorporated in Aquinas' list of special
supernatural gifts superadded to unfallen man's own na-
ture: the true knowledge of God, the sincere love of God
and neighbor, the knowledge of and dominion over all crea-
tures, eternal life, and everything that is good.[32] Because of
original sin this image is almost totally destroyed, resulting
in the depravity of the intellect and the abject bondage of
the will:

[29] *Ibid.*, *S.T.* I-II, Q. lxxxiii, Art. 4; Q. lxxxv, Art. 1-2, *Works*, II,
684-685, 694-697.

[30] An exception is Jerome Zanchius, who located the image in the
whole man, body as well as soul. See Arnold Williams, *The Common
Expositor* (Chapel Hill, 1949), pp. 81-82.

[31] Martin Luther, *Lectures on Genesis*, ed. Jaroslav Pelikan, *Works*,
vols. I— (St. Louis, Mo., 1958—), I, 60-61.

[32] *Ibid.*, I, 62-63; cf. Luther, *Commentary on Genesis*, trans. J.
Theodore Mueller, 2 vols. (Grand Rapids, Mich., 1958), I, 31-33.

Memory, will, and mind we have indeed; but they are most depraved and most seriously weakened, yes, to put it more clearly, they are utterly leprous and unclean. . . . If some assert nevertheless that these powers are that image, let them admit that they are, as it were, leprous and unclean. Similarly, we still call a leprous human being a human being even though in his leprous flesh everything is almost dead and without sensation, except that he is rather violently excited to lust.[33]

Calvin was no less adamant in refusing to distinguish between image and likeness. He defined the image as "the perfect excellence of human nature which shone in Adam before his defection," and he glossed the phrase "image and likeness" as "the whole integritie of nature . . . when Adam was indued with a right understanding, when all his affections were ordered by reason, when all his senses were uncorrupted, and when he truly excelled in all graces."[34] Arguing that the Pauline discussion of the renewed image of God in man (Ephesians 4:24) affords the best insight into the original image, Calvin declared that the chief seat of God's image was the mind and heart, although "there was no parte wherein some sparckes did not appeare."[35] As for the effects of original sin, Calvin asserted that God's image in man, though not totally destroyed, was "so corrupted that whatever remains is frightful deformity." His qualification, that "certeine obscure lineaments and markes of that image remaine in us" means little, for "they are so corrupted and lame, that we may truly say that it [the image] is blotted out," and "nothing remains after the Fall except what is confused, mutilated, and disease-ridden."[36] From

[33] "Lectures on Genesis," *Works*, I, 61-62.

[34] John Calvin, *Institutes of the Christian Religion*, I.xv, ed. John T. McNeill, in *Library of Christian Classics*, xx (Philadelphia, 1960), p. 190; *A Commentarie . . . upon the first booke of Moses called Genesis*, trans. Thomas Tymme (London, 1578), p. 44.

[35] *Commentarie . . . upon . . . Genesis*, p. 44.

[36] *Institutes* I.xv, LCC, xx, 189-190; *Commentarie . . . upon . . . Genesis*, p. 44.

man now, therefore, "in place of wisdom, virtue, holiness, truth, and justice, with which adornments he had been clad, there came forth the most filthy plagues, blindness, impotence, impurity, vanity, and injustice."[37] This is not primarily a matter of the rebellion of the senses, as in the Thomistic formulation, but rather of corruption of the mind and heart: "the mind is given over to blindness and the heart to depravity."[38] Enough of reason is spared us to distinguish us from brute beasts and to achieve some knowledge in the natural order, but all knowledge of God and his kingdom is wholly lost and we are left in these matters "blinder than moles." The heart is rendered deceitful and corrupt, and the will is in such bondage that "it cannot move toward good, much less apply itself thereto."[39] These formulations became classic for English Protestantism; they were reiterated in the Geneva bible, in countless commentaries and doctrinal treatises, and in many secular works as well.[40]

Donne's formulation in regard to the image of God as originally created in man is that of Augustine and Bernard rather than Calvin: the image resides in the powers of the soul and cannot be effaced. Yet, preaching on Genesis 1:26, Donne proposed to treat the two terms "image" and "like-

---

[37] *Institutes* II.i, *LCC*, xx, 246.   [38] *Institutes* II.i, *LCC*, xx, 253.

[39] *Institutes* II.ii, II.iii, *LCC*, xx, 277-294.

[40] The Geneva Bible (*The Holie Bible* [London, 1599], "Genesis," fol. 1ᵛ) defined image and likeness from the description in Ephesians 4:24 of the restored image in the new man; the two terms were thereby treated as synonyms, indicating that "man was created after God for righteousnesse and true holinesse, meaning by these two words, all perfection, as wisedome, trueth, innocencie, power, etc." Andrew Willet (*Hexapla in Genesin, that is, A Sixfold Commentary upon Genesis* [London, 1608], p. 15) also distilled in brief compass the essence of this position: the image consists in "righteousness and true holines"; the faculties of the soul are not themselves obliterated in the Fall but the Divine image (as defined) is utterly lost and extinguished. Cf. John Weemse, *The Portraiture of the Image of God in Man* (London, 1636), pp. 61-68; Sir Walter Raleigh, *The History of the World* (London, 1614), pp. 23-27.

ness" as synonyms, in the Protestant way, even though he felt that some significant differences must be pointed to by the presence of the two distinct words in the scripture text.[41] For a specific definition of the image he appealed to Augustine's discussion of the trinity in the soul's faculties—memory, understanding, and will—as a reflection of the Divine Trinity and its chief attributes, power, wisdom, and goodness.[42]

Because he took the image to be in the powers of the soul themselves, Donne held with Augustine and the Roman Catholic theologians generally that original sin could not efface it. Bernard's striking comment, "*Imago Dei uri potest in Gehenna, non exuri*" comes close to being his favorite quotation: "Till the soul be burnt to ashes, to nothing, (which cannot be done, no not in hell) the Image of God cannot be burnt out of that soule."[43] At times Donne invoked this quotation to stress man's dignity, but often also to emphasize his culpability in bringing that image of God into vileness and sin: "we draw the image of God into all our incontinencies ... we carry his image, into all foul places, which we haunt upon earth; yea ... even in Hell ... The image of God burns in us in hell, but can never be burnt out of us."[44]

Moreover, Donne's conception of the way original sin affects the soul's faculties is not the Thomistic or Tridentine view; rather it approximates Augustine's and even approaches Calvin's position. That the image of God is in man by nature and cannot be destroyed means in this context merely that the natural powers themselves remain capable of functioning; they are, however, horribly defaced, and are wholly useless for supernatural purposes. For Donne the condition of man in sin is such that "he hath no interest in his own natural faculties; He cannot think, he cannot wish, he cannot do any thing of himself" toward supernatural

[41] Donne, *Sermons*, IX, 70-73. See note 9.
[42] *Ibid.*, IX, 82-85; cf. II, 73.   [43] *Sermons*, IX, 81.
[44] *Ibid.*, I, 160. Sermon on Isaiah 52:3, at Greenwich, April 30, 1615.

ends; his will is a "dead will."[45] Original sin is "that indeleble foulnesse, and uncleanesse which God discovers in us all," and the death attendant upon it "hath invaded every part and faculty of man, understanding, and will, and all."[46]

B. The Restored Image

Christians of Donne's era generally agreed that the image of God in man could be restored only through the grace of God, merited for man by the sacrifice and satisfaction of Jesus Christ. They also agreed that the process of restoring the image must be initiated by God, that it cannot be begun by man's will and effort. But just what that process involved was variously understood and formulated.

The Church Fathers had emphasized the sacrament of baptism as the means by which grace was infused into the soul, removing the defilement of sin and brightening the image of God. Chrysostom declared that restoration to be instantaneous and complete at baptism: "As soon as we are baptized, the Soul beameth even more than the Sun, being cleansed by the Spirit; and not only do we behold the glory of God, but from it also receive a sort of splendour. . . . So also doth the soul being cleansed, and made brighter than silver, receive a ray from the glory of the Spirit, and glance it back."[47] Again, referring to Galatians 3:27, he equates the restored image with the manifestation of Christ in the self: "He that was a Greek, or Jew, or bond-man yesterday, carries about with him the form, not of an Angel or Archangel, but of the Lord of all, yea displays in his own person the Christ."[48] This restored image is defaced and defiled

[45] *Ibid.*, I, 155; I, 292-293. Sermon on I Tim. 1:15, at Whitehall, April 19, 1618.

[46] *Ibid.*, VI, 116-117. Sermon on I Cor. 12:3 [1624?].

[47] St. John Chrysostom, *Homilies on the Second Epistle of S. Paul to the Corinthians*, trans. J. A. Ashworth, *Library of the Fathers*, 27 (Oxford, 1848), p. 98.

[48] Chrysostom, "Homilies on Galatians," trans. anon., *LF*, 5 (Oxford, 1840), p. 61.

again and again by postbaptismal sins (for the predisposition to sin remains in man as a result of original sin), but it is restored again and again by penitence and it is heightened and enhanced by the practice of virtue and by superadded graces.

Augustine, by contrast, distinguished between the "first cure" or remission of sins in baptism, which is instantaneous, and the "second cure" or restoration of the image, which "takes place by daily additions" in grace and virtue.[49] Citing II Corinthians 4:16, "the inward man is renewed day by day," and Ephesians 4:24, he describes a progressive movement toward perfection:

> He, then, who is day by day renewed by making progress in the knowledge of God, and in righteousness and true holiness, transfers his love from things temporal to things eternal. . . . And he does this in proportion as he is helped by God. . . . And when the last day of life shall have found any one holding fast faith in the Mediator in such progress and growth as this, he will . . . be made perfect by Him [God]. . . . For the likeness of God will then be perfected in this image, when the sight of God shall be perfected. And of this the Apostle Paul speaks: "Now we see through a glass, in an enigma, but then face to face."[50]

Because the will in bondage to sin can "do absolutely no good thing," God's grace through Christ is necessary to renew its freedom; man's new righteousness is therefore a free gift of God which he can do nothing to merit. Paul's phrase, "through a glass, in an enigma" is a key metaphor for Augustine's (and for Donne's) conception of the restored image in man, for that gradually brightening image is itself the "dark glass" through which (here) we best see God: "In a glass nothing is discerned but an image. We have endeavoured, then, so to do; in order that we

[49] Augustine, *De Trinitate* XIV.xvii (#23), *Works*, VII, 472.
[50] *Ibid.*, XIV.xvii (#23), *Works*, VII, 472-473. The biblical quotation is I Cor. 13:12.

might see in some way or other by this image which we are, Him by whom we are made, as by a glass."[51] However, since the Christian always bears the root of original sin in his nature, and since he cannot avoid some venial sins however saintly he may become, the perfect restoration of the image in man cannot be achieved in this life.

St. Bernard discussed the restoration of the image in baptism as a resealing, as of an impression in wax, whereby a stronger impression of the image in man is made by means of the seal which is Christ: "I will make then, He [God] seems to say, a new union [of man's spirit and flesh], on which I will place a seal clearer and more strong; a seal not made after My image and likeness, but which is My likeness itself; the brightness of My glory, the figure of My substance; not made, but begotten before all ages."[52] Like Augustine, Bernard conceives the total restoration as a process which is initiated by God at every stage; the soul seeking God must know that it has been anticipated by him, and even its desiring to be sought is from God.[53] But being thus enabled and constantly sustained by grace, the soul is to seek God constantly and to work out its salvation through good works: it is "to adorn and embellish by good and vertuous thoughts and actions, as by rich colours, that illustrious image which has been impressed upon the depths of its nature at its creation."[54]

As he did on many other matters, Thomas Aquinas formulated the concepts of justification, grace, and merit in terms which became classic in Roman Catholic discourse about the restored image for several centuries. According to Thomas, the sacrament of baptism infuses grace into the soul, thereby remitting sin and changing the state of ungodliness to a state of justice like that which Adam received

[51] *Ibid.*, XV.viii (#14), *Works*, VII, 393.

[52] Bernard, "Sermon II. On the Nativity of our Lord," *Sermone De Tempore*, *Works*, III, 415.

[53] *Sermons on the Song of Songs*, *Works*, IV, 511-515.

[54] *Ibid.*, *Works*, IV, 461-467, 508.

originally from God. This justice "signifies a certain recti-
tude of order in the interior disposition of a man"; its res-
toration is wholly the effect of God's grace and is instan-
taneous, although God first moves man's free will to turn
from sin and to accept the gift of grace.[55] Whenever man
falls again into mortal sin he must again be restored
through new infusions of grace attending upon his repent-
ance and issued through the sacrament of penance. After
restoration to the state of justice by God, man can advance
in charity and can further perfect the image within him by
acting in cooperation with God's grace; he can refrain from
mortal sin, although not from all venial sin because of the
corruption of his lower appetites by original sin. Perfecting
himself thus, he really merits eternal life, both on account
of the dignity of grace, "whereby man, being made a par-
taker of the divine nature, is adopted as a son of God, to
whom the inheritance is due by right of adoption," and also
by congruity or proportion, "for it would seem congruous
that, if a man does what he can, God should reward him ac-
cording to the excellence of His power."[56] The Douay-
Rheims scholars, under pressure of controversy with the
Calvinists, developed this position, distinguishing a "first
justification" effected "merely by Christ's grace and mercie,"
which remits sin and restores order in the soul, and also a
"second justification" or progressive increase of the former
justice, whereby the Christian, employing his free will as a
secondary cause, cooperates with God's grace in the per-
formance of good deeds—which are thereby meritorious.[57]
The Roman Catholic version of the restored image, then,
proclaims it to be "a very qualitie, condition, and state of
vertue and grace resident in us."[58]

[55] Aquinas, *Summa Theologica* I-II, Q. cxiii, Art. 1-7, *Basic Writings*,
II, 1020-1032.

[56] *Summa Theologica* I-II, Q. cxiv, Art. 3, *Basic Writings*, II, 1042.

[57] *The New Testament . . . By the English College at . . . Rheims*
(Antwerp, 1600), note to Rom. 3:24, p. 398; note to Rom. 2:13, p.
387; note to Ephes. 1:5, p. 513.

[58] *Ibid.* note to Gal. 6:15, p. 511; see also note to Col. 3:9-10, p. 543.

For the Protestant, by contrast, man's salvation is wholly the work of God, and the decisive moment in the process is the conversion experience rather than the ceremony of baptism. Because the image of God in man is almost wholly destroyed by original sin its restoration must be wholly God's work, effected by the merits of Christ and apprehended by a faith which is itself the gift of God. For the Protestant also, since man in this life is unable to perform the righteous works demanded by the Law and since sin can never be totally eradicated in him, man's works cannot be said to merit salvation in any degree or sense.

Luther's primary emphasis throughout his writings is upon the righteousness of justification, which alone brings about salvation.[59] Denying the Catholic version of righteousness as a quality infused into the soul, he argues rather that God imputes to us Christ's righteousness, which in itself is formally outside us, like a cloak or covering hiding our sins: "These two things . . . worke Christian righteousnesse: namely, faith in the hart, which is a gift of God . . . and also that God accepteth this imperfect faith for perfect righteousnesse, for Christs sake. . . . Because of this faith in Christ, God seeth not [the] . . . sinnes which are yet in me. . . . I am covered under the shadow of Christs wings, and . . . dwell without all feare under that most ample and large heaven of the forgivenesse of sinnes, which is spread over me."[60] Noting however that this righteousness is also in us, since Christ lives in us, Luther highlights the paradox whereby this righteousness is both ours and not ours: "True Christian righteousnes is . . . that righteousnes whereby Christ liveth in us, and not that which is in our person. . . . Now because Christ liveth in me, therefore looke what grace, righteousnes, life, peace, and salvation is in me, it is his, and yet notwithstanding the same is mine also by that unseparable union and conjunction which is through faith:

[59] Luther, *A Commentarie of . . . Martin Luther upon . . . Galathians* (London, 1602), fols. 110ᵛ-111.

[60] *Ibid.*, fol. 112.

by the which Christ and I are made as it were one body in spirite."[61] For St. Bernard, it will be remembered, original sin was that which covered the soul with a mantle of unlikeness hiding its true form as image of God, and that form was restamped in it by justification. For Luther, original sin wholly destroys the image and likeness in the soul, and justification, which cannot actually restore that image, provides the covering or cloak which hides the defaced image from God's sight and presents Christ's merits to view instead. Accordingly, the justified Christian can be said to be perfectly holy with Christ in heaven, even while in his earthly state he remains radically sinful.[62]

Yet Luther held also that at the time of justification a "new life" or actual repairing of the image (sanctification) is gradually begun in the soul. But since this actual restoration "has merely its beginning in this life, and it cannot attain perfection in this flesh,"[63] we must joyfully await the full restoration of the image of God in us in heaven. In this process there can be absolutely no question of human merit, and men can attain forgiveness of sins, quiet, happiness, and peace in this life only by relying upon the imputed righteousness of Christ. Nevertheless the Christian will perform such good works as he can in obedience to God, since "as a good tree he will bring forth good fruites."[64]

Calvin's formulation defines justification and sanctification in terms which constantly recur in English theological

[61] *Ibid.*, fols. 82-83.

[62] For a careful analysis of this complex and paradoxical position see F. E. Cranz, *An Essay on the Development of Luther's Thought on Justice, Law, and Society*, Harvard Theological Studies, XIX (Cambridge, 1959). Cranz cites Luther's *Kirchenpostille* (1522) x, 1, 2, pp. 36, 22 ff., to highlight Luther's mature view of the Christian as at once totally justified in Christ and totally sinful in himself: "Therefore, all the life of a good believing Christian after Baptism is nothing more than an awaiting the revelation of a holiness which he already has. He surely has it whole, though it is still hidden in faith" (pp. 55-56).

[63] *Lectures on Genesis*, *Works*, I, ed. Pelikan, 64-65.

[64] *Commentarie ... upon ... Galathians*, fol. 76ᵛ.

tracts. For Calvin, as for Luther, justification is in no way related to the soul's actual condition but arises from the imputation of Christ's merits to men. But whereas Luther's metaphors presented Christ's righteousness as covering us or paradoxically dwelling "in" us, Calvin's characteristic figure—our "ingrafting in Christ" as described in Romans 11:7—emphasizes our participation in Christ's merits through this spiritual union: "We do not . . . contemplate him [Christ] outside ourselves from afar in order that his righteousness may be imputed to us, but . . . we put on Christ and are engrafted into his body. . . . Our righteousness is not in us but in Christ, that we possess it only because we are partakers in Christ."[65] By Calvin's terms also, when God regards the justified man he sees not that sinner but his own perfect image, Christ himself: "He does not justify in part but liberally, so that they may appear in heaven as if endowed with the purity of Christ."[66]

The process of sanctification (or regeneration) is the actual, though partial, restoration of God's image in man's own soul. Calvin gives somewhat larger scope than Luther does to the partial restoration of the image in this life. Defining the restored image in terms of Ephesians 4:24—"righteousness and true holiness"—Calvin holds that the elect strive toward this goal throughout life, though the process of sanctification no less than justification is wholly God's work: "This restoration does not take place in one moment or one day or one year; but through continual and sometimes even slow advances God wipes out in his elect the corruptions of the flesh, cleanses them of guilt, consecrates them to himself as temples renewing all their minds to true purity. . . . This warfare will end only at death."[67] This partial restoration is pleasing to God, since "wherever God contemplates his own face, he both rightly loves it and holds it in honor," and a man so restored "doeth represent the wisdome, righteousnesse and goodnesse of God as it

[65] Calvin, *Institutes* III.xi, *LCC*, xx, 737-739, 753.

[66] *Ibid.*, III.xi, *LCC*, xx, 739.   [67] *Ibid.*, III.iii, *LCC*, xx, 601-602.

were in a loking glasse."[68] But because the godly are still sinners, and their good works are as yet incomplete and redolent of the vices of the flesh they are always in themselves liable to the judgment of death, so that only justification in Christ and not this partial sanctification can give them assurance of being among the elect.[69] Yet because the two kinds of grace always go together, an indication and proof of election is the performance of the works of righteousness, the commandments.

Luther, Calvin, and Augustine as interpreted by Calvin profoundly influenced English theological conceptions of the restored image during the period 1560-1640. English Protestants, of whatever persuasion regarding church order and discipline, showed remarkable unanimity on such key issues as the all but total depravity of man's faculties for spiritual uses as a result of original sin, the impossibility of man's meriting grace or salvation in any degree or sense, the continuation of sin even in the elect, the description of good works as the fruits of faith rather than as works earning salvation, and the all-important distinction between justification and sanctification.[70] Even Richard Hooker, that

---

[68] *Ibid.*, III.xvii, *LCC*, xx, 807; *Commentary . . . upon the Epistle to the Colossians*, trans. R. V. [aux] (London, 1581), p. 68.

[69] *Institutes* III.iii.10-16, *LCC*, xx, 602-610.

[70] The Geneva Bible (London, 1599), "Romans" fol. 63ᵛ, defines justification as "the gift of Christes righteousnesse imputed or put upon us by faith, which swalloweth up that unrighteousnesse which flowed from Adam into us," and sanctification as the process which "killeth by litle and litle" the corruption yet remaining in us, so that in its place succeeds "the cleannesse and purenesse of nature reformed." Thomas Rogers in his often republished commentary on the Thirty-nine Articles also urged the Protestant commonplaces: the utter bondage of the will due to original sin; the corruption which persists in the regenerate, making it impossible for them to be sinless in this life or to perform meritorious works; and the cardinal principle that "we are accounted righteous before God, only for the merit of our Lord, and Saviour Jesus Christ, by faith, and not for our owne workes, or deservings" (*The Faith, Doctrine, and Religion, Professed and Protected in the Realme of England . . . Expressed in 39 Articles* [Cambridge,

eloquent defender of church establishment, liturgy, sacraments, and of the natural law's comprehensibility even to fallen reason, distinguished the doctrine of English Protestants sharply and with admirable clarity from that of Rome. On the question of justification he observed:

> When they [the Roman Catholics] are required to shew what the righteousnes is, whereby a Christian man is justified: they answere that it is a divine spirituall quality, which qualitie receaved into the soul, doth first make it to be one of them who are borne of God, and secondly indue it with power, to bring forth such workes, as they doe that are borne of him . . . that it maketh the soule amiable and gratious in the sight of God . . . that it purgeth, purifyeth, and washeth out all the staines, and pollutions of sinne. . . . This grace they will have to be applied by infusion . . . so the soule might be righteous by the inherent grace: which grace they make capable of increase . . . the augmentation whereof is merited by good workes, as good works are made meritorious by it. Wherefore, the first receipt of grace in their divinity, is the first justification; the increase thereof, the second justification. . . . But the righteousnesse wherein we must be found if we wil be justified, is not our owne: therefore we cannot be justified by any inherent quality. Christ hath merited righteousnesse for as many as are found in him. In him God findeth us, if we be faithfull, for by faith we are incorporated into Christ. Then although in our selves we be altogither sinnefull, and unrighteous, yet even the

---

1607], pp. 46-50). Cf. William Perkins, "A Golden Chaine: or, The Description of Theologie," and "A Treatise Tending unto a Declaration, whether a Man be in the Estate of Damnation, or in the Estate of Grace," in *The Works of that Famous and Worthie Minister of Christ . . . M. W. Perkins* (Cambridge, 1603), pp. 82, 441; and Perkins, *A Commentarie or Exposition, upon . . . Galatians* (Cambridge, 1604). See also the book of homilies, *Certaine Sermons, Appointed by the Queens Majestie, to be declared and read* (London, 1595), pp. 31-32.

man which is impious in him selfe . . . him God upholdeth
with a gracious eie; putteth away his sinne by not imput-
ing . . . and accepteth him in Jesus Christ, as perfectly
righteous, as if he had fulfilled all that was commanded
him in the lawe: shall I say more perfectly righteous, then
if him selfe had fulfilled the whole law?[71]

Similarly, with regard to sanctification, Hooker asserts the
Protestant view that this real but very partial restoration of
the divine image in no way merits salvation:

Now concerning the righteousnesse of sanctification, we
deny it not to be inherent; wee graunt that unlesse we
worke, we have it not: . . . [It] consisteth of faith, hope
and charitie, and other Christian vertues. . . . God giveth
us both the one justice and the other. . . . The proper and
most immediate cause in us of this later, is the spirit of
adoption we have received into our hearts. . . .

The best things which we doe, have somewhat in them
to be pardoned. How then can wee doe any thing meri-
torious, or worthy to be rewarded? . . . We acknowledge
a dutifull necessity of doing well; but the meritorious dig-
nity of doing well, wee utterly renounce.[72]

Donne's view of man's regeneration is essentially Prot-
estant, with a few modifications. The familiar Calvinist
terms for the various stages of regeneration—election, voca-
tion, justification, sanctification, glorification—come readily
from his pen. For Donne, as for Calvin, justification involves
the imputing of Christ's merits to us through faith, uniting
us to Christ as the body to the head. That faith is wholly
God's gift, which we can do nothing to merit. Explaining
that this union takes place in baptism, Donne uses the famil-
iar metaphor of clothing to describe the "putting on" of the
divine nature:

[71] Richard Hooker, *A Learned Discourse of Justification, Workes,
and how the foundation of faith is overthrowne* (Oxford, 1612), pp.
4-7.
[72] *Ibid.*, pp. 8, 26, 11.

To be baptized is to put on Christ: . . . By his pretious promises we are made *partakers of the Divine nature*; yea, we are discharged of all bodily and earthly incumbrances, and we are made *all spirit*; yea the spirit of God himselfe, *He that is joyned to the Lord, is one spirit with him*. . . . This act of Christ, this redemption makes us onely *servants*. . . . But the *application* of this redemption (which is the *putting on of Christ*,) makes us *sons*; for we are not to put on Christ, onely as a *Livery*, to be distinguished by externall marks of *Christianity*; but so, as the sonne puts on his father; that we may be of the same nature and substance as he. . . . We shall so appeare before the Father, as that he shall take us for his owne Christ; we shall beare his name and person, and we shall every one be so accepted, as if every one of us were *all Mankind*; yea, as if we were he himselfe. . . . He shall doe this by imputation.[73]

For Donne, somewhat untypically, Christ's incarnation argued for the possibility of salvation to all, not for a Calvinistic predestination of the elect: "As all mankinde was in *Adam*, all mankinde was in *Christ*: and as the *seale of the Serpent* is in all, by *originall sinne*, so the *seale* of God, *Christ Jesus*, is on us *all*, by his assuming our *nature*."[74] Like others of his contemporaries Donne was engaged in working out a personal, often original, theological synthesis. But the important point here is that for Donne, even as for Calvin and Luther, the process of justification involves not a cleansing of our guilt but the imputation of Christ's perfections to us so as to cover our sinfulness: "we are so washed in his bloud, as that we stand in the sight of the Father, as cleane, and innocent, as himselfe, both because he and we are thereby become one body, and because the garment of

[73] Donne, *Sermons*, v, 153-160. Sermon on Gal. 3:25 (uncertain date).

[74] *Ibid.*, vi, 159. Sermon on Apoc. 7:9, to the Earl of Exeter, at St. John's, Jan. 13, 1624.

his righteousnesse covers us all."[75] In Donne's formulation, this justification is applied to man through faith and tendered through preaching and the sacraments, but there is no question of any infused or personal righteousness resulting therefrom: "No man hath any such righteousness of his own, as can save him; for howsoever it be made his, by that Application, or Imputation, yet the righteousness that saves him, is the very righteousness of Christ himself."[76]

Donne's conception of sanctification is also firmly Protestant, though he perhaps envisioned a more complete restoration of the soul's faculties than Calvin would admit. It is the gradual process whereby the image of God is partially restored in the soul, and the soul begins to be conformed to the perfect Image of God, Jesus Christ. The process begins in baptism, which partly restores our faculties, giving us again "the good use of our own Will . . . for, without such Grace . . . we have . . . no power to doe any thing of, or with our selves, but to our destruction."[77] Donne insists that grace in no way violates man's will, and he concedes that our good works may be called ours in some sense whereas faith is wholly God's gift.[78] Yet despite these reservations, he is staunchly Protestant in insisting that man's sanctification is wholly God's work, in no way related to human merit or good works or cooperation with grace: "*David* does not say, Do thou wash me, and I will perfect thy worke. . . . Let him that is holy be more holy, but accept his Sanctification from him, of whom he had his Justification; and except he can think to glorifie himself because he is sanctified, let him not think to sanctifie himself because he is justified; God does all."[79]

[75] *Ibid.*, v, 173. Sermon on Cant. 5:3, at Essex House at the churching of Lady Doncaster, Dec., 1618.

[76] *Ibid.*, VII, 158-159. Sermon on Matt. 9:13, to the household at Whitehall, April 30, 1626.

[77] *Ibid.*, I, 292-293. See note 45.

[78] *Ibid.*, VII, 353. Sermon on Isaiah 65:20, to the king at Whitehall, Feb., 1626/7. See also x, 89.

[79] *Ibid.*, v, 316. Sermon of uncertain date on Psalm 51:7.

C. The Divine Image in Man as Donnean Poetic Symbol

It is a legitimate question whether the idea of the image of God in man gleaned from Donne's sermons and later theological works can properly be used to explicate the poetic, symbolic uses he makes of the concept a decade or so earlier in his occasional poems of compliment and in the *Anniversaries*. Yet the consistency of Donne's ideas about the image of God throughout his theological writings, and their close resemblance to the views of Augustine, Hooker, and numerous Protestant contemporaries, affords some basis for confidence in using these formulations to explicate the metaphysical dimension of these poems of praise; surely this context is more apt than any other to reveal what these poems intend to praise when they celebrate a human person as image of God. As we have seen, Donne believed with Augustine and Bernard that the divine image at man's original creation was located in the powers of the soul (memory, understanding, will) and so was ineffaceable, but that at the same time he had an Augustinian-Calvinist conception of the almost total corruption and deformity of that image due to original sin. His idea of the restoration of the image through grace was firmly Protestant, even Calvinist, in its insistence that justification is imputed to us so that in regarding us God does not see our actual wicked state but Christ's merits; and that our sanctification is wholly effected by God and not at all by any meritorious works on our part.

It was precisely because of these theological assumptions that Donne's praises of persons assumed to be regenerate Christians could sustain extreme hyperbole and even language assimilating the person praised to Divinity. Since the justified Christian presents to view Christ's merits and not his own sins, and since whatever progress is made toward the actual restoration of God's image within him is entirely God's work, the object of poetic praise cannot be the individual's own worth but, rather, God manifested in or working in him. The sermons constantly invite such a perspective upon the self or upon another Christian: "we cannot see the *Essence* of God, but must see him in his *glasses*, in his *Images*, in his *Creatures*."[80] Or again, "the glory of God shines through godly men."[81] Praise of any Christian may therefore become a means to contemplate God, to know ourselves as his image in us defines our potentialities, and to understand the human condition as it is characterized by the destruction or the restoration of that image in mankind. These terms bring us close to the fundamental assumptions of the *Anniversary* poems.

Donne's identification with the Protestant consensus regarding the process of salvation permitted him to exploit in the *Anniversary* poems the multiple perspectives upon the Christian as restored image of God which are possible from that theological position. Since from the standpoint of justification the perfect Image of God, Christ himself, is as it were substituted for, regarded in place of, the soul's actual deformed image, this theology can view any regenerate individual as at once radically corrupt, and as perfect. Luther dwelt constantly on this paradox: "A Christian man is both righteous and a sinner, holy and profane, an enemy of God and yet a childe of God. . . . These two things are quite contrarie: to wit, that a Christian is righteous and beloved of God, and yet notwithstanding he is a sinner . . . most worthy of Gods wrath and indignation."[82] Donne's imagination was also fired by this paradox, and he tended to give it yet more extravagant formulation:

The perfectest order was Innocency; that first integrity in which God made all. All was disordered by sin. . . . But . . . every man, howsoever oppressed with the burden of sin, may, in the application of the promises of the Gospel by the Ordinance of preaching, and in the seales thereof

[80] *Ibid.*, v, 161. Sermon on Gal. 3:27, at a christening (uncertain date).

[81] *Ibid.*, VII, 238. Sermon on Psalm 64:10, at St. Paul's, Nov. 5, 1626.

[82] Luther, *Commentarie . . . upon . . . Galathians*, fols. 112ᵛ-114.

in the participation of the Sacraments, be assured, that he hath received his Absolution, his Remission, his Pardon, and is restored to the innocency of his Baptisme, nay to the integrity which *Adam* had before the fall, nay to the righteousnesse of Christ Jesus himselfe.[83]

So with Elizabeth Drury considered as regenerate Christian. The speaker of the *Anniversary* poems can view in her, as God does, the perfections of Christ himself, and so can ascribe to her restorative powers only appropriate to Christ:

> She that had all Magnetique force alone
> To draw, and fasten sundred parts in one;
> She whom wise nature had invented then
> When she observ'd that every sort of men
> Did in their voyage in this worlds Sea stray,
> And needed a new compasse for their way.
>
> (I *Ann.* 221-226)

Donne also characteristically extends and elaborates the paradox inherent in the Protestant doctrine of sanctification, whereby the title of "saint" is appropriate to any Christian in whom the mere beginnings of the restoration and reformation of the soul's defaced image are evident. Denouncing the Roman Catholic reservation of the appellation "saint" to a spiritual elite, Luther had revelled in the paradox of that term's broad applicability:

> [There are] not one but many Saints, yea an infinite number of true Saints: . . . These things do sufficiently declare who be the true Saints indeede, and which is to be called a holy life: Not the life of those which lurke in caves and dennes, which make their bodies leane with fasting, which weare haire, and do other like things with this perswasion and trust, that they shall have some singular reward in heaven above all other Christians: but of those

[83] Donne, *Sermons*, VII, 229-231. Sermon on John 16:8-11, on Whitsunday [1626].

which be baptised and beleeve in Christ, which put off
the old man with his works, but not at once: For con-
cupiscence and lust remaineth in them so long as they
live.[84]

Heightening this paradox, Donne often assumes God's point
of view, in which the end and the beginning are one. He
characteristically telescopes the process of sanctification, so
that its inchoation (one of Donne's favorite words) on earth
is one with the fulfillment, the perfection of the Divine
image in heaven:

If God take thee out of the world, before thou think it
[thy sanctification] throughly accomplished, yet he shall
call thine inchoation, consummation, thine endeavour,
performance, and thy desire, effect. For all Gods works
are intire, and done in him, at once, and perfect as soon
as begun; And this spiritual Resurrection is his work and
therefore quickned even in the Conception, and borne
even in the quickning, and grown up even in the birth,
that is, perfected in the eyes of God, as soone as it is seri-
ously intended in our heart.[85]

Accordingly, at times Donne all but merges the conditions
of grace and glory:

The pure in heart are blessed already, not onely compara-
tively . . . but actually in a present possession of it: for
this world and the next world, are not, to the pure
in heart, two houses, but two roomes, a Gallery to passe
through, and a Lodging to rest in, in the same House,
which are both under one roofe, Christ Jesus; The Mili-
tant and the Triumphant, are not two Churches, but this
the Porch, and that the Chancell of the same Church,
which are under one Head, Christ Jesus; so the Joy, and
the sense of Salvation, which the pure in heart have here,

---

[84] Luther, *Commentarie . . . upon . . . Galathians*, fols. 268-268ᵛ.
[85] Donne, *Sermons*, IV, 76-77. Sermon on I Thess. 4:17, on Easter
[1622].

is not a joy severed from the Joy of Heaven, but . . . a present inchoation of that *now*.[86]

So, quite apart from the actual imperfections and sins which Elizabeth Drury, like any other human being, must possess, Donne has a basis for praising her as a manifestation of the perfections of Christ himself, and can virtually equate the goodness exhibited in her regenerate condition on earth with that of her glorified state in heaven.

In the *Anniversary* poems, Donne could also exploit the contemporary practice of analyzing the human condition according to the various states of the Divine image in man —his "*Created holinesse* in his innocencie; His *Sinfulnesse* since the fall of *Adam*; His *Renewed* holinesse in his regeneration," according to Thomas Morton's formulation.[87] Identifying Adam as the epitome of mankind "in whome onely all these three estates did concurre, and may be seene, as an anatomie of the soule."[88] Morton points out that in another sense any regenerate person might provide such an epitome, since on earth he experiences the estates of sinfulness and regeneration, and in heaven such a perfection of the renewed image as recapitulates but also surpasses the condition of primal innocence.[89] The method of

---

[86] *Ibid.*, VII, 340-341. Sermon on Matt. 5:8, on Candlemas Day [1626/7].

[87] Thomas Morton, *A Treatise of the Threefolde State of Man* (London, 1596), title page.

[88] *Ibid.*, preface.

[89] *Ibid.*, pp. 423-426: "In the life to come, the elect shall be restored to that perfect inherent holinesse, wherein *Adam* was created: by vertue whereof, without any imputed righteousnesse borrowed from anie other, they shall looke for happinesse, even as the holie Angels doe. . . . Now as touching the difference, it is this, celestiall holinesse is more excellent and exceedeth the other: for as the bodies of the faithfull shalbe more glorious, pure, and after a sort spirituall, then was the bodie of *Adam* in his innocencie. . . . So also shall the faculties of the soule and bodie be more able, readie, & quicke in performing their severall duties and functions. . . . Our mindes shalbe more capable of knowledge and more enriched with actuall knowledge . . .

the *Anniversary* poems involves just such careful discriminations among estates of human goodness (and evil) through analysis of the regenerate Christian, Elizabeth Drury, as an epitome of these various estates and as a means to an "anatomie of the soule."

Donne could also exploit the shifting value which the Protestant theologians accorded to the regenerate state when they compared it with the primal innocence, and with the heavenly perfection. On the one hand he could adopt the formula which takes the situation of the regenerate Christian as a state less perfect than either of the others since in this life only a partial cleanness can be achieved. In this vein Donne denounced the "imaginary and illusory purities" pretended to by the ancient Cathari and the modern Roman Catholics,[90] limiting the purity required of the regenerate to cleanness of heart, which is the concomitant of wisdom. This wisdom he defined as "the knowledge, the right valuation of this world, and of the next; To be able to compare the joyes of heaven, and the pleasures of this world, and the gaine of the one, with the losse of the other. . . . To understand the wretchednesse of this world, is to be wise, but to make this wisedome apprehend a happinesse in the next world, that is to be blessed."[91] In Donne's *Anniversary* poems the speaker seems to be striving to attain this kind of wisdom by just this method.

On the other hand, Morton could present the regenerate state as superior to Adam's on the ground of being "certaine, immutable, and eternall," whereas Adam's was mutable, and also on the ground that regenerate man can lay claim to the holiness of Christ himself.[92] And Donne, elab-

---

& as full & perfect a knowledge of God, of his will, word, actions, and creatures, yea greater then that which man had by his first creation."

[90] Donne, *Sermons*, VII, 334.   [91] *Ibid.*, VII, 336, 339. See note 86.

[92] Morton, *Treatise of the Threefolde State*, pp. 22-23. Cf. Robert Pollock, *Lectures upon the Epistle of Paul to the Colossians* (London, 1603), pp. 298-299.

orating upon Cyril's exalted description of regenerate man —"I being in the forme of a servant, may, nay must take upon me the forme of God, in being *Deiformis homo*, a man made in Christ, the Image of God"—could also argue that the Christian's privileges in the order of grace are such that he images more fully than Adam did God's power, wisdom, and goodness.[93] In this argument the regenerate state is presented as the mean between the original perfection and the highest perfection of the image in the Kingdom of Glory where, as Donne says, "I shall be so like God, as the Devill himselfe shall not know me from God, so far, as . . . to conceive any more hope of my falling from that Kingdome. . . . I shall be as immortall, as God."[94] This shifting perspective permits the presentation of Elizabeth Drury as a regenerate soul who in some essential ways recapitulates the original innocence but also surpasses it in respect of the nearness her regenerate condition has to the heavenly perfection, and the purchase that state gives her upon heavenly glory.

Donne's ordering symbol in the *Anniversary* poems has its basis, I have been arguing, in his definition of the Archetype or Idæa of the human person in terms of the image of God he or she bears, and specifically in the multiple perspectives which Donne's Protestant theology permitted him to employ in analyzing a regenerate Christian as the restored image of God. It is important to reiterate here that Elizabeth Drury (like Lady Bedford and the others) carries the significances explored in these poems not because of her personal merits but only as any regenerate Christian may do. In Donne's theological terms, an individual cannot be praised in terms of his own moral and spiritual worthiness, as a Catholic saint might be praised; but only as he is the vehicle for God's work and the manifestation of his image. This is the point which Ben Jonson, speaking from the vantage point of a Roman Catholic (and classical) conception of personal merit and virtue, quite failed to under-

[93] Donne, *Sermons*, IX, 86. See note 9.
[94] *Ibid.*, IX, 89.

stand when he complained about the inappropriateness of this mere girl as object for all the hyperbole, declaring that the poem might better have been written of the Virgin Mary. In point of fact, of course, the neutral, insignificant figure of Elizabeth Drury is ideal for Donne's metaphysical argument; since she obtrudes no generally known individual virtues or vices before the reader's vision she is perfectly suited to manifest the general human situation of man seen as image of God. Just how such symbolism functions in Donne's *Anniversaries* can be better understood through a study of contemporary Protestant—and Donnean—formulations concerning symbolism and figurative expression in God's Word and world.

Chapter V

Donne's Poetic Symbolism and
Protestant Hermeneutics

RECOGNIZING that the symbolic dimension of Elizabeth Drury—and of several other personages celebrated in Donne's poetry of praise—involves the manifestation of the restored image of God in man, we are ready to examine Donne's symbolic method in some detail. I suggest that the scope and function of Donne's symbolism in the *Anniversary* poems evidently derives from and can best be illuminated from certain contemporary trends in Protestant hermeneutics. But investigation of this context leads also to a recognition of the significant role of Donne's own sermons and poems in developing and exploiting the potential for symbolic expression inherent in these trends, and in promoting such symbolism in the seventeenth-century sermon and in "metaphysical" poetry.

In reference to the *Anniversary* poems, we may begin by asking how far we are intended to focus upon the fifteen-year-old Elizabeth as the symbolic center of the poems, and in what ways the poems' vehement expression of misery and extravagant theological hyperbole pertain to her? We have observed the tendency to regard Elizabeth Drury as one term of a rather contrived allegory in which some lines of the poem concern the real girl and some the allegorical referent—whether Queen Elizabeth, St. Lucy, or *Sapientia Creata*. We have also noted another prevalent critical assumption, that the real Elizabeth Drury either does or should evanesce from our consciousness as we contemplate the profound issues of the poems. I propose here a different view: that Elizabeth Drury functions in these poems as a poetic symbol, somewhat as modern critics understand that term—that is, as "an object which refers to another object but which demands attention also in its own right, as a presentation."[1] To the point here is Coleridge's classic definition of the symbol, set forth, it is well to remember, in a "lay sermon" discussing the kinds of significance and signification to be found in the Bible: "A Symbol . . . is characterized by the translucence of the Special in the Individual or of the General in the Especial or of the Universal in the General. Above all the translucence of the Eternal through and in the Temporal. It always partakes of the Reality which it renders intelligible; and while it enunciates the whole, abides itself as a living part of that Unity, of which it is the representation."[2]

The very diverse conceptions of the way Donne's symbol works makes apparent the truth of Warren and Wellek's observation that "one has to know intimately both language and literary convention to be able to feel and measure the metaphoric intention of a specific poet."[3] It is also necessary to have intimate knowledge of contemporary ideas and attitudes about language and about the nature of things. We are hampered in our measurement of the metaphoric and symbolic intentions of Elizabethan and Jacobean poets by the absence of contemporary discussions of symbolism in the theoretical treatises of the period (the term itself rarely appears in Elizabethan rhetorics and *artes poeticae*), and also by the intrusion of anachronistic modern distinctions degrading allegory and exalting symbolism.[4]

Throughout the Middle Ages and the Renaissance allegory was the umbrella term for all patterns of signification

[1] René Wellek and Austin Warren, *Theory of Literature* (New York, 1956), p. 189.

[2] S. T. Coleridge, *The Statesman's Manual . . . A Lay Sermon* (London, 1816), p. 37.

[3] Warren and Wellek, p. 196.

[4] See, e.g., C. S. Lewis, *The Allegory of Love* (Oxford, 1951), pp. 44-48; K. G. Hamilton, *The Two Harmonies: Poetry and Prose in the Seventeenth Century* (Oxford, 1963), p. 151.

which involved, broadly speaking, the process of saying one thing and meaning or pointing to another; other terms invoked (sometimes interchangeably, sometimes with a clear sense of distinction) to convey such a relationship are myth, figure, symbol, type.[5] Attention to the particular term used, then, often does not reveal very much about the kind of symbolic process at work in a given poem; rather, we have to examine underlying assumptions. One crucial theoretical distinction can be made at the outset. Modern critics tend to speak of poetic allegory as a pattern of significances made or meant by the poet, created through his own poetic strategies. By contrast, classical, medieval, and Renaissance theorists almost universally assume that the allegorist, whatever his method, is concerned to veil, or obscurely point to, or in some way render a truth which inheres in the nature of things.

These earlier theorists recognize, in general, two distinct ways in which the allegorist may render the truth of things. On the one hand, he may create a fiction or myth which hides or obscures the essential truth (as the hard shell of a nut does the kernel) so as to deflect the unworthy and exercise the wits of the wise in a salutory and pleasant fashion. Dante assumes this understanding of the allegorical process in his *Convivio*, in which he defines the allegory of the poets, in contradistinction to the allegory of the theologians, as "A truth hidden under a beautiful fiction."[6] On the other hand, many texts assume that both the literal level and the ontologically higher meanings it signifies, together with the allegorical relationship itself, emerge from the nature of the universe, and that all are grounded firmly upon

[5] I am indebted for some of the distinctions in these paragraphs to an unpublished essay by Edward Cranz, "Some Changing Historical Contexts of Allegory," which he has kindly permitted me to read. An impressive guide through the materials bearing upon the theory and practice of allegory, symbol, and myth from classical times through the seventeenth century is Don C. Allen, *Mysteriously Meant* (Baltimore and London, 1970).

[6] Dante, *Convivio*, trans. W. W. Jackson (Oxford, 1909), p. 34.

truth. Portrayals of the Greek cosmos in such terms undertake to present the very structure of reality—sensible images and intelligible exemplars, copies and originals. Similarly, Christian allegory may portray the natural world as a created order incorporating images and vestiges of its Divine maker, and the course of history as a providential order in which types are recapitulated and fulfilled in antitypes. St. Thomas distinguished clearly between the two allegorical methods when he referred to the poets' contrived use of "other words or feigned likenesses to signify something," in contrast to God's use of "the very course of things themselves for signifying other things."[7] This distinction would seem to explain why Dante's "Letter to Can Grande della Scala" discusses the *Commedia* in terms which pertain to the allegory of the theologians rather than the allegory of the poets. In that poem (unlike the *Convivio*) he is presenting significations which have their ground in the nature of things, the relationships God has contrived: "The subject of the whole work, then, taken merely in its literal sense, is simply the state of the souls after death, for from that subject comes the course of the whole work and with that it is occupied. But if the whole work is taken allegorically, the subject is man as by reason of meriting and demeriting through the freedom of the will he is liable to the rewarding and punishing of justice."[8] In poetry based upon this assumption the allegorical relationships between the images, symbols, or types and their onto-

[7] Aquinas, "Quodlibet VII, Art. 16, Ad 3, Responsio," [Quodl. VII, Q. vi, Art. 16] in *Quodlibetales Questionnes* (Venice, [1501]), fol. 37: "Sicut enim homo potest adhibere ad aliquid significandum aliquas voces vel aliquas similitudines fictas: ita deus adhibet ad significationem aliquorum ipsum cursum rerum suae providentiae subjectarum. Significare autem aliquid per verba vel per similitudines fictas ad significandum tantum ordinatas: non facit nisi sensum literalem." See the full discussion of poetic language and the various senses of scripture, *Quodlibet* VII, Q.vi, Arts. 14-16, fols. 36-37.

[8] "Letter to Can Grande Della Scala," in *Literary Criticism: Plato to Dryden*, ed. and trans. Allan H. Gilbert (Detroit, 1962), p. 203.

logically higher referents are to be understood as something *found* by the poet, not made by him; he merely renders significations which God has produced.

Important theoretical discussions of allegory and symbolic language understood in this second sense are of course to be found in the Christian hermeneutical tradition in relation to the text of scripture—in St. Paul and the Epistle to the Hebrews, and in many patristic and medieval theologians such as Tertullian, Origen, Augustine, and Aquinas. Several distinguished literary critics, among them Erich Auerbach, Rosemond Tuve, and Ruth Wallerstein,[9] have applied these conceptions brilliantly to poetic texts. But it is a matter of sharp dispute how far theories of biblical symbolism were relevant even in the Middle Ages to the writings of poets other than the Holy Spirit, and the matter is even more problematic with regard to Renaissance writers. In relation to this issue, Helen Gardner's observation that "the insistence of Protestantism on . . . the primacy of the literal sense of the Scriptures is not unconnected with the flowering of our literature in the reign of Elizabeth"[10] would seem to discourage attempts to use theories of biblical symbolism in the study of Renaissance poetry. But the argument as formulated militates only against the use of medieval theory: indeed, Dame Helen's reference to the influence of Protestantism on English Renaissance literature draws attention to a most important though unexplored contemporary context for defining Donne's symbolic manner.

The fact is that in the course of defining the "literal sense" the Protestant theologians developed the most serious and extended discussions of poetic language and the nature of

---

[9] Auerbach, *Mimesis*, trans. Willard Trask (Princeton, 1953); Auerbach, "Figura," *Scenes from the Drama of European Literature* (New York, 1959), pp. 11-76; Tuve, *A Reading of George Herbert* (Chicago, 1962); Wallerstein, *Studies in Seventeenth-Century Poetic* (Madison, Wis., 1965), pp. 11-148.

[10] Helen Gardner, *The Business of Criticism* (Oxford, 1959), p. 139.

symbolism to be found in sixteenth- and seventeenth-century England, and certainly those with the widest readership. It seems highly probable that these discussions about the poetic language and symbolism of the scripture were influential in shaping attitudes toward literature generally, especially as some writers consciously proposed the Bible to themselves as literary model. To this end, the eloquent Puritan preacher Thomas Adams cited God's constant use of metaphor and simile in scripture as providing a warrant for those men (ministers) who are "the dispensers of Gods secrets," to express "in borrowed formes . . . the meditations of their harts . . . to lay downe the truth . . . with the helpes of Invention, Wit, Art."[11] There is ample evidence that Donne made a similar connection. In his book of meditations, the *Devotions upon Emergent Occasions*, Donne observed that scripture had served as a stylistic model for many writers, including himself:

> This hath occasioned thine ancient *servants*, whose delight it was to write after thy *Copie*, to proceede the same way in their *expositions* of the *Scriptures*, and in their composing both of *publike liturgies*, and of *private prayers* to thee, to make their accesses to thee in such a kind of *language*, as thou wast pleased to speake to them, in a *figurative*, in a *Metaphoricall language*; in which manner I am bold to call . . . now.[12]

Also, he frequently urged that sermons be modeled upon the poetic texture of scripture in regard to their manner and eloquence. For example,

> There are not so eloquent books in the world as the Scriptures: . . . Whatsoever hath justly delighted any man in any mans writings, is exceeded in the Scriptures. The style of the Scriptures is a diligent, and an artificial style.

[11] Adams, *The Sinners Passing-Bell*, in [*Sermons*] (London, 1614), pp. 214-216.
[12] *Devotions*, pp. 486-487.

> . . . So the Holy Ghost hath spoken in those Instruments, whom he chose for the penning of the Scriptures, and so he would in those whom he sends for the preaching thereof.[13]

And directly to the present purpose, the speaker of Donne's *Anniversaries* presents himself as imitating in his measure the biblical poets and prophets. In the *First Anniversarie* he "boldly" invades Moses' "great Office," producing an analogue to the Mosaic song in Deuteronomy 31 (I *Ann.* 461-468); in the *Second Anniversarie* he is the Trumpet "at whose voice the people came" to receive God's proclamation, Elizabeth (II *Ann.* 527-528).

I suggest, then, that an important body of theoretical material for understanding the symbolism of the *Anniversary* poems is to be found in Donne's sermons and theological writings, studied in the context of contemporary Protestant theory concerning allegory and figurative language in the scriptures. Some critical attention has been given to Protestant hermeneutics as it bears upon seventeenth-century literature, but since most of these studies have focused upon Puritan writers, and specifically Milton,[14] they do not indi-

[13] *Sermons*, II, 170-171. Sermon on Ezek. 33:32, at Whitehall, Feb. 12, 1618. See also *Sermons*, VI, 56: IX, 122-124.

[14] See, e.g., Victor Harris, "Allegory to Analogy in the Interpretation of Scripture," *Philological Quarterly*, 45 (1966), 1-23; Murray Roston, *Biblical Drama in England* (Evanston, Ill., 1968), pp. 69-78, 152-164; H. R. MacCallum, "Milton and Figurative Interpretation of the Bible," *UTQ*, 31 (1962), 397-415; B. K. Lewalski, *Milton's Brief Epic* (Providence and London, 1966), pp. 165-321; Joseph Aloysius Galden, S.J., "Typology and Seventeenth-Century Literature," Unpub. Columbia Univ. dissertation, 1965; William Madsen, *From Shadowy Types to Truth* (New Haven, 1968), pp. 27-53; Sacvan Bercovitch, "Typology in Puritan New England: The Williams-Cotton Controversy Reassessed," *American Quarterly*, 19 (1967), 167-191; Kaufmann, *Puritan Meditation*, pp. 25-60; J. Paul Hunter, *The Reluctant Pilgrim: Defoe's Emblematic Method and Quest for Form in "Robinson Crusoe"* (Baltimore, 1966), pp. 93-124; B. K. Lewalski, "*Samson Agonistes* and the 'Tragedy' of the Apocalypse," *PMLA*, 85 (1970), pp. 1050-1061. For a most useful bibliography of materials

cate the range and complexity of earlier Protestant views on biblical language. My concern here is to discover what Donne seems to have understood about symbolism from contemplating the symbolic method of the scriptures as the Protestant theologians described it, and also to indicate his own seminal role in developing and extending that method through his own contributions to seventeenth-century sermon literature, devotional prose and poetry, and especially the poetry of praise.

To begin with, a brief resumé of medieval exegetical principles may be in order, to state the norm against which Protestant changes in focus can be measured.[15] The fundamental formula, enunciated by Augustine and repeated constantly, recognized a literal or historical meaning of scripture residing in the signification of the words (which necessarily includes such figurative devices as metaphor, parable, and metonymy), and in addition, a spiritual meaning whereby the things or events signified by the words point beyond themselves to other things or events.[16] This is so because God as creator has invested the things of crea-

---

bearing upon typological exegesis and its literary applications in all periods, but with particular emphasis upon Puritan developments, see Sacvan Bercovitch, "Selective Check-List on Typology," *Early American Literature*, 5, No. 1, Part 2 (Spring, 1970), 1-76.

15 See, e.g., Henri de Lubac, *Exégèse Médiévale*, 4 vols. in 2 (Paris, 1959-1964); Jean Daniélou, *From Shadows to Reality*, trans. Wulstan Hibberd (Westminster, Md., 1960); Daniélou, "The Problem of Symbolism," *Thought*, 25 (1950), 423-440; G.W.H. Lampe and K. J. Woollcombe, *Essays on Typology* (London, 1957); H. Flanders Dunbar, *Symbolism in Medieval Thought* (New Haven and London, 1929); D. W. Robertson, Jr., *A Preface to Chaucer* (Princeton, 1962), pp. 286-390; A. C. Charity, *Events and their Afterlife: the dialectics of Christian typology in the Bible and in Dante* (Cambridge, Eng., 1966); J. S. Preus, *From Shadow to Promise: Old Testament Interpretation from Augustine to the Young Luther* (Cambridge, Mass., 1969).

16 Augustine, *De Doctrina Christiana* I.ii (#2), II.xvi (#23-24); III.v (#9), x-xii (#19-20), trans. D. W. Robertson, Jr. (Indianapolis and New York, 1958), pp. 8-9, 50-51, 83-84, 87-92.

tion with rich emblematic significance, and as designer of providential history has invested the persons, things, and events recorded in scripture with symbolic significance. Aquinas' classic formulation of the so-called fourfold method of exegesis recognized, in addition to the literal meaning, three spiritual senses of scripture: allegorical (in the limited sense which came to be termed typological) in which persons and events in the Old Testament prefigure Christ and various events in the New Testament and sometimes prefigure also the Christian Church as Body of Christ; tropological or moral, in which what our Head Christ has done is an example of what we ought to do; and anagogical, in which Old and New Testament events prefigure the end of time or "eternal glory."[17] As Auerbach has demonstrated, many medieval exegetes recognized the primacy of the literal sense of scripture, and, in addition, made a generally consistent conceptual though not linguistic distinction between typological symbolism and various kinds of allegorical meaning in scripture.[18] The allegorical method was understood to involve the use of fictions or contrived sequences of signs which are not true or real in themselves but refer or point to underlying spiritual truths. The typological process by contrast is a pattern of signification in which type and antitype, as historically real entities with independent meaning and validity, form patterns of prefiguration, recapitulation, and fulfillment by reason of God's providential control of history. But this clarity was constantly blurred by the widespread use of the general term "allegory" for both kinds of signification; it was further confounded in practice since medieval exegetes characteristically intermixed a plethora of allegorical interpretations with their stricter typological readings as equivalent levels of meaning to be derived from a given scripture text. These

[17] Aquinas, *Summa Theologica* I, Q. I, Art. 10, *Basic Writings*, I, 16-17.
[18] Auerbach, *Mimesis*, pp. 63-66, 170-176.

practices promoted the conception of the Bible as a multi-level allegorical work.[19]

As everyone knows, the cardinal principle of Protestant hermeneutics was the "one sense of scripture," the sole authority of the literal meaning. We are coming to understand, however, that this Reformation rallying cry did not entail a literalist or antiliterary stance. For one thing, Protestant exegetes invited the closest attention to the figurative elements of biblical language in order to ascertain the exact literal meaning with precision. The characteristic medieval exegesis, though often insistent upon careful grammatical and rhetorical analysis, had approached the verbal texture of scripture differently: Augustine had waxed eloquent over the language of scripture, but his profound sense of the inadequacy of words to render divine mysteries and ineffable realities led him to discount the possibility of determining the exact meanings of texts, and to accept any interpretations which made for charity and devotion.[20] And Aquinas, although he included poetic figures as part of the literal meaning of scripture, observed that the common function of metaphor in poetry is to "draw the reason off to the side"—poetry being of matters deficient in truth and so below reason even as theology is of matters superior to reason.[21]

But the new, sharply focused Protestant emphasis upon the Word made for new attention to the words through

[19] See Preus, *Shadow to Promise*, pp. 61-149; Madsen, *From Shadowy Types to Truth*, pp. 22-26.

[20] Augustine, *De Doctrina Christiana* I.xxxvi (#40-41); II.vii-ix (#9-14); III.x-xii (#14-20), xvii-xviii (#25-27), Robertson, pp. 30-31, 38-43, 87-92, 94-95.

[21] Aquinas, *Scriptum super libros sententiarum Magistri Petri Lombardi*, Prolog., Q. 1, Art. 5, ad. 3, ed. Pierre Mandonnet, Tom. 1 (Paris, 1929), p. 18: "Ad tertium dicendum, quod poetica scientia est de his quae propter defectum veritatis non possunt a ratione capi; unde oportet quod quasi quibusdam simultudinibus ratio seducatur: theologia autem est de his quae sunt supra rationem; et ideo modus symbolicus utrique communis est, cum neutra rationi proportionetur."

which it is conveyed. While Protestant exegetes continued to analyze scripture language according to the medieval discriminations of *res* and *verba*, using the properties of the *res* to illuminate the metaphorical dimensions of words,[22] they also gave new attention to the text itself, to its grammatical, syntactical, and figurative terms, as the ground of religious significance. J. S. Preus notes this trend in Luther's developing attitude toward scriptural language, whereby the "naked word" and not simply what it points to is seen as the source of religious meaning and power.[23] Calvin attributed many misinterpretations of scripture to failures to respond properly to literary devices, noting, for example, that in interpreting the phrase "This is my body" Roman Catholics read literally what was intended as metonymy, a common scriptural figure whereby a sign is called by the name of the thing it signifies; he complains of them, ironically, "These good masters, that they may appear men of letters, forbid even the slightest deviation from the letter."[24] And Thomas Adams' two sermons on Jeremiah 8:22, "Is there no Balme in Gilead? Is there no Phisitian there? why then is not the health of the daughter of my people recovered?" develop in detail the figurative dimensions of this text considered as "a tripartite *metaphor*, that willingly spreads itselfe into an Allegorie."[25] This kind of attention to the figurative aspects of language rather than primarily to the qualities of things as a key to scriptural meaning may well have ramifications for poetry.[26]

[22] See Winfried Schleiner, *The Imagery of John Donne's Sermons* (Providence, 1970), pp. 164-185.

[23] Preus, *Shadow to Promise*, pp. 252-254.

[24] Calvin, *Institutes* IV.xvii.23, ed. McNeil, II, 1388. Cf. Calvin, *Opera Selecta*, ed. Petrus Barth, 5 vols. (Munich, 1926), V, 373: "Vetant boni isti magistri, ut literati appareant, vel tantillum a litera discedere." See Wallace, *Calvin's Doctrine of Word and Sacrament*, p. 227.

[25] Adams, *The Sinners Passing-Bell*, pp. 203-341, esp. p. 211. See also his four sermons on Prov. 9:17-18 entitled, *The Divels Banket*, [*Sermons*], pp. 1-197.

[26] See, e.g., Edward Vaughan, *Ten Introductions: How to read, and in reading, how to understand . . . the Holy Bible* (London, 1594);

John Donne's discussions of scriptural language affirm the common Protestant position both as regards his insistence that the literal sense always be preserved, and his conviction that the literal sense is often rendered through poetic figures which must be apprehended and analyzed as such. In common with Reformation theologians he insists that the words of scripture are not obscure enigmas but offer plain sense to the understanding, yet at the same time tender that sense through a poetic texture, making poetic analysis the means to the sense:

> The literall sense is always to be preserved; but the literall sense . . . is not alwayes that, which the very Letter and Grammar of the place presents, as where it is literally said, *That Christ is a Vine*, and literally, *That his flesh is bread*. . . . But the literall sense of every place, is the principall intention of the Holy Ghost, in that place: And his principall intention in many places, is to expresse things by allegories, by figures; so that in many places of Scripture, a figurative sense is the literall sense.[27]

But there must be few if any contemporary analogues for Donne's sheer delight in the pervasive poetic texture of God's literal word—his joy in discovering that the Holy Spirit is a poet:

> My *God*, my *God*, thou art a *direct God*, may I not say, a *literall God*, a *God* that wouldest bee understood *lit-*

Robert Cawdrey, *A Treasurie or Store-House of Similies* (London, 1600); Richard Bernard, *The Faithfull Shepheard* (London, 1607), pp. 40-60); Solomon Glassius, *Philologiae Sacrae, qua totius sacrosanctae veteris et novi testamenti scripturae, tum stylus & literatura . . . expenditur, libri duo* (Jena, 1623); Flacius Illyricius, *Clavis Scripturae, seu de sermone sacrarum literarum, plurimas generales regulas continens* (Basel, 1617); Maximilianus Sandaeus, *Symbolica. Ex omni antiquitate sacra, ac profana in artis formam redacta, oratoribus, poetis, & universe philologis ad omnem commoditatem amoenae eruditionis concinnata* (Mainz, 1626).

[27] Donne, *Sermons*, VI, 62. Sermon on Apoc. 20:6, at St. Paul's, Easter, 1624.

erally, and according to the *plaine sense* of all that thou saiest? But thou art also . . . a *figurative*, a *metaphoricall God* too; A *God* in whose words there is such a height of *figures*, such *voyages*, such *peregrinations* to fetch remote and precious *metaphors*, such *extentions*, such *spreadings*, such *Curtaines of Allegories*, such *third Heavens of Hyperboles*, so *harmonious eloquutions* . . . as all *prophane Authors*, seeme of the seed of the *Serpent*, that *creepes*, thou art the *dove*, that flies. O, what words but thine, can express the inexpressible *texture*, and *composition* of thy *word*.[28]

Also, although the reformers discounted allegories and spiritual interpretations imposed wholesale upon the text of scripture, all accepted typological symbolism, recognizing New Testament and especially Pauline warrant for the typological reading of various Old Testament events: the ceremonies of the Law are "a shadow of things to come" (Colossians 2:16-17); the tabernacle of the Law and the rock struck by Moses are types of Christ (Hebrews 9:8-11, 1 Corinthians 10:4); Adam is everywhere a type of Christ. The difference lies in the insistence of the Protestants that typological symbolism is a part or dimension of the literal meaning rather than a distinct "spiritual" sense. This may seem to be a distinction without a difference but, from a literary point of view at least, it is not; the Protestant emphasis makes for a different sense of the Bible as a unified poetic text, and for a much closer fusion of sign and thing signified, type and antitypical fulfillment. This characteristic Protestant approach does not take the Bible as a multilevel allegory, but as a complex literary work whose literal meaning is revealed only by careful attention to its poetic texture and to its pervasive symbolic mode—typology. The incorporation of typological symbolism as an integral part of the literal meaning was a concomitant of the

[28] Donne, *Devotions*, pp. 479-81.

154

Protestant sense of the types not merely as signs or shadows pointing toward the truths to come, but as genuine symbols participating in the spiritual truth they present. Calvin, insisting that all revelation is of Christ the Mediator, "the archetype of the figures,"[29] declared that the people of Israel figured forth the experience of the Christian church not merely as a shadow of the truth to come, or as an example for our instruction, but as participants, though less fully, in the spiritual reality they present: "For that people was a figure of the Christian Church in such wyse, that it was also a true Church: their condition did so delineat and represent ours, that nevertheless it was even then the proper state of the Church: those promises that were geven unto them, did so shadow and prefigure the Gospell, that they did include the same within them selves."[30]

English Protestants contemporary with Donne discussed typological symbolism in these terms, as a dimension of the literal sense. A favorite biblical text for making the necessary distinctions was Galatians 4:22-24:

> For it is written, that Abraham had two sons, the one by
> a bondmaid, the other by a freewoman.
> But he who was of the bondwoman was born after the
> flesh; but he of the freewoman was by promise.
> Which things are an allegory: for these are the two
> covenants; the one from Mount Sinai, which gendereth
> to bondage, which is Agar.
> For this Agar is mount Sinai in Arabia, and answereth to
> Jerusalem which now is, and is in bondage with her
> children.
> But Jerusalem which is above is free, which is the mother
> of us all.
>
> (A. V.)

[29] Calvin, *Institutes*, II.xvi.6, ed. McNeill 1, 510.
[30] Calvin, *A Commentarie upon S. Paules Epistles to the Corinthians*, trans. Thomas Tymme (London, 1577), fol. 116ᵛ-117.

Commenting on this text, William Perkins begins by dismissing the traditional Roman Catholic formulation of a literal meaning and three spiritual senses, declaring:

> There is but one full and intire sense of every place of scripture, and that is also the literal sense. . . . To make many senses of scripture, is to overturne all sense, and to make nothing certen. . . . It may be said, that the historie of Abrahams familie here propounded, hath beside his proper and literall sense, a spiritual or mysticall sense. I answer, they are not two senses, but two parts of one full and intire sense. For not onely the bare historie, but also that which is therby signified, is the full sense of the h[oly] G[host].[31]

This position was perhaps most subtly articulated at the close of the sixteenth century in William Whitaker's *Disputation on Holy Scripture*, directed chiefly against Robert Bellarmine.[32] Whitaker's writings are central to English hermeneutics, and this work especially is of the first importance in estimating English attitudes toward the symbolism of scripture. In it he insisted firmly upon the one sense of scripture, relegating allegories and tropologies to the category of applications or accommodations of the text, though he allowed that such meanings might be intended by the Holy Spirit, and thus might properly be extrapolated from the text.[33] But he affirmed that the types, including anagogical references to the end of time, constitute an inseparable component of the literal meaning, and that, as symbols, they

[31] William Perkins, *A Commentarie or Exposition upon the Five First Chapters of the Epistle to the Galatians* (Cambridge, 1604), p. 346. See also Illyricius, *Clavis Scripturae*, Part II (Basel, 1611), pp. 66-76.

[32] Robert Bellarmine, *Disputationes Roberti Bellarmini . . . de controversiis fidei adversus hujus temporis haereticos* (Ingoldstadt, 1588-1593).

[33] Whitaker, *A Disputation on Holy Scripture against the Papists, especially Bellarmine and Stapleton*, trans. William Fitzgerald (Cambridge, 1847), pp. 404-405.

convey the full significance of the text. As Charles K. Cannon has observed, Whitaker's argument here turns upon a sophisticated sense of metaphor and symbol as conveying meaning through the mutual relation between the sign and the thing signified, a "comparison or conjunction of signs and things."[34] Accordingly, Whitaker does not base his discussion of typology upon the Thomistic formula whereby the things referred to by the words of scripture themselves refer to other things, but rather upon the symbolic reach of language itself, which forces the conjunction in our minds between the symbol (type) and the antitypical revelation of the meanings obscurely contained within the symbol. Explicating Galatians 4:24 in these terms, Whitaker declares:

> The apostle . . . interprets the history of Abraham's two wives allegorically, or rather typically, of the two Testaments; for he says in express words, ἅτινά ἐστιν ἀλληγορούμενα, &c. [which things are an allegory]. . . . Indeed, there is a certain catechresis in the word ἀλληγορούμενα, for that history is not accommodated by Paul in that place allegorically, but typically; and a type is a different thing from an allegory. The sense, therefore, of that scripture is one only, namely, the literal or grammatical. However, the whole entire sense is not in the words taken strictly, but part in the type, part in the transaction itself. In either of these taken separately and by itself, part only of the meaning is contained; and by both taken together the full and perfect meaning is completed. . . . When we proceed from the sign to the thing signified we bring no new sense, but only bring out into the light what was before concealed in the sign.[35]

Donne, like the Protestant commentators though again more ecstatically, views the types as the symbolic dimension

[34] Charles K. Cannon, "William Whitaker's *Disputatio de Sacra Scriptura*: A Sixteenth Century Theory of Allegory," *HLQ*, 25 (1962), 136-137.

[35] Whitaker, *Disputation*, pp. 405-406, 407.

of the literal meaning. In God's Word, as in his created world, literal and spiritual are fused into symbols, and, as Joan Webber has observed,[36] both Word and world are to be explicated in much the same fashion. Specifically, as a passage from Donne's *Devotions upon Emergent Occasions* indicates, Donne sees typology and anagogy as together constituting the figural dimension of scripture, and further conflates God's mode of working in biblical history with his continuing work in nature, so that the two make up a common symbolical mode:

> Neither art thou thus a *figurative*, a *Metaphoricall God*, in thy *word* only, but in thy *workes* too. The *stile* of thy *works*, the *phrase* of thine *Actions*, is *Metaphoricall*. The *institution* of thy whole *worship* in the *old Law*, was a continuall *Allegory*; *types* and *figures* overspread all, and *figures* flowed into *figures*, and powred themselves out into *farther figures*; *Circumcision* carried a *figure* of *Baptisme*, and *Baptisme* carries a *figure* of that *purity*, which we shall have in *perfection* in the *new Jerusalem*.[37]

What implications for poetry reside in these trends? The constants we have noted in Protestant hermeneutics—the careful attention to varieties of figurative discourse as a means of exposing the full literal meaning, and more importantly, the insistence upon a fully symbolic reading of the types which fuses the sign with the thing signified—may have influenced the retreat from the Spenserian allegorical mode in poetry with its multiple levels or juxtaposed planes of meaning. Moreover, in a general way these attitudes perhaps contributed to the development in England of the metaphysical literary mode, which embodies symbolic meanings within particular situations and events. But whether or not the shift in the approach to the text of scripture contributed to these larger shifts in literary style, I suggest that

[36] Joan Webber, *Contrary Music: The Prose Style of John Donne* (Madison, Wis., 1963), p. 124.

[37] Donne, *Devotions*, pp. 484-485.

it does bear directly upon Donne's way of exploring the significance of the real individuals, notably Elizabeth Drury, whom he undertakes to praise. In his poetry of compliment generally, but especially in the *Anniversaries*, Donne's witty but not frivolous technique is to take hyperbolic tropes and figures seriously, probing and exploring their grammar, syntax, and metaphoric meanings as revelatory of truth—even as the biblical exegetes did. He does this throughout the *Anniversaries*, analyzing in great detail the conceits of the world dead and anatomized, and of the girl as the world's form or soul. The figural extravagance, those "third heavens of hyperbole" which he understands to constitute the texture of scripture, may be the warrant for his own hyperbolic extravagance, since the speaker of the *Anniversaries* claims to be invading the Mosaic poetic office.

More important, this context indicates Donne's theoretical basis for making the fifteen-year-old Elizabeth Drury the symbolic center of the *Anniversary* poems. The model of God's own symbolic writing in scripture suggests, for the poet intending to imitate that model, the choice of a subject from the real world or from historical events or personages, and the revelation of the spiritual significances embodied and manifested in such subjects.[38] Donne's book of meditations, the *Devotions upon Emergent Occasions*, is evidently designed according to just such principles, in imitation of God's typological method in the scriptures; in it, Donne presents his own actual physical illness and recovery—an event in the order of nature—as type of his sickness of soul and regeneration in the order of grace, and both these experiences as adumbrations of that eternal suffering and death which he hopes to escape through a resurrection to eternal life. He can treat the event in this fashion because it is a real event in the course of providential history: the

[38] Anthony Raspa, "Theology and Poetry in Donne's *Conclave*," *ELH*, 32 (1965), 478-489, argues that such aesthetic principles as these are implicit in Donne's *Ignatius His Conclave* and *Essays in Divinity*.

speaker does not create but finds the symbolic relationships which God has contrived. And so with Elizabeth Drury's death: the girl can embody the spiritual significances explored in the poems precisely because she was a real individual, not a fiction, and is therefore part of God's total revelation. She is God's "Proclamation," the *Second Anniversarie* states, and so may be read by her poet and by his readers through the explication of God's symbolic method, which reveals the symbolic meanings contained within historical reality.

The context we have been examining, Protestant conceptions of typological symbolism in the sixteenth and seventeenth centuries, affords still other grounds for Donne's characteristic identification of a particular Christian as locus of spiritual meaning. What occurs in Protestant typology is a shift of emphasis, modifying the medieval focus upon Christ's life and death as the primary antitype to which all the Old Testament types refer, by developing a further focus upon the contemporary Christian as an antitype.[39] Though the Christian was traditionally understood to share in Christ's antitypical role of recapitulating and fulfilling Old Testament types *forma perfectior*, the locus of antitypical significance now tends to be primarily the in-

---

[39] Murray Roston, in *Biblical Drama in England* (pp. 67-78), discusses such a shift of emphasis briefly in relation to sixteenth- and seventeenth-century biblical drama, using the term "postfiguration" to describe the tendency of English Protestants in the period to see themselves and their nation as the direct antitypes of Israel of old. Some Miltonic uses of what I call "correlative typology"—the disposition of many Protestants and especially Puritans to regard the contemporary Christian and the events of his life as correlative types with Old Testament personages and events, both exemplars existing on essentially the same spiritual plane and alike looking for fulfillment at the end of time—are indicated in my article, "*Samson Agonistes* and the 'Tragedy' of the Apocalypse," PMLA, 85 (1970), pp. 1050-1061. Other literary implications of correlative typology with special relevance to John Dryden are traced by Steven Zwicker in *Dryden's Political Poetry: The Typology of King and Nation* (Providence, 1972).

dividual Christian, who is said to recapitulate in himself the experiences recorded in both the Old and the New Testaments.[40] Such application of scripture to the individual is of course akin to what medieval exegetes called the tropological or moral sense—"so far as the things done in Christ, or so far as the things which signify Christ, are signs of what we ought to do."[41] But the Protestant sense of the desperate condition of fallen man shifts the emphasis from *quid agas* to God's activity, and led the Protestants to find that God works in us precisely as he works in history. Accordingly, the pattern of individual lives is readily assimilated to the pervasive typological patterns discerned throughout history. Calvin's comment on Psalm LXI exemplifies this shift in focus from Christ as antitype of David's experience to the repetition of both David's and Christ's experience in each of Christ's members: "It was necessary that what was begun in David should be fully accomplished in Christ; and, therefore, it must of necessity come to pass, that the same thing should be fulfilled in each of his members."[42]

Donne carried the Protestant tendency to view the individual Christian as recapitulation of Old Testament types and New Testament experience much further still, developing from it an all-encompassing "incarnational" symbolism whose focus is the individual. In the poems in question, the *Anniversaries*, it is evident that Elizabeth Drury as image of God functions in some sense as a Platonic symbol, an earthly image rendering and reflecting the absolute. But as Robert Ellrodt has noted, the direction in which this symbolism works is in important respects anti-Platonic, if a Platonic symbol be understood as a particular which (as

[40] J. S. Preus, *Shadow to Promise*, pp. 245-252, works out some theoretical bases for these tendencies in Luther, as does J. S. Wallace, *Calvin's Doctrine of Word and Sacrament*, pp. 27-58, for Calvin.

[41] Aquinas, *Summa Theologica* I. Q. 1, Art. 10, *Basic Works*, I, 17.

[42] Calvin, *Commentary on . . . the Book of Psalms*, trans. James Anderson, 5 vols. (Edinburgh, 1845), II, 122. See also Calvin, *Psalms* II, 366; *Geneva Bible* [1599]; "Psalms," fol. 14, notes to Psalm lxix.

in Keats's *Endymion*) leads the mind toward the eternal Idea and then is itself transcended.[43] For Donne, by contrast, the universals are apprehended as they are embodied, epitomized, incarnated in particular individuals: Elizabeth Drury herself, as image of God, is designated in life as well as after death as the true Platonic Idea—the "best, and first originall/ Of all faire copies" (I *Ann.* 227-228). Moreover, instead of the vertical frame of reference, from image to archetype, which is appropriate to Platonic symbolism, Donne invokes the typological symbolic mode, viewing Elizabeth Drury in terms of prefigurations and fulfillments within the order of time. She is described as the one of whom "th'Auncients seem'd to prophesie,/ When they call'd vertues by the name of shee" (I *Ann.* 175-176); in her, Beauty's ingredients grew "As in an unvext Paradise" (I *Ann.* 363); in whatever she did, "Some Figure of the Golden times, was hid" (II *Ann.* 69-70); she was "here/ Betrothed to God, and now is married there" (II *Ann.* 461-462). Our world, on the other hand, finds recapitulated in itself the notable biblical calamities and evils: "One woman at one blow, then kill'd us all,/ And singly, one by one, they kill us now" (I *Ann.* 106-107); the world's present vanity repeats that of the builders of Babel and the idolators of "Wine, and Corne, and Onions" (II *Ann.* 417-433); and moreover, "a new Deluge, and of Lethe flood,/ Hath drown' us all," a Deluge "grosse and generall" (II *Ann.* 27-30).

Such references indicate that Elizabeth Drury is to be understood as a typological symbol, though not, as is sometimes suggested, in the conventional medieval sense as a type (recapitulation) of Eve, or of the Virgin, or of Christ.[44] Rather, Donne's typological method is illuminated

[43] Ellrodt, *L'Inspiration Personnelle et L'Esprit du Temps chez les Poètes Métaphysiques Anglais.* 3 vols. (Paris, 1960) I, 137; Cf. John Crowe Ransom, "Poetry: A Note in Ontology," *The World's Body* (New York, 1938), p. 122.

[44] Galden, "Typology and Seventeenth-Century Literature," pp. 180-186; William Empson, *Some Versions of Pastoral* (New York, 1935), p. 84.

by Luther's development of a future-oriented typological system in which the words of scripture, regarded as God's promises, are seen to refer to the three advents of Christ—in the flesh, in our souls by grace, and in glory—with the eschatological advent, rather than Christ's life, serving as the great antitype.[45] These are the categories with which Donne constantly works—nature, grace, and glory—and he understands these orders to be related typologically, with our state in glory presenting the ultimate fulfillment. So in the *Anniversary* poems, the symbolic meanings attaching to Elizabeth Drury pertain to her as regenerate Christian bearing the image of God restored by grace, and by that token both recapitulating and foreshadowing the other conditions of human goodness past and to come. She recapitulates in some sense that image of God in the order of Nature which we had in the created perfection of our first innocence; she bears that image robed with Christ's perfections in the order of grace; and both these conditions prefigure what the image of God we bear will be in the condition of glory.

What remains is to suggest the range of meanings Donne is able to locate in Elizabeth Drury by means of his incarnational and typological focus. His sermons, meditations, and other poems of praise and compliment provide the key to these meanings, and they reveal that the praises accorded Elizabeth Drury are quite in harmony with the terms he habitually invokes in discussing any human being, or any regenerate Christian, as image of God. Although Donne can praise Elizabeth Drury in the *Anniversaries* as image of God only because she is a real person, yet the praises he accords to her on this ground are in no sense particular to her as an individual. The fact is, however, that the language of the *Anniversary* poems constantly asserts that she has a unique worth and value vis-à-vis all others. This apparent contradiction is a paradox central to Donne's manner of praising: we recall that claims for uniqueness of the

[45] Preus, *Shadow to Promise*, pp. 185-194.

same order, though less fully developed, were made for the subjects of several of Donne's verse letters and epicedes and obsequies examined earlier.[46] Indeed, Donne consistently exploits the tensions created from such attribution of uniqueness, on the one hand, and, on the other, his readers' awareness that what is attributed to Elizabeth Drury and all those other persons can apply to any regenerate soul. The hyperbolic claim to uniqueness is witty and we are intended to appreciate that wit, as well as the rich and complex poetic texture it helps to create. And the hyperbole itself—though wildly and wittily extravagant—will not alienate us once we recognize that it is based solidly upon the unique worth that can quite validly be predicated of *any* particular regenerate soul considered in itself. The paradox the reader is expected to perceive is that through an analysis of Elizabeth Drury's uniqueness as a regenerate soul, Donne is examining the condition of humankind as its potentialities are defined by the creation in the order of nature of God's image in us, its restoration in the order of grace, and its forthcoming glorification in heaven.

In the first instance, Elizabeth Drury is presented as recapitulating the created perfection of the order of nature, the Book of the Creatures. Taking as truth the familiar microcosm/macrocosm *topos*, Donne characteristically notes that the human individual is himself the abridgment and compendium of the Book of the Creatures that constitutes God's creation: "Gods abridgement of the whole world was man."[47] As man incorporates all, so can he be equated with the world itself: "man is not onely a contributory Creature, but a totall Creature; He does not onely make one, but he is all; He is not a piece of the world, but the world it selfe; and next to the glory of God, the reason why there is a world."[48] Probing the microcosm/macrocosm *topos*,

---

[46] See above, chap. II.

[47] Donne, *Sermons*, IX, 83. See chap. 4, note 9.

[48] *Sermons*, VI, 297-298. Sermon on Psalm 62:9, preached at St. Paul's, May 8, 1625.

Donne can reverse its terms to argue that man is not so much *microcosmos*, the abridgment of the world, as himself the macrocosm of which that world is the abridgment. In one sermon he declares that,

> The properties, the qualities of every Creature, are in man; the Essence, the Existence of every Creature is for man; so man is every Creature. . . . The Philosopher draws man into too narrow a table, when he says he is *Microcosmos*, an Abridgement of the world in little: *Nazianzen* gives him but his due, when he calls him *Mundum Magnum*, a world to which all the rest of the world is but subordinate: For all the world besides, is but Gods Foot-stool; Man sits down upon his right hand.[49]

The point is made most eloquently in the *Devotions upon Emergent Occasions*:

> It is too little to call *Man* a *little World*; Except *God*, Man is a *diminutive* to nothing. Man consistes of more pieces, more parts, then the world; then the world doeth, nay then the world is. And if those pieces were extended, and stretched out in Man, as they are in the world, Man would be the *Gyant*, and the world the Dwarfe; the world but the *Map*, and the man the *World*. If all the *Veines* in our bodies, were extended to *Rivers*, and all the *Sinewes*, to *vaines* of *Mines*, and all the *Muscles*, that lye upon one another, to Hilles, and all the *Bones* to *Quarries* of stones, and all the other pieces, to the proportion of these which correspond to them in the *world*, the *aire* would be too litle for this *Orbe* of Man to move in, the firmament would bee but enough for this *star*; for, as the whole world hath nothing, to which something in man doth not answere, so hath man many pieces, of which the whol world hath no representation.[50]

---

[49] *Sermons*, IV, 104. Sermon on II Cor. 4:6, preached at Spital Cross in the Churchyard of St. Mary's without Bishopsgate, Easter Monday, 1626.

[50] *Devotions upon Emergent Occasions*, pp. 64-66.

Donne can ring still further changes upon this identification of man and world. Just as man may be seen as an abridgment or an enlargement of the entire world, so is any one man a conflation of all men: "all mankind is of one author, and is one volume . . . any man's death diminishes me, because I am involved in mankind."[51] Or again, "God hath made all *mankinde* of *one blood*, and all *Christians* of *one calling*, and the sins of every man concern every man, both in that respect, that *I*, that is, *This nature*, is in that man that sins that sin; and *I*, that is, *This nature*, is in that Christ, who is wounded by that sin."[52]

As epitome of the Book of the Creatures, then, a man may see in himself or in any other man, or woman, the best image of God to be found in any created being. He may find in himself, and in any other human being, the compendium of all the creatures, an abridgment and enlargement of all the world, and, withal, he will find that any man in some sense incorporates all mankind. Accordingly, Elizabeth Drury's poet is making no excessive claims, and is invoking a *topos* which Donne invests with precise meaning, when he declares that to her, "This world must it selfe refer,/ As Suburbs, or the Microcosme of her" (I *Ann.* 235-236). Moreover, as compendium of all the creatures, she reflects and recapitulates the primal innocence which was the essence and definition of the first-created world, when God pronounced that it was very good. The departure of that goodness, that innocence, is figured in Elizabeth's death:

> Thou [world] hast forgot thy name, thou hadst; thou wast
> Nothing but she, and her thou hast o'repast.
>
> .   .   .   .
>
> Her name defin'd thee, gave thee forme and frame.
> I. Ann. 31-37

<hr/>

[51] *Ibid.*, pp. 108-109.
[52] *Sermons*, II, 122. Second Sermon on Psalm 38:4, preached at Lincoln's Inn, 1618.

Elizabeth Drury's potentialities—any man's potentialities —as image of God are also defined in relation to the order of grace. The book of revelation in the order of grace is scripture as interpreted by the Church, and this book also Donne finds epitomized within man as Christian. Donne shares the Protestant theologians' tendency to find in the Christian's life a recapitulation of Old and New Testament experience: as member of Christ's body he participates in Christ's antitypical fulfillment, *forma perfectior*, of such Old Testament types as Adam; and as himself a *figura* of Christ he imitates and reflects what Christ was and did. Accordingly, Donne characteristically explains scripture texts and events in terms of their recapitulation in himself and his hearers—"a repeating againe in us, of that which God had done before to Israel, or . . . a performing of that in us, which God promised by way of Prophesie to Israel."[53] Or he finds that "*David* was not onely a cleare Prophet of Christ himselfe, but a Prophet of every particular Christian; He foretels what I, what any shall doe, and suffer, and say."[54] But, again characteristically, Donne intensifies this Protestant impulse so as to find the whole of scripture and also the Church located in, incarnated in, the individual Christian. He observes in one sermon, "As every man is *a world* in himself, so every man hath *a Church* in himselfe; and as Christ referred the Church for hearing to the Scriptures, so every man hath Scriptures in his own heart, to hearken to."[55] Expanding this theme on another occasion, he declares,

He that hears no Sermons, he that reads no Scriptures, hath the Bible without book; He hath a *Genesis* in his

---

[53] *Sermons*, III, 313. Sermon on Psalm 2:12, on Trinity Sunday [1621?].

[54] *Sermons*, VII, 51. Sermon on Psalm 63:7, at St. Paul's, Jan. 29 [1625/6].

[55] *Sermons*, VII, 403. Sermon on Mark 4:24, to the King at Whitehall, April 1, 1627.

memory; he cannot forget his *Creation*; he hath an *Exodus* in his memory; he cannot forget that God hath delivered him, from some kind of *Egypt*, from some oppression; he hath a *Leviticus* in his memory; hee cannot forget, that God hath proposed to him some Law, some rules to be observed. He hath *all* in his memory, even to the *Revelation;* God hath *revealed* to him, *even at midnight alone*, what shall be his portion, in the next world.[56]

Or again, more fully:

By this light of *Faith* . . . all that is involved in *Prophecies*, is clear, and evident, as in a History already done; and all that is wrapped up in *promises*, is his own already in *performance*. . . . He hath a whole *Bible*, and an abundant Library in his own heart, and there by this light of *Faith*, (which is not onely a knowing, but an applying, an *appropriating* of all to thy benefit) he hath a better knowledge then all this, then either *Propheticall*, or *Evangelicall*. . . . And as he needs not looke back to *Esay*, nor *Abraham*, nor *Adam*, for the Messias, so neither needs he to looke forward. . . . He hath already *died the death of the righteous;* which is to die to sinne; He hath already had his *buriall*, by being *buried with Christ in Baptisme*, he hath had his *Resurrection* from sinne, his *Ascension* to holy purposes of amendment of life, and his *Judgement*, that is, *peace of Conscience*, sealed unto him, and so by this light of applying Faith, he hath already apprehended an eternall possession of Gods eternall Kingdome.[57]

In Donne's poetry the most striking example of this disposition to incarnate the whole process of providential history in the individual Christian is the striking passage from the "Hymn to God my God in My Sicknesse":

[56] *Sermons*, II, 74. Sermon on Psalm 38:3, at Lincoln's Inn, 1618.
[57] *Sermons*, III, 365-366. Sermon on John 1:8, at St. Paul's, Christmas Day, 1621.

Looke Lord, and find both *Adams* met in mee;
As the first *Adams* sweat surrounds my face,
May the last *Adams* blood my soule embrace.

In the *Anniversary* poems, the girl Elizabeth Drury and the occasion of her death are shown to recapitulate the paradigm of biblical history in the Pauline version: as regenerate Christian she reflects the innocence of our first creation in the image of God; our postlapsarian subjection to misery and death; the regenerate state in which Christ the perfect Image of God is as it were substituted for our defaced image; and our forthcoming glorification in heaven. Accordingly, heavenly perfection and even a *logos*-role can be ascribed to her simply as regenerate Christian: in heaven she only enhances the perfection she manifested in the order of grace, so that, "by making full perfection grow,/ [She] Peeces a Circle, and still keepes it so"; she is the form of the world, and our essential joy while yet on earth (II *Ann.* 507-508, 470). Elizabeth also incarnates Church and Bible within herself: "religion/ Made her a Church" (II *Ann.* 374-375) the speaker declares, and in addition, having thoroughly read "all Libraries . . ./ At home, in her own thoughts," she was herself "our best, and worthiest booke" (II *Ann.* 303-304, 320).

Elizabeth Drury is also viewed as image of God in regard to the realm of heavenly glory. The book rendering knowledge of God in relation to that third realm is the Book of Life, the scroll containing the names of the elect who will enjoy that glory. This book is inscrutable, sealed up, Donne declares in his *Essays in Divinity*, but it can be "insinuated and whisper'd to our hearts,"[58] offering us some intimations of future glory for our continual study:

All this life is but a *Preface*, or but an *Index* and *Repertory* to the book of *life*; There, at that book beginnes thy study; To grow perfect in that book, to be dayly con-

---

[58] *Essays in Divinity*, p. 7. See also *Sermons*, v, 160-161, on Gal. 3:27 (uncertain date).

versant in that book, to find what be the marks of them, whose names are written in that book, and to finde those marks, ingenuously, and in a rectified conscience, in thy selfe . . . this is to goe *forth*, and see thy self, beyond thy selfe, to see what thou shalt be in the next world.[59]

These beams of future glory are refracted to us chiefly through Christ, the best glass by which every Christian may see himself as he will be in glory, but also through other Christians. Because a Christian is united to Christ by justification, and because the inchoate beginnings of the Christian's sanctification in this life image his final perfection in the realm of glory, every Christian is a shadow, a foreshadowing, a type of what he is to be, and, as such, a glass by which others may view the heavenly condition. United with Christ we are "changed in *naturam Dei*, as S. *Peter* expresses it: . . . This transmutation is a glorious restoring of Gods image in us . . . which admits no re-transmutation. . . . They who are thus changed into him, are so much His, so much He, as that nothing can separate them from him."[60] And so any Christian may be a glass to reflect the light of God's essence in glory: "By the light of faith, and grace in *sanctification*, we may come to such a *participation* of that light of Essence, or such *reflection* of it in this world, that it shall be true of us, which was said of those Ephesians, *You were once darknesse, but now are light in the Lord*; he does not say *enlightned*, nor *lightsome*, but *light* it selfe, light *essentially*, for *our conversation is in heaven*."[61] Extending this typological perspective, Donne invites the Christian to find certain events or conditions of life to be types of the glory to come. Thus, "*Peace* in this world, is a precious *Earnest*, and a faire and lovely *Type* of the ever-

[59] *Sermons*, VI, 286. Sermon on Cant. 3:11, at King James's death, April 26, 1625.

[60] *Sermons*, I, 164. Sermon on Isaiah 52:3, at Greenwich, April 30, 1615.

[61] *Sermons*, III, 363. Sermon on John 1:8, at St. Paul's, Christmas Day, 1621.

lasting peace of the world to come."[62] Or again, "Long life is a blessing, as it is . . . a Type of Eternity."[63] Or yet again, "God gives us a type, and figure of the eternity of the *joyes* of heaven, in the succession and propagation of children here upon the earth."[64]

This typological perspective is obviously relevant to the presentation of Elizabeth Drury, whose goodness on earth is to be seen as type of her now achieved heavenly glory. For that Queenly "rich soule," this earthly life was her "progresse time" and heaven is her "standing house"; (I *Ann.* 1-8); here those "rich joyes" possessed her heart and now she is both "partaker, and a part" of them (I *Ann.* 433-434); she was "here/ Betrothed to God, and now is married there" (II *Ann.* 461-462); she "made this world in some proportion/ A heaven" but now is gone "Both where more grace, and more capacitee/ At once is given" (II *Ann.* 466-469). Though in general Donne's speaker presents Elizabeth's goodness on earth as type of her achieved glory in heaven, he can from time to time take up God's vantage point, whereby inchoate sanctification is viewed as full perfection, so that he sometimes finds little to choose between Elizabeth Drury's perfections in this world and in the next. She was grown to such perfection in the "Art of knowing Heaven" here that she "but read the same" since coming to heaven—in, however, "a far fairer print" (II *Ann.* 311-314). Or again, with no qualification at all, she could plead on earth a long possession of heaven since "they'are in Heaven on Earth, who Heavens workes do" (II *Ann.* 154). One basis for this conflation is Donne's sense of the entire creation, heaven and earth, as a temporal and spatial continuum: "God . . . made but one World; for, this, and the

---

[62] *Sermons*, IV, 182. Sermon on Judges 5:20, at Paul's Cross, April 15, 1622.

[63] *Sermons*, VII, 357-358. Sermon on Isaiah 65:20, at Whitehall, Feb., 1626/7.

[64] *Sermons*, V, 116. Sermon on Ephes. 5:25, 26, 27, at a christening (uncertain date).

next, are not *two Worlds*; This is but the *Morning*, and that the *everlasting Noon*, of one and the same Day, which shall have no Night: They are not *two Houses*; This is the *Gallery*, and that the *Bed-chamber* of one, and the same Palace, which shall feel no ruine."[65]

Particularly illuminating analogues for Donne's symbolic method in the *Anniversary* poems are to be found in many of his sermons on special occasions, particularly weddings and funerals, where he characteristically undertakes to develop typological relationships between the event in the order of nature, the course of providential history in the order of grace, and the fulfillment of both in the anagogical realm. The sermon for Margaret Washington on a text from Hosea 2:10, "And I will marry thee unto me for ever" may serve as illustration.[66] Donne presents the particular secular marriage as type of all the figural relationships between the marriages of Adam and Eve, of Christ and the Soul, and of the Lamb and his Bride:

> The first mariage that was made, God made, and he made it in Paradise. . . . The last mariage which shall be made, God shall make too, and in Paradise too; in the Kingdome of heaven. . . . The mariage in this Text hath relation to both these mariages: It is it self the spirituall and mysticall mariage of Christ Jesus to the Church, and to every mariageable soule in the Church: And it hath a retrospect, it looks back to the first mariage; . . . And then it hath a prospect to the last mariage. . . . Bless these thy servants, with making this secular mariage a type of the spirituall, and the spirituall an earnest of that eternall, which they and we, by thy mercy, shall have in the Kingdome which thy Son our Saviour hath purchased.[67]

[65] *Sermons*, IV, 240. Sermon on Lament. 4:20, at St. Paul's, Nov. 5, 1622.

[66] *Sermons*, III, 241-255, preached on May 30, 1621, at St. Clement Dane.

[67] *Ibid.*, 241, 255.

For Donne's speaker, Elizabeth Drury's death is such an event, and the complex meanings it conveys will be discussed more fully in subsequent chapters. But enough has been said here to differentiate Donne's characteristic use of typological symbolism from medieval practice, to indicate its basis in Protestant hermeneutics, and to display Donne's own significant contribution to the development and literary use of such symbolism. In the *Anniversary* poems, as we have seen, Elizabeth Drury is made a type both of the condition of original created perfection and of the heavenly glory to come; her untimely death is a type (recapitulation) of the death brought upon us all by original sin; her religious death is an event (like the illness which occasions Donne's *Devotions*) in which the speaker finds a figure of his own renunciation of the world; her actual ascension to heaven is a *figura* of Christ's ascension, even as the imagined flight of the speaker's own soul is a *figura* of hers, and the projected spiritual progress of the fit audience of the poems will recapitulate both her progress and his.

Such significances could be applied, it must be remembered, to any historically real personage supposed (in charity) to be a regenerate Christian. We can come closest to understanding how Donne came to invest these meanings in a dead fifteen-year-old girl, and how he came to produce poems conjoining such a variety of generic and theological elements, by examining what is in some respects the nearest seventeenth-century analogue to the *Anniversary* poems, the funeral sermon. As Donne and his contemporaries preached them, these contemporary funeral sermons link meditation, instruction, and praise; commonly, they recognize an obligation to praise an unknown and unremarkable person; and they normally ground these praises upon the assumption that the deceased was a regenerate Christian who has now attained the glorious perfection of the heavenly state.

173

CHAPTER VI

The Funeral Sermon: The Deceased as Symbol

THE *Anniversary* poems have occasionally been discussed in relation to certain kinds of oratory. George Williamson has suggested that the poems bear some structural resemblance to the classical funeral oration and especially to the Christian funeral sermon, whose two parts, according to Puttenham, are instruction and eulogy—"teaching the people some good learning, and also saying well of the departed."[1] Harold Love has proposed the judicial oration, with its special emphasis upon argument and proof, as generally relevant to the form of the *Anatomy*.[2] I wish to examine here a specific, contemporary context as the principal channel through which such rhetorical forms influenced Donne's poems—the English Protestant funeral sermon.

In terms of theory, the Protestant funeral sermon, like the *Anniversaries*, is a mixed genre incorporating instruction, meditation, and praise. As practiced, it provided certain standard topics, such as the eulogy of the deceased as a regenerate soul and the presentation of the dead person in typical or symbolic terms, which are suggestive for the conceptual framework and for the language of the *Anniversaries*. Not surprisingly, Donne's own funeral sermons were themselves important in developing and extending the meditative and symbolic characteristics of the genre. More-

[1] Williamson, "The Design of Donne's *Anniversaries*" (1963), in *Milton and Others* (Chicago, 1965), pp. 150-164. See [George] Puttenham, *The Arte of English Poesie* [1589] (facsim. ed., Scolar Press, Menston, Eng., 1968), p. 39.

[2] Love, "The Argument of Donne's *First Anniversary*," MP, 63 (1966), 125-131.

over, though they were written several years after the *Anniversary* poems, Donne's funeral sermons are in some respects the nearest analogues to them, and illuminate some important aspects of the poems' conception and structure.

A. THE THEORY OF THE PROTESTANT FUNERAL SERMON

Although any full account of the theory of the Protestant funeral sermon would have to relate it to medieval and Protestant sermon theory generally, as well as to typical Roman Catholic models of the funeral sermon, my special concern here with the *Anniversary* poems permits a more limited focus.[3] The important points for consideration in the theoretical accounts are the elements supposed to be incorporated in the funeral sermon, the purposes it is presumed to serve, and the precepts which govern the conception and praise of the deceased.

Protestant theorists recognized that the sermon bore some relation to the classical funeral oration, which itself developed from more general forms of demonstrative oratory such as the encomium and the panegyrical biography. The authority of Menander and the writer of the *Ad Herennium*, as well as the example of notable classical texts in these kinds, established that the demonstrative oration should concern itself with three categories of praise: celebrations of the goods bestowed by nature upon the person in question (his family, physical features, health), the

---

[3] For the larger question see, e.g., G. R. Owst, *Literature and Pulpit in Medieval England* (Cambridge, 1933); W. Frazer Mitchell, *English Pulpit Oratory from Andrewes to Tillotson* (London, 1932); William Haller, *The Rise of Puritanism* (New York, 1938); Thomas M. Charland, *Artes praedicandi* (Paris, 1936); Millar MacLure, *The Paul's Cross Sermons* (Toronto, 1958); Dietrich Arno Hill, "The Modus Praedicandi of John Donne," unpub. Ph.D. dissertation, Univ. of Illinois, 1962; Dennis Quinn, "Donne's Christian Eloquence," *ELH*, 27 (1960), 276-297; William R. Mueller, *John Donne, Preacher* (Princeton, 1962).

goods bestowed by fortune (his wealth, power, fame), and his goods of mind and character.[4] Educated clergymen knew also that Cicero, Quintilian, and most Renaissance rhetoricians had proclaimed virtue to be the chief or only true basis for praise, and had recognized the didactic possibilities such praises of virtue might have for promoting virtue in the auditory.[5] Indeed, this didactic function had been emphasized in the *Evagoras* of Isocrates, a funeral oration addressed to Evagoras' son Nicocles, to inspire him to emulate the ideal set forth. Isocrates had declared:

> I have undertaken to write this discourse because I believed that for you [Nicocles], for your children, and for all the other descendants of Evagoras, it would be by far the best incentive, if someone should assemble his achievements, give them verbal adornment, and submit them to you for your contemplation and study. For we exhort young men to the study of philosophy by praising others in order that they, emulating those who are eulogized, may desire to adopt the same pursuits.[6]

Though the orator's appeal to didactic intention to explain an admixture of fiction and hyperbole in his praises was sometimes a cynical effort to defend the crassest flattery, on its positive side it justified the "ideal type" as more suitable for didactic purposes than the particulars of an indi-

---

[4] See Hardison, *Enduring Monument*, pp. 24-58, 194-196; Theodore Burgess, *Epideictic Literature* (University of Chicago Studies in Classical Philology, III [Chicago, 1902]); Menander, ed. Leonhard Spengal, *Rhetores Graeci*, 3 vols. (Leipzig, 1854-1885), III, 329-446; [Cicero], *Ad C. Herennium, de ratione dicendi. Rhetorica ad Herennium*, ed. Harry Caplan (Loeb, London, 1954), pp. 173-175.

[5] Cicero, *De Oratore* II.lxxxiv.84, 342, ed. H. Rackham, 2 vols. (Loeb Classical Library, London, 1942), I, 459; Quintilian, *Institutes of Oratory* III.vii.12-15, ed. H. E. Butler (Loeb, London, 1907), I, 469-471; Thomas Wilson, *The Arte of Rhetorique* (1553), facsim. ed. Robert H. Bowers (Gainesville, Fla., 1962), pp. 24-30. See Hardison, *Enduring Monument*, pp. 24-58.

[6] "Evagoras," 75-76, *Isocrates*, 3 vols., trans. Larue van Hook (Loeb, London, 1945) III, 47.

vidual life could be. On these grounds, the demonstrative orator claimed the right to present what ought to be instead of what is. Isocrates told Nicocles, "It is my task, therefore . . . to speak and write in such fashion as may be likely to incite you to strive eagerly after those [good] things . . . that you may be worthy of your father and all your ancestors," and to this end he portrayed Evander as the ideal type of the good king.[7]

The fact that several of the Church Fathers—notably Gregory Nazianzen, Athanasius, Ambrose, and Jerome—were known to have delivered funeral orations modeled closely upon classical precedent, provided some warrant for utilizing classical theory and example in the Christian funeral sermon. Gregory's orations were essentially eulogies of the deceased as paradigms of virtue; they were organized in terms of the goods of nature, fortune, and character, and incorporated passages of Christian consolation, but the lament or expression of personal grief was almost wholly absent.[8] By contrast, St. Ambrose's orations fused lamentation, consolation, and praise. Ambrose's two funeral exercises *On his Brother Satyrus* are of particular interest as complimentary works in somewhat different modes—a funeral oration charged with personal lament and grief, and an "Anniversary" oration delivered on the seventh day, which emphasizes consolation and is intended as "a general exhortation applicable to all."[9] But although the earlier sev-

[7] *Ibid.*, p. 49.

[8] Four of Gregory's orations are extant: *On his Brother St. Caesarius; On St. Basil the Great; On his Sister, St. Gorgonia; On his Father.* See the edition, *Funeral Orations by Saint Gregory Nazianzen and Saint Ambrose*, ed. Martin R. P. McGuire (Fathers of the Church, xxii, New York, 1953).

[9] McGuire, *ibid.*, p. 197. Four orations of Ambrose are extant: *First Oration: On the Death of His Brother Satyrus; Second Oration [on Satyrus]: On Faith in the Resurrection; Consolation on the Death of the Emperor Valentinian; Funeral Oration on the Death of Emperor Theodosius.* The last-mentioned of these is also an "Anniversary" sermon, on a fortieth day's anniversary.

enteenth century affords a few examples of funeral orations written in direct imitation of the Fathers,[10] Catholics and Protestants for the most part agreed that these patristic orations with their strong panegyric element were inappropriate as models for the Christian funeral sermon—indeed that they belonged to another genre.[11]

Nevertheless, the fact that the Fathers had emphasized the didactic purposes of praises of the deceased far more strongly than had the classical orators remained important

[10] See, e.g. [Anthony Nixon], *London's Dove: Or, A Memoriall of the Life and Death of Maister Robert Dove* (London, 1612); Phillip Stubbes, *A Christall Glasse for Christian Women, Containing a most excellent Discourse, of the Godly life and Christian death of Mistress Katherine Stubbes, who departed this life in Burton-upon-Trent in Staffordshire, the 14 day of December* (London, 1606); William Walker, *A Sermon Preached at the Funerals of the Right Honourable, William Lord Russell, Baron of Thornhaugh . . . the 16 of September, 1613* (London, 1614). Walker felt it necessary to justify his use of the funeral oration form for his sermon:

> Some will admit funerall pompe, which yet will condemne funerall Orations. But these men are either ignorant of the laudable practice of the Saints of the primitive Church; or else no well-willers to Antiquitie. And therefore let all men know, that if any condemne our practise herein, they must withall condemne those worthy lights of the ancient Church of God, which are our Precedents, viz. *Nazianzene*, whose funerall Orations are to be seene in his works made for his brother *Caesarius*, his sister *Gorgonia*, his father *Gregorie*, his friend *Basilius Athanasius*, and others; And *Ambrose* also, who commends his brother *Satyrus*, and the Emperour *Valentinian* and *Theodosius*. And *Hierome*, who praises *Nepotian*, *Marcella*, *Blaesilla*, *Pauline*, *Paula*, *Fabiola*. And *Bernard*, who extols *Malachy*, and his brother *Gerrard*: and divers others.

[11] Catholic writers of *Artes concionandi* such as Erasmus (*Ecclesiastae, sive de ratione concionandi* [Basel, 1535], p. 151) and Luis de Granada (*Ecclesiasticae Rhetoricae, sive de ratione concionandi* [Lisbon, 1576], pp. 170-178) discussed sermon-writing in terms of Ciceronian rhetorical precepts and the classical categories of orations, locating sermons praising God and the saints in the demonstrative category, but they observed that funeral sermons are not now rendered in that form in the Church. Protestant theorists usually repudiated the classical formulas even more sharply, and of course had no use for demonstrative sermons in praise of the saints.

for Christian preachers of various religious persuasions, as did the affirmation that praises of the deceased should be the strict, unvarnished truth. As St. Gregory put it in his oration *On his Sister, St. Gorgonia*, "we should not . . . praise undeservedly the qualities of others nor should we disparage what is found in our own [family], if it be truly praiseworthy. . . . We [should] make the truth our standard and rule."[12] Particularly influential for both Catholic and Protestant theorists was St. Augustine's formulation of these principles, to the effect that although the preacher might learn from classical rhetoricians he should chiefly imitate the writers of sacred scripture, who did not aim primarily at eloquence (though they achieved it) but at wisdom and truth. Moreover, the sermon concerned with praise should seek not chiefly to please but rather to show "that those things which it praises are to be desired or firmly adhered to."[13]

Baptized according to such precepts, certain aspects of the demonstrative funeral oration or the encomium of the Saints found their way into Protestant funeral sermons, and Protestant theology provided a firm basis for accommodating them. The Protestant denial of purgatory meant that the departed soul could be envisaged as enjoying heavenly glory at once, and the Protestant disavowal of the idea of personal merit meant that any praise of the deceased's good life redounded not to that individual but to God working in him. Moreover, the Protestant insistence upon the priesthood of believers made for an equalization of spiritual categories such that all the elect (and not only designated saints or those exercising religious vocations) were understood to be called to and capable of the highest spiritual attain-

[12] Gregory Nazianzen, ed. McGuire, trans. Leo P. McCauley, p. 101. In his oration *On St. Basil the Great*, Gregory declared to his auditory that his intention was not so much to lament and praise Basil as to "counsel you . . . that you may be perfected by the Spirit," *ibid.*, p. 97.

[13] Augustine, *De Doctrina Christiana* IV. 26 (#56), trans. D. W. Robertson (New York, 1953), p. 163.

ments.[14] Given these premises, the charitable understanding must have it that the subject of any funeral sermon—however lowly or ordinary his life—was at the very time he lay in state a glorious saint of God.

The most complete statement of the Protestant theory of the funeral sermon and the best explanation of the Protestant model for this genre are to be found in Andreas Hyperius' Latin tract translated into English in 1577 as *The Practis of Preaching*; it was constantly cited in subsequent discussions of the preacher's art. Hyperius set aside the demonstrative, deliberative, and judicial categories as not very suitable for classifying sermons, and proposed instead to "draw out of the entrailes of the scriptures, both what and howe many kindes of divine Sermons there bee."[15] Appealing chiefly to Paul's epistles, he discovered five classes, locating praises of various kinds and also funeral sermons under the fourth kind, moral instruction.[16] Hyperius insisted further that Christian praises cannot be founded upon the classical categories of the goods of nature, fortune, and character: for one thing, the Church cannot sanction orations to living men but only to those "whom all good men trust assuredly to be now translated into the felowshippe

---

[14] For development of these points, see Charles and Katherine George, *Protestant Mind of the English Reformation*, pp. 29-38. Luther emphasized these points strongly in his *Commentarie . . . upon . . . Galathians* (fol. 268): "He hath given me the grace to see, not one but many Saints, yea an infinite number of true Saints: . . . Wherefore rejecting this foolish and wicked opinion concerning the name of Saints (which in the time of Popery and ignorance we thought to pertaine onely to the Saints which are in heaven, and in earth to the Heremites and Monks which did certaine great and strange workes): let us now learne by the holy Scripture that al they which faithfully beleeve in Christ are saints."

[15] Andreas Hyperius [Gerardus], *De formandis concionibus sacris: seu de interpretatione scripturam populi* (Basel, 1579); *The Practis of Preaching, otherwise called the Pathway to the Pulpet: Conteyning an excellent Method how to frame Divine Sermons*. Trans. John Ludham (London, 1577), fol. 18.

[16] *Practis of Preaching*, fols. 18-18ᵛ.

and societie of Saints."[17] Even in those cases the classical bases for praise should be used only to show "how that blessed man trusted not or abused not those giftes and benefites,"[18] since the preacher's primary aim is not to evoke admiration or worship for that man, but rather to effect that "by hearinge the gracious and excellent deedes of worthy and famous men the godly hearers may be provoked to prayse and magnifie GOD, who vouchedsafe to elect and call them, and to bringe to passe through them great and mightye thinges. . . . The other [purpose is], that the multitude maye be stirred and enflamed to the imitation of their so notable deedes."[19] His general model for a Christian epideictic sermon proposes the development and explanation of some text of scripture, and the gradual relation of certain aspects of the departed worthy's life to it,[20] thereby treating a particular individual as illustration or manifestation of the text.

Turning to funeral sermons directly, Hyperius recommended the form he declared to be in general use among Protestants, in which a biblical text gives rise to topics for development appropriate to the occasion.[21] The list of recommended topics is quite suggestive for the *Anniversaries*:

Of preparation unto death, that death is the penaltye of sinne, of the miseries of mannes lyfe, of the delyveraunce from them by death, of the contempt of the world and all earthely things, of desiring ye felicitie of the lyfe to come, of the immortalytye and eternall blessednes of sowles, of the resurrection of bodyes, of the last judgement . . . that the deade are delivered . . . out of the most filthy prison of theyr body, that the death of the sayntes is pretious in the lordes sight.[22]

---

[17] *Ibid.*, fol. 153.   [18] *Ibid.*   [19] *Ibid.*, fol. 153[v].
[20] *Ibid.*, fol. 153.
[21] *Ibid.*, fol. 155: "They [the Protestants] handle not prayses curiouslye contrived and couched togyther, but other places much more holesome and fitte for the enformation of the hearers."
[22] *Ibid.*

Hyperius recommended great restraint in the usual brief concluding account of the life and virtues of the deceased—which often incorporated elements of the funeral oration or panegyrical biography—so as to make it serve the glory of God and the purpose of moral instruction:

> Where if so be it be thought good after these places declared, that somewhat be sayde of the brother which is brought to buriall, then add they briefely, and (as ye woulde say) shamefastely some thinge touchinge the kinde of life that he imbraced, and shewe how devoutly he served God therin, by diligent performinge of those thinges that were his dutye to doe. Whereby ye hearers also are given to understand what great industry it behoveth them to employe, to the intent every of them in their callinge and kinde of life may become acceptable to God.[23]

Besides being open to the abuse of overpraising or wrongly praising the dead, this kind of funeral sermon could lack unity if the biographical matter were merely tacked on as an appendage. Preachers often tried to prevent this by discussing the individual as a manifestation and illustration of the text, or by a close integration of the praises with the explication of the text and doctrine, in accordance with Hyperius' general prescription for the Christian epideictic sermon. Richard Harris, for example, defended his decision to forbear "personall praise in the close" of his funeral sermon for Sir Anthony Cope (1618), as allowing for a more decorous and more integrated sermon:

> My text gave me occasion of saying something before, & me thought it handsomer to lay al my stuffe upon the foundation, then to set up a leane-to. . . . I finde the practice (though in it selfe lawful) exceedingly abused, I have no leisure now to take up the complaints of worthy Writers against this abuse; only I could wish, that our

23 *Ibid.*, fols. 155-155ᵛ.

age would distinguish betwixt funerall Orations, and funerall Sermons, as former ages have done, and not confound so different things.[24]

Taking his text from the life of the biblical Samuel, he identified Cope's life with Samuel's so closely as to make Cope a direct contemporary referent of that text, "both so neare in agreement, that in the storie of the one, you may reade the life of the other."[25]

One additional element, meditation, was associated with the Protestant theory of the funeral sermon. This is hardly surprising, given the general Protestant tendency to conflate meditation and sermon in regard to method, presenting the sermon as at once the publication of the preacher's meditations and as the model for and stimulus to the auditory's meditation.[26] Often citing Seneca to the effect that the life of a wise man is a continual meditation on death, and designating the death or funeral at hand as a fitting occasion for his hearers to meditate upon the death they must all undergo soon, the preacher would propose his own sermon as a directive to or an example of such meditation. Samuel Hieron, in a funeral sermon entitled *The Life and Death of Dorcas* (1613), urged the congregation to "take occasion thereby" for "a due meditation of our end. For surely if even the holiest die, then all must die."[27] John Warren offered his published sermon for his kinswoman Mis-

---

[24] Robert Harrice [Harris], *Samuels Funerall. Or, a Sermon Preached at the Funerall of Sir Anthonie Cope, Knight, and Baronnet* (London, 1618), "Epistle to the Reader."

[25] *Ibid.*, p. 25.

[26] See above, chap. 3.

[27] Samuel Hieron, *The Life and Death of Dorcas*, in *All the Sermons of Samuel Hieron* (London, 1614). Similarly Robert Pricke in his sermon at the joint funerals of Sir Edward and Lady Susan Lewkenor (*A Verie Godlie and Learned Sermon, treating of mans mortalitie, and of the estate both of his bodie and soule after death* [London, 1608] p. 391) urged his hearers to take the occasions of such funerals and such events to "seriously meditate of death, and as it were to continually set it before our eyes."

tresse Needes (1618) to the readers as a stimulus to their meditations on death, even as (reportedly) it had stimulated his original auditory: "That it may now bring forth fruit in thee (Reader) let it bee in thy hands, as a *Deaths head*, to remember thy end: take it as the clock striketh . . . apply it line by line." Preaching upon Isaiah 38:1, "Put thy house in order, for thou shalt die and not live," he urged meditation as the means to this ordering, and presented the sermon itself as an example of how "first to meditate of death, secondly of this life: and thirdly of the great change which will happen to diverse men presently after death."[28] The Protestant funeral sermon had, then, the threefold function of instructing the auditory, praising the deceased, and promoting by directive and example the hearers' meditations upon their own mortality.

B. English Funeral Sermons, 1600-1630

The funeral sermons of Donne's contemporaries have a fairly standard format, closely approximating that recommended by Hyperius. They set forth and expound a biblical text; divide it into set topics; develop doctrines and uses, with the arguments and proofs for them, in relation to the topics proposed;[29] and conclude with a brief account of and eulogy for the deceased. My focus here is upon funeral sermons for relatively undistinguished persons, often unknown

[28] John Warren, *Domus ordinata. A Funerall Sermon, preached in the City of Bristol, June 25, 1618, at the buriall of his kinswoman, Mistress Needes* (London, 1618), "To the Reader," sigs. A 2-A 2ᵛ, p. 23. Moreover Thomas Gataker in the subtitle of his funeral sermon for Richard Stock (*Abrahams Decease. A Meditation on Genesis 25:8* [London, 1627]) testified to the near identity of the modes of meditation and sermon in the common usage.

[29] The concern with argument and proof in the *Anatomy of the World* seems to me most likely to derive from the presence of these elements in the funeral sermons, rather than directly from the traditions of the *oratio judicalis*, as Harold Love has suggested (see above, note 2).

gentlewomen, since such works afford the nearest approximation to the circumstances and occasion of Donne's *Anniversaries*. Three elements of these sermons are particularly suggestive for the method of Donne's poems: the topics commonly developed to instruct the auditory and assist their meditations; the bases upon which the eulogies of the dead are constructed; and the symbolic dimensions which the dead customarily assume in these exercises.

Most of the funeral sermons of the period, whatever the text chosen and whoever the corpse, propose for consideration the same two contrasting topics, and these topics are also the subjects of the two *Anniversaries*: the wretchedness, misery, and degeneration attending upon the human condition in this life as a result of original sin, and the joys of the regenerate state and of heaven. These topics are of course obvious ones which might be expected to occur in any Christian discussion of or meditation upon death. But their ubiquity as paired topics and the language used to explore them in the funeral sermon suggest the direct generic influence of that form upon Donne's poems.

The typical development accorded the first of these topics, the omnipresence of human misery, degeneration, and death resulting from sin, provides analogues for the chief subject matter and many of the striking images of *The First Anniversarie*. The scope of the topic is suggested by Richard Carpenter (1612): "Thinke on thy naked nativity and blush for shame; on this worlds wretchednesse and misery, and Sigh for griefe, on death's approaching tyranny, and tremble for feare."[30] In developing the topic, some preachers emphasized man's physical sufferings and griefs: William Forde, at the sermon for Lady Anne Glover (1616), urged consideration of "how manie diseases we continuallie carrie about us, what aches affect our bones, what heavinesse our bodies, what dimnesse our eies, what deafenesse our eares, what trembling our hands, what rot-

---

[30] Richard Carpenter, *The Soules Sentinall . . . preached . . . at the funeral of Sir Arthur Ackland* (London, 1612), pp. 34-35.

185

tennesse our teeth."[31] By contrast, at his sermon for Lady
Strode, John Barlow dwelt upon the appalling moral evils
accompanying the physical loathsomeness of this world:

> What is she tooke from? and what is the world and all
> therein, but . . . a *Sodom*, where men burne in lust? . . .
> Whereto shall I further liken it? Why, to an Hospitall,
> where be both deafe, dumbe, lame and blinde; a very
> Pesthouse, where be many sicke of every soare, die of
> each disease. . . . Truely, it's a very Bedlem, pestered with
> fooles, filled with madde and franticke fellowes; who
> know not, either their owne misery, or can endure to be
> cured . . . it's a sinke, a whirle-poole . . . of all un-
> cleanesse.[32]

Still others emphasized the world's and man's continuing
degeneracy, citing as evidence the shortness and transitori-
ness of the present life. John Preston's development of this
commonplace at the funeral of Josiah Reynel (1614) recalls
the way in which this topic is explored in *The First
Anniversarie*:

> Our lives shorten as if the booke of our daies were by the
> pen-knife of Gods judgement cut loose. Before the Flood
> they were in Folio, they lived almost a thousand yeares,
> *Methushelah* lived nine hundred sixty and nine yeares,
> *Gen.* 5.27. the whole chapter will shew us how long the

[31] William Forde, *A Sermon Preached at Constantinople, in the
Vines of Perah, at the Funerall of the vertuous and admired Lady
Anne Glover, sometime Wife to the Honorable Knight Sir Thomas
Glover, and then Ambassadour Ordinary for his Majesty of Great
Britain, in the port of the Great Turk* (London, 1616), p. 31. Cf.
Thomas Gataker, *The Benefit of a Good Name, and a Good End.
A Funerall Sermon on Eccles 7:1* (London, 1612), p. 20: "Our life is
begun with weeping and teares, and continued in greife and cares;
full fraught with crosses and calamities from one end of it to the
other."

[32] John Barlow, *The True Guide to Glory. A Sermon Preached at
Plympton-Mary in Devon, at the Funerals of . . . the Lady [Strode
of Newingham]* (London, 1619), p. 45.

men lived before the Floud. After the Floud in Quarto, then they lived an hundred and twenty, and an hundred and seventy. *Gen.* 25.7. In *Davids* time in Octavo, three-score and foure score yeares, but with us in the daies of the Gospell, in Decimo Sexto in the least volume, now at forty, fifty, or sixty yeares, old men, and so we are dying almost so soone, as we beginne to live. The Elements are more mixed, drossie, and confused, our new sins call for new plagues; the aire is more infected and contagious, and our sins of drunkennesse and surfeiting do not want to second all the rest: we may observe that neither planets above, nor plants below, yeeld us expected comfort.[33]

Commonly, all these evils are shown to stem from the omnipresence of death (the wages of Adam's sin) and the paradox that human life is itself death is constantly propounded.[34] Charles Fitz-Geffrey in the sermon for Lady Philippe Rous (1620) declared that every man is dying while yet in life: "The Wormes take possession of us, almost

[33] John Preston, *A Sermon Preached at the Funerall of Mr. Josiah Reynal, Esq., the 13 of August 1614* (London, 1615), sig. B 4. Much to the same point, Humphry Sydenham in his sermon for Sir John Sydenham (*Natures Overthrow, And Deaths Triumph.* [London, 1626], p. 12) complained of the inaccuracy of David's similitude about man's life: "*David* was too prodigall in his similitude, when he beat out the age of a man to the dimensions of a *span*; an inch, a *punctum* had been bountifull enough, the least Atome types out his glory here, the glory of life here, 'tis breath on steel, no sooner on than off; Sunne-burnt stubble, at once flame, and ashes."

[34] William Forde in his *Funerall of . . . Lady Anne Glover* (pp. 6-7) described vividly the spectacle of death taking possession of the entire world after Adam's sin: "How did death enter by sinne? even as an effect that followeth yts cause, or as a shadowe that accompanieth a bodie in the sunne. And how went death over all; as a plague *grassantis in domo*, depopulating the citie or a house where it entereth: or like an enemie *pervagantis, vastantis, sternentis*, raging, ranging, destroying, all that he meets with, or like a hidden poyson that diffuseth its venome, unto every member, and penetratheth unto all and everie part . . . unto all, high and lowe, rich and poore, bond and free."

187

as soone as we doe of life, and have bespoken us even in our Cradles, for their fellowes that awaite us in the Earth. Thus have we Death alreadie in us and on us. . . . We put it on our backs in our clothes, and are clad in Death from top to toe; we cramme it into our mouthes with our meate, we have it in our bones, we carrie the handsell of it in our bowels."[35] Developing the same point, Thomas Gataker observed in his sermon for Richard Stock (1627): "The whole course of our life is nothing else but a passage to death: the severall ages of our life so many severall degrees of death: we are dying daily by degrees. No sooner are we (I say not, borne, but even) bred, but wee are dying and decaying. Every minute and moment that seemeth added to our life, is taken from it. For our life it is as a taper, that being once lighted, never linneth spending, till it be wasted all at last."[36]

As a counterpoise to such instructions and meditations upon the miseries of the human condition, these sermons customarily treat the second topic, the joys of the life of grace and of the world to come: its development suggests the chief subject matter and imagery of *The Second Anniversarie*. The pairing was considered to be natural and inevitable: Thomas Gataker in his sermon for Mistress Rebekka Crisp (1620) advised, "when thou meditatest on death, meditate withall on those benefits that shall accrue unto thee by death."[37] In his sermon on William, Lord Russell (1613) William Walker summarized those benefits as follows:

Health without sickness, youth without olde age, liberty without bondage, satiety without loathing, fairenesse

[35] Charles Fitz-Geffry, *Deaths Sermon unto the Living, Delivered at the Funerals of the Religious Ladie Philippe, late Wife unto the Right Worshipfull Sr. Anthonie Rous* (London, 1620), p. 11.

[36] Gataker, *Abrahams Decease*, p. 42.

[37] Gataker, *Pauls Desire of Dissolution, and Deaths Advantage. A Sermon Preached at the Funerall of that right vertuous and religious Gentlewoman Mrs. Rebekka Crisp* (London, 1620), p. 26.

without deformitie, abundance without want, knowledge without ignorance, glory without ignominie . . . and life without inconvenience, or end of happinesse.

Wouldest thou have beauty and excellency of body, there shalt thou be like unto the Angels, and shalt *shine as the Sunne, in the kingdome of thy Father.* Wouldest thou have pleasure and delight, there shalt thou *be satisfied with the fatnesse of Gods house, who shall drench thee with the river of his pleasures.* Wouldest thou have wisedome, there thou shalt injoy the full view of Wisedom it selfe, and see God face to face. Dost thou desire friendship, concord, and unitie, there thou shalt love God above thy selfe, and God shall love thee better than thou canst love thy selfe: and there all the Saints and Angels shall have but one will.[38]

And in his sermon for Mistress Crisp, Thomas Gataker emphasized especially the superiority of the soul's perfections in heaven to those of its life of grace here, and even to those of the first Edenic innocence:

Death, it strippeth us of our old man, our old skin, all at once, not, as sanctification doth it here, by degrees: yea it placeth us in far better estate then our first parents were in before their fall. For they were so free from sinne, that yet they might have will to sinne: we shall be so freed by death from sinne, that we shall never have

[38] Walker, *A Sermon Preached [for] . . . Lord Russell,* p. 29. William Forde in the *Funerall of . . . Lady Anne Glover,* pp. 56-57, noted many of the same goods, paraphrasing as it were the departed soul's report on its new condition: "I am not perished, but am rather perfected. I am now in the state of perfection, where I feele no infirmitie, where I am not tempted unto sinne, but sing a continuall Halleluiah to the Lord. I am now where I behold the glorious Majestie of the Trinity, where I looke on the amiable countenance of my Saviour, where I enjoy the sweet society of Saints and Angels, where I have satiety without loathsomenesse; love, without hatred; peace, without discord; joy, without sorrow; eternall blisse, without end or intermission."

either will or minde againe thereunto. . . . When the sunne of righteousnes shall shine full upon us, and shining full upon us, shall make us like unto himselfe; so that we shall *also shine as the sunne in the kingdome of heaven.*[39]

In addition to these common topics, the Protestant funeral sermon also supplied the basis for the eulogies of Elizabeth Drury in the *Anniversary* poems—the presumption of her regenerate condition. In his sermon for Sir Philip Boteler (1607), George Downame explains what is obvious enough once stated—that this assumption must naturally be made regarding the subject of any funeral exercise:

The faithfull are in Christ; and . . . all which bee in Christ, are happie and blessed. . . . Wee are not onely made partakers of his merits to our justification; but also being in him, we are made partakers of his graces unto sanctification. . . .

This opinion, which the holy Ghost doth here teach us in general, to conceive of all those that die in the Lord, Christian charity bindeth us to entertaine, concerning this our worthy brother departed in the faith of Christ.[40]

Typically—and seemingly unlike Donne in the *Anniversary* poems—the preacher of funeral sermons in a brief concluding encomium recounted from his own observations certain facts concerning the dead person's good life. However, except for cursory enumeration of the particular virtues accordant to his state of life, and repetition of stock formulas praising, for example, a deceased matron as the best wife, best mother, best neighbor, best friend, best example to the church, the lives described turn out to be much the same

[39] Gataker, *Pauls Desire of Dissolution*, p. 9.

[40] George Downame, *A Funerall Sermon Preached at Watton in Hertfordshire, at the buriall of the ancient and worthy Knight, Sir Philip Boteler* (London, 1607), pp. 23-25, 61.

whoever the corpse. This is so because the emphasis falls upon the evidences of regeneration, and any regenerate life is understood to conform in its basic contours to the conventional Protestant paradigm: conversion experience, daily readings in the Bible and other religious books, daily meditation upon scripture passages and sermons, daily examinations of conscience and repentance for any failings, pious observance of the Sabbath, works of mercy and charity, manifestation of patience and faith in sickness and suffering, and final victory in the awful deathbed struggle with Satan. Lancelot Langhorne made explicit this basis for his praise when he declared of Mistress Mary Swaine, "I come not to extoll flesh and bloud, but to describe those graces God had endowed her withall, and not onely from report, for I have conversed with her almost these four yeares, and was present with her most part of her sicknesses."[41]

Moreover, since the dead were praised according to this well-established pattern, a preacher could and often did extoll in elaborate encomiastic language the life of one not personally known to him, appealing confidently to the reports of others. John Warren accordingly recorded the praiseworthy life of his kinswoman Mistresse Needes (1618) from hearsay, noting that despite the kinship, "in respect of conversation, I was a stranger."[42] William Forde, preaching for Lady Anne Glover, also admitted to reliance upon second-hand evidence for his encomium: "it was not my hap (which I count a great part of my unhappinesse) either to see her living or to heare of her life, before I heard of her death. . . . I speake not from my selfe, but from the mouth of such who being eie and eare witnesses of her actions and speeches, I presume have informed me nothing but the

[41] Lancelot Langhorne, *Mary Sitting at Christs Feet. A Sermon Preached at the Funerall of Mistris Mary Swaine, the wife of Mr. William Swaine, at Saint Buttolph's without Aldergate* (London, 1611), p. 6.

[42] John Warren, *Domus Ordinata*, sigs. A 4-A 4ᵛ.

truth."[43] The grounds for a preacher's confidence that the praises he speaks are justified, even when he has no direct knowledge of the subject, are most fully presented in a funeral sermon entitled "A Tryall of Sinceritie." They involve the familiar appeal to the didactic usefulness of the ideal type, and also the assumption that any regenerate Christian's life must follow in its religious dimensions the classic paradigm, and so must fit the portrait drawn:

Happily some may scoffe, and some may doubt, as though this commendation flew too high, or out of sight. To whom I shall briefly answer both. For the former . . . the ordinary observation of the wits of the time was . . . they thought that *Euripides* that presented them bad, presented women as they were: and *Sophocles* that presented them good, presented them [women] as they should bee. If I had nothing else to say to the scoffes of any, but only this, I suppose it would be sufficient: I doe believe fully, that I have presented her as she was: but howsoever you can take no hurt if you doe but consider, that it is spoken as what you should be. I am sure, and I know I have presented what you should be.

And for any that shall doubt yet, that it may seeme too

---

[43] Forde, *Funerall of . . . Lady Anne Glover*, pp. 73, 77. Similarly, in the absence of the regular minister the preacher of the sermon *Lifes Apparition: And Mans Dissolution* for a young woman dead in childbirth admitted that "my knowledge of her was but a few weekes or moneths, by reason of our neighbourhood in the Countrey," and that he visited her only once, a brief visit during her last illness. The sermon appears in ΘΡΗΝΟΙΚΟΣ *The House of Mourning; Furnished with Directions for, Preparations to, Meditations of, Consultations at the hour of Death* (London, 1640), p. 494. This collection constitutes the most complete compilation of funeral sermons of the earlier seventeenth century. The title page identifies the authors as "Daniel Featly, Martin Day, Richard Sibbs, Thomas Taylor . . . and other Reverend Divines," but particular sermons are not identified as to preacher, deceased, or date, either in this edition or in the somewhat expanded edition of 1660. Nor do the sermons contained here appear among the published sermons of the divines mentioned.

high, I would desire them only to consider this: I describe in the Text, the very temper and character of one that is truly godly (such as I conceive her to have beene) and the truth is, there is none that is truly godly, but in some degree or measure must attaine, and doe attaine to participate in a conformitie with this Character: and therefore I have neither done you (as I conceive) any wrong, and yet done her right too.[44]

We find here a basis for Donne's apparent expectation that the audience of the *Anniversary* poems would understand his praises to be grounded upon the presumption of Elizabeth Drury's regenerate condition, rather than upon the specifics of her life. Given the ubiquity of this presumption by preachers of funeral sermons it was not an unreasonable expectation, even though Ben Jonson, by reason of his theological and classicist bias toward individual virtue and merit, could not understand the terms. Indeed, in a letter written on April 14, 1612, to George Gerrard, Donne justified his praises of Elizabeth Drury on precisely the grounds contemporary ministers were using when they were called upon to praise a deceased person not personally known to them. Donne wrote:

Of the imputation of having said so much, my defence is, that my purpose was to say as well as I could; for since I never saw the gentlewoman, I cannot be understood to have bound myself to have spoken just truth; but I would not be thought to have gone about to praise anybody in rhyme, except I took such a person as might be capable of all that I could say. If any of those ladies think that Mistress Drury was not so, let that lady make herself fit for all those praises in the book, and it shall be hers.[45]

[44] *A Triall of Sinceritie, or, The Desire of the Faithfull*, in *House of Mourning*, p. 316. This sermon is ascribed to Richard Sibbes in a contemporary hand on the title page of the Harvard University copy.

[45] Edward Gosse, *The Life and Letters of John Donne*, 2 vols. (New York, 1899) I, 302.

Donne here denies any intent to describe the actual Elizabeth: he had no first-hand knowledge and so did not attempt a "just"—i.e., factual—account. He does not claim, however, to have created an ideal type for didactic purposes. Rather, he asserts that he had taken an appropriate figure, one who "might be capable" of his best praises. That her appropriateness rests upon her regenerate condition is evident from Donne's final retort to the complaining ladies Gerrard had mentioned to him, that any of them who would make herself "fit" for those praises would be a suitable subject for his poem. He clearly assumes, with the preachers of funeral sermons, that any regenerate person can properly be praised according to the marks of that condition, without necessary reference to the actual particulars of his or her life. However, Donne is not concerned in the *Anniversary* poems, as the preachers often were and as he himself was in some funeral sermons, with the conventional indicators of the regenerate life, but rather with the metaphysical and symbolic dimensions of Elizabeth Drury's regenerate status—that is, with the "Idea of a Woman" as the image of God. For that symbolic perspective the contemporary funeral sermon also offers some precedent.

As righteous soul—however known to be such—the deceased could be perceived and portrayed in various symbolic ways in the sermons. Most often, he was presented as example, embodiment, or manifestation of the text chosen for the sermon, or of some topics derived from it. In such usage the term "example" does not mean a case history cited to teach a lesson: rather, the dead person is a particular which presents a general and makes it more comprehensible, as when we say in explaining something, "Let me give you an example." In literary terms, the deceased is treated as a particular or part which presents, or embodies, or participates in the universal or the abstraction—that is to say, a symbol. The usual rationale for considering the deceased as a "commentary on the text," that is, as a particular manifestation or symbol of the truth contained in the biblical text, is spelled out in the sermon, *The Desire of the Saints after Immortall Glory*: "Examples have in them an universalitie of Doctrine and instruction, especially the examples of the Saints, because *Praxis Sanctorum*, is *Interpres praeceptorum*, the practice of the Saints, is the best interpretation of the precept."[46] The sermon *The Platforme of Charitie, or the Liberall Mans Guide*, on Galatians 6:10, approaches the deceased in just these terms: "It is for their sakes that survive, that God hath given us these occasions; and for your sakes that are yet living, that I have chosen this Text; where you have the rule and the example concurring together. The life of our deceased Sister, was but a commentarie upon this Text."[47]

One of the most common texts chosen for or alluded to on funeral occasions, and often explicated by reference to the deceased as its commentary or contemporary exemplar, was Isaiah 57:1: "The righteous perisheth, and no man considereth it in his heart: And mercifull men are taken away, and no man understandeth that the righteous is taken away from the evil to come."[48] That the death of princes portends evil is a time-honored concept, given special biblical sanction by the contemporary Protestant view of the Book of Lamentations as a funeral elegy for the righteous King Josiah, whose death inaugurated the catastrophe of the Babylonian Captivity and foreshadowed the final destruction of the city and temple of Jerusalem. It is hardly surprising, therefore, to find the death of Queen Elizabeth, and even more of Prince Henry, cited as illustrations of the Isaiah text. But, in fact, the death of any righteous person could be pre-

[46] *The House of Mourning*, p. 419. The sermon *Lifes Apparition: And Mans Dissolution* (*House of Mourning*, p. 419) approaches the deceased in just these terms: "Wee have a spectacle here before us, that was a reall comment upon this Text; She did understand the Doctrine of it, and was excellent in the practice of it."

[47] *House of Mourning*, p. 792.

[48] Isaiah 57:1, as pronounced in the funeral sermon by William Harrison, *Deaths Advantage Little Regarded . . . at the buriall of Mistris Katherin Brettergh the third of June, 1601* (London, 1602).

sented as referent for this text—as manifesting the continuing degeneration of the world and portending yet worse evils to come, from which the righteous person is delivered. William Harrison chose this text for his funeral sermon for Mistress Katherine Brettargh, wife of William Brettargh, Gentleman (1601), a young woman of modest social prominence, but no special distinction or fame, who died at the age of twenty-two of an ague. After defining righteousness in classic Protestant terms and listing at length the evils of the world from which the righteous are delivered, Harrison insists that the death of any such person may portend extraordinary evils and judgments of God. He makes Katherine the contemporary referent of the text, figuring forth symbolically just what such deaths mean to the world:

> Those which survive the righteous have just cause to feare some present evils, and labour by unfained repentance, if possible, to prevent them. Their death is a plaine prognostication of some evils to come, and should be as a trumpet to awaken others out of the sleepe of sinne. . . . The Lord himselfe doth often make the death of the righteous to be lamented, by sending of extraordinary judgements immediately after their death. . . . A *righteous* woman is *perished*: a *mercifull* woman is *taken away*: let us lay it to our hearts, and consider that *she is taken away from evill*. I am fully perswaded that she is delivered from ordinary evils: and it may be her death hath in her self prevented some extraordinarie judgements which remaine for us that are left behinde. Sin is now so rife and ripe among us, that we may justly feare some strange future evils.[49]

[49] *Ibid.*, pp. 71-77. Richard Stock in his sermon for Lord Harrington (*The Churches Lamentation for the Losse of the GODLY. Delivered . . . at the funerals of . . . John Lord Harington . . . who yeelded to nature the 27 of February, when he wanted two months of 22 yeeres of his age* [London, 1614]) makes the same kind of argument and the same use of the deceased as a contemporary referent for this text. Noting that the apostles made great lamentations for

On the same basis, William Fuller derives from the death of Lady Frances Clifton (1627) grounds for universal fear and grief: "all that but remember that the righteous are taken away from the anger to come, howsoever they have no part in our private losse, may joyne themselves in our publicke feare, knowing that the death of saints trencheth to further danger."[50] Here surely is one frame of reference which helps to substantiate Donne's assertion that Elizabeth Drury's death reveals, even causes, the death of the world.

Another important way of exploiting the symbolic potential of the deceased was in terms of correlative typology, whereby the dead person was equated with, or presented as a contemporary reiteration of, one or more of the great Old Testament or New Testament personages. In funeral sermons for monarchs the practice is not surprising; Queen Elizabeth in life and in death was the Moses, the Deborah,

---

the death of Stephen the first martyr, although by his death "the number of the good was lessened but by one," he advances the following reasons (pp. 12-14):

> First, because by this meanes the Church & the land is exceedingly weakned, and unarmed: for not one of them [the good] but they are in their rank . . . *The Charet of Israel, and the horsemen of the same*: not for their persons, who are men inferiour to many others, not for their pollicie, which are of inferiour reach then many thousands, but for their pietie and praiers: *For the innocent shall deliver the Iland, and it shall be preserved by the purenes of his hands*. . . . The walles of the Citie are the praiers of the saints, or at least they uphold the wals. As at the shoutings of the people, *the walles of Jerico fel downe*, so at the prayers and cries of the godly, the walles of the Church and countrey stand up. . . .
>
> Secondly, because this is a forerunner, and certaine immediate signe and prediction of some fearefull judgement & plague of God at hand ready to breake in upon them. . . . Their taking away, doth then directly presage an evil to come. . . . These, while they are, with-hold and keepe back the plague.

[50] William Fuller, *The Mourning of Mount Libanon: Or, The Temples Teares. A Sermon Preached at Hodsocke, the 20 day of December, 1627, In Commemoration of the Right Honourable and Religious Lady, the Lady Frances Clifton* (London, 1628), p. 37.

the Judith, the Sampson, the David of her people; King
James succeeding her was a Solomon following after David;
and Prince Henry was the young Josias who reformed reli-
gion and was reft from his people young.[51] But this correla-
tive typology was also readily available for any subject of
a funeral sermon: anyone, however insignificant, might re-
iterate in modern times the ancient types and their mean-
ings. Indeed, the presentation of a deceased woman as the
reiteration and compendium of all the holy women of scrip-
ture became a constantly repeated *topos*, whose use can be
exemplified in William Fuller's praise of Lady Frances Clif-
ton: "she was a *Mary* to God, a *Martha* to the world, a *Sara*
to her husband, a *Lois*, an *Eunice* to her children, a *Lydia*
to the Disciples."[52]

---

[51] See, e.g., William Leigh, *Queene Elizabeth, Paraleld in her
Princely Vertues, with David, Joshua, and Hezekia. In three Sermons
as they were preached through severall Queenes Dayes* (London,
1612); Miles Mosse, *Scotlands Welcome. A Sermon Preached at
Needham in the Countie of Suffolk, on Tuesday, April 5, 1603* (Lon-
don, 1603), pp. 57-58; John Hayward, *Gods Universal Right Pro-
claimed. A Sermon Preached at Paules Crosse, the 27 of March, 1603,
being the next Sunday after her Majesties departure* (London, 1603);
Daniel Price, *Sorrow for the Sinnes of the Time* [on the third
Sunday after Prince Henry's death] (Oxford, 1613), p. 21. See chap.
1, pp. 27-28, and chap. 5, pp. 160-161; also chap. 5, note 39.

[52] Fuller, *Mourning of Mount Libanon*, p. 33. Similarly, Launcelot
Langhorne taking his text from Luke 10:42, "Mary hath chosen that
good part, which shall not be taken away from her," for his sermon at
Mary Swaine's funeral (*Mary Sitting at Christs Feet*, p. 15), associ-
ates Mary the sister of Martha with the just deceased Mary: "This
Mary being a chosen and elect vessell of God, sanctified from the
Wombe, by Gods grace did *choose the better part*: not at her *Death*,
but *all the time of her pilgrimage*, shee led an *Angelicall* and *holy
life*." Also Richard Chambers in a sermon entitled *Sarahs Sepulture*
(London, 1620) finds his subject, Lady Dorothy, Countess of North-
umberland, to be a correlative type with Sarah, wife of Abraham:
"This good gracious Lady, one of the daughters of the faithfull, was
for all the world like *Sarah* the mother of the faithful" (p. 20). See
also e.g., *A Christians Victorie; or, Conquest over Deaths Enmitie*,
and *Lifes Apparition: And Mans Dissolution*, in *House of Mourn-
ing*, pp. 280, 495.

But the symbolic dimension which was of chief importance for Donne's *Anniversary* poems was the subject's manifestation (as restored and now glorified image of God) of the order of human perfection and even of God himself. Miles Mosse, preaching on the occasion of Queen Elizabeth's death, emphasized that she was the image of God not so much as monarch but as righteous soul displaying the perfections of Christ: "All are righteous men before God, that love him and keepe his commandments: God accepting their good indeavours in Christ, and imputing unto them for perfection, the perfect *Righteousnesse of Christ. . . .* A good man is the image of God."[53] Perhaps the most striking development of this symbolism is to be found in a sermon entitled *The Carelesse Merchant; or, the wofull losse of the precious soule*, on Matthew 16:26, "What is a man profited, if hee shall gaine the whole world, and lose his soule?" Here the deceased is presented as a specific manifestation of the general truths about the soul's incalculable worth in regard to the realms of nature, grace, and glory. The preacher first expatiates on the image in nature, the original created image:

First of the surpassing excellencie, and dignitie of mans soule: it is valued and prized here above the whole world.

[53] Mosse, *Scotlands Welcome*, pp. 13-14, 39. Similarly, in the dedication of his funeral sermon on Lord Harrington's death (*The Churches Lamentation*, sigs. A 4-A 4ᵛ) Richard Stock proposed Harrington as a glass by which to see and imitate God, by reason of the restored image of God which he bore: "*Be partakers of the godly nature*. Seeing we are the generation of God, made to his image, what greater glory can we have then to preserve that image and be like unto him to whose similitude wee were made, for as one saith, *There is no honour to the imitation of God*: which is then performed when we imitate those who have walked with God." In this vein also Richard Harris (*Samuels Funerall*, p. 10) undertook to portray Anthony Cope's soul as it now is, with the image of God perfectly restored in it: "all the powers and faculties thereof are perfected and advanced above the ordinary straine of nature. . . . [and] the soul is furnished with . . . Christs image, everlasting joy, perpetuall peace, a constant correspondency and communion with God."

It was the plausible conceit of certaine Philosophers, that the world was a great man, and that man was a little world: a little world indeed, but as Saint *Austin* tearmes him, a great wonder: for within this little world, there is a reasonable soule worth all the world. . . . For the Image, the soule is most like God . . . and the Lord himselfe signifies so much, *After our Image let us make man.* Then the soule of man is not stamped with a Roman *Caesar,* but with Gods owne Image and superscription.[54]

He then turns to the image renewed by grace after the Fall:

In the Kingdome of grace, the price of the soule is farre above the dignitie of the world. . . . In the grace of renovation, nothing is able to cleanse it from sinne, but the Spirit of God. The Spirit alone must enlighten the understanding, and rectifie the affections, and purifie the will, and sanctifie the conscience, and seale up the Image of God in righteousnesse, and true holinesse. And the soule thus renewed, is as a Garden inclosed, a spirituall Paradise, where the God of heaven delights to dwell. . . . Seeing it appeares that the universall World is not able to redeeme, or being redeemed, to renew, or renewed to paralell the soule; let grace subscribe to that which nature concludes, that the soule is of greater value then the whole world.[55]

Finally, he extolls the glory of the soul in heaven, the perfected image:

Lastly, for the passage of glory, the contents of the whole Universe are not able to come neere the soule. . . . The world is transitorie like the dew of the morning, it fades as the grasse, and as the flower of the field; whereas on the contrarie, the soule of man is the subject of immortalitie, capable of an exceeding, surpassing, eternall weight of glory. . . . How resplendant shall the soules of the

[54] *The Carelesse Merchant; or, The Wofull Losse of the Precious Soule,* in *House of Mourning,* pp. 438-439.

[55] *Ibid.,* pp. 439-440.

righteous bee, in the beatificall vision of Gods excellencies? How wonderfull shall that divine capacitie be, that shall be capable of God himselfe for a perpetuall residence? Insomuch that the most ancient of dayes shall give fulnesse to the Soule, of knowledge and wisdome, and his sacred Spirit that shall fill it *with the fulnesse of God*.[56]

In these terms any deceased Christian in his highest symbolic function presents the image of human perfection which is at the same time the image of God: in life, as regenerate saint, he manifested the (partly) restored image as originally created in nature and he enjoyed also the added spiritual privileges accruing to the image of God restored by grace in Christ; now in heaven he bears the perfected and glorified image. The particular advantage of the funeral occasion for the development of these symbolic meanings is precisely that the dead person, having attained to heavenly glory, can present the full range of symbolic meanings and implications attendant upon the concept, image of God, in relation to all three orders. Here we approach Donne's stance in his own funeral sermons, as well as his formula for presenting Mistress Elizabeth Drury.

C. JOHN DONNE'S FUNERAL SERMONS

Donne had opportunities in many Lenten and Easter sermons to develop the standard funeral topics of death and resurrection, but he preached only five sermons which have a direct relation to funeral occasions. Of these only the sermon for King James on April 26, 1625, and that for Sir William Cokayne on December 12, 1626, were funeral sermons in the strict sense of being delivered in the presence of the unburied body.[57] Another, for Magdalen Herbert (Lady

[56] *Ibid.*

[57] Donne, *Sermons*, VI, pp. 280-291. *Preached at Denmark house, some few days before the body of King James, was removed from thence, to his buriall, April 26, 1625; Sermons*, VII, pp. 257-278. *Preached at the funerals of Sir William Cokayne Knight, Alderman of London, December 12, 1626.*

Danvers) on July 1, 1627, is technically an anniversary sermon, though for a month's anniversary rather than a year's; other "Pre-obligations" and "Pre-contracts" had prevented Donne from preaching Lady Danvers' funeral sermon, as he had been asked to do.[58] But Donne treats the situation much like a funeral occasion, proposing to consider Lady Danvers not "as thou art a *Saint in Heaven*" but "as thou didst appeare to us a moneth ago."[59] The fourth is a genuine anniversary sermon of uncertain date on an unnamed parishioner some years dead, whom Donne seems not to have known.[60] The sermon preached at St. Dunstan's on January 15, 1626, and subtitled "The First Sermon after Our Dispersion, by the Sickness" can be added to these as a fifth, because Donne himself characterized it as "a general Funeral Sermon, both for *them that are dead in the flesh*, and for our selves, that are *dead in our sins*."[61] The specific reference is to the victims of the epidemic of bubonic plague in 1625, perhaps the worst of all such epidemics in England, except for the great plague of 1665.[62]

There are similarities among these five sermons which are

[58] Donne, *A Sermon of Commemoration of the Lady Danvers, late Wife of Sir John Danvers. Preach'd at Chilsey, where she was lately buried. Sermons*, VIII, 61-63. See also introduction, *Sermons*, VIII, 3.

[59] *Sermons*, VIII, 85.

[60] Donne, *An Anniversary Sermon preached at St. Dunstans, upon the commemoration of a Parishioner, a Benefactor to that Parish, Sermons*, X, 178. See also introduction (*Sermons*, X, 24-26) for the suggestion that this is the first sermon (June 29, 1624) for one Mr. Adams, whose anniversary Donne commemorated four times, according to the St. Dunstan's Churchwardens Accounts.

[61] Donne, *A Sermon Preached at St. Dunstans January 15, 1625* [1625/6]. *Sermons*, VI, 351.

[62] *Sermons*, VI, "Introduction," p. 33. The subtitle refers to the wholesale dispersal of court, parliament, merchants and citizens to the countryside in an effort to escape the sickness. Donne himself described the dispersal in a letter to Thomas Roe, November 25, 1625: "The Citizens fled away, as out of a house on fire, and stuffed their Pockets with their best ware, and threw themselves into the highways, and were not received, so much as into barns, and perished so."

related to the general characteristics discerned in the funeral sermons of Donne's contemporaries. One is their evident adherence to the theory that the funeral sermon should combine meditation, instruction, and praise. Another is the tendency to proceed by dichotomies and contraries, in some fashion contrasting the evils and miseries and moribund state of the natural order with the joys and benefits of the orders of grace and glory. Yet another is the presentation of the dead person(s) as commentary on, or symbolic presentation of, the meaning of the text, and also as image of God manifesting to us the order of human perfection. But the sermons proceed variously in developing these concerns, so that it will be useful to examine them separately, noting how their respective emphases extend and heighten these common Protestant elements, and also highlight different aspects of Donne's method in the *Anniversary* poems.

Though it is the longest, the sermon for Lady Danvers is perhaps the simplest in conception, and the nearest to the conventional funeral exercises performed by Donne's contemporaries. No doubt long friendship with her led Donne to incorporate an extended eulogy (much more personal and specific, indeed, than such notices usually were); his other funeral sermons either omitted or greatly abbreviated such appendages, thereby achieving greater unity and conciseness. In this respect the sermon for Lady Danvers provides documentation for Donne's self-judgment that he "did best when I had least truth [e.g., factual reality] for my subjects."[63]

Stating his conviction that the purposes of the funeral sermon are instruction and commemoration (praise), Donne undertakes to derive both from the same biblical text:

I propose to my selfe, and to this Congregation, two Workes for this day; That wee may walke together two miles, in this Sabbath daies journey; First, *To instruct the*

[63] Letter "To Sir Robert Carr," (1625) accompanying "An hymne to the Saints, and to Marquesse Hamilton," in Grierson, *Poems*, I, 288.

Living, and then *To commemorate the Dead.* . . . Whether I looke up to the *Throne* of *Heaven* and that *Firmament*, for my first worke, *The Instruction of the Living*, or downe to the *stones* of the *Grave*, and that *pavement*, for my second worke, *The commemoration of the Dead*, I need no other words than these which I have read to you, for both purposes.[64]

The words read (the text) were from 2 Peter 3:13, "Neverthelesse, we, according to his promises, looke for new heavens, and new earth, wherein dwelleth righteousnesse," and they provide Donne with two central dichotomies. First, he portrays the godly as they are subjected on the one hand to the scorns and taunts of the worldly and to apprehensions of the terrors of the last day, but on the other hand as they constitute a greatly privileged regenerate society consoled by the evidences of their election and able to contemn the world. His second dichotomy develops the amazing contrast between the conditions of this world and the next in regard to justice and righteousness:

Justice dwels there, and there *dwels Righteousnes*; Of which there is none in this world; None that growes in this world; none that is mine owne. . . . But in this new *state*, these *new Heavens*, and *new Earth*, *Justicia habitat*, This *Righteousnesse* shall dwell; I shall have an *innocence*, and a *constant innocence*; a present *impeccancy*, and an *impeccability* for the future. But, in this especially, is *Righteousnes* said to *dwell* there, because this *Righteousnesse*, is the very *Son of God*, the *Sonne* of *Righteousnesse* himselfe. And, this day, the day of his second Comming, is the last day of his *Progresse*; For, ever after that day, these *new Heavens*, and *new Earth* shall bee his *standing house*, where hee shall *dwell*, and wee with him . . . shall all, not onely *have*, but *be* a part of that *Righteousnes*.[65]

[64] *Sermons*, VIII, 63. [65] *Ibid.*, pp. 84-85.

The eulogy of Lady Danvers contains the conventional *topoi*: she is best wife, best mother, best neighbor, best friend, best example to the world. Her possession of the goods of nature, fortune, and character is duly recorded, but she is praised especially as a regenerate soul whose life and manner of death provide all the typical religious evidences of that condition. Donne adds several personal testimonials as well, from his own experience of her. At the beginning of his eulogy he offers to fuse all this with his scripture text, and to present Lady Danvers as a true "commentary" on it: "Close we here this *Booke of life*, from which we have had our *first text*, And, *Surge quae dormis in pulvere*, Arise thou *Booke of Death*; thou, that sleepest in this *consecrated dust*; and hast beene going into *dust*, now, almost a Moneth of *dayes*. . . . Arise thou, and bee another *Commentary* to us; and tell us, what this *new Heaven*, and *new Earth* is, in which, now, thou *dwel'st*, with *that Righteousnesse*."[66] But then he deliberately turns from that high symbolic realm back to the simply human, and offers to present her as she was a month ago, or "in thy history." In accordance with this shift, he revises his method, proposing at length to reapply "some parts of this *Text* . . . unto thee."[67] Suggestive in relation to the *Anniversaries*, however, is the passage quoted above, which uses the metaphors of "Progress" and "standing house" for the respective states of developing and attained perfection, and which proposes the plan (subsequently revised) of fusing instruction and praise by deriving them from the same text. Moreover, the double perspective on Lady Danvers' death contained in a later passage might almost be a thematic statement for the *Anniversary* poems: "Consider us fallen in *Adam*, and wee are miserable, that wee must die; But consider us restor'd and redintegrated in *Christ*, wee were more miserable if wee might not die; Wee lost the *earthly Paradise* by death then; but wee get not *Heaven*, but by *death*, now."[68]

[66] *Ibid.*, p. 85.   [67] *Ibid.*, pp. 85-86.   [68] *Ibid.*, p. 91.

The sermon after the plague and the anniversary sermon on the unnamed parishioner are alike and are significant here for their method of developing two contrary arguments, two quite distinct and opposed interpretations of our situation, from the same text, by giving that text different grammatical and interpretive emphases. In the sermon after the plague, the plague victims take the place of the dead body in supplying the particular occasion, and Donne proposes them as at once our catechism (instruction) and our topic for meditation. He first links law and example: "He [God] gives us his Law in *Exodus* and *Leviticus* . . . he accompanies, he seconds his Law with examples . . . in the Historical [Books]." We may recall in this connection that Elizabeth Drury was "A strong example gone equall to Law."[69] He then relates instruction and meditation, finding both purveyed to us in the great calamities recorded in scripture, and in the private calamities of our friends' deaths: "God would catechise us in the knowledge of our *mortality*; since we have divested our *immortality*, he would have us understand our *mortality*; since we have induced *death* upon our selves, God would raise such a benefit to us, out of *death*, as that by the continual *meditation* thereof, *death* might the less terrifie us, and the less damnifie us."[70] He presents his sermon as such an instruction-*cum*-meditation on the text from Exodus 12:30, "For there was not a House where there was not one dead."

Donne's first reading of the text develops the case for the ubiquity of death—with literal reference to God's slaughter, through Moses' instrumentality, of the first-born of the Egyptians, and with applicatory references to "deaths" in three other houses. One is our domicile, for there are some spiritually dead in each family. Another is our body, "this House of Clay, and of Mudwalls . . . [which] is ready to fall as soon as it is set up."[71] The last is the church itself and the churchyard, where the plague victims have recently been

[69] *Sermons*, VI, 350-351; *First Anniversarie*, l. 48.
[70] *Sermons*, VI, 354-355.   [71] *Ibid.*, p. 356.

brought in great numbers: "In this house you have seen, and seen in a lamentable abundance, and seen with sad eyes, that for many monehts there hath scarce been one day in which there hath not been one dead."[72] But he then proceeds to develop the opposite case, reinterpreting his text through an emphasis upon the past tense of the verbs. The skill with which this shift is made is worth noting:

> Thus far we have survey'd these four Houses, *Egypt*, our families, our selves, and the Church, as so many places of Infection, so many temporal or spiritual Pesthouses, into which our sins had heaped powder, and Gods indignation had cast a match to kindle it. But now the very phrase of the Text, which is, *That in every house there was one dead, There was*, invites us to a more particular consideration of Gods mercy, in that, howsoever it were, it is not so now; in which we shall look how far this beam of mercy shines out in every of these houses, that it is not so now, There is not one dead in every house now; but the Infection, (Temporal and Spiritual Infection) is so far ceased, as that not only those that are alive, do not die, as before; but those whom we call dead, are not dead; they are alive in their spirits, *in Abrahams bosome*; and they are alive in their very bodies, in their contract and inherence in Christ Jesus in an infallible assurance of a joyfull Resurrection.[73]

Applying the new terms to each of the houses, he finds that all (except for the literal Egyptians) are through Christ capable of life: "though we were dead, dead in our several houses, dead in a sinful *Egypt*, dead in our family, dead in our selves, dead in the Grave, yet we shall be received, with that . . . glorious consolation, you were dead, but are alive."[74]

The anniversary sermon "preached at St. Dunstans, upon the commemoration of a Parishioner, a Benefactor to that

[72] *Ibid.*, p. 357.　　[73] *Ibid.*, p. 358.　　[74] *Ibid.*, p. 364.

Parish," takes as text God's curse on the serpent in Genesis 3:14, "And Dust shalt thou eat all the dayes of thy life." Here the contrasting arguments or interpretations derived from the text are developed concurrently, not consecutively, and the unnamed parishioner by a few casual allusions becomes the exemplar of both meanings. The first interpretation finds him, and us, subjected to the serpent's eating in that we are all dust, having been made of dust:

> And of that part of the Judgement, which was inflicted upon the Serpent, and Satan in him, this dead brother of ours who lyes in this consecrated earth, is an experimentall witnesse, who being by death reduced to the state of dust, for so much of him, as is dust, that is, for his dead body, and then, for so long time, as he is to remaine in that state of dust, is in the portion, and jurisdiction, and possession of the Serpent, that is, in the state which the Serpent hath induced upon man, and dust must he eat all the dayes of his life.[75]

Later, generalizing, Donne observes that the serpent has power over our bodies, and carnal affections, and can feed "upon our living dust, that is, induce sicknesses, and hunger, and labour, and colde, and paine upon our bodies here." Also, "when we are dead dust too, in the grave, he feeds upon us, because it proceeds from him both that we die, and that we are detained in the state of exinanition and ingloriousnesse, in the dust of the earth."[76]

The contrary argument is developed through emphasizing the limitations upon what is given to the serpent: "it is a great degree of mercy to man, that the Serpent must eate but dust, because mans best part is not subject to be served in at his table, the soule cannot become dust, (and dust must he eate all the dayes of his life)."[77] Moreover, insofar as we are not dust but (in Christ) new creatures, regenerate, and ultimately to be glorified, we quite escape subjection to his eating:

[75] Donne, *Sermons*, x, 179.   [76] *Ibid.*, p. 188.   [77] *Ibid.*, p. 179.

I shall make the Serpent see, I am a God; thus far a God, that by my adhering to Christ, I am made partaker of the Divine Nature. . . . Then I may say to the Serpent, Your meat is dust; and I was dust; but *Deposui terram*, I have shak'd off my dust, by true repentance, for I have shak'd off my self, and am a new creature, and am not now meat for your Table. . . . I am a branch of that Vine, (Christ *is the Vine, and we are the branches*) I am a leafe of that *Rose of Sharon*, and of that *Lilly of the valleys*; I am a plant in the *Orchard of Pomegranats*, and that Orchard of Pomegranats is the Church; I am a drop of that *dew*, that *dew* that lay upon the *head* of Christ. And this Vine, and this Rose, and Lilly, and Pomegranats, of Paradise, and this Dew of heaven, are not Dust, *And dust must thou eate all the dayes of thy life.*[78]

These contrary readings are brought together again in regard to the particular parishioner, and both are shown to be appropriate to him: it is simply a matter of the perspective taken: "In this state of dust, and so in the territory of the Serpent, the Tyrant of the dead, lies this dead brother of ours, and hath lien some years, who occasions our meeting now, and yearly upon this day; and whose soul, we doubt not, is in the hands of God, who is the God of the living."[79]

Both these sermons turn upon a double argument and present a dual perspective upon the human condition: the omnipresence of death and corruption on the one hand, and the limitation upon or transcendence of that death and corruption on the other. These dichotomies in themselves, but especially Donne's method of developing these contrary views and arguments from one text by giving that text different interpretive emphases, offer a close parallel to the method of the *Anniversary* poems. From the "text" of Elizabeth Drury's death, seen in different perspectives, two contrary but not contradictory arguments are proposed:

[78] *Ibid.*, pp. 186-187.   [79] *Ibid.*, p. 190.

"Wherein, by occasion of the *untimely* death of Mistris Elizabeth Drury, the frailty and the decay of this whole world is represented"; "Wherein: By occasion of the *religious* death of Mistris Elizabeth Drury, the incommodities of the Soule in this life and her exaltation in the next, are Contemplated."[80]

The sermon preached for Sir William Cockayne, Alderman of London, incorporates most of the elements we have been considering. For one thing, it formally conjoins instruction, meditation, and praise. Indeed, the brief and carefully integrated eulogy affords striking evidence of how irrelevant the subject's personal moral virtue was to Donne's concern, for Alderman Cockayne's disastrous projects and shady financial transactions in relation to the English cloth trade were notorious.[81] But Donne could regard even such a man in symbolic terms as image of God, since that condition depends upon justification by grace, not merit. The element of instruction is indicated as Donne proposes to his auditory two texts, "This Text which you Heare, *Martha's* single words, complicated with this Text which you See, The dead body of this our Brother, makes up between them this body of Instruction for the soule."[82] The meditative term is introduced when, after making his *Divisio*, Donne offers to proceed "to the furnishing of them [the headings proposed], with meditations fit for this Occasion."[83]

From his scripture text—Martha's words to Christ after the death of Lazarus, "Lord, if Thou hadst been here, my Brother had not died" (John 11:21)—Donne develops two dichotomies. On the basis of the weaknesses in faith, hope and charity displayed by Martha's words, the first dichotomy affirms the radical imperfection of all our spiritual

[80] Emphases mine.

[81] See Astrid Friis, *Alderman Cockayne's Project and the Cloth Trade* (London, 1927), pp. 224-381.

[82] Donne, *Sermons*, vii, 259.   [83] *Ibid.*, p. 260.

acts but, nevertheless, their acceptance by God.[84] The second dichotomy asserts that in temporal things there is nothing permanent, but that nevertheless this mortal body will be eternal. The language used in developing this last dichotomy is reminiscent of the imagery of the *Anniversaries*:

> I need not call in new Philosophy, that denies a settlednesse, an acquiescence in the very body of the Earth, but makes the Earth to move in that place, where we thought the Sunne had moved; I need not that helpe, that the Earth it selfe is in Motion, to prove this, That nothing upon Earth is permanent. . . . Nothing needs be done . . . by God, or Destiny; A Monarchy will ruine, as a haire will grow gray, of it selfe. . . . The world is a great Volume, and man the Index of that Booke; Even in the body of man, you may turne to the whole world; This body is an Illustration of all Nature; Gods recapitulation of all that he had said before . . . and yet this body must wither, must decay, must languish, must perish.[85]

The counterproposition is developed in the following terms:

> For all this dissolution, and putrefaction, he affords this Body a Resurrection. . . . We die in the light, in the sight of Gods presence, and we rise in the light, in the sight of his very Essence. . . . And as God shall know no man from his own Sonne, so as not to see the very righteousnesse of his own Sonne upon that man; So the Angels shall know no man from Christ, so as not to desire to looke upon that mans face, because the most deformed wretch that is there, shall have the very beauty of Christ himselfe. . . . And everything that we can call good, shall first be infinitely exalted in the goodnesse, and then infinitely multiplied in the proportion, and againe infinitely extended in the duration.[86]

[84] *Ibid.*, pp. 259-269.   [85] *Ibid.*, pp. 271-272.
[86] *Ibid.*, pp. 272-273.

The praises of Cockayne are integrated with this sermon-meditation by means of a slight recasting of the text which permits a further dichotomy. As the text in its original formulation led to a mortified sense of the miseries of the human condition (but yet their remedies) so the new phrasing affords consolation through assurance of life through Christ: "we dismisse you with Consolation, by a[n] . . . occasionall inverting the Text, from passion in *Martha's* mouth, *Lord, if thou hadst been here, my Brother had not dyed*, to joy in ours, *Lord, because thou wast here, our Brother is not dead*."[87] The praise then is deftly transformed from a series of biographical details into an indication that "The Lord was with him in all these steps."[88] In this way Cockayne is made a true symbol, a manifestation of the reformulated text: "Even hee, whom we call dead, is alive this day. In the presence of God, we lay him downe; In the power of God, he shall rise; In the person of Christ, he is risen already."[89]

The points of contact with the *Anniversaries* are the explicit presentation of the exercise as a mixed genre incorporating instruction, meditation, and praise; the development of the several dichotomies; and especially the presentation of Cockayne as a counterweight to the human defects highlighted in the biblical text. The auditory would have known that, in personal terms, Cockayne's defects were far more serious than Martha's, yet his special privilege as regenerate soul justified by Christ permits him to be an exemplar of the loftiest perfections enjoyed by the regenerate. If such terms as these are available for a man like Cockayne, their application to Elizabeth Drury scarcely presents a problem.

The sermon preached before the body of King James is especially relevant to the method of the *Anniversaries* for its fusion of instruction and meditation, and for the way in which it develops the symbolism of James as image of God.

[87] *Ibid.*, p. 273.   [88] *Ibid.*   [89] *Ibid.*, p. 278.

The text is from Canticles 3:11, "Goe forth ye Daughters of Sion, and behold King Solomon, with the crown, wherewith his mother crowned him, in the day of his espousals, and in the day of the gladnesse of his heart." Donne identifies the speaker in the text as the Church, the auditory as her faithful children, and Solomon as Christ, but then he finds the text's meaning manifested also in himself, this auditory, and the dead king. The usual Donnean dichotomies of argument are not in evidence here: there is only one paradox, briefly developed, which identifies the "crown" of the text as Christ's humiliation and suffering, and then points out that this same crown is a token of his glad espousals to the church and his exaltation to glory. At the center of the sermon is its interpretation of the words "Goe forth" as a dictate to us to meditate upon our death and what is beyond it. Directing and demonstrating such meditation, the sermon displays the two glasses in which we are to see ourselves—Christ, and James:

Walke in thine own *ashes*, in the meditation of thine own death, or in the *ashes of Gods Saints*, who are dead before thee ... *Goe forth*, that is, *goe farther then thy selfe*, out of thy selfe.... Get beyond thine own circle; consider thy selfe at thine end, at thy death, and then *Egredere*, Goe further then that, *Go forth and see* what thou shalt be after thy death.

Still that which we are to look upon, is especially *our selves*, but it is *our selves*, enlarg'd and extended into the *next world*; for till we see, what we shall be then, we are but *short-sighted*.... All this life is but a *Preface*, or but an *Index* and *Repertory* to the book of *life*; There, at that book beginnes thy study ... to goe *forth*, and see thy self, beyond thy self, to see what thou shalt be in the next world. Now, we cannot see our own face, without a glasse: ... Here, at your coming hither now, you have *two glasses*, wherein you may see your selves from head to foot; One in the Text, your *Head, Christ Jesus*, represented unto you, in the name and person of *Solomon, Behold King Solomon crowned, &c.* And another, under your feet, in the dissolution of this great *Monarch*, our *Royall Master*, now layd lower by death then any of us, his Subjects and servants.[90]

The Protestant exegetical habits of applying scripture to the self, and of shifting the focus from Christ as antitype to the Christian who shares that role with him are here evident: the auditor is both subject and object of this sermon-meditation, and the recommended meditations upon the first glass, Christ, focus primarily upon how "we" will be brought from passion to glory.

In proposing James to us as the second glass, Donne does not explore the contemporary typological identification of James with King Solomon, though he evidently expects it to help establish the aptness of his text.[91] Rather, Donne proposes James as a glass for our meditation and as a referent for the text in hand because he is the image of God— not in the special sense in which a monarch images God's power and authority, but precisely as any regenerate saint now in heaven is a glorious image of God and of what we shall be:

> The hand of God, hath *not set up*, but *laid down another Glasse*, wherein thou maist see thy self; a glasse that reflects thy self, and nothing but thy selfe. Christ, who was the other glasse, *is like thee in every thing* but not absolutely, for *sinne* is *excepted*; but in this glasse presented now (*The Body of our Royall*, but *dead Master and Soveraigne*) we cannot, we doe not except sinne. ... Those therefore that are like thee in all things, subject to humane *infirmities*, subject to *sinnes*, and yet are trans-

[90] Donne, *Sermons*, VI, 285-286.

[91] See, e.g., John [Williams, Lord Bishop of Lincoln, Lord Keeper of the Great Seal], *Great Britains Solomon. A Sermon Preached at the Magnificent Funerall, of the most high and mighty King, James* (London, 1625).

lated, and *translated* by *Death*, to everlasting *Joy*, and *Glory*, are nearest and clearest glasses for thee, to see thy self in; and such is this glasse, which God hath proposed to thee, in this house. . . . Looke upon him as a beame of that Sunne, as an abridgement of that *Solomon* in the Text; for every Christian truely reconciled to God, and *signed* with his hand in the *Absolution*, and *sealed* with his bloud in the *Sacrament*, (and this was his case) is a beame, and an abridgement of *Christ* himselfe.[92]

This directive as to how we are to meditate upon any dead Christian—as an abridgment of Christ and as the means to see what we shall be—sheds light upon the *Logos* allusions often noted in the *Anniversary* poems, and also upon the speaker's relation to Elizabeth Drury in those poems. Her progress to her standing house foreshadows his own, and he projects for himself the stages of that progress in the *Second Anniversarie*. The speaker in the *Anniversary* poems takes Elizabeth Drury as a "glass" and invites "us" to do so also, using the method Donne in this sermon demonstrates for his auditory in relation to their dead King.

Donne's remarkable funeral sermons draw together the various Protestant trends we have noted in regard to meditation, preaching, and focus upon the symbolic dimensions of the individual life. Characteristically, Donne also extends and exploits as only a master poet could the rich potential for paradox, psychological analysis, and symbolism inherent in these Protestant developments. In so doing he produced a group of funeral sermons which, despite the difference in genre from the *Anniversary* poems, yet provide important and illuminating analogues to them in regard to conception, structure, stance of the speaker, and exploration of the symbolic meaning of the deceased.

[92] Donne, *Sermons*, VI, 289-290.

PART III

THE SYMBOLIC MODE OF DONNE'S
ANNIVERSARIES

CHAPTER VII

The First Anniversarie

THE TRENDS we have been examining in the poetry of
praise and in Protestant meditation, doctrine, herme-
neutics, and funeral sermons—trends which Donne himself
in various ways furthered and redefined—are brought to-
gether in the *Anniversary* poems, in a highly complex and
sophisticated way. Accordingly, we may now examine how
these and some other literary and intellectual traditions il-
luminate those remarkable poems. My reading of the *Anni-
versaries* focuses primarily upon the theological ideas and
generic forms which give substance and structure to the
central metaphysical argument of the poems, and this focus
has led inevitably to some scanting of the witty pyrotech-
nics and tonal complexities which so greatly enrich their
texture. The rationale for this emphasis is simply that the
logical coherence and consistency of the poems' central ar-
gument has gone virtually unrecognized, though it is in fact
the basis for all their gyrations of wit and astounding flights
of fancy.

At this point the question whether the *Anniversary* poems
succeed as literary works must be raised directly, for poems
cannot be simply equated with their conceptual framework.
These poems may continue in some degree to repel or an-
tagonize us as readers by reason of Donne's hyperbolic in-
sistence upon the uniqueness of Elizabeth Drury, even
though we recognize that we are to take Elizabeth as image
of God. Of course we know that she is not the only or even
the most excellent image of God that might be celebrated,
despite the fact that Donne's speaker, framing his remarks
in terms of a particular occasion, vehemently asserts that
she is precisely that. Donne indeed exploits for literary ef-
fect the slight shock and tension which even the informed

reader must experience in being told insistently, on the one hand, that Elizabeth Drury's perfections are unique, and being expected to remember, on the other, that what is said of her applies to any regenerate soul. Yet I submit that, far from destroying the poems, this tension will be found to be a source of their special power once we have understood enough of the assumptions involved to recognize that the apparent contradiction is in fact a true paradox—witty, not fully explicable, but in no sense absurd. I suggest further that Donne makes this delicate maneuver work by restricting the frame of reference of the poem to the realm of metaphysics: Elizabeth, we will discover, is seldom presented to us as model or pattern for our imitation, but rather (in typical Donnean fashion) as a glass by which we can see something—in this case, the nature and potential of man as image of God.

A. "A Funerall Elegie" and Hall's "Praise"

Evidently by November, 1611—precisely when is not known since the book was not entered in the Stationers Register—John Donne published *An Anatomy of the World*;[1] in 1612 the poem was given the added title, *The First Anniversarie*. It is preceded in the 1611 volume by a short poem, presumably by Joseph Hall,[2] entitled "To the Praise of the Dead, and the *Anatomy*," and it is followed by another poem by Donne about Elizabeth Drury called "A Funerall Elegie." This placement of the "Funerall Elegie"—which is retained in the 1612 edition of the *Anniversary*

---

[1] For dating see R. C. Bald, *Donne and the Drurys* (Cambridge, 1959), pp. 68-103.

[2] The attribution to Hall is based upon Ben Jonson's statement to Dummond of Hawthornden that Hall was "the Herbenger to Dones Anniversarie." The reference is to the lines headed "The Harbinger to the Progres" prefixed to the *Second Anniversarie*, but the two prefatory poems are so similar in style and purpose that critics uniformly attribute them to the same author. See "Conversations with Drummond of Hawthornden," in *Ben Jonson*, ed. Herford and Simpson, I, 149.

poems so that it comes between the first and second *Anniversaries*—is also retained in Frank Manley's important modern edition of these poems. Challenging the general assumption that "A Funerall Elegie" was written first, Manley argues that the placement in the editions indicates the order of composition, or at least the intended reading order, and that the "Funerall Elegie" derives its meaning from the symbolic processes developed in the *Anatomy*.[3] However, the weight of internal and external evidence, most recently reviewed by R. C. Bald, appears to support the traditional view of the evolution and relationship of the poems.[4]

That traditional theory holds that "A Funerall Elegie" was written shortly after the death of Elizabeth Drury in December, 1610, and was presented by Donne to the girl's still grief-stricken parents.[5] Bald suggests that the idea for expanding some of the themes of this poem must have occurred to Donne shortly thereafter, since *The First Anniversarie* was ready for print or actually in print before he left England with Sir Robert Drury in November, 1611. Moreover, from the text of *The Second Anniversarie* (ll. 3-6), and from the fact that the poem was published in London together with the second edition of the *Anatomy* in time for criticism of both poems to reach Donne in France by April, 1612, Bald concludes that *The Second Anniversarie* was probably begun in December, 1611—perhaps on the very anniversary of Elizabeth's death, as Donne's second year's "true Rent" paid in advance.[6]

This relationship among the three poems is also indicated in the titles, which carry conventional generic significations. A funeral elegy is properly a poem composed on the occasion of a funeral (sung before or presented to the unburied body), and an anniversary is a poem or a sermon commemorating some periodic anniversary of a death. Furthermore,

[3] See Frank Manley, *The Anniversaries*, "Introduction," pp. 1-4.

[4] See R. C. Bald, *John Donne: A Life* (New York and Oxford, 1970), pp. 240-252.

[5] *Ibid.*, pp. 240-241.

[6] Bald, *Donne and the Drurys*, pp. 87-93.

the subsidiary status of "A Funerall Elegie" is reinforced by the typography of both the 1611 and 1612 editions, which use the same type face for this poem and the prefatory poem(s), distinguishing all of the shorter works from the more significant *Anniversary* poem(s). The placement of the "Funerall Elegie" after *The First Anniversarie* in the 1611 edition may well have been intended to designate this subsidiary status, and the retention of this order in 1612 (when Donne was abroad) is likely to have been simply a matter of the printer's following the previous convention. Also, Bald's conclusion that the two *Anniversary* poems were composed within a few months of each other supports the argument I am proposing here regarding their structural unity as parallel poems.

Internal evidence also reinforces this order of development. The "Funerall Elegie" uses, as the *Anniversary* poems do not, the conventions of Petrarchan hyperbole and of panegyric celebrations of the ideal through a particular example.[7] The focus is upon the girl herself, seen in terms of these conventions. Her value is above that of the marble which entombs her, or the verse which would elegize her: she herself is precious jewels, a tabernacle, and the poet conventionally wonders how his elegy can house her and bring her fame: "Can these memorials, ragges of paper, give/ Life to that name, by which name they must live?" (ll. 11-12). He says that her death wounded the world which will not long endure: this is the germ of the *Anatomie*, but here the conception is much more modest. In the *Anatomie* "she" is the sole source of value in the world, but in the "Elegie" she is merely *one* source of the world's good:

> But those fine spirits, which doe tune and set
> This Organ, are those peeces which beget
> Wonder and love; And these were shee, and shee
> Being spent, the world must needes decrepit bee.
> (ll. 27-30)

---

[7] See above, chap. 1.

She is one of those "peeces" who do the office for the world which the "fine spirits" do for the body, that is, tuning and setting the whole; they do this by producing wonder and love. As those qualities were her essence, her death left the world decrepit by exhausting her large stock of those qualities. The subsequent proposition, that death "can finde nothing, after her, to kill,/ Except the world it selfe, so great as shee" (ll. 32-33) is a Petrarchan hyperbole very different from superficially similar statements in the *Anatomy*, in which she is always described as greater than the world and as the source of its value. Here the world is as great as—or greater than—she: the "Elegie" simply utilizes as a vehicle of praise the commonplace equivalence of macrocosm and microcosm whereby a virtuous man is a world and worth a world. In subsequent lines the world is presented as agent bestowing all its "force and vigor" upon her when it felt the last fire approaching (this last fire being anticipated *before* her death, ll. 55-58), whereas in the *Anatomy* it is she who gave life to the world and her death which caused its final demise.

In the rest of the poem the praise is even closer to conventional Petrarchanism. Elizabeth is praised for her near noncorporeality resulting from her extreme youth, thus far spared the encroachments of adult grossness: her "cleare body was so pure, and thin" that it seemed a mere "exhalation breath'd out from her soule" (ll. 59-62). But her mere humanity is evident from the statement that she was admired by all men and desired by those who "had worth enough" (ll. 63-64); no such statement is possible about the symbol she becomes in *The First Anniversarie*. She is praised for leaving the world with her "Virgin white integrity" intact: since she died just after attaining "yeares of Reasons use," she presumably retained her baptismal innocence, and she had not yet surrendered her virginal integrity in marriage, which "though it doe not staine, doth dye" (ll. 75-76, 91-92). She is praised for virtues specifically appropriate to her state as young virgin—"How faire and chast, humble and high shee'ad beene" (l. 85)—and these characteristics by their very specificity are limiting. Indeed, the poem explicitly admits the narrow scope of her actions and life, "Shee did no more but die" (l. 97); the effect of the admission is not obliterated by the presentation of death as her conscious heroic choice to escape the infirmities of adult womanhood and of the world through yielding too long to an ecstasy, and as the effect of a modesty which would not permit her to be "Fellow-Commissioner with des-tinee" (l. 96) in working out her own life. Ultimately she is presented as an ideal whose example will inspire others to virtuous deeds that will "accomplish that which should have beene her fate" (l. 100)—another recognition of her personal lack of accomplishment despite her great promise and great worth.

These conventional Petrarchan and panegyric praises are obviously a far cry from the theologically based symbolism of the *Anniversaries*, yet the "Funerall Elegie" contains the seeds of that subsequent development. The bases upon which Donne could locate in Elizabeth Drury the symbolic meanings she incarnates in these later poems are suggested here: her extreme youth, her "Virgin white integrity" which is an emblem of baptismal innocence, her reputation for goodness and virtue, and the assumption of her regenerate status conveyed in the expectation that the grave will yield her "greater, purer, firmer, then before" (l. 46). When Donne conceived the idea of a longer poem or poems deriv-ing from the occasion of Elizabeth Drury's death, he must have seen immediately that Petrarchan hyperbolic exag-geration of her personal qualities and situation would not suffice. But Donne, who could find in any good Christian the (restored) image of God and the recapitulation of God's three books, could readily enough find in these quali-ties a basis for viewing this young girl as a symbol of human perfection, and her death as revelatory of the human condition.

Hall's rather conventional prefatory poem, "To the Praise of the Dead, and the *Anatomy*," affords certain insights into

The First Anniversarie, such as the fact that the poem's elaborate praises are grounded upon Elizabeth's manifestation of the Divine image. Also, by directing its praises to the poet (who praised Elizabeth and through her the God whom she praises directly) the dedicatory poem suggests something of the way in which Donne's speaker stands between "us" and the subject, mediating it to us:

> Enough is us to praise them that praise thee,
>
> . . . .
> So these high songs that to thee suited bine,
> Serve but to sound thy makers praise, in thine,
> Which thy deare soule as sweetly sings to him
> Amid the Quire of Saints and Seraphim,
> As any Angels tongue can sing of thee.
>
> (ll. 21, 35-39)

Through the song of the lesser angel (Donne's speaker) we come to apprehend something of the song of the higher seraphim (Elizabeth) and the object of her praise, God. Finally, however, Hall's terms do not prove very useful, for they accommodate Donne's symbolic method more closely than seems warranted to the Petrarchan or Neoplatonic stance.

B. *An Anatomy of the World*

In *The First Anniversarie* the long introductory section (ll. 1-90) and the conclusion (ll. 434-474) together constitute a frame which sets forth the terms necessary for reading that poem, terms which may be elucidated by reference to the literary and theological traditions we have been exploring and to some others. Our attention is first directed to the speaker, and to the genre of the poem he voices, by the fact that the lengthy title and subtitle of the poem seem to point in various generic directions at once: *An Anatomy of the World. Wherein, By Occasion of the untimely death of Mistris Elizabeth Drury the frailty and the*

225

decay of this whole world is represented. Then the speaker introduces himself as the celebrator of Elizabeth. In regard to her his work is a public song of praise, and the praise he accords to that "rich soule" itself testifies to the speaker's spiritual awareness: "For who is sure he hath a soule, un-lesse/ It see, and Judge, and follow worthinesse,/ And by Deedes praise it?" (ll. 2-5). In regard to the world, the speaker is a public teacher, a preacher upbraiding the world for its failure to comprehend its loss: "So thou, sicke world, mistak'st thy selfe to bee/ Well, when alas, thou'rt in a Letargee" (ll. 23-24). And again, "Thou hast lost thy sense and memory" (l. 28). And yet again, "Thou hast for-got thy name, thou hadst" (l. 31).

At length, despairing of the sick world, the speaker iden-tifies himself as a specific kind of public teacher, an anato-mist.[8] That stance proved to be a popular one for late six-teenth- and early seventeenth-century writers of tracts, poems, sermons, and romances, and the term "anatomy" took on, accordingly, several generic and metaphorical sig-nificances. Donne's speaker is an anatomist first of all in the general rhetorical sense of the term—one who undertakes to analyze a subject methodically, rigorously, point by point. This is the stance and method employed in several contem-porary analogues on subjects thematically related to the concerns of Donne's poems, such as *A Lively Anatomie of Death* (1596), *The Anathomie of Sinne* (1603), *The Anat-*

[8] Ralph Maud ("Donne's *First Anniversary*," *Boston University Studies in English*, 2 [1956], 218-225) has challenged Louis Martz's objections to the poem in part by emphasizing the fact that it is to be read as an anatomy rather than as a meditation. However, his very general discussion of the anatomy genre as "a demonstration of parts" does less than justice to the several generic forms and metaphoric meanings Donne imports into his poem through this designation. Rosalie Colie's discussion of Donne's use of the "Anatomy" genre emphasizes Donne's witty extension and literalizing of the common *topos* of the decay and deterioration of man and the world, "All in Peeces," pp. 200-203.

omie of a Christian Man (1613), *Times Anotomie* (1606).[9]
These works, and many others such as *The Anatomie
of Ananias* (1616), *The Anatomie of Sorcerie* (1613), *A
New Anatomie* [*of*] . . . *The Body of Man* (1605) are re-
plete with definitions, divisions, and subdivisions precisely
and methodically set forth, a type of structure which re-
ceives an unforgettable *reductio ad absurdum* formulation
in Robert Burton's lengthy title:

> *The Anatomy of Melancholy, What it is. With all the
> Kindes, Causes, Symptomes, Prognostickes, and Severall
> Cures of it. In Three Maine Partitions, with their severall
> Sections, Members, and Subsections. Philosophically, Me-
> dicinally, Historically, opened and cut up.*[10]

[9] John More, *A Lively Anatomie of Death: wherein you may see
from whence it came, what it is by nature, and what by Christ* (Lon-
don, 1596); [Anon.], *The Anathomie of Sinne, Briefly discovering the
braunches thereof, with a short method how to detest and avoid it*
(London, 1603); William Cowper, *The Anatomie of a Christian Man.
Wherin is plainly shewed out of the Word of God, what manner
of man a true Christian is in all his conversation, both inward and
outward,* 2nd ed. (London, 1613); [Robert Pricket], *Times Anot-
omie: Containing: The poore mans plaint, Brittons trouble, and her
triumph* (London, 1606).

[10] Burton (Oxford, 1621). Cf. Roger Gostwyke, *The Anatomie of
Ananias: Or, Gods Censure against Sacriledge* (Cambridge, 1616);
John Mason, *The Anatomie of Sorcerie. Wherein the Wicked
Impietie of Charmers, Inchanters, and such like, is discovered and
confuted* (London, 1612); Robert Underwood, *A New Anatomy:
Wherein the Body of Man is very fit and aptly (two wayes) com-
pared: 1. To a Household. 2. To a Cittie.* (London, 1605). See also,
in somewhat similar vein, [Thomas Bell], *The Anatomie of Popish
Tyrannie* (London, 1603); and [Anon.], *A Myrrour for English
Souldiers: Or, An Anatomy of an Accomplished man at Armes*
(London, 1595). In the romance mode are John Lyly, *Euphues. The
Anatomy of Wit* (London [1590]), and Robert Greene, *Arbasto:
The Anatomie of Fortune* (London, 1594), both of which develop
the conceit of the anatomy as a schematic and elaborately detailed
picture or drawing.

Given this conventional expectation for the genre of the anatomy, the somewhat rigid and schematic organization of *The First Anniversarie*, to which Louis Martz objects,[11] is wholly appropriate. For one thing, Donne sets forth numerous definitions and distinctions—of the world(s) addressed, of the various evils and miseries of mankind, of the qualities and powers pertaining to the lady. For another, the structure of the poem is a four-part argument, with introduction and conclusion, and each of the four sections contains three subsections—a complaint or denunciation of evils, a eulogy, and a *contemptus mundi* moral. It will be evident, however, that Donne takes care to provide aesthetic variation within his schematic structure. Also, as it happens, some of the contemporary analytic anatomies afford interesting analogues to the companion-poem form of the two *Anniversaries. The Lively Anatomie of Death* (whose subtitle promises an analysis of what death "is by Nature, and what by Christ") is suggestive thematically and structurally for the contrary perspectives on death developed in the two *Anniversary* poems. A similar structural parallel occurs in the pairing of *The Anathomie of Sinne* with a companion tract, *The Geneologie of Virtue*, and in the two-book organization of Thomas Rogers' *Anatomie of the Minde*, the first of which "is of Perturbations, and discourseth of that part of the minde of man which is voide of reason," and the latter "of Morall vertues (so called because it is of that parte of the minde, which is endued with reason)."[12]

In addition to the methodical, analytic character appropriate to the rhetorical anatomy, some of the sixteenth- and seventeenth-century anatomies incorporate a satiric, wryly ironic, denunciatory, or complaining tone which links them generically with satire. With specific reference to Burton's

[11] See *Poetry of Meditation*, p. 233.
[12] "The Geneologie of Virtue" does not have a separate title page. Thomas Rogers, *A Philosophicall Discourse, entituled, The Anatomie of the Minde* (London, 1576).

Anatomy and to Donne's, Northrop Frye associates the anatomy with Menippean satire, a stylized, encyclopaedic form which satirizes ideas and mental attitudes rather than individuals and which "presents us with a vision of the world in terms of a single intellectual pattern."[13] This group of anatomies seems to resemble most closely that mode of satire known as complaint, which John Peter characterizes as conceptual, impersonal, concerned with mankind generally rather than with particular men, and engaged with themes of the Fall, the moral and physical vileness of man and the world, and the *contemptus mundi*.[14] *The Anatomie of Abuses* (1595) is designed after such a model: it deplores mankind's and particularly England's evils and follies, as they originate in the Fall of Adam and as they are displayed through the several branches of the seven deadly sins and the Commandments. So also is the *Anatomie of Humors* (1609), which deprecates the defects and declinations in all strata of society in relation to the ideals appropriate to each social class or calling.[15] A wryly ironical view of the full range of human follies is afforded by the "Satyricall Preface" and the digressions of Democritus Junior in Burton's *Anatomy* (1621).

The most interesting contemporary analogue for Donne's *Anatomy* in the complaint mode is Robert Pricket's long poem in heroic couplets entitled *Times Anotomie: Contain-*

---

[13] Frye, *Anatomy of Criticism*, pp. 298, 309-312.

[14] John Peter, *Complaint and Satire in Early English Literature* (Oxford, 1956), pp. 9-13, 60-103.

[15] [Philip Stubbs], *The Anatomie of Abuses. Containing a Description of such notable Vices and enormities, as raigne in many Countries of the world, but especially in this Realme of England* (London, 1595); Simion Grahame, *The Anatomie of Humors* (Edinburgh, 1609). For a more sharply satiric note, see John Andrews, *The Anatomie of Basenesse. Or the Four Quarters of a Knave: Flatterie, Ingratitude, Envie, Detraction* (London, 1615), and John Oberndorff, *The Anatomyes of the True Physition and Counterfeit Mounte-banke, wherein both of them are graphically described, and set out in their Right, and Orient Colours.* Trans. F. H. (London, 1602).

ing the poore mans plaint (1606). The speaker of the plaint
is conceived as a poor, honest soldier roundly denouncing
his age's abuses: "In this little worke, which I have called,
Times Anotomie . . . I doe with a religious anger chide, the
violent, and presumptious rage of unrul'd abuses, because
I grieve to see those grosse impieties which our time com-
mits; briefly therefore, I have Anotomis'd those evills which
do afflict the world."[16] Like Donne's speaker, he dis-
tinguishes three separate audiences for his plaint, the poor-
er sort like himself who are to be led to repentance and
given consolation, the "idle vaine misgoverned dissolutes
who do seeme as if they scornde both heaven and hell"; and
the "least and almost unseene number" of the righteous.[17]
Like Donne's speaker also, the poor soldier expatiates on all
mankind's moral ills, stemming from Adam's sin:

> This rotten world, doth painted garments weare,
> Leaves without fruite, professions name doth beare.
> Blest charity, divine religions grace,
> Now stearv'd to death, hath but a pictures place.
> Celestiall *Love*, the goulden chaine of piety,
> Is turn'd to lust, and cloth'd in sinnes variety.
> Friendships best shew, deceipt and fraud doth cloake,
> dissembling friends, are wrapt in flatteries smoake.
>
> . . . .
>
> What *Adam* lost, all humaine race did lose,
> And what he kept, that for our part we chose,
> Will, to doe good, that force in *Adam* died,
> Since when, that grace was to his seed denied.
> So in our selves, sinne every action staines,
> That to doe good, in us no power remaines.[18]

He also finds evidence of general dislocations in the uni-
verse, portending the relentless spread of corruption and
death, and the imminence of God's judgment:

[16] *Times Anotomie*, sig. A.   [17] *Ibid.*, sigs. A 2-A 3.
[18] *Ibid.*, sigs. B 1ᵛ, B 4.

Peace smiles on us, but view heavens motion well,
Combustious times doth *Sunne* and *Moone* foretell.
This yeares *Eclipse*, a fatall period maketh,
And God thereby all earths foundation shaketh.
The *Planets* in their aspects differ farre,
From former time by course *irregular*.
The *Crab*, and *Goate*, whose *Circles* doe devide,
The sweating Summer, from frostie Winters tide.
Keepe still the times, of auncient nomination,
But want the force, of wonted operation,
Ver, Eastus, Autumne, Hymen, all growne strange,
Seeme as they would, their seasons each exchange.
Celestiall *fyers*, that round this world impale,
And should from hence, corruptions dregs *exhale*.
Leaves them beneath, that noysome pestilence,
On earth, might fetch, materiall cause from thence.

. . . .

Corruption grosse, thick, fatte sad, slimie, slowe,
Shall by the Sunne, to a combustion growe.[19]

In striking contrast to Pricket's pedestrian piece and the
other complaint-satires, the satiric element in Donne's *Anatomy*
is produced by a highly sophisticated complex of tones
and devices. The speaker can lament in doleful phrases the
miseries and paradoxes of the human predicament: "This
man, so great, that all that is, is his,/ Oh what a trifle, and
poore thing he is!" (ll. 169-170); "For the worlds subtilst
immateriall parts/ Feele this consuming wound, and ages
darts" (ll. 247-248). Within a few lines, he can modulate
from shock and dismay over the physical disintegration of
the cosmos to sharp denunciation of human solipsistic
pride:

And freely men confesse, that this world's spent,
When in the Planets, and the Firmament
They seeke so many new; they see that this
Is crumbled out againe to his Atomis.

[19] *Ibid.*, sigs. C 3-C 3ᵛ.

'Tis all in pieces, all cohærence gone;
All just supply, and all Relation:
Prince, Subject, Father, Sonne, are things forgot,
For every man alone thinkes he hath got
To be a Phoenix, and that there can bee
None of that kinde, of which he is, but hee.

(ll. 209-218)

He can also observe with wry amusement the cosmic jokes
perpetrated upon us all, and our own active cooperation in
bringing them off:

How witty's ruine? how importunate
Upon mankinde? It labour'd to frustrate
Even Gods purpose; and made woman, sent
For mans reliefe, cause of his languishment.
They were to good ends, and they are so still,
But accessory, and principall in ill.
For that first mariage was our funerall:
One woman at one blow, then kill'd us all,
And singly, one by one, they kill us now.
We do delightfully our selves allow
To that consumption; and profusely blinde,
We kill our selves, to propagate our kinde.

(ll. 99-110)

The contemporary writers of anatomies were not un-
aware of the satiric possibilities inherent in the role of the
medical anatomist, though they invoked it chiefly as occa-
sional reference or metaphor rather than as a sustained
stance with its own generic associations. John Lyly charac-
terized himself playfully as an anatomist in explaining how
thoroughly he has dissected Euphues' wit: "The Surgion
that maketh the Anatomie, sheweth as well the muscles in
the heele, as the vaines of the hart. If then the first sight
of Euphues shall seem too light to bee read of the wise . . .
they ought not to impute it to the iniquitie of the Authour,

but to the necessity of the History."[20] Robert Burton also alluded casually to the way in which Melancholy under his hand would be "medicinally . . . opened and cut up."[21] Similarly, the frontispiece to William Cowper's *The Anatomy of a Christian Man* fuses for the moment the idea of medical and rhetorical dissecting by presenting a detailed drawing of the human body with various scriptural precepts pertaining to the various parts and aspects of man written on the appropriate anatomical parts.[22] When the medical aspect of the anatomy figure is taken seriously, as in Robert Pricket's poem, the metaphor is not normally pursued in its own grisly terms, but is transmuted into the image of the surgeon probing corrupt flesh in order to heal it:

> *Corsive* useth not to be applied unto the flesh that's sound, and where it hath no power to touch, it procures no smart. . . . But . . . if then it be their chance to light uppon an ill compounded outside closd up ulcer, whose unseene hollownesse in it selfe containes, the poyson of some grosse corruptions *Core*, there let them sinke, and worke, and purge, and by the rootes pluck up that which plucks downe the race of man.[23]

Simion Grahame also explained his exercise as painful but curative surgery for morbid corruption: "I have searched thy feastred wounds, I have bared thy ulcered sores, and for feare of putrifying cankers I have tainted thee to the very quick: so to keepe thy weaknes in a good temper, I have applied this *Cataplasme*, to appease thee of all thy paines."[24] Similarly, Henry Hutton in his verse satires con-

---

[20] Lyly, *Euphues*, sig. A 2.

[21] Burton, *Anatomy of Melancholy*, title page.

[22] Cowper, *Anatomy of a Christian Man*, frontispiece. Many who, like Cowper, use the medical figure evoke rather the idea of the anatomist's detailed drawing of the human body than of his actual dissecting of it.

[23] Pricket, *Times Anotomie*, sig. A.

[24] Grahame, *Anatomie of Humors*, sigs. A 3-A 4.

sidered but rejected the idea of conducting a surgical anat-
omy of the glutton:

> Ile therefore leave him in his pan-warm'd bed,
> Resting on's pillow his distempr'd head.
> Wer't not for censures, I should make him prance
> Skip at the Satyr's lash, leade him a dance,
> Unrip his bowels, and Anatomize
> His filthy intrailes, which he doth much prize.[25]

Donne, of course, does not hedge on this matter, but ex-
plicitly defines his anatomist as surgical dissecter as well as
rhetorical analyst and satirist. His speaker proposes himself
at the outset as the teacher of an anatomy lesson with the
dead world as corpse: "I (since no man can make thee live)
will trie,/ What we may gaine by thy Anatomy" (ll. 59-60).
The identification is reinforced periodically throughout the
poem, and at its conclusion the speaker again reminds us
that he has been engaged in dissecting a cadaver, and re-
vealing its defects and diseases:

> But as in cutting up a man that's dead,
> The body will not last out to have read
> On every part, and therefore men direct
> Their speech to parts, that are of most effect;
> So the worlds carcasse would not last, if I
> Were punctuall in this Anatomy.
> Nor smels it well to hearers, if one tell
> Them their disease, who faine would think
>   they're wel.
> Here therefore be the end.
>
> (ll. 435-443)

The speaker's exploitation of the character of medical anat-
omist greatly heightens the satiric thrust of his rhetorical
dissecting, especially since, as Donne's satire "Upon Mr.
Thomas Coryats Crudities" reminds us, anatomies were
customarily performed upon the bodies of executed crimi-

---

[25] Henry Hutton, *Follie's Anatomie. Or Satyres and Satyricall
Epigrams* (London, 1619), sig. B 5ᵛ.

nals: "Worst malefactors, to whom men are prize,/ Do publique good, cut in Anatomies."[26]

It seems clear that the frame of the poem insists upon the speaker's role as a public teacher, an anatomist, whose teaching is primarily the revelation and dissecting of corruption, disease, evils: he is not a solitary, meditating in his chamber. Nevertheless, we can recognize, in those sections of the poem which Martz has termed meditations upon the evils of the world, that the speaker's voice takes on a more reflective tone, signalled by the shift in his style of address from *Thou* to *We*: "Of nothing he made us, and we strive too,/ To bring our selves to nothing backe" (ll. 156-157). At such times, like the Protestant theorists who tended to fuse sermon and meditation,[27] the speaker identifies himself with his audience as sharing with them in the sad conditions of the world, and he reflects—meditates aloud, as it were—upon those conditions, with and for his audience.

The introduction contains a few such shifts from the second person direct address to the reflective "we"—"none/ Offers to tell us who it is that's gone" (ll. 41-42); "our weakenes was discovered" (l. 52); "Her death hath taught us dearely" (l. 61)—which prepare us for a continuing pattern of clearly defined and thematically appropriate changes in the speaker's stance toward his audience. In the long reflective sections on the evils of the world the speaker's "we" announces his involvement with his auditory in those miserable and evil conditions; in the eulogies of "she" he focuses his eyes (and ours) upon her, and by this means distances himself and his hearers from those conditions; and consequently, after the eulogies he can forgo the involved "we" for a hortatory style, thereby taking his stance above the world, as its judge, and inviting his auditory to the same perspective: "Shee, shee is dead; shee's dead: when thou knowest this,/ Thou knowest . . ." (ll. 183-184). Structurally and thematically, then, the eulogies are not excrescences, but are intrinsically involved in the poem's dialectic

[26] *Satires*, etc., ed. Milgate, p. 48, ll. 53-54.
[27] See above, chaps. 3 and 6.

and in the psychological and spiritual growth of the speaker; they are indeed the specific means by which he achieves and manifests that distancing from the world which he urges upon his auditory. Following the eulogies he addresses the audience as "thou," thereby signifying that he and they are no longer "we," caught up necessarily in the mundane conditions, but that both can learn to judge and to reject this world.

The speaker presents himself, then, as public celebrant and public teacher (anatomist), in which latter role he incorporates a meditative element. These roles are fused and further clarified in the final identification the speaker makes of himself—as a latter-day Moses whose song is an analogue of the Mosaic song in Deuteronomy 32. Defending the appropriateness of his form to those who might think the matter "fit for Chronicle, not verse" he asks them to,

> Vouchsafe to call to minde, that God did make
> A last, and lastingst peece, a song. He spake
> To *Moses*, to deliver unto all,
> That song: because he knew they would let fall,
> The Law, the Prophets, and the History,
> But keepe the song still in their memory.
> Such an opinion (in due measure) made
> Me this great Office boldly to invade.

(ll. 460-468)

Formally, the song in Deuteronomy is a precise analogue for Donne's *Anatomy* in that it combines praise (of God) and instruction to the Israelites—an instruction that is primarily a berating of them for their ingratitude and idolatry. As Calvin observes, the song begins and ends "in a strain of magnificence,"[28] praising God for his absolute righteousness:

> Because I will publish the name of the Lord: ascribe ye greatness unto our God.

[28] Calvin, *Commentaries on the Four Last Books of Moses*, trans. Charles W. Bingham, 4 vols. (Edinburgh, 1852-1855) IV, 335.

He is the Rock, his work is perfect: for all his ways are
  judgment: a God of truth and without iniquity, just
  and right is he.

  .   .   .   .

Rejoice, O ye nations, with his people: for he will
  avenge the blood of his servants, and will render
  vengeance to his adversaries, and will be merciful
  unto his land, and to his people.
                    (Deuteronomy 32; 3-4, 43, A.V.)

But the burden of the song is the instruction of the Israelites
through denunciation of their iniquities and perversities, for
the Lord intended that by singing it they should continually
condemn themselves out of their own mouths: "Now there-
fore write ye this song for you, and teach it the children of
Israel: put it in their mouths, that this song may be a witness
for me against the children of Israel" (Deuteronomy 31:19).
Explaining God's declared purpose, Calvin noted that this
song was to be, like the minister's sermons, "the means of
assisting the elect to seek after repentance, when they were
smitten by the hand of God . . . whilst the reprobate should
be more and more condemned."[29] Accordingly, the theme
of the wickedness and impending destruction of the people
looms large:

They have corrupted themselves, their spot is not the
  spot of his children; they are a perverse and crooked
  generation.

  .   .   .   .

Of the Rock that begat thee thou art unmindful, and hast
  forgotten God that formed thee.

  .   .   .   .

The sword without, and the terror within, shall destroy
  both the young man and the virgin, the suckling also
  with the man of gray hairs.

  .   .   .   .

---

[29] *Ibid.*, IV, 328, 334.

> O that they were wise, that they understood this, that
> they would consider their last end.
>
> (Deuteronomy 32:5, 18, 25, 29)

The idea that the Deuteronomaic song fuses praise and instruction through censure is widespread, and is obviously accepted by Donne's speaker, who "invades" the Mosaic office in composing his own song of praise and censure. Calvin declared that the Mosaic song contrasts "the perfection of Gods works, the rectitude of his ways . . . with the rebellion of the people,"[30] and the Geneva Bible annotating Deuteronomy 32:2 reaffirms Moses' dual purpose, "that he may speak to Gods glory, and that the people, as the greene grasse, may receive the dew of his doctrine."[31] The Junius-Tremellius annotations also assign to the song the two functions of praising the past and present favors of God to his people, and censuring their ungrateful spirit.[32] In his *Essays in Divinity*, Donne comments on the Song in Deuteronomy in just these traditional terms:

> God himself in that . . . Heavenly Song which onely himself compos'd . . . [chose] this way and conveyance of a Song, as fittest to justifie his future severities against his children, because he knew that they would ever be repeating this Song, (as the Delicacy, and Elegancy therof, both for Divinity and Poetry, would invite any to that) and so he should draw from their own mouthes a confession of his benefits, and of their ingratitude.[33]

Moreover, in one of his sermons Donne suggestively referred to this song, the sermon, and the meditation, as related forms:

> And so likewise, long before, when God had given all the Law, he provided, as himself sayes, a safer way, which

---

[30] *Ibid.*, IV, 338.   [31] *Geneva Bible* (1599), fol. 77v.
[32] Immanuel Tremellius and Franciscus Junius, *Testamenti Veteris Biblia Sacra* (London, 1581), fol. 209.
[33] Evelyn M. Simpson, ed. *Essays in Divinity* (Oxford, 1952), p. 92.

238

was to give them a heavenly Song of his owne making: for that Song, he sayes there, he was sure they would remember. So the Holy Ghost hath spoken in those Instruments, whom he chose for the penning of the Scriptures, and so he would in those whom he sends for the preaching thereof: he would put in them a care of delivering God's messages, with consideration, with meditation.[34]

Clearly, Donne's speaker has identified the genre of his poem with some precision: it is a "mixed genre" but the mixture has both contemporary and biblical precedent.

Moreover, the perspective and tone of Donne's speaker is clarified by this "invasion" of the Mosaic office. As Manley points out, Donne is giving the standard contemporary gloss on the song from Deuteronomy when he terms it the summary or epitome of the old dispensation, "The Law, the Prophets, and the History."[35] Sebastian Munster observes, "Dicunt Hebraei canticum istud esse . . . *summarium totius Legis*"; the Douay Bible terms the song an "abridgement of the Law";[36] and Luther explains just how the fundamental significance and the very tone of the Law are mirrored in this song:

The Song of Moses is full of denunciations and reproof respecting the many great benefits shown by God to an ungrateful and evil people. . . . In it Moses carries out an office worthy of himself, that is, worthy of the ministry of the Law. He bites, prosecutes, denounces, threatens, curses, and shows nothing but wrath throughout his song. Nevertheless, he feels that the peeple is not improved as

[34] Donne, *Sermons*, II, 171. Sermon on Ezek. 33:32, at Whitehall, Feb., 1618/19.

[35] Manley, "Commentary," pp. 167-168. P. G. Stanwood, "Essentiall Joye in Donne's *Anniversaries*," pp. 230-231, develops some of the implications of this association of the speaker with Moses and the Law.

[36] Sebastian Munster, in *Critici Sacri*, I, p. 1351, cited in Manley, p. 168; *The Holie Bible faithfully translated . . . by the English College of Doway* (Douai, 1609-1610), I, 459.

a result of this. Here one can see as in a mirror the power and nature of the Law, that it works wrath and holds under the curse.[37]

In Donne's *Anatomy* the speaker on the occasion of an *untimely* death undertakes to analyze, denounce, and curse that realm—the order of nature—in which such deaths occur. As Mosaic singer he intimates that the standard of judgment is the perfect righteousness of the Law of Works, whose author is the same righteous God who inspired the Mosaic song. Judged by that standard the order of nature is revealed to be utterly corrupt, lost in sin, given over to death, and abandoned to God's wrath and judgment.

The introductory lines of the *Anatomy* also serve to define the speaker's audience as—in various senses—the world. Analyzing the world's responses to her death, the speaker notes that at first it languished in a "great earth-quake" of bloody sweat and tears (ll. 11-12). Then, realizing that to see her again (as all desired) "All must endeavour to be good as shee," it had fits of alternating consumptive mourning and hectic, feverish joy (ll. 14-20). Now it is sunk in a coma of forgetfulness which it mistakes for recovery: "So thou, sicke world, mistak'st thy selfe to bee/ Well, when alas, thou'rt in a Letargee" (ll. 23-24). The metaphor of the world's sickness is continued throughout the poem in references to its "generall sickenesse" (l. 240), its "Hectique fever" (l. 243), its "consuming wound" (l. 248), its condition as a "lame . . . cripple" (l. 238). Yet the problem becomes more complex because the world is not only sick and moribund but, from another metaphoric point of view, actually dead and the subject of an anatomy lesson: "Sicke world, yea dead, yea putrified" (l. 56). It is an utterly "drie . . . Cinder" which nothing can soften (l. 428), and its "carcasse" will not last to complete the anatomy (ll. 439-440). In addition to these "worlds" there is also a "new world" somehow emerging from the carcass of the dead world. The

[37] Luther, *Lectures on Deuteronomy*, ed. Pelikan, *Works*, IX, 290.

passage in the introduction which presents all these terms, and shows the speaker discriminating among worlds and audiences will repay close attention:

> But though it be too late to succour thee,
> Sicke world, yea dead, yea putrified,
>
> . . . .
>
> I (since no man can make thee live) will trie,
> What we may gaine by thy Anatomy.
> Her death hath taught us dearely, that thou art
> Corrupt and mortall in thy purest part.
> Let no man say, the world it selfe being dead,
> 'Tis labour lost to have discovered
> The worlds infirmities, since there is none
> Alive to study this dissectione;
> For there's a kind of world remaining still,
>
> . . . .
>
>   ... And though she have shut in all day,
> The twi-light of her memory doth stay;
> Which, from the carcasse of the old world, free,
> Creates a new world; and new creatures be
> Produc'd: The matter and the stuffe of this,
> Her vertue, and the forme our practise is.
> And though to be thus Elemented, arme
> These Creatures, from hom-borne intrinsique harme,
> (For all assum'd unto this Dignitee,
> So many weedlesse Paradises bee,
> Which of themselves produce no venemous sinne,
> Except some forraine Serpent bring it in)
> Yet, because outward stormes the strongest breake,
> And strength it selfe by confidence growes weake,
> This new world may be safer, being told
> The dangers and diseases of the old.
>
>   (ll. 55-88)

Commenting in one of his sermons on a text from John 16:8, "And when he is come, he will reprove the World of Sin, and of Righteousnesse, and of Judgment," Donne offers four definitions of the term "world" which illuminate the distinctions in this passage: one sense is "the whole frame of the world . . . now subject to mutability and corruption"; a second is the world of men; a third sense "signifies only the wicked world"; and the last "signifies the Saints, the Elect, the good men of the world."[38] Further clarification of the final two senses is afforded by John More's *Lively Anatomie of Death*, which emphasizes the universal condition of spiritual death caused by original sin and avoided only by those who live in Christ:

> All are subject to the spirituall death, being full of sinne and disobedience, and so remaine, (those onely excepted) which are quickened by Christ, and are buryed by Baptisme into his death, to die to sinne, and live to righteousnesse. . . . They are sayd to be dead in their sinne, who cannot so much as moove themselves to any goodnesse, who have no sence or feeling either of Gods mercie or their owne miseries.[39]

The sick world, "this world," which Donne's speaker first addresses and with which he associates himself and his auditory, is the "whole frame of the world" we live in, the human condition as men experience it. The dead world, the "old world" upon which the anatomy is performed, is the natural world wholly perverted by original sin and utterly "dead" in that it cannot of itself produce any spiritual good. Men must transcend it through grace and the new life in Christ or be utterly lost—"Be more then man, or thou'rt less then an Ant" (l. 190). "This world" is from one point of view identifiable with the mere natural order dead in sin, since it is so profoundly affected by that original sin and that universal death as to be "rotten at the heart" and doomed. But in another sense "this world" somehow endures—as a sick world languishing and in desperate straits; through his

---

[38] Donne, *Sermons*, VI, 322-327. Sermon on John 16:8-11, on Whitsunday [1625?].

[39] More, *Lively Anatomie of Death*, sigs. C iii^v-C iv.

anatomy and his praise of Elizabeth Drury the speaker hopes to stir this audience from lethargy to some "feeling . . . of their miserie." He can dissociate himself in some degree from the sick world, since by undertaking the praise of Elizabeth he demonstrates possession of a "soul" which follows worthiness and is not sunk in lethargy. But periodically throughout the poem he associates himself and his listeners with this world's diseases and miseries—as all men must.

There is also another audience which the speaker distinguishes—the "new world" of the regenerate who are "free" from the carcass of the old world, the natural order dead in sin, and by grace are "assum'd unto this Dignitee" of being "weedlesse Paradises." That is, they are safe from "venemous sin" (elected to salvation) but are still endangered by attacks of the serpent, outward storms, and spiritual presumption so long as they live in the sick world. For their sake especially—to make them safer—the speaker proposes to anatomize the natural order destroyed by sin, and to trace the dire effects of its spiritual death upon this, our sick world. For the *Anatomy* is undertaken to this end: to lead the auditory to repudiate the sick world insofar as it is mere nature, and to take their places in the "new world" of grace.

The third term identified in the introduction is the "she" of the poem, the girl Elizabeth Drury—or more precisely her "rich soule"—portrayed as a Queen who has ended her progress on earth and has taken up residence in her heavenly palace. As is Donne's custom when using real persons as symbols, that soul is regarded as a glass to manifest something to us (certain states of human goodness) and her untimely death is presented as an occasion fraught with spiritual significance for the speaker and his audience: "since now no other way there is/ But goodnes, to see her, whom all would see,/ All must endeavour to be good as shee" (ll. 16-18). Like any Christian preacher or poet addressing a funeral or anniversary occasion, Donne assumes Elizabeth Drury to be a regenerate soul bearing on earth the (partly)

243

restored image of God, and now enjoying the perfect res-
toration of that image in heavenly glory.[40] Therefore she
can present all the significances and symbolic dimensions
which Donne customarily attaches to the regenerate soul,[41]
and so can serve as type of two modes of human goodness.
As regenerate soul and restored image of God, she recapitu-
lates and manifests the natural innocence in which man was
first created as image of God, and which he lost utterly by
original sin. She also manifests the height of goodness con-
ceivable in the order of grace on earth, becoming thereby
a type of the perfection which she and we will attain
in heaven, a perfection even surpassing that of the first in-
nocence in its glory and permanence. It should be empha-
sized that the restored image of God in Elizabeth Drury is
apprehended as the measure of human goodness rather
than as the means for a Neoplatonic contemplator of her to
ascend to God: Donne's focus throughout both poems is
sharply upon the human condition, its actual misery and its
conceivable perfection. According to the usual Donnean
conflations, she is portrayed as manifesting these two modes
of human goodness as if they were fully realized and per-
fected in her, even though he and we know that in all the
regenerate such goodness can be only partly realized in this
world.

In *The First Anniversarie* the focus is upon Elizabeth
Drury's regenerate status as it recapitulates and manifests
to us the created perfection of man and nature, the inno-
cence and goodness man first enjoyed when made in the
image of God. Her untimely death is a fit occasion for ex-
ploring in an anatomy the effects of original sin, since all
death is an effect of that first sin, and a virgin untimely dead
in the first blush of youth is a particularly apt recapitulation
of that first mortal loss. Elizabeth Drury's death can then
serve as both cause and revelation of the dismal condition
of "this world," blasted by the death of the young world's

[40] See chap. 6.
[41] See chap. 4, pp. 134-141, and chap. 5, 163-173.

innocence—the destruction of the created goodness of the natural order. Her death, manifesting the loss of this created perfection, wounded and tamed our world which "mightst have better spar'd the Sunne, or Man" (l. 26), but the world is yet more damaged by forgetting what it has lost:

> Thou hast forgot thy name, thou hadst; thou wast
> Nothing but she, and her thou hast o're past.
>
> . . . .
>
>   Thou unnam'd hadst laid,
> Had not her comming, thee her Palace made;
> Her name defin'd thee, gave thee forme and frame
> And thou forgetst to celebrate thy name.
> Some moneths she hath beene dead (but being dead,
> Measures of times are all determined)
> But long shee'ath beene away, long, long, yet none
> Offers to tell us who it is that's gone.
>
>   (ll. 31-42)

The name given to the world in its innocent state was goodness: "And God saw every thing that he had made, and behold, it was very good" (Genesis 1:31). The name which defined man as originally created was *image of God*: "Let us make man in our image, after our likeness" (Genesis 1:26). Man's goodness and dignity as image of God defined the order of nature, which was made for him as his palace, and man, in Adam, gave their names to everything in nature. That primal goodness, as recapitulated in Elizabeth Drury, has been gone some months, but of course it has been long gone. Elizabeth Drury herself was "A strong example gone equall to law" (l. 48), for she was a *figura* of that innocent state in which man lived by the law of nature without need of other law. As regenerate soul, she was a glass to manifest that primal innocence which was "The Cyment which did faithfully compact/ And glue all vertues," and which was the world's "ntrinsique Balme, and . . . preservative [that]/ Can never be renew'd" (ll. 49-50, 57-58).

245

This reading of the symbolic value attaching to her good-
ness in *The First Anniversarie* is reinforced by several ser-
mons in which Donne identifies the spiritual analogue to the
body's natural preservative—its *Balsamum Suum, Nardum
Suam*—as that natural disposition of the soul toward good-
ness which has been lost in original sin: "We are so far from
that naturall Balsamum, as that we have a naturall poyson
in us, Originall sin . . . that indeleble foulnesse, and unclean-
nesse which God discovers in us all."[42] And again,

> We have lost the sweet savour of our own Spikenard. . . .
> There was a time, when we had a Spikenard, and a sweet
> savour of our own, when our own Naturall faculties, in
> that state as God infused them, in *Adam*, had a power to
> apprehend, and lay hold upon the graces of God. . . . We
> have lost that good and all possibility of recovering it, by
> our selves, in losing *Nardum nostram*, The savour of our
> Spikenard, the life, and vigour of our naturall faculties,
> to supernaturall uses. For though the soule be *Forma
> hominis*, it is but *Materia Dei*; The soule may be the
> forme of man, for without that, Man is but a carcasse; But
> the soule is but the matter upon which God works; for,
> except our soule receive another soule, and be inani-
> mated with Grace, even the soule it selfe, is but a
> carcasse.[43]

Since this primal goodness, this intrinsic balm, cannot be
renewed in nature, the order of nature is unquestionably
dead and may be anatomized; moreover, since it cannot be
renewed the actual world has proved to be "Corrupt and
mortall in thy purest part" (l. 62)—i.e., the rational facul-
ties of man himself are subject to corruption and spiritual
death, and even such regenerate persons as Elizabeth
Drury prove to be subject to natural death. The new world,
the regenerate state as experienced in this world, is only a

[42] Donne, *Sermons*, VI, 116-117. Sermon on I Cor. 12:3, preached
on Whitsunday [1624?].

[43] *Sermons*, VII, 108-109. Sermon on I Cor. 15:29, at St. Paul's,
Easter Day, 1626.

pale reflection of that first innocence as far as its achieved moral virtue and goodness is concerned; the matter of this new world is the goodness which defined the innocent world, and the form is our imperfect practice of that virtue:

> For there's a kind of world remaining still,
> Though shee which did inanimate and fill
> The world, be gone, yet in this last long night,
> Her Ghost doth walke; that is, a glimmering light,
> A faint weake love of vertue and of good
> Reflects from her, on them which understood
> Her worth; And though she have shut in all day,
> The twi-light of her memory doth stay;
> Which, from the carcasse of the old world, free,
> Creates a new world; and new creatures be
> Produc'd: The matter and the stuffe of this,
> Her vertue, and the forme our practise is.
>
> (ll. 67-78)

But though the new world's actual goodness is only a pale reflection of that first innocence, the regenerate have special privileges attendant upon election and grace, in that as "weedlesse Paradises" these new creatures will not of themselves produce deadly sins, will not again lose the paradise within.

We have then the terms—the speaker, the audience, the girl and her symbolic significance—set forth in the frame of the poem complexly, but yet with precision. After the introduction the speaker proceeds with the analysis of the desperate state of the sick world, which is at the same time an anatomy of the spiritually dead natural order. An anatomy is properly performed on a body, and that framework is maintained throughout: in accordance with the terms developed in those sermons in which Donne discussed the loss of our soul's *balsamum* or preservative through original sin, the *Anatomy* addresses itself to the question of what man and this world are like now that the purest part, man's soul, has lost its informing principle—the natural goodness in which we were created as images of God. My reading of the poem intends to display the logical development of this central metaphysical argument, which has gone virtually unrecognized amidst the barrage of criticism addressed to the poems' hyperbolic language and audacious wit.

Structurally, the argument of the *Anatomy* is carried forward in four large sections, the third of them subdivided into two parts. Although of course various patterns of organization may be discerned in the poem, its basic structure, I suggest, is that of a four-stage dissection and analysis of parts of various "bodies" in accordance with the genre of the anatomy, rather than the five-part meditation formula which Professor Martz proposes.[44] Section one (ll. 91-190 is concerned especially with the microcosm—the deterioration and decay of man's substance and faculties toward their original nothingness. The desperateness of his condition is ascribed to the loss, the perishing, of his heart —the vital organ properly given central attention in an anatomy lesson. Section two (ll. 191-246) shows the macrocosm, "the world's whole frame," to be diseased, decaying, disintegrating due to the loss of, the rottenness of, *its* heart, man. The third section (ll. 247-376) is concerned with the world's beauty, with the "subtlest immaterial parts" of the world's body (both macrocosm and microcosm); these are proportion and color, the two components of beauty which correspond in the anatomy to the external features and appearance of the body. The fourth section (ll. 377-434) deals with the "body" of the cosmos—the disruption of correspondence between heaven and earth, and the near cessation of heavenly influence upon the world as well as of the order of grace upon the natural order. Within each section the analysis of the world's corruption and disintegration is followed by a description of its original perfection, recapitulated in Elizabeth as a regenerate soul: her death is thereby made to display the full extent of the world's loss from the death of the first innocence, and to display also its utterly hopeless state, since the death of the regenerate removes any slender possibility for the world's

[44] Martz, *Poetry of Meditation*, pp. 221-228.

recovery that their presence in the world might have of-
fered. Each section concludes with the speaker's transcend-
ence of the natural order and the sick world, a transcend-
ence he urges upon his auditory as the only possible result
of these exercises in proper valuation. Such ordering of
values is the stated purpose of the *Anatomy*, made explicit
at the conclusion of the introduction: "For with due temper
men do then forgoe,/ Or covet things, when they their true
worth know" (ll. 89-90).

The first concern, then, is with disease, decay, deteriora-
tion, and disintegration in man's substance and faculties
(ll. 91-190). Identifying himself with the audience and with
the sick world, the speaker reflects upon our sad state:
there is no health; we are born ruinous (ruining) and our
very process of birth mimics the fall; the first marriage was
our funeral, and each subsequent marriage recapitulates
that condition, as we shorten our lives in the act of procrea-
tion. We cannot even be called men as men once were, for
we steadily decline in longevity and size. In the silver age
of the patriarchs men seemed of equal longevity with the
world but now, "Alas, we scarse live long enough to trie/
Whether a new made clocke runne right, or lie" (ll.
129-130). Then men were of a size equal to elephant
or whale, each soul controlling a fair kingdom and large
realm, whereas now, "As in lasting, so in length is man/
Contracted to an inch, who was a span" (ll. 135-136). This
would not matter if we still contained all our former worth
in epitome, but, instead, in mind as well as body we are
moving back to the nothingness out of which we were
created:

> 'Tis shrinking, not close-weaving, that hath thus
> In minde and body both bedwarfed us.
> We seeme ambitious, Gods whole worke t'undoe;
> Of nothing he made us, and we strive too,
> To bring our selves to nothing backe; and we
> Do what we can, to do't so soone as hee.
>   (ll. 153-158)

The speaker opposes to this dismal vision a brief, ecstatic remembrance of what man was as created: the world's vice-emperor, containing all the faculties and graces pertaining to all other creatures, though now a mere trifle, a nothing. His condition is utterly hopeless because he has lost his "heart"—his vital principle—whose loss would afford a satisfactory explanation of the "death" in any anatomy lesson;

> This man, so great, that all that is, is his,
> Oh what a trifle, and poor thing he is!
> If man were any thing, he's nothing now:
> Helpe, or at least some time to wast, allow
> T'his other wants, yet when he did depart
> With her, whom we lament, he lost his hart.
>
> (ll. 169-174)

These concluding lines are difficult, but again quite precise. As regenerate soul, she manifests the created innocence and goodness of the natural order; when man parted with her (or when his essential being, his soul's spiritual life, departed—left—with her) he lost his heart also. This means on a simple level that the body's life principle is dependent upon the soul (with sin the body became mortal) but it means also the utter corruption, the death of the will and affections, whose seat was traditionally understood to be the heart, so that natural man can now make no motion toward spiritual good. In one of his sermons, after describing the loss of our proper *balsamum* through original sin Donne analyzes this "death" of the heart: "Man hath lost his *paratum cor meum*; he cannot say, *his heart is prepared*; that he hath lost in originall sin. . . . He hath lost his *variis odoribus delectatum cor*, the delight which his heart heretofore had . . . in those good actions, in which formerly he exercised himself, and now is falne from."[45] Having thus lost

---

[45] *Sermons*, VII, 113. Thomas Adams' sermon entitled *Mysticall Bedlam: Or, The World of Mad-men* (1615), in *Workes* (London, 1629), on Eccles. 9:3, affords a further gloss on these lines:

The *Heart* [is] the receptacle of life. . . . It is the member, that

his heart, man may still have some time to waste in the sick world, but as mere natural man there is no hope for him.

The eulogy of Elizabeth is a counterstatement: the primal goodness is (partially) reiterated and restored in her, as a regenerate soul—through grace, the only way in which it can be regained by man. This goodness is antitype or fulfillment, *forma perfectior*, of all that the ancient philosophers understood as virtue, and it can drive out "The poysonous tincture, and the stayne of *Eve* . . . by a true religious Alchimy" (ll. 180-182). Realizing then that even she is subject to the death which pervades the entire natural order, the speaker detaches himself from any involvement with man as natural man and urges his auditory to a similar abnegation. Man's sole hope now is to "feed" upon the supernatural food, religion, and so to nurture in himself a better growth which can recompense the decay of nature:

> Shee, shee is dead; shee's dead: when thou
>   know'st this,
> Thou knowest how poore a trifling thing man is.
> And learn'st thus much by our Anatomee,
> The heart being perish'd, no part can be free.
> And that except thou feed (not banquet) on
> The supernaturall food, Religion,
> Thy better Grouth growes withered, and scant;
> Be more then man, or thou'rt lesse then an Ant.
>
> (ll. 183-190)

In the second section (ll. 191-246), the speaker traces the same pattern of disease, corruption, and disintegration in

---

hath first life in man, and is the last that dyes in man; and to all the other members gives vivification.

As man is *Microcosmus*, an abridgement of the world, he hath *heaven* resembling his *soule*, *earth* his *heart*, placed in the midst as a center. . . . Every perpetrated sinne doth some hurt to the wals; but if the *Heart* be taken, the whole *Corporation* is lost. . . . The *Heart* leades, directs, moves the parts of the body, and powers of the soul (pp. 482-483).

"the worlds whole frame" (l. 191), the macrocosm, and once again he associates himself and his audience with this decaying world. This section is linked structurally to the first in that the macrocosm's decay is plotted according to the same graph as man's—from the world's "birth" to its present state. As man's birth images the fall of the first man "killed" by the first woman, so the "world did in her Cradle take a fall": the macrocosm's created goodness began to fail with the fall of the angels even before the creation was finished. Then man, the noblest creature of the world, felt the effect, and beasts and plants were cursed in the curse of man. The present world shows an acceleration of this deterioration, even as man's present short life and small stature are evidence of the accelerating rate of his regression toward nothingness. The disruption of the planetary system and of the traditional four elements signals the world's approaching dissolution into chaos: it "Is crumbled out againe to his Atomis./ 'Tis all in pieces, all cohærence gone" (ll. 212-213). Then, even as the microcosm proved to be "dampt" in mind as well as body, so in the macrocosm society is shown to be deteriorating like the physical universe, and mere individualism is rampant: "Prince, Subject, Father, Sonne, are things forgot,/ For every man alone thinkes he hath got/ To be a Phoenix, and that there can bee/ None of that kinde, of which he is, but hee" (ll. 215-218).

Elizabeth is then eulogized as a regenerate soul displaying a force—the image of primal goodness restored—that might have been able to reorder the world (just as, in relation to the microcosm, she pointed natural man to that supernatural food, religion, to drive out the stain of Eve). Recapitulating the first innocence, she seemed able to provide a "Magnetique force . . . / To draw, and fasten sundred parts in one"; she was invented by "wise nature" to be a "new compasse" for mankind straying in the world's sea (ll. 221-226). Since in her was restored and manifested the image of God, the Idea by which all things were initially made, she therefore was the "best, and first originall/ Of all faire copies" (ll. 227-228) and could be a pattern for the world's remaking—the world itself being but a microcosm or suburbs to her. However, her death demonstrated that the powers of the regenerate soul, great as they are potentially, are yet located in a person subject to the death that pervades nature, and so cannot restore nature. Seeing this, the speaker detaches himself from the whole natural order, and urges his audience again to abnegate all the world:

> Shee, shee is dead; shee's dead: when thou
>   knowst this,
> Thou knowst how lame a cripple this world is.
> And learnst thus much by our Anatomy,
> That this worlds generall sickenesse doth not lie
> In any humour, or one certaine part;
> But, as thou sawest it rotten at the hart,
> Thou seest a Hectique fever hath got hold
> Of the whole substance, not to be contrould,
> And that thou hast but one way, not t'admit
> The worlds infection, to be none of it.
>
> (ll. 237-246)

The final lines ascribe the hopelessness of the macrocosmic infection to the state of the heart, even as was the case with the microcosm. As man's heart—his vital principle, the goodness of his will and affections—was "lost" with the departure of his primal innocence, so the world's heart is also rotten. The world's heart, "the noblest part" is evidently man himself, even as the angels are termed the world's "brains" (ll. 195-200). The passage states that we *have seen* the world to be "rotten at the heart" and because of this condition we find now that a hectic fever or infection has seized the entire substance of the macrocosm. This statement alludes to the curse upon all the world because of man's sin and fall, and leads to the speaker's rejection of the entire natural order.

The third large section (ll. 247-376) is concerned with the "worlds subtilst immateriall parts," its beauty, whose components are "colour, and proportion"; these parts also

"Feele this consuming wound, and ages darts"—the loss of primal innocence (ll. 247-250). In the anatomy these are the outward parts which first greet and attract our senses, as opposed to the decay of substance and matter, the "faults in inward parts,/ Corruptions in our braines, or in our harts" (ll. 329-330), with which the speaker has hitherto been concerned. In this section the schematic ordering of subsections is altered somewhat, to the advantage of the poem's aesthetic effect: lack of proportion in the macrocosm is first considered; then, following the eulogy and as part of the conclusion from it, comes a description of disproportion in the microcosm which serves as a bridge to the subsection dealing with color; and in the brief color passage the faults in both orders are considered together. This treatment links the subsections closely, and also merges the eulogies and conclusions with the analytic portions, thereby achieving a pleasing variety within the schematic organization.

Turning to the new question, the speaker reverts to his reflective style of address, laced from time to time with pungent satire as he associates himself and his auditory with the world's disproportions, and, especially, with the foolish astronomers who try vainly to impose their own order upon the cosmos. He finds distressing evidence of distortion and disruption in the Ptolemaic cosmic order: the heavens present a "various and perplexed course" (l. 253), new stars appear and old ones vanish "As though heav'n suffred earth-quakes, peace or war" (l. 261); the sun and the stars fail to preserve their circular motion. The sun itself is discovered to be a devious creature that must be fettered by the astronomers' signs lest he run away to the poles:

> For his course is not round; nor can the Sunne
> Perfit a Circle, or maintaine his way
> One inche direct; but where he rose to day
> He comes no more, but with a cousening line,
> Steales by that point, and so is Serpentine.
>
> (ll. 268-272)

But these actual cosmic distortions are increased by men, by foolish astronomers who devise "Eccentrique parts" for the Ptolemaic cosmic system, and make other absurd schematizations of the heavens which "disproportion that pure forme." Unable to fathom the stars' paces, man brashly sets his own paces for them:

> Man hath weav'd out a net, and this net throwne
> Upon the Heavens, and now they are his owne.
> Loth to goe up the hill, or labor thus
> To goe to heaven, we make heaven come to us.
> We spur, we raine the stars, and in their race
> They're diversely content t'obey our pace.
>
> (ll. 279-284)

Moreover, the earth itself has not a perfect, round shape, if we take into account the height of the mountains, the depth of the seas, and the infernal vault of hell beneath. And especially if we consider the social order, whose disfigurement is evident in the fact that "those two legges whereon it doth relie,/ Reward and punishment are bent awrie" (ll. 303-304). The speaker then is certain that "beauties best, proportion, is dead" (l. 306).

In the eulogy Elizabeth Drury is praised as the measure of symmetry because, by reflecting the goodness of created nature, her regenerate soul embodies the very principle of proportion, harmony itself:

> Whom had that Ancient seen, who thought
>   soules made
> Of Harmony, he would at next have said
> That Harmony was shee, and thence infer,
> That soules were but Resultances from her.
>
> (ll. 311-315)

Manifesting the harmony of the primal innocent world, and man's perfect proportions in it, she is a type for the Ark (which theologians such as Ambrose and Augustine declared to have been made to man's, or Christ's, propor-

255

tions).[46] And the harmony of the various creatures on the ark is a type of the harmony of her own nature: "Both Elements, and Passions liv'd at peace/ In her, who caus'd all Civill warre to cease" (ll. 321-322). As Manley notes, the use of the ark as type of the just man's inner harmony was traditional,[47] and after the manifestation of this harmony in her any form we see in nature seems "discord, and rude incongruitee" (l. 324). After eulogizing her thus, the speaker can again stand above and judge the natural order which has utterly lost its lovely created proportions, and can urge the audience (thou) to repudiate the now ugly and repellant world:

> Shee, shee is dead, she's dead; when thou knowst this,
> Thou knowst how ugly a monster this world is:
> And learnst thus much by our Anatomee,
> That here is nothing to enamor thee.
>
> (ll. 325-328)

Serving as part of this lesson and also as a bridge to the next subsection is the speaker's brief analysis of loss of proportion in the microcosm—which shows itself as lack of discretion in man's behavior. Though the speaker admits his and our involvement in this condition by reverting to the "we" form, he yet retains his achieved stance of superiority to the natural order and invites his audience to adopt the perspective of "wise, and good lookers on" in recognizing how far our actions are from satisfying a proper standard of decorum, and how loathsome they therefore seem:

> If every thing
> Be not done fitly'nd in proportion,
> To satisfie wise, and good lookers on,

---

[46] See Ambrose, "De Noe et Arca," *Pat. Lat.*, ed. Migne, XIV, cols. 387-388; Augustine, *City of God*, xv.26, trans. Marcus Dods (New York, 1950), pp. 516-517.

[47] Manley, *Commentary*, p. 156.

(Since most men be such as most thinke they bee)
They're lothsome too, by this Deformitee.
For good, and well, must in our actions meete:
Wicked is not much worse then indiscreet.

(ll. 332-338)

Indiscretion and indecorum in the microcosm again demonstrate that, with the loss of primal harmony, the mere natural order can hold no attraction for us.

The speaker then analyzes the loss of beauty's second element, color and luster, contrasting this world's wan and sickly complexion with the riot of color which characterized it during the first week of creation:

When nature was most busie, the first weeke,
Swadling the new-borne earth, God seemd to like,
That she should sport herselfe sometimes, and play,
To mingle, and vary colours every day.
And then, as though she could not make inow,
Himselfe his various Rainbow did allow.

(ll. 347-352)

Now color is decayed in both macrocosm and microcosm: summer's robe grows dusky, and we men are so hardened in sin that we are unable to blush with shamefastness: "onely our soules are redde" with sin (l. 358). This image, based upon the meaning of the name *Adam* (red earth) and its near identity in Hebrew with the word for blushing, is best explicated by a passage from one of Donne's sermons:

He made us all of earth, and all of red earth. Our earth was red, even when it was in Gods hands; a rednesse that amounts to a shamefastnesse, to a blushing at our own infirmities, is imprinted in us, by Gods hand. . . . But that redness, which we have contracted from bloud shed by our selves, the bloud of our own souls, by sinne, was not

257

upon us, when we were in the hands of God. . . . We have dyed our selves in sinnes, as red as Scarlet.[48]

In the eulogy Elizabeth Drury is proclaimed as a possible agent for restoration of color in the universe, since, in recapitulating the primal perfection, she manifests the colors of Paradise and so can be regarded as the principle of color. This is so not only because the white and red of her complexion and the blue of her eyes are beauty's ingredients, but also because these colors are emblems of the theological virtues, faith, charity, and hope, which belong to her as regenerate soul:

> Shee, in whom all white, and redde, and blue
> (Beauties ingredients) voluntary grew,
> As in an unvext Paradise; from whom
> Did all things verdure, and their lustre come,
> Whose composition was miraculous,
> Being all color, all Diaphanous.
>
> (ll. 361-366)

Moving to his objective stance the speaker concludes, and invites his audience to agree, that since even she who displayed this paradisal color is subject to death, beauty in the natural order is destroyed beyond all hope of renewal. This world then is a wan Ghost that "should more affright, then pleasure thee" (l. 372), and all use of color now is a mere deception, "to color vitious deeds" (l. 375).

In the final section (ll. 377-434) the focus is changed somewhat: the previous concern was the effect of her loss upon the microcosm, and upon the substance and beauty of the macrocosm, whereas here it is the disruption, the near cessation, of the influence of heaven upon earth. In this last section the effects of her loss extend to the heavens, and the object of the anatomy becomes the "Body of the universe"—the relations and interactions obtaining between

[48] Donne, *Sermons*, IX, 64-66. Sermon on Gen. 1:26, to the king at court, April, 1629.

this world and the heavens. This subject is examined first in relation to physical influences, then in terms of the influence the order of grace may have upon the order of nature —the question being how she might yet influence us from heaven and how she was able to do it while still on earth. This last inquiry merges with the eulogy, so that again the rather rigid thematic organization of the anatomy is adjusted for artistic variety.

Noting first the physical failures of correspondence and influence between heaven and earth, the speaker ascribes them both to heaven's withholding and to earth's insensitivity: "For heaven gives little, and the earth takes lesse" (l. 397). Nature is seen to be almost devoid of influences beyond itself which might mitigate its defects. The clouds do not impregnate the earth with their rain; the air does not "motherly" hatch the seasons and produce their vegetation but rather produces prodigious meteors; earth suffers false pregnancies, her springtime cradles are turned into tombs, and the "new worms" her carcass breeds are such serpents as would overmatch those of the Egyptian magicians who contested with Moses in turning their rods into serpents. Nor can alchemists or alchemical physicians really achieve any constellations or cures on earth by bringing the influence of the stars to bear, for that "art is lost, and correspondence too" (l. 396).

All this sets up an analogue in the physical universe for Elizabeth's inability to exert her influence upon us from heaven. Using *virtue* in its multiple meanings—power (*virtù*), alchemical or medical effects, *areté* (moral goodness)—and also with reference to her particular quality as a regenerate soul manifesting the restored image of God and so figuring our primal perfection, the speaker imagines that her virtue could still work on us after death if correspondence between heaven and earth were not interrupted. At least, all the world would be so attracted by her virtue that, like a dying swan, it would "sing her funerall prayse, and vanish than" (ll. 407-408). Instead, as we remember from the introduction, the world has sunk into a lethargy and forgets to celebrate her. In a daring metaphor which builds upon the earlier allusion to the Egyptian serpents, the speaker then declares,

> But as some Serpents poison hurteth not,
> Except it be from the live Serpent shot,
> So doth her vertue need her here, to fit
> That unto us; she working more then it.
>
> (ll. 409-412)

Besides introducing a witty bit of reptilian lore, this allusion conflates that poison with which the first Serpent infected us all with that which the fiery serpents inflicted upon the murmuring Israelites in the desert (Numbers 21:6-9); more especially, it identifies her virtue with the curative power against snakebite (sin) exercised by the Serpent of Brass which Moses raised up, uniformly interpreted by Christian biblical commentators as a type of Christ.[49] Here, as a regenerate soul united with Christ and bearing the restored image of God, Elizabeth Drury was a type (recapitulation) of Christ, and manifested in her own mature virtue the curative power of grace. Yet her removal from us makes that manifestation of no effect, for unless that example is an active power working among us it cannot overcome "Receivers impotencies" (l. 416).

Then the speaker takes up the question of what effect the order of grace can have upon nature in this world. While on earth, reflecting the (restored) perfection of our primal innocence, the Golden Age, she had some—though woefully limited—effect in stimulating moral virtue. Even strict Calvinists admitted the possibility that unregenerate fallen man could develop some natural and civil virtues, but thought that such virtues would be so marred by man's blighted nature that they could not be called genuinely good or in any way meritorious. Such natural virtues—a

---

[49] See, e.g., *Douay Bible*, I, 366; Calvin, *Four Last Books of the Pentateuch*, IV, 154-157.

"gilding" rather than a transmutation—she could inspire in the natural world while she lived in it:

> She from whose influence all Impressions came,
> But, by Receivers impotencies, lame,
> Who, though she could not transubstantiate
> All states to gold, yet guilded every state,
> So that some Princes have some temperance,
> Some Counsaylors some purpose to advance
> The common profite; and some people have
> Some stay, no more then Kings should give, to crave;
> Some women have some taciturnity;
> Some Nunneries, some graines of chastity.
> She that did thus much, and much more could doe,
> But that our age was Iron, and rusty too,
> Shee, shee is dead; shee's dead: when thou knowst this,
> Thou knowest how drie a Cinder this world is.
>
> (ll. 415-428)

Clearly, even while they coexist, the order of grace can have comparatively little influence upon the order of nature as such, because of the breakdown of correspondence, and even the limited influence she was able to exercise was deprived of permanent effect when she proved to be subject to the death pervading all nature. The speaker therefore assumes his juridical stance again and concludes, definitively, that the world is beyond hope—a "drie Cinder" which cannot be "mollified" by any beneficent influences from heaven or from those regenerate who occupy the order of grace, or by our "Teares, or Sweat, or Bloud" (l. 431). As natural order, then, this world can only be abandoned for something better—"those rich joyes, which did possesse her hart,/ Of which shee's now partaker, and a part" (ll. 433-434).

The method of the *Anatomy* is analytic rather than progressive; it gains its force by reiterating her loss and tracing its effects upon the bodies of all the "worlds" which constitute the order of nature. The organization of the topics is strictly logical, beginning with man whose Fall was the root of all the evils described, and then taking up the ever-widening ramifications of that Fall throughout the world and the universe. The first section displays the loss of man's heart, and the consequent rottenness and decay of man's whole substance, who is himself a microcosm and the "heart" of the macrocosm. The second section analyzes the corruption and decline of the whole world's frame and substance due to the rottenness of its heart, man. Part three shows the extension of this decay to the exterior and immaterial parts which constitute the beauty of both microcosm and macrocosm. And part four shows the further expansion of these effects throughout the entire body of the universe, as interaction between the realms of earth and heaven, nature and grace, are almost wholly disrupted.

The significance of Elizabeth Drury as manifestation of our primal innocence is similarly extended. In the first section, her recapitulation of that primal perfection is seen to intensify the almost total corruption of man's substance and faculties now, demonstrating thereby that man's only hope lies in transcending the natural order by religion. In regard to the macrocosm, the world's substance and beauty, her manifestation of primal innocence serves not only to emphasize the world's loss but for a time seemed to offer some hope for its restoration, a hope blasted by her death. In regard to the failure of correspondence, her life demonstrated the limited effect which even the manifestation of primal innocence restored by grace could have in stimulating natural virtue, and her death removed all hope for any amelioration of nature by higher influences. This brings us directly to the focus of *The Second Anniversarie*, the order of grace, which, though it does not restore nature as such, does regenerate man.

In the final lines of the poem (ll. 435-474), the speaker terminates his anatomy, and offers his anniversary tribute formally to Elizabeth Drury as his first year's rent, promising yearly celebrations of "thy second birth,/ That is, thy death" (ll. 450-451). He also identifies his song and office with Moses' Song in Deuteronomy, which was at once a praise of God, an instruction for and judgment against the people, and an epitome of the Old Law. The concluding couplet is lighter in tone, wittily reminding us that the song paradoxically intends praise and the preservation of Elizabeth Drury's fame in this world, even while it anatomizes and displays the world's rottenness:

> Verse hath a middle nature: heaven keepes soules,
> The grave keeps bodies, verse the fame enroules.
>
> (ll. 473-474)

CHAPTER VIII

The Second Anniversarie

D ONNE'S *Second Anniversarie* was evidently in print early
in 1612. Joseph Hall produced a new prefatory poem
for *The Second Anniversarie*, and also, in all probability,
conducted the book containing that poem as well as the sec-
ond edition of the "Funerall Elegie" and the *Anatomy of
the World* through the press in Donne's absence.[1] In his
"Harbinger to the Progres" much more than in his introduc-
tory poem for the *Anatomy*, Hall emphasizes the mediating
role of the poet, thereby underscoring the central impor-
tance for *The Second Anniversarie* of the progress of the
speaker's soul, as an imitation of Elizabeth's progress, and
as a model for ours. First there was her "Rich soule" which
"Mov'd from this mortall sphere to lively blisse" (l. 4) and
which will still move and aspire until the last day. Then
there is the poet whose spirit follows hers:

> And thou (Great spirit) which her's follow'd hast
> So fast, as none can follow thine so fast;
> So farre as none can follow thine so farre,
> (And if this flesh did not the passage barre
> Had'st raught her) let me wonder at thy flight
>
> . . . .
>
> So while thou mak'st her soules Hy progresse knowne
> Thou mak'st a noble progresse of thine owne.
>
> (ll. 19-28)

And there is also Hall himself, spokesman for us, who re-
sponds to both progresses: "Two soules move here, and
mine (a third) must move/ Paces of admiration, and of
love" (ll. 1-2). The "Harbinger" insists, as did the prefatory

---

[1] See chap. 7, pp. 220-221; chap. 3, p. 83.

poem to the *Anatomy*, that the object of the praise is God in her, but here the terms are more explicitly Petrarchan: "let thy makers praise/ Honor thy Laura, and adorne thy laies" (ll. 35-36). This emphasis misses the incarnational direction of Donne's symbolism, and the fact that Elizabeth especially mirrors certain conditions of human goodness rather than divinity as such. Yet as Hall rightly senses, the praises of her are based upon her dignity as image of God.

Donne's new poem is entitled *The Second Anniversarie. Of the Progres of the Soule. Wherein: By Occasion of the Religious Death of Mistris Elizabeth Drury, the incommodities of the Soule in this life and her exaltation in the next, are Contemplated.* This title and the introduction to the poem (ll. 1-84) establish a new set of terms, characterizing speaker, audience, and symbolic lady in such a way as to relate this poem to *The First Anniversarie*, but also to establish its very different character. The titles themselves suggest that the two poems relate according to the method we have discovered in several of Donne's funeral sermons, in which he builds two distinct and contrary arguments upon the same text by giving that text two different readings or emphases. In this poem the text—the girl's death—is given a different reading from that offered in *The First Anniversarie*: it is no longer an untimely but is now a religious death, and by consequence it displays not the frailty and decay of the world but the state of the soul in this world and the next. The method of this poem, accordingly, is not that of an anatomy of the (world's) body, but rather of a contemplation, a meditative analysis, of the soul.

The introductory passage (ll. 1-84) renders more precise the relations and the distinctions between the two poems, indicating in the first place that the speaker is now concerned with a different audience and a different genre of poem. The speaker's repudiation of the world as the order of nature, achieved by means of the *Anatomy* and reiterated in the introductory passage to the new poem, necessitates a change of audience: no longer will the speaker address

the world directly or relate himself to it as one caught up
in its corruptions and evils, though of course he cannot es-
cape its incommodities. After registering surprise that the
world still endures a year after her death (and after his
anatomy of it) he finds its continued movement to be mere-
ly the post-execution spasm of a beheaded man; the gory
metaphor recalls and intensifies the repulsive aspects of the
world revealed by the *Anatomy*. The speaker completely
separates himself from the dead world he now understands
so well: he sees it engulfed in a second deluge (of evil and
forgetfulness) far more disastrous than the lethargy which
characterized it at the beginning of the *Anatomy*, and he
sees himself as a new Noah striving to save himself from
this deluge by means of the praises of her which he has
undertaken:

> Yet a new Deluge, and of Lethe flood,
> Hath drown'us all, All have forgot all good,
> Forgetting her, the maine Reserve of all;
> Yet in this Deluge, grosse and generall,
> Thou seest mee strive for life; my life shalbe,
> To bee hereafter prais'd, for praysing thee,
> Immortal Mayd.
>
> (ll. 27-33)

He speaks then as a regenerate soul who has repudiated
corrupted Nature, but is still endangered and must strive
hard to progress.

In this passage and at some other points in the poem the
new audience addressed (the new "thou") is Elizabeth her-
self as the object of his "hymns"; as we know, hymns custo-
marily address and apostrophize the one whom they praise:

> Immortal Mayd, who though thou wouldst refuse
> The name of Mother, be unto my Muse,
> A Father since her chast Ambition is,
> Yearely to bring forth such a child as this.

These Hymes may worke on future wits, and so
May great Grand-children of thy praises grow.

. . . .

These Hymns thy issue, may encrease so long,
As till Gods great Venite change the song.

(ll. 33-44)

According to one generic association, then, this poem is a
hymn, whereas *The First Anniversarie* was a song modelled
upon the Mosaic song in Deuteronomy.[2] The identification
is to be taken seriously, despite Donne's punning assertion
that his "hymes" will impregnate future wits just as her in-
fluence has impregnated his muse to produce this hymn. In
antiquity and in the Renaissance a hymn was defined as a
praise of God or the gods. Menander and Scaliger list many
classical varieties of hymns, including invocations, descrip-
tions of the gods, myths about a god's birth, background, or
acts, and stories of his ancestors or descendants.[3] Scaliger
observes that while classical poets made hymns of many
Gods, the Christian poet writes hymns in praise of the one
true God, although he may address any one of the three di-
vine persons or focus upon any of the divine attributes.
Scaliger also relates the Greek genre ὕμνος and the Latin
celebratio, pointing thereby to a precise meaning behind
Donne's frequently used term, celebration.[4] The Psalms

[2] Some implications of this designation are noted by Rosalie Colie,
"All in Peeces," pp. 212-213, and P. G. Stanwood, "Essentiall Joye,"
pp. 236-238.

[3] See Hardison, *Enduring Monument*, pp. 195-198; Philip Rollin-
son, "The Renaissance of the Literary Hymn," *Renaissance Papers*,
ed. George W. Williams (Durham, N. C., 1969), pp. 11-20; and
Rollinson, "A Generic View of Spenser's *Four Hymns*," SP, 68 (1971),
292-304. See also the forthcoming monograph by Sears Jayne, "The
Genre of Spenser's *Fowre Hymnes*."

[4] Scaliger, *Poetices libri septem* ([Heidelberg], 1581), pp. 411-412.
Dennis Quinn's essay, "Donne's *Anniversaries* as Celebration," *SEL*, 9
(1969), 97-105, characterizes the poems as possessing a liturgical, cele-

were widely recognized as the most notable examples of or models for the Christian hymn. Sir Philip Sidney parallels them with hymns by classical poets in his discussion of divine poetry: "In this kinde, though in a full wrong divinitie, were *Orpheus, Amphion, Homer* in his Hymnes, and many other, both Greekes and Romaines: and this Poesie must be used, by whosoever will follow S. *James* his counsell, in singing Psalmes when they are merry."[5] Puttenham, in his *Arte of English Poesie*, usefully summarizes the received theory of the classical hymn and its Christian analogues:

> The gods of the Gentiles were honoured by their Poetes in hymnes, which is an extraordinarie and divine praise, extolling and magnifying them for their great powers and excellencie of nature in the highest degree of laude. . . . The Poets first commended them by their genealogies or pedigrees, their mariages and aliances, their notable exploits in the world for the behoofe of mankind. . . . Such of them as were true, were grounded upon some part of an historie or matter of veritie, the rest altogether figurative & misticall. . . . To the God of the Christians, such divine praise might be verified: to th'other gods none, but figuratively or in misticall sense as hath bene said. . . . And these hymnes to the gods were the first forme of Poesie and the highest & the stateliest, & they were song by the Poets as priests, and by the people or whole congregation as we sing in our Churchs the Psalmes of David.[6]

The Psalms were generally identified as the Judeo-Christian equivalent of the classical hymns, in that they were understood to be, in essence, praises of God. Nevertheless, commentators often indicated distinctions of genre among

---

bratory tone, but does not note this specific contemporary meaning of celebration.

[5] Sir Philip Sidney, *An Apologie for Poetrie* (London, 1595), sigs. C 2ᵛ-C 3.

[6] Puttenham, *The Arte of English Poesie* (London, 1589), pp. 21-23.

them on the basis of the categories of divine lyric enumer-
ated in Ephesians 5:19, "Speaking to yourselves in psalms
and hymns and spiritual songs, singing and making melody
in your heart to the Lord," and also in Colossians 3:16,
"teaching and admonishing one another in psalms and
hymns and spiritual songs." The result was to sharpen the
generic conception of the Christian hymn as, specifically,
a praise of God. Glossing Colossians 3:16, the Geneva Bible
commented, "By Psalmes he meaneth all godly songs, which
were written upon divers occasions, and by hymnes, all
such as conteine the prayse of God, and by spirituall songs,
other more peculiar and artificious songs which were also
in prayse of God, but they were made fuller of musicke."[7]
Henry Ainsworth used these distinctions formally in an-
notating the Psalms: "Ther be three kinde of songs men-
tioned in this book: 1. *Mizmor*, in Greeke *Psalmos*, a Psalm:
2. *Tehillah*, in Greeke *hymnos*, a *hymn* or *Prayse*: 3. and
Shir, in Greeke *Odé*, a *song* or *Laie*. All these three the
Apostle mentioneth together, wher he willeth us to speak
to our selves with *Psalmes*, & *hymnes*, & *spirituall* songs:
Ephe. 5:19."[8] Similarly, in his *Preparation to the Psalter*
George Wither began from these categories, but then he
expanded them somewhat to include other kinds suggested
by the headings of particular psalms; his categories also re-
inforce the specification of the hymn as a lofty praise of
God:

> The Names of the *Psalmes* are many: such as these, A
> Psalme: A Song: A Hymne: a Prayer: Instructions: Re-
> membrances: Of Degrees: Halleluiah, or Praises. . . . By
> a *Psalme*, the Auncient Expositors understood such verses
> as being composed in the honour or prayse of some Sub-
> ject, were indifferently intended, to be either read or
> sung, as our ordinary English Sonnets, consisting of foure-

[7] *Geneva Bible* (1599), fol. 90.

[8] Henry Ainsworth, *Annotations upon the Booke of Psalms*, 2nd.
ed. (London, 1617), sig. B 2; first ed., 1612.

teene lines. A *Song* was made of *Measures*, composed
purposely to be Sung. *Hymnes* were Songs, in which
were the praises of God onely, and that with joy and tri-
umph; and therefore the Songs of *Jeremy* cannot be prop-
erly called *Hymnes*, but rather Tragedies, or Lamenta-
tions: those that are intituled *Halleluiah*, are *Hymns* also,
mentioning particularly the praises of God for benefits
received. Now of what nature they are which be called
Prayers, Psalms of Instruction, or such like; the very
names of some of them doe plainely enough declare.[9]

John Donne, who chose texts for his sermons from the
Book of Psalms far more often than from any other biblical
book, also found among them a wide variety of forms. He
rejoiced that they were all poems, and therefore familiar
and particularly attractive works to him.[10] Some of them
(Psalms 6, 38) he designated prayers: "This whole Psalm
is a *Prayer*, and recommended by *David* to the Church."[11]
He also thought of Psalm 38 as a meditation or contempla-
tion of the human condition: it is a "*Psalm for Re-
membrance*," in which "we contemplate *man*, as the Re-
ceptacle, the Ocean of all misery."[12] Another, Psalm 32, he
terms "David's Catechism," which proceeds "by way of
Catechisme, of instruction in fundamentall things, and Doc-
trines of edification."[13] On another occasion he took delight
in quoting St. Jerome to the effect that the Psalms served
the early Christians as love songs and ballads, eclogues
and pastorals; he also cited with approval Bede's considera-
tion of them as "The Booke of Meditations upon Christ."[14]

[9] George Wither, *A Preparation to the Psalter* (London, 1619),
p. 54.

[10] Donne, *Sermons*, II, 49. Sermon on Psalm 38:2, at Lincoln's Inn
[1618].

[11] *Sermons*, II, 50; *Sermons*, V, 338. Sermon on Psalm 6:2-3.

[12] *Sermons*, II, 75-78. Sermon on Psalm 38:3, at Lincoln's Inn [1618].

[13] *Sermons*, IX, 251. Sermon on Psalm 32:1-2 [at St. Paul's].

[14] *Sermons*, V, 288-289. Sermon on Psalm 90:14, at St. Paul's. The
conception of the Book of Psalms as containing examples of pastoral

Yet like Calvin, whose comment on Ephesians 5:19 recognized no essential difference in the three categories of "Psalmes, Praysings, and spirituall songs," since all serve to "the glorifying of God,"[15] Donne found that the various kinds of poems in the Book of Psalms may all be subsumed under the general category of praise, which he saw as the defining characteristic of the entire Book:

> The whole Book of Psalms is called *Sepher Tehillim*, that is, *Liber Laudationum*, the Book of Praise, yet this Psalme [Psalm 90], and all that follow to the hundredth Psalme, and divers others besides these . . . are called Prayers; The Book is Praise, the parts are Prayer. The name changes not the nature; Prayer and Praise is the same thing.

> There are eleven Psalmes that have that Title, *Psalmes of Instruction*; the whole booke is *Sepher Tehillim, The booke of prayses*; and it is a good way of praysing God, to receive Instruction, Instruction how to praise him. Therefore doth the holy Ghost returne so often to this Catechisticall way, Instruction, Institution, as to propose so many Psalmes, expresly under that Title purposely to that use.[16]

This conflation of the various generic forms in the Book of Psalms under the modality of praise bears upon Donne's incorporation of various generic elements in *The Second Anniversarie* within the broad category of hymn, which is by definition a praise of God.

---

poetry is advanced by Thomas Jackson in *Davids Pastorall Poeme: or Sheepheards Song. Seven Sermons, on the 23. Psalme* (London, 1603).

[15] John Calvin, *The Sermons of M. John Calvin upon the Epistle of S. Paule to the Ephesians*, trans. Arthur Golding (London, 1577), fol. 269ᵛ.

[16] Donne, *Sermons*, v, 270, on Psalm 90:14, at St. Paul's; *Sermons*, IX, 350. Sermon on Psalm 32:8 [at St. Paul's].

As a hymn, then, *The Second Anniversarie* proposes itself as lofty and elevated praise or celebration of God. The designation is appropriate in that this poem formally disclaims lamentation for celebration: "Looke upward; that's towards her, whose happy state/ We now lament not, but congratulate" (ll. 65-66). And again, "Shee whom we celebrate, is gone before" (l. 448). It is also appropriate because the focus is now upon Elizabeth as she manifests the perfection of the order of grace (not, as before, of primal nature restored); thus like all the elect she has become "*Deiformem hominem*, man in the forme of God," and is "an abridgement of *Christ* himselfe."[17] As the conclusion of the poem makes explicit, God in her—that is, God's image restored in her and his Image, Christ, united to her—is the proper object of this hymn of praise:

> Immortall Maid, I might invoque thy name.
> Could any Saint provoke that appetite,
> Thou here shouldst make mee a french convertite.
> But thou wouldst not; nor wouldst thou be content,
> To take this, for my second yeeres true Rent,
> Did this Coine beare any other stampe, then his,
> That gave thee power to doe, me, to say this.
>
> (ll. 516-522)

Besides Elizabeth, there is another audience in the poem, appropriate to that other generic identification suggested in the subtitle—a "contemplation," or meditation of the soul's state. As we have seen, Donne's sermons identify the Psalms as hymns of praise which are also sometimes meditations, and he has precedent for this view not only in Bede, whom he cites, but also in Aquinas, who glossed the phrase in Ephesians, "speaking to yourselves in psalms," as a reference to that meditation which precedes vocal praise: "The first effect of the Holy Spirit is a holy meditation, and the second is a spiritual exultation."[18] After his initial address

---

[17] *Sermons*, IX, 86; VI, 290. See chap. 4, pp. 131-133.

[18] Thomas Aquinas, *Commentary on Saint Paul's Epistle to the Ephesians*, trans. Matthew L. Lamb (New York, 1966), p. 214.

to Elizabeth, then, the speaker turns directly to this other audience, the self, refusing to waste speech in this poem upon a world he has already rejected as worthless:

> Thirst for that time, O my insatiate soule,
> And serve thy thirst, with Gods safe-sealing Bowle.
> Bee thirsty still, and drinke still till thou goe;
> 'Tis th'onely Health, to be Hydropique so.
> Forget this rotten world; And unto thee,
> Let thine own times as an old story be.
>
> (ll. 45-50)

He therefore urges upon his soul a lethargy or forgetfulness of the world which is very different from the world's lethargy in forgetting her: "To be thus stupid is Alacrity;/ Men thus lethargique have best Memory" (ll. 63-64). The world is not even worth an anatomy revealing its worthlessness: "He honors it too much that thinks it nought" (l. 84).

The speaker turns then to that standard *topos* of *meditatio mori*, the benefits and joys accruing to us by death, but his tone is as much hortatory as reflective: he seems to be preaching a sermon to his own soul, directing its meditations, urging it forward, analyzing topics for it as a clergyman might for a congregation. This familiar Protestant fusion of sermon and meditative techniques was also found in *The First Anniversarie*, though in somewhat different form. That poem is set forth as a public address in which the speaker sometimes assumes a meditative reflective tone as he laments the miseries and evils he shares with his auditory, whereas this poem is addressed primarily to the speaker's own soul, though in hortatory tones as if to an audience: "Thinke then, My soule, that death is but a Groome" (l. 85); "Thinke thee laid on thy death bed" (l. 93); "Returne not, my soule, from this extasee,/ And meditation of what thou shalt bee" (ll. 321-322). Important in this connection is the typical Protestant directive to the Christian to preach over again to his own soul the sermons which he hears, and also the meditative model consciously provided in Protestant funeral sermons, leading the auditory to consider first the evils of this world and then, as a counterpoise, the benefits gained by death.[19] Also relevant is Donne's characterization of some of the Psalms (which are all praises) as catechetical exercises and instructions.[20]

This meditation-sermon is at the same time a "Progress" for the speaker, as he urges his own soul to progress towards her soul, which has now ended its progress-time in the world. In this respect the poem has some relation to the dream-vision/pilgrimage poem—most notably, perhaps, to the *Divine Comedy*—though Donne's staggering conflations have worked a sea change in most of these generic features. In Donne's poem, a particular event, the occasion of a "religious death," stimulates a spiritual progress in which the speaker imagines his own soul following in the path her soul must have taken: its release on the deathbed, its flight to heaven, its new perfections and new pleasures there—"This must, my soule, thy long-short Progresse bee" (l. 219). In the course of that imagined flight to heaven, the speaker's address to his own soul as "she" tends to merge it with that other she who has gone before, and he finds his meditation turning at times into an "extasee" as he takes up a more constant imaginative stance in the heaven she has attained.

We have, then, a hymn of praise, but a hymn which is also the analysis of the speaker's own spiritual experience, his own "striving for life" and progress toward her; it is a meditative analysis which sounds like a sermon preached to the self. For this generic mix there is (in addition to the Psalms) an analogue in Donne's Hymn to God my God in my Sicknesse. The first stanza of that highly complex poem alludes to the tuning of the soul as instrument for producing music:

> Since I am comming to that Holy roome,
>   Where, with thy Quire of Saints for evermore,

---

[19] See chaps. 3 and 6.

[20] Similarly, Victorinus Strigelius designates certain of the Psalms as sermons. See *A Third Proceeding in the Harmonie of King David's Harp*, trans. Richard Robinson (London, 1595), p. 36.

> I shall be made thy Musique; As I come
>   I tune the Instrument here at the dore,
>   And what I must doe then, thinke now before.[21]

What happens is that the *Hymne*, as a paean of praise, is referred to the future, when the speaker himself will be music; the present poem as hymn is not so much music as preparation for music, a tuning of the instrument by means of analytic thought—specifically, meditation upon the death-bed occasion, its sufferings, and their spiritual significance. And this hymn/meditation is at length identified as a sermon preached to the self:

> So, in his purple wrapp'd receive mee Lord,
>   By these his thornes give me his other Crowne;
> And as to others soules I preach'd thy word,
>   Be this my Text, my Sermon to mine owne,
>   Therfore that he may raise the Lord throws down.[22]

The Second Anniversarie as hymn seems to assume the generic relationships which are stated explicitly in this *Hymne*. It is a hymnic praise or celebration of Elizabeth as image of God, but for the still earthbound speaker such a hymn of necessity is primarily a tuning of the instrument by means of meditation and preaching to the self.

One further generic element warrants attention here, the public character finally established for this hymn-cum-meditation/sermon. This is not only because celebration is by definition a communal act as Dennis Quinn has argued,[23] but specifically because the speaker sets the work in a public context. He reverts from time to time to his involved "we" form, taking cognizance of an audience overhearing his words even though they are not directly addressed: "Looke upward; that's towards her, whose happy state/ We now lament not, but congratulate" (ll. 65-66); "Shee . . . is gone,/

[21] Helen Gardner, ed. *The Divine Poems* (Oxford, 1952), p. 50.
[22] *Ibid.*
[23] Quinn, "Donne's *Anniversaries* as Celebration," pp. 97-105.

275

As well t'enjoy, as get perfectione./ And cals us after her"
(ll. 315-319); "[Shee] became unto us all,/ Joye, (as our
joyes admit) essentiall" (ll. 469-470). Such passages charac-
terize the speaker as spokesman for a community, the new
world of the elect who also strive for life; as in many Prot-
estant (and Donnean) sermons,[24] the speaker sets forth his
own meditations as model and stimulus for the auditory's
own exercises in that kind.

Furthermore, the satiric tone occasionally adopted by the
speaker (though much less often than in *The First Anni-
versarie*) reinforces the public character of the work, for
satire, though its themes may be private, is a public mode,
assuming an audience who will be reformed by or at least
will respond to the ridicule. In this poem that audience is
usually the world of the regenerate, and the satire takes the
form of wry irony and gentle chiding of its folly in failing
to perceive the full extent of the "incommodities" of this
life:

> Shee, shee, thus richly, and largely hous'd, is gone:
> And chides us slow-pac'd snailes, who crawle upon
> Our prisons prison, earth, nor thinke us well
> Longer, then whil'st we beare our brittle shell.
>
> (ll. 247-250)

Or again:

> What hope have we to know our selves, when wee
> Know not the least things, which for our use bee?
> We see in Authors, too stiffe to recant,
> A hundred controversies of an Ant.
> And yet one watches, starves, freeses, and sweats,
> To know but Catechismes and Alphabets
> Of unconcerning things, matters of fact;
> How others on our stage their parts did Act;
> What Caesar did, yea, and what Cicero said.
>
> (ll. 279-287)

[24] See chap. 3.

Only once is the sharper satiric bite of *The First Anniver-sarie* felt, in the passage stirring the soul (and the regenerate "we") to revulsion at the inescapable corruption dominating all walks of life:

>   What station
> Canst thou choose out, free from infection,
> That wil nor give thee theirs, nor drinke in thine?
> Shalt thou not finde a spungy slack Divine
> Drinke and sucke in th'Instructions of Great men,
> And for the word of God, vent them agen?
> Are there not some Courts, (And then, no things bee
> So like as Courts) which, in this let us see,
> That wits and tongues of Libellars are weake,
> Because they doe more ill, then these can speake?
> The poyson'is gone through all.
>
> (ll. 325-335)

The speaker's identification of himself in the final lines of the poem as a Trumpet unites these various generic elements—hymn, sermon, meditation, progress—and reinforces the public character of the exercise:

> Since his [Gods] will is, that to posteritee,
> Thou shouldest for life, and death, a patterne bee,
> And that the world should notice have of this,
> The purpose, and th'Autority is his;
> Thou art the Proclamation; and I ame
> The Trumpet, at whose voice the people came.
>
> (ll. 523-528)

The trumpet image activates rich and precise significances arising from the relevant biblical passages and the commentary on them. The speaker's characterization of himself as Trumpet calling the people to hear the Lord's proclamation, Elizabeth, alludes generally to the biblical metaphor of the prophet as trumpet of the Lord, blasted by inspiration and proclaiming God's will to the people (Judges 6:34, Ezekiel 33:3-5, 32). It alludes more specifically to the special responsibility and privilege of the priests under the Law to blow trumpets to assemble the congregation for war and for various civic functions, and also to solemnize feasts and celebrations. Moses was commanded to make

> two trumpets of silver . . . that thou mayest use them for the calling of the assembly, and for the journeying of the camps.
> And when they shall blow with them, all the assembly shall assemble themselves to thee at the door of the tabernacle of the congregation. . . .
> Also, in the day of your gladness, and in your solemn days, and in the beginnings of your months, ye shall blow with the trumpets over your burnt offerings, and over the sacrifices of your peace offerings; that they may be to you for a memorial before your God.
>
> (Numbers 10:2-3, 10)

Commenting upon these passages, Calvin observed that the silver trumpets gave the signal "so that the people should always be attentive to the voice and will of God," and that the priests "when they sounded, were the organs or interpreters of God . . . as if, by the mouth of the priests, He Himself published the holy assemblies."[25] The annual Feast of Trumpets (Leviticus 23:24) was thought by Cornelius à Lapide to be a memorial of the deliverance of Isaac from death, and by Calvin to be a reminder that the people must "be attentive to God's voice throughout their lives."[26] The sounding of the trumpets by the priests was an important part of the great celebrations of praise to God described in I Chronicles 15:16-28, II Chronicles 5:12-13, II Chronicles 7:6, and II Chronicles 29:27-28; the image also alludes to the several trumpets which are to sound at the last day, calling mankind to a general resurrection from the dead.

[25] Calvin, *Four Last Books of Moses*, ii, 458.
[26] Cornelius à Lapide, *Commentaria in Pentateuchum Mosis* (Antwerp, 1648), p. 737; Calvin, *Four Last Books of Moses*, ii, 458.

Christian commentators generally agreed that all these trumpets figure the Christian minister preaching the Word. Ambrose, noting that the word "trumpet" also means a voice, and interpreting the priests' role described in Numbers 10 as type both of the Christian minister's preaching and of the trumpets at the end of time, emphasized the trumpets' function in the spiritual awakening of the people:

> If anyone, therefore, desires to behold this image of God . . . let him fashion for himself two spiritual trumpets of pure and beaten silver, that is, composed of and adorned with precious speech. And let them not emit harsh and raucous tones inspiring fear, but let them pour forth thanks in the highest to God in continuous exultation. By the call of such trumpets the dead are raised. They are aroused, of course, not by the sound of the metal but by the word of Truth. . . . It is not everyone's prerogative, however, to sound both trumpets, nor is it everyone's prerogative to call together the whole assembly; that privilege is granted to the priests and ministers of God who are the trumpeters.[27]

But the best gloss for the speaker's designation of himself as a trumpet in *The Second Anniversarie* is supplied by Donne himself in his sermon on Ezekiel 33:32, "And lo, thou art unto them as a very lovely song, of one that hath a pleasant voyce, and can play well on an instrument; for they hear thy words, but they doe them not." The entire sermon develops the minister's double role, as trumpet, and as musical harmony (hymn):

> God for his own glory promises here, that his Prophet, his Minister shall be *Tuba*, as is said in the beginning of this Chapter, a Trumpet, to awaken with terror. But then, he shall become *Carmen musicum*, a musical and harmonious charmer, to settle and compose the soul again in a

[27] *On his Brother Satyrus: Second Oration*, in *Funeral Orations*, ed. McGuire, pp. 248-249.

reposed confidence, and in a delight in God. . . . God shall send his people preachers furnished with all these abilities, to be *Tubae*, Trumpets to awaken them; and then to be *carmen musicum*, to sing Gods music in their ears, in reverent, but yet in a diligent, and thereby a delightful manner. . . . The same trumpet that sounds the alarm (that is, that awakens us from our security) and that sounds the Battail (that is, that puts us into a colluctation with our selves, with this world, with powers and principalities, yea into a wrastling with God himself and his Justice) the same trumpet sounds the Parle too, calls us to hearken to God in his word, . . . and the same trumpet sounds a retreat too, that is, a safe reposing of our souls in the merit, in the wounds of our Saviour Christ Jesus.[28]

The sermon emphasizes also the tuning of the instrument, the life and example of the minister which makes him a fit trumpet for God's word: "[They] should first be Trumpets, and then Musick: Musick, in fitting a reverent manner, to religious matter; and Musick, in fitting an instrument to the voyce, that is, their Lives to their Doctrine."[29]

In the poem the speaker declares that Elizabeth is God's proclamation (his image, a manifestation to us of the paradigm of regeneration and salvation), and that he is the trumpet (the poet-prophet/priest/preacher) calling the people to hear the proclamation. His meditative progress becomes the means for transforming him into a fit and worthy instrument, and is itself the means by which he sounds, mediates, that proclamation to the assembly as an instruction calling them forth from spiritual death, and as a hymn of praise, *carmen musicum*. As trumpet his voice awakens from the dead the assembly of the elect even as he hymns the power of God manifested in and through Elizabeth Drury.

The title and the eighty-four-line introductory passage

[28] Donne, *Sermons*, II, 166-170, at Whitehall, Feb. 12, 1618/19.
[29] *Ibid.*, II, 173.

also indicate the symbolic values attaching to Elizabeth Drury in this poem. The occasion, her death, is now seen as a *religious death*, and this shift radically changes its significance. As any *untimely* death recapitulates the death of the young world's primal innocence and its subsequent corrupted state, so any religious death restates the archetypal pattern of the transcendence of nature and resurrection to glorified life for which Christ's death and resurrection provide the paradigm. Accordingly, as type (reflection) of Christ, this "Immortal Mayd" has now wholly transcended the dead world and has attained immortality in heavenly glory. By *occasion* of this religious death, and by means of his own poem, the speaker also undertakes his own recapitulation of the paradigm: a "death" to sin and nature, and a resurrection to the "new life" of grace.

As before, Elizabeth Drury is seen as a regenerate soul manifesting the restored image of God in man, but now that identification carries a different symbolic significance. In the *Anatomy* she chiefly imaged the perfection of the order of nature (understood to be partly restored in the regenerate, but by Donne's characteristic symbolic conflations seen in her as completed). That restoration in her emphasized by contrast the all-pervasive death of the order of nature, and the ubiquitous decay, ugliness, and morbidity of this world. As manifestation of the (restored) perfection of primal innocence she seemed at times to offer hope for the recovery of the world, but her death, recapitulating that first loss, demonstrates that nature itself, and this world as part of nature, are beyond hope. This range of significance and this argument for rejecting the world are reiterated and even extended in the introductory passage to *The Second Anniversarie*, as the appropriate beginning point for the new poem. The world's rottenness, its condition as a wormy "carcas" are again emphasized, in contrast to her recapitulation of the perfected nature of our primal innocence: "in all, shee did,/ Some Figure of the Golden times, was hid./ Who could not lacke, what ere this world could give,/ Because shee was the forme, that made it live" (ll. 69-

72). This world's form, we recall, was its created natural goodness, and more specifically man in the condition of primal innocence, who, as image of God, was the world's reason for being, and who by his original sin destroyed the world. That created natural perfection, that primal innocence gone—and departed again with her—the speaker dismisses the world once and for all as "fragmentary rubbidge" (l. 82).

In the introductory passage to *The Second Anniversarie* (ll. 1-84), Elizabeth as regenerate soul signifies our first innocence, but subsequently, with the final repudiation of the order of nature, she symbolizes the perfection of the order of grace on earth and its translation into the condition of heavenly glory. The speaker, having rejected nature, is in the body of this poem concerned wholly with the "world" of the regenerate, and he examines in Elizabeth the transcendence of nature by grace. The order of grace is in some respects a more perfect state than our first innocence because it involves participation in the divine life of Christ, whereby every Christian becomes "an abridgement of Christ himself." According to Donne's characteristic formulations, the elect Christian is viewed by God as if he were Christ himself; his inchoate sanctification may be viewed by God as if it were perfected, and his regenerate life here is a type of what he will be in heavenly glory when the perfections of the primal innocence are wholly restored and even enhanced.[30] Since Elizabeth Drury has now completed her earthly progress, she can well be taken as having achieved the highest degree of perfection grace can accomplish in the regenerate on earth, perfecting but also transcending the moral virtues of the natural order by religion, and prefiguring, foreshadowing, our "Paradise" to come:

> Shee that first tried indifferent desires
> By vertue, and vertue by religious fires,
> Shee to whose person Paradise adhear'd.
>
> (ll. 75-77)

[30] See chap. 6, pp. 210-215.

In keeping with this significance, occasional allusions in this poem present her as a type (recapitulation) of certain aspects of Christ's life and role. The poem does not thereby come to be an allegory about Christ, nor are we led to regard Elizabeth as a Petrarchan or Neoplatonic symbol pointing us away from herself and toward God; in accordance with Donne's characteristic incarnational focus, we are invited to contemplate God not in himself but in her—the human goodness possible in the order of grace. The opening lines describing her death in terms of the traditional Christ/Sun symbolism—"the Sunnes Sunne,/ The Lustre and the vigor of this All,/ Did set"—do not in themselves establish her significance as type, though the suggestion gains probability from the analogous image used of Christ in "Good Friday, 1613. Riding Westward": "There I should see a Sunne, by rising set,/ And by that setting endlesse day beget." In another passage the allusions to the eighty-fifth Psalm—the harmony of opposites supposedly effected at Christ's nativity[31]—seem uncontrovertable, as are the allusions presenting her goodness as a recapitulation of Christ's acts in her own sphere:

> ... shee made peace, for no peace is like this,
> That beauty and chastity together kisse:
> Shee did high justice; for shee crucified
> Every first motion of rebellious pride:
> And shee gave pardons, and was liberall,
> For, onely herself except, shee pardond all:
> Shee coynd, in this, that her impressions gave
> To all our actions all the worth they have.
>
> (ll. 363-370)

She too crucifies sin (in herself), she too pardons all the world, and, from Christ's grace which she manifests, all our otherwise unworthy actions receive their value. The re-

---

[31] Psalm 85:10, "Mercy and truth are met together; righteousness and peace have kissed each other." For the application to Christ see, e.g., *Geneva Bible* (1599), Part II, fol. 17ᵛ-18; *Douay Bible*, II, 158-159.

demptive powers ascribed to her in *The Second Anniver-sarie* have their basis in this identification of her as type of Christ.

The introduction also indicates the focus of this poem in the lines, "Looke upward; that's towards her, whose happy state/ We now lament not, but congratulate" (ll. 65-66), a focus consonant with the subtitle which promises to treat "the incommodities of the Soule in this life and her exalta-tion in the next." However, her heavenly state is not direct-ly described, but rather the way in which her perfections manifested on earth in the order of grace foreshadowed that heavenly condition. We are to look up to heaven where she now is, but we are invited to consider her especially as she manifested in life the possibilities of human goodness. This goodness, it should be reiterated, pertains to Elizabeth Drury by reason of her justification by grace; it is on this basis—not as a "symbol of virtue" as Louis Martz has argued[32]—that she functions in this poem as image of God, manifesting specifically the perfections of the orders of grace and glory. As with the *Anatomy*, my analysis of *The Second Anniversarie* is concerned chiefly to demonstrate the coherence and force of this central argument.

Throughout the previous discussion I have considered the first eighty-four lines of the poem as an introductory passage, departing thereby in some degree from Professor Martz's analysis of them as constituting a forty-four-line in-troduction and the first of the seven basic sections into which he divides the poem.[33] In my view this eighty-four-line passage is a close structural analogue of the ninety-line introduction to *The First Anniversarie*, and I hope that I have demonstrated the ways in which it serves as a bridge between the two poems—disposing, once and for all, of the issues important in *The First Anniversarie* and setting forth the terms for the new poem as regards speaker, audience, and the symbolic significance of Elizabeth Drury. Struc-

---

[32] Martz, *Poetry of Meditation*, p. 239. See above, chap. 4.
[33] *Ibid.*, pp. 236-248.

turally, then, I find this poem's basic argument disposed in six rather than seven sections: it begins with the deathbed meditation (l. 85) and advances through a logically ordered sequence of topics concerned with the soul's benefits from death; in relation to this sequence Elizabeth Drury is described as embodying ever more exalted perfections. I am in complete agreement with Professor Martz's cogent analysis of the demarcations of these six sections, though I find his structural formula for the individual sections—meditation, eulogy (and sometimes moral)—to be a less than complete account of their organization.

In my view, each of the six sections presents a four-part argument (with the partial exception of the deathbed meditation, in which the first two of these steps are combined).[34] In each of the six sections, the first step of the argument presents the restrictions upon and the incommodities of the elect soul in this world, as they are experienced by the speaker and all the regenerate who are as yet in the midst of their progress. Second, this experience is contrasted with a vision of the soul's exaltation in heavenly glory, where all these incommodities will be transcended. Third, Elizabeth Drury is presented as one who, having completed her earthly progress, can be assumed to have displayed the perfections possible in the order of grace on earth—a remarkable though not complete transcendence of nature and foretaste of heavenly glory. Finally, addressing his own soul in the name of all the regenerate, the speaker concludes each section with the observation that if one whose goodness in the state of grace so largely foreshadowed heavenly perfection yet wished to die so as to enhance that perfection, then we who are much more deeply enmeshed in the world's incommodities must perforce long for escape and perfection through death.

[34] Hardison (*Enduring Monument*, pp. 180-182) also recognizes a four-part argument in each section, though his formulation of it differs section by section; I suggest rather that the same basic formula for the four stages recurs in each of the six sections of the *Progres*.

As the first stage of his progress (ll. 85-156), the speaker urges his soul to meditate upon death. Here, exceptionally, the argument is in three parts rather than four: Death is to be viewed as our approach to heaven and heaven's approach to us (a merging of the usual two-part presentation of our present state and our future glory); Elizabeth Drury in life seemed already immortal because of the balance and harmony of her composition; but even she had to die in order to attain true immortality in heaven. The scene for this traditional deathbed meditation is graphically rendered by means of a personification of death as a servant approaching slowly with a taper, which is the light of heaven:

> Thinke then, My soule, that death is but a Groome,
> Which brings a Taper to the outward roome,
> Whence thou spiest first a little glimmering light,
> And after brings it nearer to thy sight:
> For such approaches doth Heaven make in death.
>
> (ll. 85-89)

With insistent and repeated directives to "Thinke then, my soule," the speaker calls up all aspects of the deathbed situation, and then transvalues every terrifying or distasteful physical aspect of death into its spiritual equivalent as an approach to heaven. The broken breath is "Division, and thy happiest Harmonee"; the loose and slack body is a pack unbound "To take one precious thing, thy soule, from thence"; the ague is a physic; the passing-bell calls us to the triumphant Church; Satan's eager bailiffs will receive only the legacy of the sins they first imparted; the weeping friends weep only that they do not die also; the worms will feed on the body only as favorites feed on a prince; the shroud is a reinvestment in white innocence; the burial is but for a St. Lucy's night before the resurrection (ll. 91-120).

Then, as an encouragement to this meditation, the speaker recalls Elizabeth—who manifested the perfections of the order of grace and who seemed so perfectly mixed and balanced in her composition as to be above nature, making cubes appear unstable, circles angular. For this reason, "No Feare, no Art could guesse" how she could die, since, as Aquinas and many others noted, death is caused by the contrarieties and oppositions which characterize all sublunary bodies.[35] Freedom from death did indeed attend upon the first innocence, although many theologians believed that man's body, made of earth, was not naturally free from death and dissolution even in the prelapsarian state, but that it enjoyed this privilege only by God's special favor.[36] Only heavenly substances are naturally incorruptible, a condition her constitution seemed to partake of since it resembled the celestial bodies of the planets and the spiritual substance of angels:

> So though the Elements and Humors were
> In her, one could not say, this governes there.
> Whose even constitution might have wonne
> Any disease to venter on the Sunne,
> Rather then her: and make a spirit feare
> That he to disuniting subject were.
>
> (ll. 135-140)

But of course these appearances are merely the types of heavenly glory, not yet its realization, and her body, however evenly balanced, is composed of contrary elements. Therefore even she had to "embrace" death as the means to heaven (the metaphor makes a positive and voluntary action out of what is an obvious necessity). The speaker concludes that if even she, who seemed already to enjoy the heavenly condition and privilege of a spiritual composition, had to die to attain true immortality in glory, clearly all the regenerate—despite the purchase they already have upon the heavenly state—must do so:

[35] *Summa Theologica* I, Q. 75, Art. 6, *Basic Works*, I, 691-693.
[36] See Arnold Williams, *The Common Expositor: An Account of the Commentaries on Genesis, 1527-1633* (Chapel Hill, 1948), pp. 104-105.

> Shee, shee embrac'd a sicknesse, gave it meat,
> The purest Blood, and Breath, that ere it eat.
> And hath taught us that though a good man hath
> Title to Heaven, and plead it by his Faith,
> And though he may pretend a conquest, since
> Heaven was content to suffer violence,
> Yea though he plead a long possession too,
> (For they'are in Heaven on Earth, who Heavens
>   workes do,)
> Though he had right, and power, and
>   Place before,
> Yet Death must usher, and unlocke the doore
>   (ll. 147-156).

The second topic, the soul's liberation by death from bodily incommodities and limitations (ll. 157-250), is developed in the customary four stages. In this life the souls of the regenerate are imprisoned and greatly encumbered by the body. In heaven the soul will be gloriously free of all material and physical hindrances. Elizabeth Drury had a body which was so commodious and lovely a habitation for her soul as to anticipate on earth the liberty and expansiveness of its heavenly dwelling. Since even she has gone to heaven, where her soul will have a yet finer habitation, we should be so much the more eager to escape from our bodies by death.

The physical incommodities suffered by the soul in this life are rendered in several typically grotesque Donnean images: the soul is urged to remember the "sinke," the foul cell of the womb in which it was made—worse than that of any Anchorite "Bedded and Bath'd in all his Ordures" (l. 171). And it is to recall its helplessness there, in that it could not avoid being instantly poisoned by original sin:

> Thinke but how poore thou wast, how obnoxious,
> Whom a small lump of flesh could poison thus.

This curded milke, this poore unlittered whelpe
My body, could, beyond escape, or helpe,
Infect thee with originall sinne.

(ll. 163-167)

And after birth it is imprisoned in a "poore Inne,/ A Province Pack'd up in two yards of skinne" (ll. 175-176), which is progressively ravaged by sickness and age.

Then the speaker presents a glorious vision of the soul's enfranchisement by death, when it will fly almost instantaneously from earth to heaven as a bullet fired from a gun or a bird hatched from its shell. In this remarkable passage the speaker exults in the speed and ease of the soul's movement and comments with wry irony upon its lack of concern for the cosmological questions plaguing foolish astronomers —questions which had also troubled the speaker in *The First Anniversarie*.[37] By use of the pronoun "she"—so constantly associated with Elizabeth Drury—in the description of the soul's flight, the speaker conflates Elizabeth's flight to heaven, which has already occurred, with this projection of his own soul's forthcoming flight. His progress (and that of every regenerate Christian) is thereby made a recapitulation of hers, and by this device the speaker is brought as it were to take up a vantage point in heaven for some of his subsequent deliberations:

> Shee staies not in the Ayre,
> To looke what Meteors there themselves prepare;
> Shee carries no desire to know, nor sense,
> Whether th'Ayres middle Region be intense,
> For th'Element of fire, shee doth not know,
> Whether shee past by such a place or no;
> She baits not at the Moone, nor cares to trie,
> Whether in that new world, men live, and die.

. . . .

[37] Compare *First Anniversarie*, ll. 205-208, 263-284.

> Nor is by Jove, nor by his father bard;
> But ere shee can consider how shee went,
> At once is at, and through the Firmament.
>
> . . . .
>
> This must, my soule, thy long-short Progresse bee.
>
> (ll. 189-219)

The passage concludes with metaphors which emerge from earlier image patterns, and resolve problems posed by them. Death, which brings about this swift flight of the soul from earth to heaven is not, as in *The First Anniversarie*, the ultimate disruptive and destructive force of the universe, but is now a new cohesive bond between heaven and earth: "As doth the Pith, which, lest our Bodies slacke,/ Strings fast the little bones of necke, and backe;/ So by the soule doth death string Heaven and Earth" (ll. 211-213). The metaphor of the taper from the deathbed meditation is continued here, to suggest the immediate approach of heaven's light at the moment when the "third birth" of death occurs: "Heaven is as neare, and present to her face,/ As colours are, and objects, in a roome/ Where darknesse was before, when Tapers come" (ll. 216-218). The reference to the three births of the soul—"Creation gave her one, a second, grace," and the third, the birth by death into glory (ll. 214-215)—makes explicit the typological framework within which Donne's *Anniversary* poems move: the three "births" of the soul, analogous to Luther's typological framework of the three advents of Christ, in nature, in our souls by grace, and in glory.[38]

Then in the third stage of this argument Elizabeth Drury is presented as manifesting the perfection of the order of grace, which is an antitype of the state of innocence and, as such, accords to the soul a bodily habitation which foreshadows its extensive and rich dwelling-place in heaven. By slight exaggeration of conventional tropes of praise—the Platonic harmony of body and soul in the virtuous person,

---

[38] See above, chap. 5, pp. 162-163, and note 45.

the body of man as a microcosm greater and more valuable than the world itself—her body is contrasted with the narrow and foul prisons that our bodies are. Hers is such that the soul "might well be pleas'd to passe/ An Age in her" (ll. 222-223); it incorporates and far surpasses the richness and scope of the macrocosm so that in one part of her is enough to make twenty such worlds, each part deserving of a tutelary angel. Already in considerable degree spiritualized, her body seemed a wholly suitable environment for her soul:

> Shee, of whose soule, if we may say, t'was Gold,
> Her body was th'Electrum, and did hold
> Many degrees of that; we understood
> Her by her sight, her pure and eloquent blood
> Spoke in her cheekes, and so distinckly wrought
> That one might almost say, her bodie thought.
> (ll. 241-246)

The conclusion follows: if she "thus richly, and largely hous'd is gone" to heaven where she will be yet more gloriously housed, then clearly we "slow-pac'd snailes" should hasten to lose our brittle shells (ll. 247-250).

The third section concerns the soul's gain by death in exchanging earthly ignorance for celestial knowledge (ll. 251-320). The argument is again in four stages: our ignorance here of all things and our defective instruments for gaining knowledge; the completeness of knowledge in heaven; Elizabeth manifesting the perfection of knowledge possible in the order of grace here and even anticipating heavenly knowledge; and finally, the necessity for even such as she to die in order to gain perfection of knowledge in heaven.

The speaker in condescending tones first condoles with the soul for its inability on earth to know itself or anything pertaining to it: "Thou art to narrow, wretch, to comprehend/ Even thy selfe" (ll. 261-262). It does not know how it came to the body, or acquired original sin, or how it is made immortal; it does not know about the elements that compose its body, or how the blood flows, or the fluid enters the lungs. And such knowledge seems especially hopeless of attainment since (and here the speaker formally relates himself to all the regenerate by his involved "we") the learned expend their time fruitlessly over unimportant and useless matters and cannot even resolve these: "We see in Authors, too stiffe to recant,/ A hundred controversies of an Ant" (ll. 281-282). Moreover, the soul is here in a "low forme"—the merest elementary class—and is hampered especially by its unreliable teachers, the senses:

> In this low forme, poore soule what wilt thou doe?
> When wilt thou shake off this Pedantery,
> Of being taught by sense, and Fantasy?
> Thou look'st through spectacles; small things seem great,
> Below.

> (ll. 290-294)

Then the contrast is stated—the soul's liberation from these senses which rather inhibit than convey knowledge to us, when it exchanges the low form of sensory knowledge for the watch-tower, intuitive knowledge in heaven:

> But up unto the watch-towre get,
> And see all things despoyld of fallacies:
> Thou shalt not peepe through lattices of eies,
> Nor heare through Laberinths of eares, nor learne
> By circuit, or collections to discerne.
> In Heaven thou straight know'st all, concerning it,
> And what concerns it not, shall straight forget.

> (ll. 294-300)

The third term in the argument is the praise of Elizabeth Drury for possessing the most complete knowledge possible to the regenerate in life, and therein foreshadowing the heavenly fullness of knowledge. The language used to describe her—"Shee who all Libraries had throughly red/ At home, in her owne thoughts, and practised/ So much good as would make as many more" (ll. 303-305)—alludes to the traditional metaphor of the Book of the Mind which contains within it an inscription of the Divine Ideas.[39] But especially it alludes to the frequently reiterated Donnean idea that all scripture is contained, incarnated, in the heart of the regenerate Christian: "He hath a whole *Bible*, and an abundant Library in his own heart, and there by this light of Faith ... he hath a better knowledge ... then either *Propheticall*, or *Evangelicall*."[40] Such knowledge can aptly be termed "all" knowledge since it is all essential knowledge (contrasting with the ignorance first described); it is knowledge of ourselves and of what pertains to us. This is in line with the Jobean definition—classic for Christian commentary on knowledge and wisdom—"The fear of the Lord, that is wisdom, and to depart from evil is understanding," and also with Paul's declaration that the essence of wisdom is knowing "Christ, and him crucified."[41] Since Elizabeth manifests such knowledge in the fullest degree possible to the regenerate, she can be portrayed as knowing all libraries, and also as foreshadowing, anticipating, the heavenly fullness of knowledge. Her knowledge of heaven in the order of grace was such that in heaven it changed only in appearance, not in essence:

> Shee, who in th'Art of knowing Heaven, was growen
> Here upon Earth, to such perfection,
> That shee hath, ever since to Heaven shee came,
> (In a far fairer print), but read the same.
>
> (ll. 311-314)

The conclusion then is that since even she, unsatisfied with her extensive knowledge on earth, went to heaven "As well t'enjoy, as get perfectione" (l. 318), we ought to follow, es-

---

[39] See Curtius, *European Literature and the Latin Middle Ages*, pp. 302-347.

[40] Donne, *Sermons*, III, 365-366. See chap. 5, pp. 167-168, and note 57.

[41] See, e.g., Augustine, *De Trinitate*, XII.xiv.22-23, *Works*, ed. Marcus Dods, VII, 302-303; also, *Geneva Bible* (1599), fol. 70, annotation on I Cor. 2:2-6, "The Gospell ... is true wisedome, but knowen to them onely which are desirous of perfection." See also Eugene R. Rice, Jr., *The Renaissance Idea of Wisdom* (Cambridge, Mass., 1958), pp. 1-92.

pecially since she has taken from us "our best, and worthiest booke," that epitome of the Book of the Creatures and that incarnate Bible which she was (l. 320).

The speaker introduces the fourth topic, our exchange by death of corrupt society here for a perfect society in heaven (ll. 321-382), by encouraging his soul to continue in the "extasee" it has attained. The suggestion that the speaker's soul has, temporarily, taken up an imagined stance in heaven is sustained by the very brief description of the world's corruptions in this section, in comparison with the vision of heaven's perfections, and Elizabeth's. The four parts of the argument are: the soul's corrupt companionship here; its perfect society in heaven among the angels and saints; Elizabeth Drury's achievement on earth, within herself, of the most perfect social order possible in the order of grace; and, her departure for heaven as an added incentive to us to seek that society.

The brief analysis of human society as the regenerate soul experiences it is sharply satiric of the "spungy slack Divine" and the courts, which are all alike in doing more evil than even libel-mongers can imagine. His attention set on Heaven, the speaker analyzes only the principal parts of the body social, which are most affected by the poison of sin, but he asserts nevertheless that "some effect/ In Nailes, and Haires, yea excrements, will show" (ll. 336-337). Then, apostrophizing his "drowsie soule," he turns its attention to Heaven's perfect society, enumerating according to the basic categories of the *Litany of the Saints* the glorious company it will enjoy there—the angels, in whose songs is no discord; the "blessed Mother-maid" who does not claim place by her maternity but attains it by her goodness; the Patriarchs, the Prophets, the Apostles, the Martyrs, and the holy Virgins (in which band of course is Elizabeth Drury). So he urges his soul, "Up, Up, for in that squadron there doth live/ Shee, who hath carried thether, new degrees/ (As to their number) to their dignitees" (ll. 356-358).

This imagination of Elizabeth as part of the heavenly society leads directly to the praise of her as manifesting the perfect society in the order of grace, in opposition to the corrupt courts and churches just described. Significantly, after the Fall the perfect society can exist only within the regenerate soul; she cannot transform the external social order, though she possesses a principle of internal order which prevents her own contamination "by company; (for shee was still/ More Antidote, then all the world was ill," ll. 377-378). Behind this praise of Elizabeth is the traditional Platonic *topos* of the kingship within the self, and the traditional Christian *topos* of the paradise within, but also that characteristic Donnean incarnational symbolism which locates the essence of the orders of nature and grace and their institutions within the individual: "As every man is *a world* in himself, so every man hath *a Church* in himselfe."[42] In these terms Elizabeth is a state and a church, manifesting within herself the highest moral and social relationships possible in the order of grace:

> Shee, who beeing to herselfe a state, enjoyd
> All royalties which any state emploid,
> For shee made wars, and triumph'd; reson still
> Did not overthrow, but rectifie her will:
> And shee made peace, for no peace is like this,
> That beauty and chastity together kisse:
> Shee did high justice; for shee crucified
> Every first motion of rebellious pride:
> And shee gave pardons, and was liberall,
> For, onely herselfe except, shee pardond all:
> Shee coynd, in this, that her impressions gave
> To all our actions all the worth they have:
>
> .   .   .   .
>
> As these prerogatives being met in one,
> Made her a soveraigne state, religion
> Made her a Church.
>
> (ll. 359-375)

42 Donne, *Sermons*, VII, 403.

She here displays that rulership over the self in respect to the dictates of morality and religion which Virgil, at the summit of the Mount of Purgatory, praised Dante the pilgrim for achieving, and thereby gaining entry into the Earthly Paradise: "Over thyself I crown and mitre thee."[43] As manifestation of this ordering grace, and as type of Christ who is its source, her "impressions" are said to give to our actions what merit they have, since they can have no intrinsic merit of their own. The conclusion follows: since she who manifested the regenerate soul's perfect internal "society" yet abandoned earth for Heaven's glorious Communion of Saints, we ought to strive for heaven too, and the more because she is now part of that heavenly society as one of its "accidental joys."

The fifth section (ll. 383-470) considers the soul's exchange of delusory joys here for essential joy in heaven. The speaker affects to retreat from the subject he seemed to be introducing, accidental joys, to consider the prior subject, essential joy. Here, as Hardison notes, Donne is finessing the matter: the proper order of climax (heretofore followed) calls for the consideration of essential joy, the vision of God, last.[44] But as will be evident, Donne's ordering is more defensible in terms of the fundamental themes of the poem than Hardison's account of it suggests. Resuming his mundane stance, the speaker develops his first approach to the topic of essential joy in a long, wryly ironic analysis of our futile search for true joys here. He follows this by a very brief account of essential joy in heaven, the vision of God. The third term presents Elizabeth's large share of that joy while on earth, and the conclusion again makes her exemplary to us in leaving this good state for that better one.

The analysis of the soul's search for essential joy on earth is a satire upon our proneness to delusion, even as regenerate souls, in that we pursue mundane, mutable goods as if they could bring essential joy. Chiding his soul in con-

[43] "Per ch'io te sopra te corono e mitrio," *Purgatorio*, xxvii.142 ("Temple Classics," London, 1956), p. 342.
[44] Hardison, *Enduring Monument*, pp. 184-186.

descending terms—"Poore couse'ned cose'nor"—the speak-
er bids it realize that if as a good Platonist it love "Beauty
. . . [which] worthyest is to move," then it will learn that
neither that love nor that beauty can endure in substance
or quality from day to day: "You are both fluid, chang'd
since yesterday; . . . Constant, you'are howrely in incon-
stancee" (ll. 389-393, 400). If it love honor, which might
seem a more worthy ideal since God himself sought it from
his creatures, then it will discover that honor derives from
the unpredictable and mutable opinions of inferiors. The
tower of Babel is a type of our folly in attempting to erect
true joy upon any mundane foundation, and the absurd
idolatry of the heathens in worshipping wine and corn and
onions is a figure of our absurdity in seeking what is only
in God in other things: "So much mankind true happinesse
mistakes;/ No Joye enjoyes that man, that many makes"
(ll. 433-434).

For the second term of his argument the speaker urges
his soul to work up again to its stance in heaven, to double
upon heaven those thoughts just expended upon earth, but
it fails in the attempt: "All will not serve" (l. 440). In ad-
mitting that he cannot describe essential joy, the speaker
advances one explanation for his reordering of topics and
for the brevity of this section: "Onely who have enjoyd/
The sight of God, in fulnesse, can thinke it;/ For it is both
the object, and the wit" (ll. 440-442). The speaker can only
give the conventional definition of essential joy—the "sight
of God, in fulnesse" as a permanent possession. The speak-
er's observation that the angels in heaven must have fallen
immediately after their creation, since they could not have
done so had they once looked upon God, affords him a witty
transition to the discussion of Elizabeth, who has come to
heaven "To fill the place of one of them, or more" (l. 447).

The third term of the argument then discusses her mani-
festation of the perfection of the order of grace on earth, in
which state she already attained in great measure the essen-
tial joy of the sight of God. She saw his image in the crea-
tion—"His face, in any naturall Stone, or Tree" (l. 453)—in

contrast to the foolish pagan and papist idolators who sought it elsewhere. Especially she saw that image in herself:

> Who kept, by diligent devotion,
> Gods Image in such reparation,
> Within her heart, that what decay was growen
> Was her first Parents fault, and not her own.
>
> (ll. 455-458)

She enjoyed here the relation of the faithful soul to the bridegroom, celebrated in the Song of Solomon: she "was here/ Betrothed to God, and now is married there" (ll. 461-462). And since she contained the restored image of God and thereby manifested him to us, she can be said to have "made this world in some proportion/ A heaven, and here, became unto us all,/ Joye, (as our joyes admit) essentiall" (ll. 468-470). The conclusion follows the usual pattern: she who on earth was filled with grace and enjoyed so abundantly the presence of God here, but yet "strove to bee,/ Both where more grace, and more capacitee/ At once is given" (ll. 465-467), obviously sets in that striving an example for us to follow.

The sixth and final section (ll. 471-510) turns back, ostensibly, to accidental joys in heaven, the topic previously postponed. But this section does not in fact explore accidental joys as such (that is, all heavenly joys that are not God) but rather sets up a contrast between the transience and reversibility of all improvements in our condition on earth and the permanence and continued growth of all our perfections in heaven. This is an appropriate thematic conclusion for the six-part sequence, given the fact that the *Anniversary* poems are concerned with states of human goodness (and evil) rather than with God or the heavenly life as such. The pinnacle of human perfection, properly climaxing the analysis of various particular goods including that of the vision of God, is the paradoxical condition of constantly increasing joys and perfections. Moreover, this section incorporates allusions to the resurrection of the body, traditionally understood to be the final perfection of man.

Again there are four parts to the argument. In regard to our condition on earth, two examples of the ephemeral and deceptive nature of earthly joys are cited: an honor given by a prince, which by "swelling" the soul in pride actually diminishes it, and the bursting of a dangerous abcess in the body, which gives temporary improvement in health but then causes death. The conclusion is, "All casuall joye doth loud and plainly say,/ Onely by comming, that it can away" (ll. 485-486). The second term is the heavenly condition, which does admit of constantly increasing joys and perfections: heaven's delight in the arrival of a new soul continues forever, and the joy of the heavenly souls steadily increases as they anticipate the forthcoming resurrection of their bodies—"When earthly bodies more celestiall/ Shalbe, then Angels were, for they could fall" (ll. 493-494). Such joy and such perfection paradoxically admit "Degrees of grouth, but none of loosing it" (l. 496).

In the third term of the argument Elizabeth Drury is envisioned as the apex of perfection in the order of grace, manifesting its particular goodness which (in Christ) is perfect and so in one sense admits of no degrees. Even her "accidental" perfections, her bodily excellencies, seem to foreshadow the celestial condition of the resurrected and spiritualized body after the judgment, when bodies also will be as souls:

> Shee, in whose goodnesse, he that names degree,
> Doth injure her; (Tis losse to be cald best,
> There where the stuffe is not such as the rest)
> Shee, who left such a body, as even shee
> Onely in Heaven could learne, how it can bee
> Made better; for shee rather was two soules,
> Or like to full, on both sides written Rols,
> Where eies might read upon the outward skin,
> As strong Records for God, as mindes within.
> (ll. 498-506)

However, in the order of grace she also foreshadowed that aspect of the heavenly condition which makes "full perfection grow": we remember that by their justification in Christ the elect are perfect in God's sight at the moment of the regeneration, but yet they steadily increase in personal virtue and sanctity. In heaven she will continue and even accelerate this paradoxical progress. The final lines are deliberately ambiguous as to whether they refer to her earthly or heavenly life, suggesting thereby the merging of grace into glory:

> Shee, who by making full perfection grow,
> Peeces a Circle, and still keepes it so,
> Long'd for, and longing for'it, to heaven is gone,
> Where shee receives, and gives, addition.
>
> (ll. 507-510)

There is no explicit conclusion for this section, but it follows from the lines cited. If she who on earth had so largely anticipated the ultimate human joys of steadily increasing perfection and the glorified spiritual body yet longed to accelerate the growth of those perfections in heaven and to give of her own perfections to that place, clearly we should also follow her there.

The Second Anniversarie presents, then, a sequence of topics concerning the soul's benefit by death, ordered as a logical progression according to an ascending scale of benefits. First, death is seen as an approach to heaven. Next, the physical encumbrances of the soul here and its freedom from them after death, in heaven, are considered. Third, the ignorance of the soul here and its fullness of knowledge there. Fourth, the soul's corrupt society here and its glorious company there. Fifth, the soul's delusory joys here and essential joy there in the vision of God. Sixth, the soul's transitory and reversible improvements here and its continual growth in perfections and joys there, leading ultimately to the resurrection of the glorified body. These are related as topics in a progressive meditative analysis, but they are also related dramatically. They define what "her" progress must have been—from earthly encumbrances to perfection in the order of grace to heavenly glory—and they display the speaker engaged in understanding these stages as part of, and as condition for, his own progress.

In relation to each of these stages, Elizabeth Drury is presented as the manifestation of the height of perfection possible in the order of grace upon earth, a condition prefiguring the still greater perfections of heaven. On her deathbed, her composition had seemed so perfectly balanced that she seemed already to be an incorruptible and immortal substance; her soul had in her earthly body a rich and extensive habitation; she possessed all (essential) knowledge, including perfection in the "Art of knowing Heaven"; she manifested here the perfection of the social order, having a kingdom and church within herself; she possessed here in large measure the essential joy of seeing God, in his creation and in his image within herself; she also enjoyed here something of the heavenly privilege of ever-increasing perfections, and even seemed to possess already a spiritual body such as the final resurrection will provide. In all these areas her perfection here was a type of that greater perfection of heaven where she has now gone and where the type is fulfilled in one of two possible ways. This sequence begins and ends with the body, and in regard to these two stages of the progress she was a type in the sense of an appearance, a shadow of the reality to come: she did not actually possess here the reality, but only the appearance, of the incorruptibility and of the glorified spiritual body she there enjoys. But in regard to the other aspects—the soul's rich and extensive dwelling, its fullness of knowledge, its harmonious society, and its vision of God—she was a type that already participated to some degree in the heavenly excellence foreshadowed. In these spiritual respects heaven will not provide a reality which before was only shadowed, but will fulfill the types *forma perfectior*.

In the concluding lines of his poem (ll. 511-528), the

speaker wittily congratulates himself (and Elizabeth) that
he has successfully withstood, while resident in France,
those prevalent idolatrous attitudes which would have per-
verted his staunchly Protestant praise. His praise does not
celebrate Elizabeth Drury as an individual, or her personal
merit as a Catholic saint, but rather God's image in her,
God's grace working upon her, which causes her to exhibit
to us the paradigm of regeneration. The focus is not upon
God but upon Elizabeth, yet upon her as she is recipient of
the grace of regeneration and thereby able to symbolize the
apex of human goodness in the orders of nature, grace, and
glory. The point is conveyed in the final images: she bears
the divine image, and therefore the poet's coin, his poem,
also bears that divine stamp, for God is the source both of her
power to do and the poet's power to say. But yet this proc-
lamation, made on God's authority and according to his
purpose, is Elizabeth Drury:

> Here in a place, where mis-devotion frames
> A thousand praiers to saints, whose very names
> The ancient Church knew not, Heaven knowes not yet,
>
> . . . .
>
> Immortall Maid, I might invoque thy name.
> Could any Saint provoke that appetite,
> Thou here shouldst make mee a french convertite.
> But thou wouldst not; nor wouldst thou be content,
> To take this, for my second yeeres true Rent,
> Did this Coine beare any other stampe, then his,
> That gave thee power to doe, me, to say this.
> Since his will is, that to posteritee,
> Thou shouldest for life, and death, a patterne bee,
> And that the world should notice have of this,
> The purpose, and th'Autority is his;
> Thou art the Proclamation; and I ame
> The Trumpet, at whose voice the people came.
>
> (ll. 511-528)

The reference to the "second yeeres true Rent" recalls the poet's promise at the conclusion of *The First Anniversarie* and in the introduction to the second, to devise yearly tributes, anniversary poems, celebrating her "birth" into heaven. These promises would seem to contradict the evidence adduced in this reading that the two poems are integrally related and constitute an artistically ordered and completed sequence. Some external evidence that the sequence as we have it represents the poet's realized intention is the fact that the two poems emphasize, respectively, the two common topics developed in most contemporary funeral sermons—the miseries of this world and the joys and benefits accruing to us by death. Also, the method in these poems is analogous to Donne's frequent practice in his own funeral sermons of developing two contrary arguments upon the same text by making slight shifts in the interpretation of that text—here, Elizabeth Drury's untimely/religious death. And, finally, there is the incontrovertible fact that Donne wrote no more anniversary poems about Elizabeth. The promises of yearly celebrations are probably best taken as a rhetorical flourish which ought not deflect us from recognizing the artistic whole Donne has in fact conceived— and executed, Bald reminds us, within a few months. Or from recognizing that Donne has here transfigured occasional poetry, making this conventional form the vehicle of a new metaphysical symbolic mode and audaciously developing that mode in the extended format of a major poetic sequence. The daring experiment was bound to have consequences both for complimentary poetry and for poetic symbolism, and we may now examine some of these.

PART IV

THE LEGACY OF DONNE'S
SYMBOLIC MODE

CHAPTER IX

The Tradition of the *Anniversary* Poems: Tributes, Echoes, and Imitations

THAT DONNE's *Anniversary* poems had a profound effect upon the idea of praise and the conception of occasional poetry in the seventeenth century seems abundantly clear. As Hardison points out, there is little evidence to support the often repeated assertion that these poems proved embarrassing to their author and incomprehensible or repugnant to his Jacobean audience.[1] They were virtually the only poems Donne gave to the press himself: his *First Anniversarie*, published in 1611, was reissued with its new companion poem in 1612, and these works went through two more editions in Donne's lifetime, in 1621 and 1625. Subsequently, they appeared in collected editions of Donne's poems in 1633, 1635, 1639, 1650, 1654, and 1669. Hardison interprets this popularity as an indication that seventeenth-century readers (with the exception of Ben Jonson) found Donne's conceptions and techniques "traditional" and "matter of course," or largely familiar to them from the writings of other poets.[2] I have been arguing, to the contrary, that these poems were genuinely innovative in their approach to poetic praise and to the genre of the funeral elegy. Yet because they drew upon ideas, attitudes,

---

[1] Hardison, *Enduring Monument*, pp. 163-166. The idea of Donne's embarrassment over these poems is based upon his letters to George Gerrard and Henry Goodyere in April, 1612, but the uneasiness expressed in these letters has to do rather with Donne's aristocratic sense that the role of the professional poet is beneath him than with any qualms about the subject or the execution of the *Anniversary* poems. See Edmund Gosse, *The Life and Letters of John Donne* (London, 1899), I, 302, 305-306.

[2] Hardison, *Enduring Monument*, pp. 163-170.

and literary forms familiar to contemporary readers from Protestant theological works, meditations, and sermons, they found a fit and numerous, though not always fully comprehending, audience that shared Donne's theological assumptions and was receptive to his metaphysical wit and style. Jonson was obviously unsympathetic on both counts, though his pointed remark to Drummond six years after the poems' publication indicates that they made a deep impression upon him.

It is not my intention here to trace the permutations of the conception and practice of funeral elegy and panegyric throughout the seventeenth century,[3] but rather to discuss the range of responses to and uses of Donne's *Anniversaries*. Although the question of influence is of course a tricky one, in that other poets might be assumed to be responding to the same intellectual and literary currents which Donne engaged with in both poetry and prose, yet the fact is that those elements received their most impressive poetic crystallization in the *Anniversary* poems. And in point of fact, several contemporary statements about these poems, as well as numerous more or less obvious verbal echoes and imitations of them, indicate that they rapidly became a model for praise and compliment generally, as well as a touchstone for judging other poetic endeavors in the panegyric and elegiac kinds. Thus the reactions to them illuminate some important matters of literary attitudes and taste, as well as questions of influence and poetic transformation in the seventeenth century.

A. Tributes and Verbal Allusions

For several decades after their publication, the *Anniversary* poems were lauded by other poets as the model and

[3] See Ruth Wallerstein, *Studies in Seventeenth-Century Poetic*, pp. 59-148, for a comparative study of the funeral elegies for Prince Henry, Edward King, and Lord Hastings, as the basis for some important distinctions concerning the various kinds of funeral elegy, and the development of the genre.

measure for poetry of praise. Also, several general eulogies of Donne's work which do not mention the *Anniversaries* by name are probably based chiefly upon those works since the fact of their publication made them the best known and most widely available of Donne's works before 1633. Joshua Sylvester's punning, deferential allusion to Donne in the opening lines of his *Lachrimae Lachrimarum* (1612), a funeral elegy for Prince Henry, seems to refer both to Donne's known accomplishment in the *Anniversary* poems and to the fact that Donne himself was planning an elegy on Henry (which was published the following year):

> How-ever, short of Others *Art and Witt*,
> I knowe my powers for such a Part unfitt;
> And shall but light my Candle in the *Sunne*,
> To doe a Work shalbe so better *Donne*.[4]

Sylvester's poem is in some respects a distant imitation of the *Anatomy* in its schematic analysis of the different elements of society whose sins helped cause Henry's death. In the same year (1612) John Davies of Hereford explicitly identified the *Anniversary* poems as the literary model he was attempting to imitate but could not hope to equal in his own elegy on a sixteen-year-old Elizabeth, Elizabeth Dutton, who died in 1611:

> I must confesse a *Priest* of *Phebus*, late,
> Upon like *Text* so well did meditate,
> That with a sinlesse *Envy* I doe runne
> In his *Soules* Progresse, till it all be DONNE.
> But, he hath got the *start* in setting forth
> Before me, in the Travell of that WORTH:

---

[4] Joshua Sylvester, *Lachrimae Lachrimarum, Or the Distillation of Teares Shede for the Untymely Death of the Incomparable Prince Panaretus* [London, 1612], sig. A 2, ll. 1-4. Sylvester's poem, somewhat expanded, was reissued the following year with a group of other elegies collected under a separate title page, *Sundry Funeral Elegies on the Untimely Death of the most excellent Prince, Henry* (London, 1613), which includes Donne's elegy and those of Sir Edward Herbert and Henry Goodyere, among others.

309

And me out-gone in Knowledge ev'ry way
Of the *Soules* Progresse to her finall *stay*.
But his sweet *Saint* did usher mine therein;
(Most blest in that) so, he must needs beginne;
And read upon the rude Anatomy
Of this dead World; that, now, doth putrifie.[5]

Another kind of testimony is provided by the elegies writ-
ten upon the occasion of Donne's death and appended to
the 1633 edition of his *Poems*. Several of these allude to the
Anniversaries as remarkable innovative works setting pro-
digiously high standards for subsequent eulogists and ele-
gists. Referring in general to Donne's achievements in the
genre of funeral elegy, Edward Hyde declared:

I cannot blame those men, that knew thee well,
Yet dare not helpe the world, to ring thy knell
In tunefull *Elegies*; there's not language knowne
Fit for thy mention, but 'twas first thy owne;
The *Epitaphs* thou writst, have so bereft
Our tongue of wit, there is not phansie left
Enough to weepe thee.[6]

Arthur Wilson remarked upon Donne's special characteris-
tic of epitomizing all the world in the woman praised:
"What ever was of worth in this great Frame,/ That Art
could comprehend, or Wit could name,/ It was thy theme
for Beauty; thou didst see,/ Woman, was this faire Worlds
Epitome."[7] Endymion Porter's rhetorical query also recog-
nized Donne's *Anniversaries* as peerless in their kind: "Tell
me, if a purer Virgin die,/ Who shall hereafter write her
Elegie?"[8] The most explicit, elaborate, and witty statement

[5] "A Funerall Elegie, on the death of the most vertuous, and no
lesse lovely, Mirs. *Elizabeth Dutton*," in *The Muses Sacrifice, or
Divine Meditations* (London, 1612) pp. 117 ᵛ-118.
[6] "On the death of Dr. Donne," *Poems by J. D. with Elegies on
the Authors Death* (London, 1633), p. 377.
[7] "*Upon Mr. J. Donne, and his* Poems," in *Poems by J. D.*, p. 398.
[8] "Epitaph upon Dr. Donne," *ibid.*, p. 405.

is that of Jaspar Mayne, which characterizes the *Anniversaries* as at once novel, inordinately complex, and normative for other elegies:

> Who shall presume to mourn thee, *Donne*, unless
> He could his teares in thy expressions dresse,
> And teach his griefe that reverence of thy Hearse,
> To weepe lines, learned, as thy Anniverse,
> A Poëme of that worth, whose every teare
> Deserves the title of a severall yeare.
> Indeed so farre above its Reader, good,
> That wee are thought wits, when 'tis understood,
> There that blest maid to die, who now should grieve?
> After thy sorrow, 'twere her losse to live;
> And her faire vertues in anothers line,
> Would faintly dawn, which are made Saints in thine.
> Hadst thou beene shallower, and not writ so high,
> Or left some new way for our pennes, or eye
> To shed a funerall teare, perchance thy Tombe
> Had not been speechlesse, or our Muses dumbe.[9]

As late as 1692 John Dryden could still appeal to the standard of the *Anniversaries* as a measure and model for his own panegyric for the Countess of Abingdon, *Eleonora*:

> It was intended, as Your Lordship sees in the Title, not for an Elegie; but a Panegyrique; a kind of Apotheosis, indeed; if a Heathen Word may be applyed to a Christian use. . . . Doctor *Donn* the greatest Wit, though not the best Poet of our Nation, acknowledges, that he had never seen Mrs. *Drury*, whom he has made immortal in his admirable *Anniversaries*; I have had the same fortune; though I have not succeeded to the same Genius. However, I have follow'd his footsteps in the Design of his Panegyrick, which was to raise an Emulation in the living, to Copy out the Example of the dead. And therefore

[9] "On Dr. *Donnes* Death," *ibid.*, p. 393.

it was, that I once intended to have call'd this Poem, the Pattern.[10]

Striking evidence of the impact of these poems upon the sensibilities of the age is also provided by numerous incidental imitations and verbal echoes of the *Anniversaries*, even though the works in which they appear often fail to assimilate the Donnean material in any profound or organic way. Because Donne's poems were published only months before that remarkable occasion for the outpouring of Protestant grief, the death of Prince Henry, they constituted a rich mine of literary resources for the muses who lamented Henry's death. Prince Henry's chaplain, Daniel Price, appropriated lines, phrases, images, and structural ideas from them for his several sermons and treatises on that woeful event. Price's general expectation of the imminent expiration of the world, "now that the Sunne is gone out of our Firmament,"[11] is a commonplace, but that can hardly be said of the application to Henry of several Donnean tropes and phrases which had been used to praise Elizabeth Drury's harmony of soul and spiritualized body:

> It is true, the very *outside* and rinde, the very raiment of his *soule*, his body was so *faire* and *strong* that a soule might have been *pleased* to live an age in it. It is *true* his soule *kept* tune so well, that *reason* sate *regent*, and the

---

[10] Dryden, "To the Right Honourable, the Earl of Abingdon," in *The Works of John Dryden*, ed. E. N. Hooker and H. T. Swedenberg, vols. 1—(Berkeley and Los Angeles, 1956—) III, 232-233.

[11] Price, *Lamentations for the death of the late illustrious Prince Henry . . . Two Sermons* (London, 1613), "The Second Sermon," sig. F 4. Cf. Donne:

> Nothing could make mee sooner to confesse
> That this world had an everlastingnesse,
> Then to consider, that a yeare is runne,
> Since both this lower worlds, and the Sunnes Sunne,
> The Lustre, and the vigor of this All,
> Did set; t'were Blasphemy, to say, did fall (II *Ann.* 1-6).

understanding Counsailour, never *captivated* with *violence* of *passions*, nor *hurried* with the *virulence* of affections, *vertue* and *valor*, *beautie* and *chastitie*, *armes* and *arts*, *met* and *kist* in him, and his goodness lent . . . mintage to other Princes.[12]

Moreover, in the same sermon Price took over virtually intact several lines from the *Second Anniversarie* to describe the benefits Henry has gained by death, and his joyful participation in the heavenly society:

He is freed from the *world*, and now being *enfranchised* enjoyes greater *good* in greater *liberty*. . . . He hath gon his *Passover* from *death* to *life*, where there is more *grace* and more *capacity* . . . where earthly *bodies* shalbe more *celestiall*, then man in his *Innocencie* or *Angels* in their *glory*, for they could *fall*: He is there with those *Patriarchs* that have expected *Christ* in *earth*, longer then they have enjoyed him in *heaven*; He is with those holy *Penmen* of the holy *spirit*, they bee now his *partners*, who were here his *teachers*.[13]

[12] Price, "Meditations of Consolation in our Lamentations," in *Spirituall Odours to the Memory of Prince Henry. In Four of the Last Sermons Preached in St. James after his Highnesse Death* (Oxford, 1613), p. 16. Cf. Donne:

> Shee, whose faire body no such prison was,
> But that a soule might well be pleas'd to passe
> An Age in her; shee whose rich beauty lent
> Mintage to others beauties (II *Ann.* 221-224).
>
>   . . . reson still
> Did not overthrow, but rectifie her will:
> And shee made peace, for no peace is like this,
> That beauty and chastity together kisse (II *Ann.* 361-364).

[13] Price, "Meditations of Consolation," pp. 16-17. Cf. Donne:

> Who being heare fild with grace, yet strove to bee,
> Both where more grace, and more capacitie
> At once is given (II *Ann.* 465-467).
>
> Joy that their last great Consummation
> Approches in the resurrection;

For his funeral sermon before the unburied body Price adapted with much else, the "Shee, shee is dead" refrain from Donne's *Anatomy*:

> *Prince Henry lieth dead before us.* He, He is dead, who while he lived, was a *perpetuall Paradise*, every season that he shewd himselfe in a *perpetuall spring, every exercise* wherein he was seene a *special felicitie*: Hee, He is dead before us. . . . *Hee, Hee* is dead; that blessed *Modell* of heaven his *face* is covered till the *latter day*, those *shining lamps* his eyes in whose *light* there was *life* to the beholders, they bee *ecclipsed* untill the *sunne* give over shining. . . . He, He is dead, and now yee see this ... *let us goe and die with him, we shall goe to him* though he shall not *returne* to us.[14]

On the first and the second years' anniversaries of Henry's death Price wrote treatises indebted to Donne's poems for titles, structure, and phrase as well as for the promise (like

---

When earthly bodies more celestiall
Shalbe, then Angels were, for they could fall (II *Ann*. 491-494).

Up to those Patriarckes, which did longer sit
Expecting Christ, then they'have enjoy'd him yet
(II *Ann*. 345-346).

[14] Price, *Teares Shed over Abner. The Sermon Preached on the Sunday before the Prince his funerall in St. James Chappell before the body* (Oxford, 1613), pp. 25-26. Cf. Donne:

But shee, in whom all white, and redde, and blue
(Beauties ingredients) voluntary grew,
As in an unvext Paradise; from whom
Did all things verdure, and their lustre come,
Whose composition was miraculous,
Being all color, all Diaphanous (I *Ann*. 361-366).

Shee to whose person Paradise adhear'd,
As Courts to Princes; shee whose eies enspheard
Star-light inough, t'have made the South controll,
(Had shee beene there) the Star-full Northern Pole
(II *Ann*. 77-80).

Donne's, unfulfilled) of producing yearly an "*Annuall* remembrance of my blessed *Master*."[15] The work entitled *Prince Henry His First Anniversary* (1613) has a structure modelled upon Donne's *Anatomy*, in which praises of Henry's goodness alternate with deprecations of the world's evil that culminate in stern warnings to the audience to learn from these contrasts. Henry is praised in Donne-like terms: "in HIM, a *glimmering light* of the *Golden* times appeared, all *lines* of expectation met in this *Center*, all *spirits* of vertue, *scattered* into others were *extracted* into him."[16] His body is again said to be such that in it "a *soule* might have contented it selfe to live an age, yea; were it *Methusulahs*: and for his *soule*, as if the *tincture* and *tainture* of original sinne, had not much infected it, it was the *Tabernacle* of all *vertue*."[17] Following meditations in this vein upon Henry's particular excellencies, the audience's sins (the world's sins) are denounced and anatomized:

O you vaine froathy *fondlings* of the world . . . learne hence . . . the *namelesse* and *helplesse* infirmities, by *outrages* and *sicknesses*, whereunto yee are subject. And upon this *consideration*, turne your eyes *inwardes* into your own *Anatomies*. . . . Learne hence yee *impatient* and *passionate whirlewinds*. . . . Learne hence yee *profane, unseasoned soules*, who never name *God* but in *oathes*. . . . Learne hence all yee unmindfull, unfaithful, unconstant, weather-beaten *worldlings*. . . . The redoubled *sound* of that *solemne* but *sorrowfull knell* [put] . . . the *world* in an *extasie*, as if some *especiall part* of *nature* were *dis-*

[15] Price, *Prince Henry His Second Anniversary* (Oxford, 1614), p. 2.

[16] Price, *Prince Henry His First Anniversary* (Oxford, 1613), p. 4. Cf. Donne:

in all, shee did,
Some Figure of the Golden times, was hid (II *Ann.* 69-70).

[17] *Ibid.*, pp. 4-5.

solving. . . . Learne hence all yee *firre trees*, that *Cedars* may fal, and *Princes* the *Gods* of the *earth* may *die.*[18]

Price's *Second Anniversary* also imitates, but much less closely, the Donnean structure of alternating praises and castigations, culminating in moralized refrains—"Learne hence yee *young Gallants!*" "Learne hence yee dunghill *muckwormes.*"[19] The language also is less imitative, but Prince Henry's perfections are still conceived in the manner of Elizabeth Drury's: his youthful goodness was "like *Adam* in his *innocencie*, it maketh the *possessor* to be *noted* and called *the childe of God.*"[20]

Several poems for Prince Henry contain elements which, though commonplace in themselves, are distinctive enough in formulation to suggest that many of them derive from the *Anniversaries*: in general these are tropes, images, and concepts which explore the death of the world with Henry's death, and the status of Henry as epitome of all good, as Divine image, and as redemptive Christ-figure. Some of these offer suggestive analogues to Donne's poems, and perhaps no more than that. In this category is George Chapman's long, sprawling *Epicede* (1612) which lauds Henry as "God-like" in his power and example, a "nothing-lesse-then-mortall Deitie" whose "worth contracts the worlds [worth]";[21] nevertheless, Chapman's claim that Henry re-

---

[18] *Ibid.,* pp. 10-11, 15, 17, 27, 31. Cf. Donne's refrain in the *First Anniversarie*:

Shee, shee is dead; shee's dead: when thou knowest this,
Thou knowest how poore a trifling thing man is.
And learn'st thus much by our Anatomee (ll. 183-185, *et seq.*)
[19] *Prince Henry His Second Anniversary*, pp. 5, 26.
[20] *Ibid.,* p. 8.
[21] George Chapman, *An Epicede or Funerall Song: On the Most Disastrous Death of the High-borne Prince of Men, Henry Prince of Wales* (London, 1612), ll. 50, 117, 438, in *The Poems of George Chapman*, ed. Phyllis B. Bartlett (New York and London, 1941), pp. 255, 256, 263. From line 354, Chapman's poem follows closely the Latin elegy of Angelo Poliziano, "In Albierae Albitiae immaturum exitum." See Franck Schoell, "George Chapman and the Italian Neo-Latinists of the Quattrocento," *MP*, 13 (1915), 215-238.

generated his followers by forming in them the Ideas of his own goodness seems much more distinctively Donnean:

> . . . they [the followers] unawares were come
> Into a free, and fresh *Elisium*;
> Casting regenerate, and refined eyes
> On him that rais'd them from their graves of vice
> Digg'd in their old grounds, to spring fresh on those
> That his divine Ideas did propose,
> First to himselfe, and then would forme in them.[22]

Another such analogue is Henry King's elegy on Prince Henry, which proclaims that the world itself will dissolve if it experiences any additional shock—"The World dares not survive/ To parallell this Woe's superlative"—and that the world's dissolution "Will be lesse grievous, though more generall" than Henry's.[23] More specifically Donnean, however, are the praises John Davies of Hereford applied to Henry, in identifying him as the epitome and masterpiece of nature, and specifically as image of God:

> He most strictly ey'de his better *Part*;
> And in the *Glasse* of *Heav'ns* eternall LAW
> Righted th'*Apparell* of his royall Heart
> As best became his FORME, which there he saw.[24]

---

[22] *Ibid.*, ll. 132-138, p. 257. Cf. Donne:

> A faint weake love of vertue and of good
> Reflects from her, on them which understood
> Her worth; And though she have shut in all day,
> The twi-light of her memory doth stay;
> Which, from the carcasse of the old world, free,
> Creates a new world; and new creatures be
> Produc'd (I *Ann.* 71-77).

[23] "An Elegy upon Prince Henryes Death," ll. 10-11, 16, in *The Poems of Henry King*, ed. Margaret Crum (Oxford, 1965), p. 65.

[24] John Davies of Hereford, *The Muses Teares for the Losse of their Hope* (London, 1613), Sig. B 1ᵛ. Cf. Donne:

> Who kept, by diligent devotion,
> Gods Image, in such reparation,
> Within her heart, that what decay was growen,
> Was her first Parents fault, and not her own (II *Ann.* 455-458).

Moreover, Davies preempted Donne's heart image, identifying Henry as our (the nation's) heart, and arguing from this that his death must needs cause the death by grief of the head (King James) and all the members (the entire nation):

> Looke how when the *Heart* is sicke, the HEAD
> And all the *Members*, of the *griefe* have part,
> But never die, untill the HEART be dead;
> So, HEAD and *Members* die with this our HEART!
> We die, though yet we move, with *griefe* conceav'd
> For this his death: whose Life gave all our Parts
> Their lively motion; which they had receav'd
> From his rare vertue, *Life* of all our *Hearts*.
> Nor can we (*ah!*) live other-wise than dead
> (Although, in *Death*, we live; or, lifeless plight)
> For him that gave us Heart; and Life, our HEAD;
> So live we now, without or *Life* or *Sp'rit*.[25]

Such Donnean tropes also recur in elegies for other persons and occasions. Patrick Hannay's elegy for Queen Anne (1619) argues that the world will inevitably fade with her death, since she was its soul:

> How can *it* then subsist?
> Can *that* be sayd to *be*, which disposest
> Of *soule*, wants *vigor*? this *Queene* was the *soule*,
> Whose *faculties* worlds *frailties* did controule.[26]

---

[25] *Muses Teares*, Sig. B 3ᵛ. Cf. Donne:

And learn'st thus much by our Anatomee,
The heart being perish'd, no part can be free (I *Ann.* 185-186).

That this worlds generall sickenesse doth not lie
In any humour, or one certaine part;
But, as thou sawest it rotten at the hart . . . (I *Ann.* 240-242).

[26] Patrick Hannay, "The First Elegie," in *Two Elegies on the Late Death of Our Soveraigne Queene Anne* (London, 1619), sig. A 4ᵛ. Cf. Donne, II *Ann.*, 72: "Shee was the forme, that made it [the world] live."

Moreover, Hannay apparently echoes Donne in making Anne the antitype whom the old poets and moralists fore-shadowed in their writings:

> Twas *she* the Antique *Poets* so admird,
> When with prophetique furie *they* inspird,
> Did faine the heavenly *powers*. . . .
> The *Morallists* did all of *her* devine,
> When *they* made every vertue foeminine;
> And but *they* knew that *such a one* should be,
> Doubtlesse with *them vertue* should have ben HE.[27]

Henry King's two poems on his dead wife, *The Exequy* (1624) and *The Anniverse* (1630), seem to show the influence of Donne's *Anniversary* poems in their general relation to each other, and in some specifics. In the first of them the poet adopts the stance of meditating upon her as "the Book,/ The Library whereon I look," and progressing steadily toward her.[28] The *Anniverse*, a sixth anniversary, uses the Donnean conceit of the world dead and putrifying as a result of her death: "So soone grow'n old? Hast thou bin six yeares dead?/ Poore Earth, once by my Love inhabited/. . . . Thou wilt bind mee Living to a Coarse."[29] Richard Brathwait's two poems for his wife Frances (1634) seem also to be indebted to Donne for their titles, *Anniversaries*, as well as for the declared intention to "reare" such an "Anniversall" each year "In Honour of her vertues";[30] though he imitated Donne in little else he also followed

[27] Hannay, "The First Elegie," *Two Elegies*, sig. B ɪ[v]. Cf. Donne:

She, of whom th'Auncients seem'd to prophesie,
When they call'd vertues by the name of shee (I *Ann.* 175-176).

[28] King, "An Exequy To His Matchlesse Never to be Forgotten Freind," ll. 8-10, in *Works*, ed. Crum, pp. 68-72.

[29] King, "The Anniverse. An Elegy," ll. 1-2, 7, in *Works*, ed. Crum, pp. 72-73.

[30] R. Brathwait, *Anniversaries upon His Panarete* (London, 1634); *Anniversaries upon his Panarete; Continued. . . . The Second Yeeres Annivers* (London, 1635), esp. sig. A 2.

Donne's lead in stopping his sequence after the *Second Yeeres Annivers.* Some poems of praise which were not funeral elegies also assimilated Donnean elements: an example is William Habington's panegyric for Lucy Hay, Countess of Carlisle (1637), which proclaims the author's intention to praise the divine image in her which, if it could be seen in pristine clarity, could restore the world:

> But I here pay my vowes to the devine
> Pure essence there inclos'd, which if it were
> Not hid in a faire cloud, but might appeare
> In its full lustre, would make Nature live
> In a state equall to her primitive.[31]

The Donnean echoes continue, though less abundantly, in later famous collections of elegies during the first half of the seventeenth century. R. Brown's elegy (1638) on Edward King (Milton's *Lycidas*), speculates in Donnean phrase, "May't not be said, the sea shall thus restore/ Our treasure greater, purer then before."[32] In the same volume, the elegy of Henry King for his dead brother employs Donnean constructions and phraseology to project what would have been the effect upon an ancient philosopher of coming to understand Edward's spiritual nature:

> His, whose perfections had that Atheist seen,
> That held souls mortall, he would straight have been
> In t'other extreme, and thought his body had
> Been as immortall, as his soul was made.

---

[31] "To the Right Honourable the Countesse of C," ll. 22-26, in *The Poems of William Habington*, ed. Kenneth Allott (London, 1948), p. 91.

[32] Brown [Elegy] *Justa Edouardo King* (Cambridge, 1638), p. 18. The echo is from Donne's "Funerall Elegie," ll. 45-46:

> May't not be said, that her grave shall restore
> Her, greater, purer, firmer, then before?

Whose active spirit so swift and clearly wrought
Free from all dregs of earth, that you'd have thought
His body were assum'd, and did disguise
Some one of the celestiall Hierarchies.[33]

And in the memorial volume for Lord Hastings (1649),
John Cave poses the problem of the world's continuation
after Hastings' death as a true Donnean paradox, arising
from the fact that Being is metaphysically dependent upon
Goodness and Hastings' death removes the source of good
from the world. How is it possible, Cave asks, "These two
flat contraries to reconcile;/ Th'*Effect* to be, and still and
still subsist;/ The *Cause* to vanish, and yet ne'er be mist"?
How can it be that goodness, "one main toward subsisten-
cie" can depart without incident, "as nothing were/ De-
pendent from it in this *Worlds* Matter"?[34] His resolution
gives a witty turn to Donne's argument that the world's
death must result from such a loss, in the explanation that
the reason Hastings' departure did not affect the mundane
supply of good was that he was so thoroughly supernatural:

[33] "Obsequies to the memorie of Mr. *Edward King*," in *Justa
Edouardo King*, p. 1. Cf. Donne:

> Whom had that Ancient seen, who thought soules made
> Of Harmony, he would at next have said
> That Harmony was shee, and thence infer,
> That soules were but Resultances from her,
> And did from her into our bodies go (I *Ann.* 311-315).

> Shee, of whose soule, if we may say, t'was Gold,
> Her body was th'Electrum, and did hold
> Many degrees of that; we understood
> Her by her sight, her pure and eloquent blood
> Spoke in her cheekes, and so distinckly wrought,
> That one might almost say, her bodie thought.
>   (II *Ann.* 241-246)

[34] Cave, "An Elogie upon the most lamented death of the Lord
Hastings," in *Lachrymae Musarum: The Tears of the Muses* (Lon-
don, 1649), p. 35.

> The Riddles out th'Abstract HE took away,
> Yet left the Concrete World Good still; to stay,
> To tell the Speculators of our time,
> How meerly supernatural, sublime
> HIS being in it was. . . .
>
> . . . .
>
>   so shall all
> That but minde HIM, grow Metaphysicall,
> Rarely transcendent, as HE was: for Minde,
> An Extract 'bove the mix of earth-Mankinde.[35]

B. IMITATIONS

Much more interesting than such cursory uses of Donnean tags and echoes are more serious poetic attempts to comprehend and respond to Donne's fundamental poetic concepts and techniques in the *Anniversaries*. These are poems which consciously undertake to imitate or qualify Donne's procedures in regard to such basic matters as the meditative/hortatory stance of the speaker; the detailed analysis of the human condition; the transformation of a real person into a symbol in some way participating in and incarnating the universal he presents; and the development of strategies to locate and explore various orders of being in the symbolic person. Several seventeenth-century poets pay Donne the compliment of attempting to imitate—usually without profound understanding—some of these innovative poetic ideas. It goes without saying, of course, that serious use of Donnean concepts is no guarantee of poetic worth: most of these poets had little ability to yoke Donne's Pegasus to their own poetic chariots, and some could lay no claim whatsoever to any such conveyance.

Two of the Prince Henry elegies, both written by members of Donne's circle, adopt without qualification the Donnean incarnational symbolism, though without developing

---

[35] *Ibid.*, p. 36.

the substantial theological and metaphysical basis for it which Donne proved able to transmute into impressive poetry. Sir Henry Goodyere's elegy (1613), the less complex of the two, is a concise, well-organized, and generally successful adaptation of Donne's techniques to rather different purposes.[36] The stance of the speaker is one of conducting an analytic examination of his own grief and the bases for it, in relation to the public grief. The series of probing questions creates a kind of anatomy of attitudes and motives, undertaken in a meditative/catechetical tone with the self as audience. Beginning with a series of parallel questions— "First, let me ask," "Next, let me ask"—he queries himself, his various hearers, and also the dead man as to whether he can possibly give appropriate expression to the universal grief, and whether to do so would not wrong Henry's present happiness. He concludes that the question is irrelevant: he must write, or be broken by grief. Then he queries whether he ought not merely state and not try to describe the grief, since the emotion is universal: every face reflects his own grief like a mirror, propagating it as some think original sin is propagated, from man to man. The people's only escape from an epidemic of grief as universal as the infection caused by original sin would be to destroy all record of Prince Henry, but this expedient is unthinkable: "Better they suffer, then His Worth should dye."[37]

Henry's true significance and the basis for resolving the speaker's dilemma are developed in terms of a metaphysical conceit identifying Henry's *head* as the source of life for our world. The origin of the conceit is obviously Donne's treatment of Elizabeth Drury (the regenerate soul which is the image of God) as the *soul* of the world. Goodyere's conceit has not Donne's metaphysical base, but the terms of its formulation are appropriate to the societal focus of Good-

---

[36] Goodyere, "Elegie On the Untimely Death of the Incomparable Prince, Henry," in *Sundry Funeral Elegies*, pub. with *Lachrymae Lachrymarum* (see note 4), sigs. F 3-F 4.

[37] *Ibid.*, sig. F 3ᵛ.

yere's poem: it is the wisdom and civilizing intelligence of Henry as monarch-to-be which is understood to create and to maintain the social order in being:

> She [Nature] made our World Then, when Shee
>   made His Head:
> Our Sense, Our Verdure, from His Brain was bred.
> And, as *Two great Destructions* have and must
> Deface, and bring to nothing, That of *Dust*;
> So Our true *World*, This PRINCES *Head* and *Brain*,
> A wastefull *Deluge* did and *Fire* sustain.[38]

The resolution builds upon the typological base suggested in this passage: As the world of dust was destroyed by flood and will be by fire, and as these destructions have been antitypically recapitulated in Henry, our true world, so the escape from the first destruction is reiterated here also. According to legend, only Seth's Columns survived the Flood, engraven with and thereby preserving the record of civilization and science to the ensuing ages.[39] So also, "what so-e're wee priz'd/ In Our lost World, is well *Characteriz'd*" in the two pillars of civilization yet preserved to us, Prince Charles and Princess Elizabeth.

More witty and tortuous in its logic, and somewhat less unified in tone and argument, is Sir Edward Herbert's elegy on Prince Henry (1613) which, according to Ben Jonson, Donne professed to be trying to over match in obscureness in his own elegy on Henry.[40] Donne's *Anatomy* was apparently the source of the fundamental paradox exploited by Herbert—the seeming life of the world despite the death of its life-principle or soul. Herbert states the metaphysical equation as a given—Henry is "our World's *Soule*"—and he

[38] *Ibid.*

[39] The legend of Seth's Columns is recounted in Flavius Josephus, *Jewish Antiquities* 1. 70-71, in *Josephus*, trans. H. St. J. Thackeray (Loeb Library, London, 1930) IV, 33.

[40] "Conversations with Drummond of Hawthornden," *Ben Jonson* I, 136.

structures his poem as an analysis of precisely how and in what senses we can be said to live and die after the death of the world's soul.[41] As in Goodyere's poem, the tone is analytic and catechetical, a series of rhetorical questions, though here they are addressed to a public audience, a generalized "we," rather than to the self.

The speaker first asks why, since Henry "had/ Our *Soules* layd up in *Him*," our love, which is the essence of souls, could not keep him alive. Since clearly it did not, he then queries whether we die in him but yet "doo appear/ To live and stirre awhile," even as the cosmic soul of the "world's *harmonick* Bodie" still moves the parts but no longer gives life to the whole.[42] Then, modulating to a more hopeful possibility, implying resurrection, he asks whether perhaps we only seem to die but are in fact asleep, as living things sleep in the earth in autumn but recover life in the spring. Then, most hopeful of all, he questions whether perhaps we yet live a life grounded upon Henry's heavenly life, which is maintained in us by his love and memory:

> May wee not be deceiv'd, and think wee knowe
> Our Selves for dead. . . .
>
> . . . .
>
>   when yet wee doo live
> A Life *His Love* and *Memorie* dooth give,
> Who was our World's *Soule*; and to whom wee are
> So re-unite, than in HIM wee repaire
> All other our Affections ill bestow'd;
> Since by This love wee now have such abode
> With *Him* in Heav'n as wee had heer, before
> *Hee* left us, *dead*.[43]

That perception changes the terms of the question, but the resolution which emerges is more witty than logically satis-

---

[41] Edward Herbert, "Elegie on the untimely Death of the Incomparable Prince, Henry," in *Sundry Funeral Elegies*, sig. F 2ᵛ.

[42] *Ibid.*, sig. F 2.   [43] *Ibid.*, sigs. F 2-F 2ᵛ.

fying, since the metaphysical equation operative here has been given no firm theological base, and Herbert does not really build (as Donne did) upon the idea of a regenerate life in the deceased and in us. We are declared to be certainly dead and our life merely a seeming life, since, if all our life is centered in his love and memory, we no longer perceive any difference between life and death, joy and pain, or have any memory of going through the motions of living. Should we (though dead) breed, this is only to keep his memory alive, although that memory (paradoxically) "being His, can therfore *never dye*."[44]

Outside Donne's immediate circle his wit, logic, conciseness, and especially his incarnational symbolism appear to have been much less perfectly understood by some would-be imitators. Sir John Davies of Hereford's poem (1612), which so explicitly and respectfully alludes to Donne's *Anniversaries* as model and measure for his praise of his sixteen-year-old subject, Elizabeth Dutton,[45] is the creation of a poet of commonplace mind and distinctly mediocre abilities. Though Davies' ineptitude caused him to produce a sprawling, disjointed mélange of praises for his Elizabeth, he undertook the project with the hope that his will and effort, together with the worthiness of his subject, would enable him to compete honorably with Donne:

> Yet greater *Will*, to this great *Enterprise*
> (Which in great *Matters* solely doth suffice)
> He cannot bring than I: nor, can (much lesse)
> Renowne more *Worth* than is in WORTHINES!
> Such were they both: for, such a worthy PAIRE
> (Of lovely vertuous *Maides*, as *good* as *faire*)
> Selfe-*Worthinesse* can scarse produce, sith they
> Liv'd like Celestiall *Spirits*, immur'd in *Clay*![46]

---

[44] *Ibid.*, sig. F 2ᵛ.

[45] Davies, "A Funerall Elegie," in *Muses Sacrifice*, pp. 111-120. See above, pp. 309-310, and note 5.

[46] *Ibid.*, p. 118.

It is instructive to observe which aspects of the *Anniversary* poems Davies endeavored to adapt, and which proved to be stumbling blocks for him. He assumed the Donnean stance of contemplating and learning from the lady, relating that stance to his particular situation as former tutor to Elizabeth Dutton and thereby heightening the paradoxes inherent in the reversal of roles. Davies also attempted a Donne-like metaphysical analysis of the question of how God will be able to reassemble our dissolved and scattered dust on the last day, but it is overlong, tedious, and digressive. He echoes certain of Donne's characteristic conceits (the lady's spiritualized body, her death which kills us all), but in general gives them conventional Petrarchan formulation: his Elizabeth is praised as Saint and Angel: her "*body* (like a soule)/ Had pow'r t'inflame the Love it did controule"; and "her *Death* must breake all *Hearts*" because her own deserts held all hearts captive to her.[47] At one point he specifically designates her a Laura-figure:

> And did my *Pow'r* but equall halfe my *Will*,
> *Laura* should be thy *Foile*: for, I (by *skill*)
> Would set thee so above her, that thy *light*
> (With poynant *Beames*) should thrust through
> *Earth* and *Night*.[48]

Like Donne, also, Davies understands his praises of the lady to be, at the most fundamental level, praises of God in and through her, but whereas Donne develops the point briefly Davies labors it, as if to obviate any possible risk of misunderstanding:

> Our *Songs* must answere the Celestiall *Quires*,
> That chant the praise of *Vertue* in their *King*,
> In whom thou art, then we on *earth* must sing
> Thy praise in *his*, sith *his* all praise containes:
> So *thine* in *his*, eternall *glory* gaines!

. . . .

---

[47] *Ibid.*, p. 113ᵛ.   [48] *Ibid.*, p. 112.

327

If some shall muse why I contemplate *Thee*
Among his *Praises* that most praisefull be,
Let it suffice them, t'was of purpose done,
To praise *thee, Starre*, for light had of this *Sunne*,
Within the *Volume* that includes his praise
(That nought includes) so *his* in *thine* to raise:
As when we laud the *light* the *Sunne* doth give
We praise the *Giver* in the *Gift*; and strive
(When most we praise the *Taker*) to renowne
The *Givers* praise for gracing so his *owne*:
So, and none otherwise, I praise the *Grace*
Appearing in the *Soule, Limbes, Eyes*, and *Face*
Of Natures *Maister-piece*, this goodly *Maide*;
Of whom all *good*, can never *ill* be said.[49]

Precisely where Donne is most innovative and daring—in the development of the symbolic value of Elizabeth as Form of the world—Davies feels called upon to take him gently to task for, as it were, overstepping the limits of the justifiable hyperbole permitted to one who praises. Despite his insistence upon praising God through the lady, Davies has not understood the metaphysical basis of Donne's incarnational symbolism (the lady as regenerate soul and image of God) and so—most respectfully—he refuses to follow Donne onto these rarefied heights:

Poets (I grant) have libertie to give
More *height* to *Grace*, then the *Superlative*:
So hath a *Painter* licence too, to paint
A Saint-like *face*, till it the *Saint* out *saint*.

[49] *Ibid.*, pp. 112, 117. Cf. Donne:

Immortall Maid, I might invoke thy name.
Could any Saint provoke that appetite,
Thou here shouldst make mee a french convertite.
But thou wouldst not; nor wouldst thou be content,
To take this, for my second yeeres true Rent,
Did this Coine beare any other stampe, then his,
That gave thee power to doe, me, to say this (II *Ann.* 516-522).

But *Truth* (which now mine *Art* to shaddow strives)
Makes *licence* larger by the *grace* she gives.
    But yet,
To say thou wast the *Forme* (that is the *soule*)
Of all this *All*; I should thee misenroule
In *Booke* of *Life*; which (on the Earth) they keepe
That of *Arts fountaines* have carowsed deepe.
Nay, so I should displease and wrong thee both:
For, *unjust praise* thou canst not chose but lothe,
That lothed'st it *here*; then *there*, more (past compare)
For, hee's the *Soule* of *All* by whom they *are*.
But I may say, (and none the same gainsayes)
Thou art the *soule* of this thy *World* of *Praise*!
Whose *soule* did animate thy *small-world* too
To be the *soule* of all that here I doe.[50]

George Chapman's poem *Eugenia* on the death of William, Lord Russell (1614)[51] is more chaotic still. It adapts some important Donnean elements from the *Anniversaries* but they are imbedded in so much that is foreign to their nature and spirit that the result is an inept mixture rather than a unified work. Organized in four *Vigiliae*, each with its *Inductio*, the poem's frame is a Spenserian allegory in which Eugenia (true nobility) and Religion (together with the Muses, the Virtues, and the Graces) retreat from the evils of the world to the House of Fame, where they hear of and are nearly destroyed by the news of Russell's death. At length they are revived by Fame's report of Russell's good life and death and his present happiness in heaven, and, further cheered by the report that Lord Russell's son

---

[50] Davies, "Funerall Elegie," pp. 113v-114. In this dismissal of Donne's method of praise there is also an echo of Donne: Donne's Elizabeth would not wish to be praised as Catholic saint (see quotation above), and Davies' Elizabeth would not wish to be praised as Donnean Form of the World.

[51] *Eugenia: Or, True Nobilities Trance; for the Most Memorable Death of the Thrice Noble and Religious; William Lord Russel* (1614), in *Poems*, ed. Bartlett, pp. 272-300.

is his true image, they return to earth to live with him. There is not much of Donne in all this, but Chapman has incorporated into Fame's lengthy reports, which constitute the bulk of the poem, several passages of metaphysical argument and numerous Donnean conceits.

In his "Epistle Dedicatory" Chapman describes his exercise as a "religious contemplation" and makes the Donnean promise of a yearly anniversary performance "for as many yeares as God shall please to give me life and facultie"; the promise is echoed in the refrain of the final hymn of praise sung by Poesie, "O heare/ These Rites of ours, that every yeare/ We vow thy Herse."[52] The chief Donnean element in the poem is the idea that by Russell's death True Nobility is stricken to death and Religion is reduced to a spider-like skeleton. The portrait of Religion as the "Form" of all the virtues and graces, and as deriving her very substance from Russell's good life and example, evidently takes off from Donne's conceit of Elizabeth Drury as Form of the world. Addressing Religion, Eugenia asks:

> How then will this poore remnant of your powres
> This cut-up-quick *Anatomie* of yours,
> This *Ghost* and shadow of you be preserv'd?
> Good life, that only feedes you, is so sterv'd,
> That you must perish; T'is not Noble now
> To be religious.[53]

Another Donnean feature is the description of the macrocosm's reaction to this death—as fact and not merely as the speaker's projection—with tempests, portentous signs, and finally a "fresh deluge" from Heaven. Still another is Fame's report of Lord Russell's deathbed meditations upon death as paradoxically light-bringing: it "presents the faire of heavenly light," and shows us "The lovely forms of our felicitie"[54] (we recall Donne's figure of death as groom bringing the taper of heavenly light into the dark death-

[52] *Ibid.*, ll. 1065-1066 *et seq.*, pp. 271, 296-299.
[53] *Ibid.*, ll. 246-251, p. 277.   [54] *Ibid.*, ll. 547-568, pp. 284-285.

chamber). Moreover, though he does not make this idea central to the poem, Chapman grounds his praise and contemplation of Lord Russell upon the fact that he presented God to us and therefore (according to the metaphysical theory of the necessary proportion between the knower and the object known) united us to God, even as his own life is now wholly "combinde" with the divine life. The speech is given to Eugenia:

> That as Philosophie
> Saies there is evermore proportion
> Betwixt the knowing part and what is knowne,
> So joynd, that both, are absolutely one;
> So when we know God, in things here below,
> And truly keepe th'abstracted good we know;
> (God being all goodnesse) we with him combine,
> And therein shew, the all-in-all, doth shine:
> This briefly, for the life of my blest love [Russell],
> Which now combinde is, with the life above.[55]

A much firmer and more unified poem is William Habington's set of eight elegies mourning his friend George Talbot (1635), entitled *The Funerals*.[56] Habington was thoughtful and selective in assimilating materials from the *Anniversaries*, and welded what he took into an organic whole. His speaker takes up the Donnean stance of contemplating the deceased soul, but—pointedly distinguishing his method from Donne's—he limits the scope of his contemplation to the sphere of Talbot's good life on earth, refusing to track the progress of his soul in the heavens:

> I can relate thy businesse here on earth,
> The mystery of life, thy noblest birth
> Outshin'd by nobler vertue: but how farre
> Th'hast tane thy journey 'bove the highest star,

[55] *Ibid.*, ll. 423-432, p. 281.
[56] Habington, *The Funerals of the Honourable, my Best Friend and Kinsman, GEORGE TALBOT, Esquire*, in *Works*, ed. Allott, pp. 99-111.

331

I cannot speake, nor whether thou art in
Commission with a Throne, or Cherubin.
Passe on triumphant in thy glorious way,
Till thou hast reacht the place assign'd.[57]

In asserting that he has no room for "witty griefe,"[58] the speaker again differentiates his poetic intention from Donne's and reaffirms the limits of his range. Yet despite these disclaimers he finds that the experience of the contemplation itself draws him beyond his intended meditation on moral virtue, creating in him a new soul which, in Donnean fashion, rises far above this world and scorns its goods:

Let me contemplate thee (faire soule) and though
I cannot tracke the way, which thou didst goe
In thy cœlestiall journey; and my heart
Expanssion wants, to thinke what now thou art
How bright and wide thy glories; yet I may
Remember thee, as thou wert in thy clay.

. . . .

Mem'ry of thy fate
Doth in me a sublimer soule create.
And now my sorrow followes thee, I tread
The milkie way, and see the snowie head
Of *Atlas* farre below, while all the high
Swolne buildings seeme but atomes to my eye.
I'me heighten'd by my ruine; and while I
Weepe ore the vault where thy sad ashes lye,
My soule with thine doth hold commerce above;

. . . .

by thee dead
I'me taught, upon the worlds gay pride to tread.[59]

He is, moreover, a meditator-cum-preacher, as Donne's speaker was, seeking to teach others what his meditations

[57] *Ibid.*, p. 101.
[58] *Ibid.*
[59] *Ibid.*, pp. 103-104.

reveal and praying that "I to the world may thy sad precepts read."[60]

Talbot is not the World's Soul, but he is the incarnation of virtue, and therefore the source of virtue in the world. Like Donne, Habington bases this conception upon the idea of the deceased as regenerate soul, restored image of God, and he takes over appropriate Donnean images to render this conception. Talbot is so virtuous that, after his death, "if yet some vertuous be,/ They but weake apparitions are of thee./ So setled were thy thoughts, each action so/ Discreetly ordered, that nor ebbe nor flow/ Was ere perceiv'd in thee." Also, the "faire republick of thy mind" presented a harmonious union of all the virtues, "where discord never swel'd."[61] Talbot was, moreover, the very incarnation of Virtue, and in manifesting Virtue to us she became "so faire" by him that "man, that blinde mole, her face did see."[62] Accordingly, like Elizabeth Drury, Talbot had been a guide in the world's tempests:

> By death extinguisht is that Star, whose light
> Did shine so faithfull: that each ship sayl'd right
> Which steer'd by that. Nor marvell then if we,
> (That failing) lost in this worlds tempest be.[63]

[60] *Ibid.*, p. 103.

[61] *Ibid.*, p. 105. Cf. Donne:

> . . . yet in this last long night,
> Her Ghost doth walke; that is, a glimmering light,
> A faint weake love of vertue and of good
> Reflects from her, on them which understood
> Her worth (I *Ann.* 69-73).

> Both Elements, and Passions liv'd at peace
> In her, who caus'd all Civill warre to cease (I *Ann.* 321-322).

[62] Habington, *Funerals*, p. 106.

[63] *Ibid.*, p. 109. Cf. Donne:

> She whom wise nature had invented then
> When she observ'd that every sort of men
> Did in their voyage in this worlds Sea stray,
> And needed a new compasse for their way (I *Ann.* 223-226).

333

His loss is therefore ruinous "To th'undone world in gen'rall," but to the speaker who lived one life of friendship with him, " 'Twas death."[64]

As regenerate soul, Talbot also presented the image of our innocent state in that he seemed to have scarcely any tincture of original sin. With him every scene of life was "from sinne so pure/ That scarce in its whole history, we can/ Finde vice enough, to say thou wert but man."[65] Therefore, again like Elizabeth Drury, it had seemed that he should be able to outlast or restore the world by his special "preservative":

> For had thy life beene by thy vertues spun
> Out to a length, thou hadst out-liv'd the Sunne
> And clos'd the worlds great eye.
>
> . . . .
>
> But thy example (if kinde heaven had daigned
> Frailty that favour) had mankind regaind
> To his first purity). . . .
>   Thou didst uncloyster'd live:
> Teaching the soule by what preservative,
> She may from sinnes contagion live secure,
> Though all the ayre she suckt in, were impure.
> In this darke mist of error with a cleare
> Unspotted light, thy vertue did appeare
> T'obrayd corrupted man.[66]

[64] Habington, *Funerals*, p. 100.   [65] *Ibid.*, p. 105.
[66] *Ibid.*, pp. 107, 108-109. Cf. Donne:

> So though the Elements and Humors were
> In her, one could not say, this governes there.
> Whose even constitution might have wonne
> Any disease to venter on the Sunne,
> Rather then her (II *Ann.* 135-139).

The Cyment which did faithfully compact
And glue all vertues, now resolv'd, and slack'd,

. . . .

Sicke world, yea dead, yea putrified, since shee
Thy'ntrinsique Balme, and thy preservative,
Can never be renew'd, thou never live (I *Ann.* 48-50, 56-58).

The conclusion of the poem posits but does not develop the Donnean distinction between the world blinded by sin and the regenerate who can respond to the beams from such a soul.

Though some of the examples cited derive from the general Petrarchan tradition of praise as well as from Donne, and though any particular reader may find certain of these examples less than convincing as illustrations of Donnean influence, this sample of tributes and imitations taken as a whole surely demonstrates the immediate and continuing popularity of the *Anniversaries*. The impact of the poems was felt immediately after their appearance, in several sermons and poems lamenting the death of Prince Henry. Though Ben Jonson's classically derived formula calling for praises directed to the specific moral qualities of individuals was probably still more influential, yet it is not too much to say that Donne's *Anniversaries* defined a significant new kind of poetry of praise which exploited the rich potentialities for symbolization and figurative expression available in the matrix of English Protestantism at the turn of the century. Moreover, as is indicated by Dryden's tribute to and imitation of the *Anniversaries* in his *Eleonora* (1692), their influence extended long after metaphysical tastes and habits of mind are supposed to have given way to neoclassicism, pointing up once more the inadequacy of sweeping generalizations relating to literary periodization.

The responses to Donne's poems suggest that the theological and metaphysical bases for his praises were at least partly perceived and accepted by his admirers and imitators for nearly a century. Not surprisingly, the imitations and adaptations also demonstrate that it is much easier to imitate a popular manner and style than to make effective use of a complex mode of symbolic thought. Donne's imitators were not notably successful in scaling his metaphysical heights, and sometimes, like Davies, they were fearful as Christians and as poets of the rarefied atmosphere on those heights. Nonetheless, the widespread admiration and tributes of imitation accorded these poems is clear evidence that they were not regarded as outlandish flattery or—*pace* Jonson—as near-blasphemy. And if their complex symbolism was not perfectly understood by less than acute contemporary readers and poet-imitators, it was well enough comprehended to establish these poems as serious, innovative, highly important models, defining a standard for eulogy and elegy.

Good poets of course do not imitate in the rather pedestrian manner I have been tracing here. They do not simply appropriate ideas or tropes from a single fashionable source, but rather transform whatever they borrow from whatever source into something new and strange. In the case of good or great poems engaged with topics and strategies resembling those of the *Anniversaries* it is much more difficult to determine specific Donnean influences or to gauge the precise effect of Donne's example. But these are the interesting cases, where the influence has led not to derivative hack-work but to fundamental poetic re-creation. A true measure of the contemporary significance of the *Anniversary* poems must take into account the stimulus they offered to good poets in the creation of important new poems.

CHAPTER X

The Tradition of the *Anniversary* Poems:
Major Poetic Responses and Re-Creations

MAJOR POETS, like minor poets, respond to poetic influ-
ences, but they normally draw upon a wide range of
literary materials and conventions, welding them into sur-
prising new syntheses informed by a powerful controlling
vision—even as Donne himself did in the *Anniversary*
poems. Jonson, Dryden, and Marvell are poets markedly
different from Donne in that they tend to be classicists in
their conceptions of genre, of decorum, and of the idea of
praise itself. Yet they all responded to and used Donne's
Anniversaries in significant and creative ways. The most
fascinating debt is Marvell's in *Upon Appleton House*,
which reworks to quite different ends the fundamental
metaphysical symbolism of the *Anniversaries*, and the po-
etic techniques which that symbolism inspires.

A. BEN JONSON

Despite his strictures upon Donne's *Anatomy*, and de-
spite his firm commitment to a poetics of praise calling for
the judicious, straightforward, and truthful estimate of the
particular virtues and qualities distinguishing the individ-
ual praised,[1] Ben Jonson was himself influenced by Donne
in certain of his longer elegies—the "Elegie On the Lady
Jane Pawlet" (1631) and particularly that on Lady Venetia
Digby (1633).[2] The elegy on Lady Jane, after a rather ro-

[1] See chap. I, pp. 36-38.
[2] *"An Elegie On the Lady* JANE PAWLET, *Marchion: of Winton"*
(d. 1631), and "EUPHEME; *Or, The Faire Fame Left to Posteritie
of that truly-noble Lady, the Lady VENETIA DIGBY, late wife
of Sir KENELME DIGBY," Under-wood, in Ben Jonson,* VIII, pp.
268-289.

mantic introduction in which the speaker imagines himself horror-stricken as the lady's ghost informs him of her death, is conceived in terms of the Jonsonian poetic: Lady Jane's particular virtues are carefully noted and evaluated; the specific events of her sickness are recounted to reveal her fortitude and piety; and an imaginative vision of her heavenly condition supplies Christian consolation. Yet, as Hardison has observed, Jonson does not simply ignore the very different Donnean conception of praise, which celebrates the individual as regenerate soul and image of God, but reacts directly to it, working out a careful justification of his own procedures as a counterstatement. Jonson's speaker pronounces himself unable and unwilling to attempt to "give her soule a Name," as if this would be near-blasphemy not unlike tendering Elizabeth Drury praises suited only to the Virgin:

> Had I a thousand Mouthes, as many Tongues,
> And voyce to raise them from my brazen Lungs,
> I durst not aime at that: The dotes were such
> Thereof, no notion can expresse how much
> Their Carract was! I, or my trump must breake,
> But rather I, should I of that part speake!
> It is too neere of kin to Heaven, the Soule,
> To be describ'd! Fames fingers are too foule
> To touch these Mysteries! We may admire
> The blaze, and splendor, but not handle fire!
> What she did here, by great example, well,
> T'inlive posterite, her Fame may tell!
> And, calling truth to witnesse, make that good
> From the inherent Graces in her blood!
> Else, who doth praise a person by a new,
> But a fain'd way, doth rob it of the true.[3]

The new but feigned way would seem to be Donne's. Yet after this statement of his own poetic platform and dismis-

[3] "Elegie," ll. 22-38.

sal of Donne's, Jonson in this very poem shows some influence of the phraseology of Donne's *Progres* as, in very brief compass, he calls up the vision of Lady Jane's flight to heaven and her privileges there:

> And now, through circumfused light, she lookes
> On Natures secrets, there, as her owne bookes:
> Speakes Heavens Language! and discourseth free
> To every *Order*, ev'ry *Hierarchie*!
> Beholds her Maker! and, in him, doth see
> What the beginnings of all beauties be.[4]

Jonson's *Eupheme*, conceived as a ten-part ode in a varied stanzaic pattern, is a much more difficult work, partly because we have it in fragmentary form. The design indicates an intention to treat the specifics of Lady Venetia Digby's life and person—her descent, her body, her mind, her offices, her match, her issue, her apotheosis. Yet the ode form, the fact that the extant parts of the poem are more panegyric than elegiac, the fact that two of the three most substantial sections deal with the abstractions of her body and mind, and the fact that the poem as we have it ends with a lengthy and lofty treatment of her apotheosis work together to exalt this subject for praise much above Jonson's usual wont. Venetia Digby is not made the Form of the world or anything like it, though she is presented throughout as a microcosm: in the section "The Picture of the Body" Jonson adapts the conventional situation of the lady sitting for her portrait as a strategy for praising her body as a universe, a paradise, which is appropriately rendered only in terms used to describe God's created universe. In the section termed "The Mind" Jonson treats the mind as the spiritual principle informing the body, thus approaching the presentation of Lady Digby as soul, and specifically as regenerate soul. In this vein, he describes that mind as bearing the image of God, and incarnating that image in the body:

[4] *Ibid.*, ll. 69-74.

A Mind so pure, so perfect fine,
As 'tis not radiant, but divine:
And so disdaining any tryer;
"Tis got where it can try the fire.

· · · · · · · · · ·

Or hath she here, upon the ground,
Some Paradise, or Palace found
In all the bounds of beautie fit
For her t'inhabit? There is it.

Thrice happy house, that hast receipt
For this so loftie forme, so streight,
So polisht, perfect, round, and even,
As it slid moulded off from Heaven

· · · · · · · · · ·

In thee, faire Mansion, let it rest,
Yet know, with what thou art possest,
Thou entertaining in thy brest,
But such a Mind, mak'st God thy Guest.[5]

The ninth section, entitled "Her Apotheosis, or Relation to the Saints" (in heroic couplets), is designed as a funeral elegy and treats the expected topics: the speaker's plaint for her death (which involves his own death as a poet since she is his muse); his perception, provoked by grief, of the world in ruins; his imagination of Venetia's glorious situation in heaven; his review of her virtuous life on earth. The strategy of the whole may owe something to Donne in its presentation of the speaker contemplating Venetia Digby and inviting her family to join in a meditative progress; interestingly, the speaker's meditations are fused with Venetia's, so that he advances in spiritual knowledge as he reviews her meditations on the incarnate Savior—his justification of us, his ascension to glory, his last judgment. In a variation of the Donnean incarnational mode Jonson fuses Christian history with her history: her death occurs during a meditative ecstasy on the last judgment so that even as she

[5] "Eupheme," ll. 25-28, 49-56, 69-72.

meditates upon the calling forth of all the dead to life and judgment, she herself is "rapt hence" from the world's death to life in heaven.

Certain details in the description of her heavenly state, though in themselves commonplaces, increase the resemblance to Donne's *Progres*. Venetia enjoys the heavenly society even as Elizabeth Drury did, "Amongst her *Peeres*, those Princes of all good!/ *Saints, Martyrs, Prophets*, with those *Hierarchies,/ Angels, Arch-angels, Principalities*."[6] Also like Elizabeth Drury, she enjoys her new freedom and glorious escape from the incommodities of this life:

> And she doth know, out of the shade of Death,
> What 'tis t'enjoy an everlasting breath!
> To have her captiv'd spirit freed from flesh,
> And on her Innocence, a garment fresh
> And white, as that, put on. . . .[7]

Moreover, in heaven she enjoys the sight of her Savior and hears him expound on those subjects which formed the theological core of the *Anniversary* poems, "his inherent righteousnesse" and our salvation "b'imputed right."[8] The passage culminates in the presentation of Christ the judge, confirming the speaker's estimate of Venetia Digby on the basis of his own thorough understanding of and anatomy of her character:

> Nor dare we under blasphemy conceive
> He that shall be our supreme Judge, should leave
> Himselfe so un-inform'd of his elect,
> Who knowes the hearts of all, and can dissect
> The smallest Fibre of our flesh; he can
> Find all our Atomes from a point t'a span!
> Our closest Creekes, and Corners, and can trace
> Each line, as it were graphick, in the face!
> And best he knew her noble Character,
> For t'was himselfe who form'd, and gave it her.[9]

[6] *Ibid.*, l. 225.   [7] *Ibid.*, ll. 84-86.   [8] *Ibid.*, ll. 91-96.
[9] *Ibid.*, ll. 135, 144, 147-156.

Despite all this, Jonson does not view Venetia Digby as image of God in Donne's metaphysical sense, preferring the more conventional understanding of her as "*Saint.*"[10] Yet his insistence upon her Divine creation, his fusion of her progress in life and death with her meditations on Christ's life, death, teachings, and judgment, and also his presentation of the meditator's progress in understanding these things by focusing on her, shows a significant debt to Donne's poetic strategy, especially in *The Second Anniversarie.* It is no small evidence of the influence of the *Anniversary* poems that they so affected the imagination even of that redoubtable classicist who was their most severe contemporary critic.

B. John Dryden

Dryden, like Jonson, was primarily concerned to praise particular virtues and qualities in the person celebrated; he was even more concerned than Jonson with the classical values of easy numbers and just poetic language. But, as several critics have observed, many of Dryden's elegies and panegyrics written throughout the long span of his literary career contain distinctive echoes and uses of Donne, most notably of the *Anniversary* poems.[11] Dryden's use of Donne is not simply a matter of echoes and conceits, though neither is it ever a matter of presenting the person praised as the Form of the world through whom to explore what can be said about man's nature and condition. Rather, Dryden's eulogized personages are conceived on an analogous though more restricted plan, according to which they epitomize some significant ranges of human experience but not, as it were, the essence of man and nature.

As Ruth Wallerstein has demonstrated, Dryden's elegy

---

[10] *Ibid.*, l. 228.

[11] See, e.g., Ruth Wallerstein, *Seventeenth-Century Poetic*, pp. 129-148; Arthur W. Hoffman, *John Dryden's Imagery* (Gainesville, Fla., 1962), pp. 123-128; Earl Miner, *Dryden's Poetry* (Bloomington, Ind., and London, 1967), pp. 206-227.

342

"Upon the Death of the Lord Hastings" (1649), written at the age of eighteen, was influenced both by classical lament and by the Donnean metaphysical elegy.[12] Some of the more extravagant conceits have long been recognized as metaphysical—derived from Donne, though often by way of Cowley or Cleveland. The *Anniversaries* were a direct influence upon this schoolboy effort. Such conceits as "His body was an Orb, his sublime Soul/ Did move on Vertue's and on Learning's Pole"[13] have the general flavor if not the logical rigor of microcosm-macrocosm figures in the *Anniversaries*. The opening paradoxes, though not Donnean in language, urge the questions posed by Elizabeth Drury's death: "Must *Vertue* prove Death's Harbinger?" "Is *Death* (Sin's wages) Grace's now?"[14] Moreover, the witty and extravagant conclusion, though drawing upon the discussion in Plato's *Symposium* of those persons, pregnant in soul, who produce and beget in others wisdom and virtue, perhaps owes something also to Donne's invitation to Elizabeth Drury to be (since she will not be a mother) a Father, impregnating his muse so that she may bring forth such hymns yearly and raise "great Grand-children of thy praises."[15] So Dryden urges Hastings' intended bride (he died on the eve

[12] See the extended discussion of the Prince Henry elegies and of Dryden's levying upon the various traditions in Ruth Wallerstein, *Seventeenth-Century Poetic*, pp. 115-148. See also her essay, "On the Death of Mrs. Killigrew: The Perfecting of a Genre," *SP*, 44 (1947) 519-528; and Hoffman, *Dryden's Imagery*, pp. 1-19.

[13] "Upon the Death of the Lord Hastings," ll. 27-28, *Works of John Dryden*, ed. Hooker & Swedenberg, I, 3-6. Unless otherwise indicated, subsequent references to Dryden's poetry are to this edition.

[14] *Ibid.*, ll. 5-7.

[15] *Symposium* 209 A-D, *Plato*, v, ed. and trans. W.R.M. Lamb (Loeb, London, 1925), 198-201. II *Ann.* 33-38:

> Immortal Mayd, who though thou wouldst refuse
> The name of Mother, be unto my Muse,
> A Father since her chast Ambition is,
> Yearely to bring forth such a child as this.
> These Hymes may worke on future wits, and so
> May great Grand-children of thy praises grow.

343

of his wedding to Elizabeth Mayerne, the daughter of a famous court physician of the era) to wed his soul since she cannot wed his body:

> Let that make thee a Mother; bring thou forth
> Th'*Idea's* of his Vertue, Knowledge, Worth;
> Transcribe th'Original in new Copies; ...
>   so shall he live
> In's Nobler Half; and the great Grandsire be
> Of an Heroick Divine Progenie.[16]

The elegy presents Hastings as the epitome of all heaven's gifts, all virtues, with something of the Donnean understanding of the "all" incarnated in the single human individual. All heaven's gifts are said to be combined in his soul, and under that freight his body is also spiritualized:

> Heav'ns Gifts, which do, like falling Stars, appear
> Scatter'd in Others; all, as in their Sphear,
> Were fix'd and conglobate in's Soul; and thence
> Shone th'row his Body, with sweet Influence;
> Letting their Glories so on each Limb fall,
> The whole Frame render'd was Celestial.[17]

In attempted rational explanation of this phenomenon, Dryden appropriates (from Donne's other *Progresse of the Soule?*)[18] the idea of metempsychosis, speculating that all the great souls of history have with all their excellencies

[16] "Upon the Death of the Lord Hastings," ll. 99-104.

[17] *Ibid.*, ll. 33-38.

[18] Donne's unfinished satirical poem, *The Progresse of the Soule*, has as its basis the conceit of the soul passing through various hosts from the forbidden apple in Paradise, through various plants and animals, to Themech, Cain's sister and wife. Where Donne intended it to end is not obvious, and Jonson's report ("Conversations with Drummond," *Ben Jonson*, I, 136) that it was to pass through the bodies of several heretics and end in Calvin seems improbable. Donne uses the fate of this "great soul" in its progress as a satiric means for castigating the world, whose various evil qualities the soul assimilates, but the experiment might have served to suggest the adaptation of the conceit to the purpose of praise. It stood first in the 1633 edition of Donne's *Poems*.

transmigrated into Hastings' soul, where they must die
again with his expiration:

> O had he di'd of old, how great a strife
> Had been, who from his Death should draw their Life?
> Who should, by one rich draught, become what ere
> *Seneca, Cato, Numa, Caesar*, were:
> Learn'd, Vertuous, Pious, Great; and have by this
> An universal *Metempsuchosis*.
> Must all these ag'd Sires in one Funeral
> Expire? All die in one so young, so small?[19]

Although the casual way in which this figure is invoked and
then dismissed prevents us from taking it seriously as a
metaphysical basis for the poem, and although the often
puerile poetry also precludes such seriousness, we can rec-
ognize in it an effort to adopt—and rationalize—an incarna-
tional symbolism on the order of that which Donne employs
in the *Anniversaries*.

The ode "To . . . Mrs. Anne Killigrew" is altogether
a more remarkable and consistent performance. There are
fewer specifically Donnean echoes or conceits, though some
familiar tropes occur. Anne's body is spiritual: "Thou hast
no Dross to purge from thy Rich Ore: / Nor can thy Soul a
fairer Mansion find, / Than was the Beauteous Frame she
left behind." She herself is such a worthy book that "to be
read her self she need not fear."[20] At the beginning of the
poem the poet undertakes to determine in which of the
heavenly spheres she is now resident, perhaps alluding to
the imagined flight of the soul to heaven in *The Second An-
niversarie*. There may also be some reference to Hall's
"Harbinger to the Progres" in the speaker's designation of
Anne as "Harbinger of Heaven" who at the last day will
point the way to the poets who follow after:

[19] "Upon . . . Hastings," ll. 67-74.
[20] "To the Pious Memory of the Accomplisht Young Lady Mrs
Anne Killigrew, Excellent in the two Sister-Arts of Poësie, and Paint-
ing. An Ode," ll. 35-37, 80, *Works*, III, 110-115.

> There *Thou*, Sweet Saint, before the Quire shalt go,
> As Harbinger of Heav'n, the Way to show,
> The Way which thou so well hast learn'd below.[21]

Dryden also makes use of a fundamental poetic strategy developed in the *Anniversaries*, that of taking the occasion of a particular death as a stimulus for analyzing and meditating upon a problem or topic somehow illustrated by that particular death. In *Anne Killigrew* the problem, as Professors Hoffman and Miner have noted,[22] concerns the ideas of poetry, art, civilization, and their relation to moral goodness. Using a strategy analogous to that of the *Anniversaries*, Dryden represents the "world" of poetry and painting as embodied in Anne Killigrew, again developing an apparently rational basis for this incarnation through whimsical speculations about metempsychosis. The proposition is that her pre-existing soul may have passed through all the great poets of the past before coming to reside in her:

> But if thy Praeexisting Soul
> Was form'd, at first, with Myriads more,
> It did through all the Mighty Poets roul,
> Who *Greek* or *Latine* Laurels wore,
> And was that *Sappho* last, which once
>   it was before.[23]

This is not to be taken seriously in itself, and is of a piece with various gentle but significant qualifications of the

---

[21] "Anne Killigrew," ll. 193-195. Cf. Hall, "The Harbinger to the Progres," ll. 19-21, 27-28.

> And thou (Great spirit) which her's follow'd hast
> So fast, as none can follow thine so fast;
> So farre as none can follow thine so farre,
>
> . . . .
>
> So while thou mak'st her soules Hy progresse knowne
> Thou mak'st a noble progresse of thine owne.

[22] Hoffman, *John Dryden's Imagery*, pp. 98-129; Miner, *Dryden's Poetry*, pp. 253-265; E.M.W. Tillyard, *Five Poems* (London, 1948), pp. 49-65.

[23] "Anne Killigrew," ll. 29-33.

praises accorded Anne as poet.[24] She is at length placed quite precisely in the ranks of the minor poets through an equation with *Orinda*, the poetess Katherine Philips. Yet the problem located in her and in the situation of her death is to be taken seriously: as in the *Anniversaries*, a slight vehicle is made to carry a weighty tenor. In analogy with Elizabeth Drury, Anne Killigrew is a very minor poet and painter who, simply because she does participate in the "world" of art and its conditions, is made to incarnate and symbolize that world in its pure, ideal state.

The analogy with the *Anniversaries* is carried further in that the world of poetry is imagined to have undergone a second fall, and Anne Killigrew is proposed as the atonement for this fall—the agent of our second redemption. The crucial stanza describing this fall of poetry contains something like the alternation of tones in the *Anniversaries*—a satirical denunciation of the fallen world (of poetry) and a eulogy of the pure regenerate artist-soul who is potentially redemptive:

> O Gracious God! How far have we
> Prophan'd thy Heav'nly Gift of Poesy?
> Made prostitute and profligate the Muse,
> Debas'd to each obscene and impious use,
> Whose Harmony was first ordain'd Above
> For Tongues of Angels, and for Hymns of Love?
> O wretched We! why were we hurry'd down
>   This lubrique and adult'rate age,
>   (Nay added fat Pollutions of our own)
>   T'increase the steaming Ordures of the Stage?
> What can we say t'excuse our Second Fall?
> Let this thy *Vestal*, Heav'n, attone for all!
> Her *Arethusian* Stream remains unsoil'd,
> Unmixt with Forreign Filth, and undefil'd,
> Her Wit was more than Man, her Innocence a Child.[25]

---

[24] For a discussion of such qualifications, see Miner, *Dryden's Poetry*, pp. 256-263.

[25] "Anne Killigrew," ll. 56-70.

The basis of her potential as redeemer is pointed to in the final line: a superhuman wit (the effect of the metempsychosis, we may suppose, or, more seriously, the divine or inspired nature of the poetic creation itself) is wedded to a childlike innocence which guarantees to her poetry the moral purity almost wholly lost in this second fall that corrupted art. Because of this innocence she can embody a regenerative possibility for poetry, even as Elizabeth Drury before her death had seemed to embody such a possibility for fallen mankind generally by manifesting the perfections of our primal innocence. Anne recalls poetry to its original purity and fusion with good life: her poetry presents love without sinful passion, and her painting (which realm she governed in right of poetry) is not restricted to externals but in its highest realization renders the hearts and souls of her subjects.[26] This utilization of Donnean strategies to explore the fall and restoration of art, together with the relation of this issue to the occasion of Mistress Killigrew's death, display Dryden's sure judgment in taking precisely what he needed and not more from the Donnean model, and reworking it brilliantly to his own purposes.

In *Eleonora* (1692) Dryden avowedly took Donne's *Anniversaries* for his model, and professed to derive his poetic strategy for praising the titular lady, the Countess of Abingdon, directly from them. Exulting in a sense of inspiration which, he declared, had lifted from him the weight of thirty years and produced in him a great "multitude and variety" of similitudes, Dryden revealed in his prefatory letter to the deceased lady's husband that he had undertaken to write a panegyric, not an elegy, and that he understood Donne's poem to be of that generic character.[27] As Earl Miner has observed, it is as if Dryden viewed the two *Anniversary* poems and the "Funerall Elegie" as one extended pane-

[26] Miner discusses the treatment of her progression from the realm of inferior French art to the nobler English mode of painting, *Dryden's Poetry*, pp. 259-262.

[27] "To the Right Honourable The Earl of Abingdon," III, 231-235.

gyric on Mistress Drury, and designed his own poem in terms of that conception.[28]

Any reader of *Eleonora* is aware that Dryden drew heavily upon Donne's three poems in regard to verbal echoes, allusions, and some structural patterns—almost all taken from the eulogistic portions of the poems. In his very perceptive essay on *Eleonora*, Miner cited more than fifteen clear echoes of Donne's three poems on Elizabeth Drury, and a dozen more doubtful or general echoes.[29] All are not equally persuasive as borrowings, but some are uncontrovertible. The opening lines of *Eleonora* strike at once the familiar Donnean chords:

> As when some Great and Gracious Monarch dies,
> Soft whispers, first, and mournful Murmurs rise
> Among the sad Attendants; then, the sound
> Soon gathers voice, and spreads the news around,
> Through Town and Country, till the dreadful blast
> Is blown to distant Colonies at last;
> Who, then perhaps, were off'ring Vows in vain,
> For his long life, and for his happy Reign:
> So slowly, by degrees, unwilling Fame
> Did Matchless *Eleonora*'s fate proclaim,
> Till publick as the loss, the news became.
>
> (Eleo. 1-11)

The passage echoes the opening lines from Donne's "Valediction Forbidding Mourning" as well as elements from the *Anatomy*:

> As virtuous men passe mildly'away,
> And whisper to their soules, to goe,

---

[28] Miner, *Dryden's Poetry*, p. 209. Miner's essay, chap. 6, pp. 206-229, is the most substantial study of the poem, and I draw heavily in what follows upon its record and discussion of the specific debts Dryden's poem owes to Donne's *Anniversaries* and "A Funerall Elegie."

[29] See discussion in pages cited above (Miner, pp. 206-229), and suggested list of borrowings in notes 1 and 6.

> Whilst some of their sad friends doe say,
> The breath goes now, and some say, no:
>
> (*Vale.* 1-4)

> But as in states doubtfull of future heyres,
> When sickenes without remedy, empayres
> The present Prince, they're loth it should be said,
> The Prince doth languish, or the Prince is dead:
> So mankind. . . .
>
> .   .   .   .
>
> Thought it some blasphemy to say sh'was dead;
> Or that our weakenes was discovered
> In that confession.
>
> (I *Ann.* 43-53)

The description of Eleonora's goodness as a perfect fusion of virtues resembling a perfectly mixed perfume recalls similar lines in *The Second Anniversarie*:

> As in Perfumes compos'd with Art and Cost,
> 'Tis hard to say what Scent is uppermost;
> Nor this part Musk or Civet can we call,
> Or Amber, but a rich Result of all;
> So, she was all a Sweet; whose ev'ry part,
> In due proportion mix'd, proclaim'd the
>   Maker's Art.
>
> (*Eleo.* 154-159)

> But as in Mithridate, or just perfumes,
> Where all good things being met, no one presumes
> To governe, or to triumph on the rest,
> Onely because all were, no part was best.
>
> (II *Ann.* 127-130)

Or again, Dryden's description of the surprise elicited by the unexpected tearing of the Lady's page in the Book of Fate closely resembles a passage from Donne's "Funerall Elegie":

Her fellow Saints with busie care, will look
For her blest Name, in Fate's eternal Book;
And, pleas'd to be outdone, with joy will see
Numberless Vertues, endless Charity;
But more will wonder at so short an Age;
To find a Blank beyond the thirti'th Page;
And with a pious fear begin to doubt
The Piece imperfect, and the rest torn out.

(Eleo. 291-298)

He which not knowing her sad History,
Should come to read the booke of destiny,
How faire and chast, humble and high shee'ad
    beene,
Much promis'd, much perform'd, at not fifteene,
And measuring future things, by things before,
Should turne the leafe to reade, and read no more,
Would thinke that eyther destiny mistooke,
Or that some leafes were torne out of the booke.

(Elegie 83-90)

Some phrases are taken over almost without alteration. Donne writes that the soul enroute to heaven, "ere shee can consider how shee went,/ At once is at, and through the Firmament," and Dryden observes of Eleonora's flight "(so smooth, so suddenly she went)/ [It] Look'd like Translation, through the Firmament."[30] Donne declares that the soul arrived in heaven "now is growen all Ey" and Dryden observes that Eleonora in heaven is become "all Intelligence, all Eye."[31] A striking evidence of Donnean influence in another kind occurs at the end of the poem as Dryden briefly abandons panegyric for a Donnean satiric tone, imitating in the passage in question the Donnean alternation between praises of the lady and castigation of the wicked world. The speaker refers to himself as one who,

[30] II *Ann.* 205-206; *Eleo.* 337-338.   [31] II *Ann.* 200; *Eleo.* 341.

> Dares to sing thy Praises, in a Clime
> Where Vice triumphs, and Vertue is a Crime:
> Where ev'n to draw the Picture of thy Mind,
> Is Satyr on the most of Humane Kind:
> Take it, while yet 'tis Praise; before my rage
> Unsafely just, break loose on this bad Age;
> So bad, that thou thy self had'st no defence,
> From Vice, but barely by departing hence.
>
> (*Eleo.* 363-370)

Finally, Dryden virtually repeats the conclusion of *The First Anniversarie* in his own conclusion:

> Verse hath a middle nature: heaven keepes soules,
> The grave keeps bodies, verse the fame enroules.
>
> (I *Ann.* 473-474)

> As Earth thy Body keeps, thy Soul the Sky,
> So shall this Verse preserve thy Memory;
> For thou shalt make it live, because it sings of thee.
>
> (*Eleo.* 375-377)

The governing conception of Dryden's poem, as Miner has persuasively shown, is the idea of Eleonora as pattern. The title of the poem was to have been "The Pattern," Dryden explains in his prefatory letter, for his design was to present the Countess as the "Pattern of Charity, Devotion, and Humility; of the best Wife, the best Mother, and the best of Friends."[32] The poem terms her a "second Eve" less brittle than the first, who, had she been the first woman, would have retained Paradise for us and remained our "Pattern."[33] Miner demonstrates, moreover, that the term "pattern," as Dryden uses it in this poem, carries two specific significances: Eleonora is a pattern or copy of God and the heavenly beings, and she is a pattern for us to copy in regard to her various excellencies and virtues.[34] In develop-

---

[32] *Works*, III, 233.
[33] *Eleonora*, ll. 170-175. For the poem see *Works*, III, 235-246.
[34] See Miner, *Dryden's Poetry*, pp. 219-227.

ing the first sense, Dryden used biblical allusions in a daring way to invest Eleonora with Godlike properties: in her charity to the poor her gift of "Manna" is as certain as the coming of dawn, a mode of action which associates her with God's providence to the Israelites; she feeds multitudes, and a mere touch of her garment "cures" poverty, allusions which associate her with Christ. This last association is pressed further with the occasion of her death at age thirty-three, "her Saviour's time," and the conclusion is, "cou'd there be/ A Copy near th'Original, 'twas she."[35] These allusions are placed in perspective and controlled, however, by the final description of her in terms of Christian sainthood of the Roman Catholic variety: as we know, the saint by virtue of that role "copies" or imitates Christ.[36]

In this presentation of the lady as pattern Dryden professed to be following Donne's precedent with Elizabeth Drury,[37] but, as we have seen, Donne's conception is more daring and more radically metaphysical. In his *Canonization* Donne uses the term "pattern" in Dryden's double sense, in order to define the status and function of the "saints" of love in accordance with the Catholic idea of sainthood. Donne's lovers are "saints" in that they enact in relation to their own sphere of lovemaking the saints' role as imitation or copy of Christ, and also in that they provide a model for us to copy—just like Eleonora. But in the *Anniversaries* Donne uses the term "pattern" only in the second sense: Elizabeth is "for life, and death, a patterne" for us, and her poet proclaims her as such.[38] She is not a pat-

[35] *Eleonora*, ll. 16-22, 38-39, 300. See Miner, pp. 216-227.

[36] *Eleonora*, l. 359. Miner discusses the way in which the biblical allusions audaciously associate her with divinity, but at the same time are often qualified to indicate her lesser status as saint or "pattern" of the divine.

[37] "To . . . the Earl of Abingdon," *Works*, III, 233: "I have follow'd his [Donne's] footsteps in the Design of his Panegyrick, which was to raise an Emulation in the living, to Copy out the Example of the dead."

[38] II *Ann.* 524.

tern in Dryden's first sense, a "Copy near th'Original," as
Eleonora was said to be. Rather, as image of God she her-
self is "first originall/ Of all faire copies" and "the forme,
that made it [the world] live."[39] For Donne the lady, as re-
generate soul and image of God, *is* the Platonic idea and not
a copy of it.

Still later, in "The Monument of a Fair Maiden Lady,
Who dy'd at Bath" (1700), Dryden produced some of his
closest verbal echoes of Donne's poems on Elizabeth Drury,
though he made no effort in this short poem to present the
lady as a symbol in any sense. This lady's body was a "Crys-
tal Case," a "transparent Veil," which seemed to be of the
same spiritual substance as her soul.[40] Her virginal purity
is described in lines taken almost unchanged from Donne:
she was "All white, a Virgin-Saint . . . / For Marriage, tho'
it sullies not, it dies."[41] And she, like Elizabeth Drury, had
little left to learn about heaven when she arrived there:

> Yet she had learn'd so much of Heav'n below,
> That when arriv'd, she scarce had more to know:
> But only to refresh the former Hint;
> And read her Maker in a fairer Print.
>
> (*Fair Maiden*, 24-28)

[39] *Eleo.* 300; I *Ann.* 227-228, II *Ann.* 72.

[40] "Monument of a Fair Maiden Lady," ll. 9-10, 16-17, *The Poems
and Fables of John Dryden*, ed. James Kinsley (London, Oxford, and
New York, 1970), pp. 814-815:

> So faultless was the Frame, as if the Whole
> Had been an Emanation of the Soul;
>
> . . . .
>
> As through a Crystall Case, the figur'd Hours are seen.
> And Heav'n did this transparent Veil provide.

Cf. "A Funerall Elegie," ll. 59-62:

> One, whose cleare body was so pure, and thin,
> Because it neede disguise no thought within.
> T'was but a through-light scarfe, her minde t'enroule,
> Or exhalation breath'd out from her soule.

[41] Cf. "A Funerall Elegie," ll. 75-76.

> Cloath'd in her Virgin white integrity;
> For mariage, though it doe not stain, doth dye.

Shee, who in th'Art of knowing Heaven, was
  growen
Here upon Earth, to such perfection,
That shee hath, ever since to Heaven shee came,
(In a far fairer print,) but read the same.

(II Ann. 311-314)

Dryden's concern with the *Anniversary* poems extends over half a century, making him the primary exponent of Donnean influence in the Restoration era and beyond. His debt to the *Anniversaries* runs the gamut from very close verbal echoes, through important poetic strategies for praise, to the large significances attaching to the lady eulogized. In all these categories Dryden skillfully reworks the Donnean precedents from his own clearly realized moral and aesthetic point of view, according to which the lady to be praised may be perceived as pattern or as microcosm of a "world" of art, but not in Donne's far-ranging metaphysical terms as that image of God which is the Idea and Form of the world itself.

C. Marvell's *Upon Appleton House*

Though it is a very different kind of poem, emerging from the classical and contemporary generic tradition of the topographical panegyric or country-house poem, Marvell's *Upon Appleton House*[42] manifests in some ways the most imaginative, complex, and significant influence of the *Anniversaries*. With Marvell this is a matter not of local al-

---

[42] Subsequent quotations from the poem are taken from *The Poems and Letters of Andrew Marvell*, ed. H. M. Margoliouth, 2nd ed., 2 vols. (Oxford, 1967), pp. 59-83. Fairfax's retirement from the army occurred in June, 1650, and Marvell's employment as tutor to Maria evidently lasted about two years—from early in 1651 to early in 1653. These facts, together with a topical reference to Davanant's *Gondibert* published in 1651, argue for that year as the probable date of composition for *Appleton House*. It was published posthumously in the first collected edition of Marvell's poems, *Miscellaneous Poems* (1681).

355

lusions or echoes, but of a thorough comprehension and creative reworking of the fundamental symbolic concepts and poetic strategies which Donne had developed for investing a real individual, praised in relation to a real occasion, with profound and metaphysically grounded significance. Don C. Allen has observed that Marvell's description of Maria owes something to Elizabeth Drury, but this is an understatement which does not take us very far; nor, I think, does his suggestion that both these ladies are somehow representations of Divine Wisdom or Sophia.[43] Maria Fairfax, I suggest, is the only worthy seventeenth-century descendant of Elizabeth Drury, having been conceived in the same symbolic mode and bearing much the same range of significance. Moreover, though the poem's texture displays a highly sophisticated assimilation of numerous literary and emblematic sources,[44] the poem is Donnean in many of its large controlling strategies and ordering conceptions. Indeed, I would argue that the "brokenness" and multiplicity of perspectives, whose centrality to the poem's art Miss Colie has brilliantly demonstrated, are made to coalesce into some overarching unity primarily by means of an incarnational/typological symbolism like that developed by Donne. For as Donne undertook to embody the "All" in the individual one, so Marvell endeavored to show how "Things greater are in less contain'd."[45]

Donne's influence is evident in certain of the poetic

[43] Don C. Allen, *Image and Meaning: Metaphoric Traditions in Renaissance Poetry*, rev. ed. (Baltimore, 1968), pp. 191, 220-225. John M. Wallace, *Destiny his Choice: The Loyalism of Andrew Marvell* (London, 1968), pp. 251-254, develops a similar interpretation of Maria. For a full discussion of Elizabeth Drury as a figure for Heavenly Wisdom, see the introduction to Manley's edition of the *Anniversaries*, pp. 20-50.

[44] The rich variety of such influence and traditions, and Marvell's complex and highly original treatment of them, is demonstrated by Rosalie Colie in *My Ecchoing Song: Andrew Marvell's Poetry of Criticism* (Princeton, 1970), pp. 181-305.

[45] *Appleton House*, l. 44.

frames which organize the poem. In the first place, there is the speaker who contemplates the house, the entire Fairfax estate, and Maria, and who learns about himself and about the nature of things as he does so. He speaks both to and for a generalized audience, a "we" who are imagined to be accompanying him on his "progress" through the parts of the estate—though we are often unsure as to when the speaker's experiences are occurring in the present and when his meditations refer to past or remembered experience. The topographical progress is also, of course, a progress of the soul toward understanding of the self and of the human condition; its stages are reflections on the garden, on the history of the Fairfax family, on the scenes in the meadow, on the retreat into the woods, on Maria as epitome and ordering principle for all these elements. And the progress is advanced by means of a retreat from the "dead" world—nature as it is corrupted and returned almost to its first chaos—into nature as it is God's "Book of the Creatures." The speaker's tone is a mixture of explanation and comment to the public audience, and personal reflective meditation. Especially does the striking shift to the first person in the section on the woods—"But I, retiring from the Flood"—designate the experience as intensely personal. Yet it has implications for the listener(s) as well, whom we are never quite allowed to forget and who at the end of the poem are invited "in" to escape the coming darkness. These frames identifying the poem as contemplation and progress, and its speaker as meditator/teacher, are directly in the tradition of the *Anniversary* poems.

Another aspect of *Appleton House*, common enough in pastoral works but probably owing its particular form to the precedent of the *Anniversaries*, is the mixture of panegyric and satire. Donne's poems display patterned alternations of denunciation and panegyric, as the speaker first analyzes the natural world dead in sin, and then the regenerate soul. In Marvell's case the satiric commentary is more often rendered in a wryly ironic tone, and is employed whenever the confusions, disorders, and follies of the world outside are viewed from, or seen in relation to, or as possibly impinging upon, the Fairfax estate, which also embodies the principle of order restored. Such alternation of tones is evident as the speaker contrasts the "unproportion'd dwellings" and the "Marble Crust" usually constructed by man— that "wanton Mote of Dust"—with the house of the Fairfaxes which is "Like Nature, orderly and near."[46] It recurs in the passage on the history of the family, whenever the eloquent praise of the founder, Sir William Fairfax (who stormed the perverted convent), and of his offspring Sir Thomas Fairfax (who was to "fight through all the *Universe;/ And with successive Valour try/ France, Poland,* either *Germany*";),[47] alternates with witty ridicule of the foolish nuns who vainly strive to prevent this noble destiny:

> Some to the Breach against their Foes
> Their *Wooden Saints* in vain oppose.
> Another bolder stands at push
> With their old *Holy-Water Brush.*
> While the disjointed *Abbess* threads
> The gingling Chain-shot of her *Beads.*
> But their lowd'st Cannon were their Lungs;
> And sharpest Weapons were their Tongues.[48]

The tonal contrast recurs again as the modest and wholly defensive posture of the Fairfax military garden of flowers is seen in relation to the aggressive stance of "proud *Cawood Castle,*" which manifests in stone the "Ambition of its *Prelate* great."[49] The tonal complexity of the harvest-cum-battle scene in the meadow is achieved in other ways. The folly, distress, and disorder of war are conveyed though the discrepancy between the harvest events and what they suggest as emblems of war—Bloody *Thestylis,* the massacred grass, the carved rail, the meadows "quilted ore" with bodies (of hay), the pitchfork-pillaging of the women, the

---

[46] *Appleton House,* ll. 21-22, 26.
[47] *Ibid.,* ll. 242-244.   [48] *Ibid.,* ll. 249-256.   [49] *Ibid.,* ll. 363-366.

newly-levelled space which is either like the *tabula rasa* before the creation of the animals, or the bullring before the bulls enter for their bloody adventure. There is nothing in the *Anniversaries* remotely like this tonal layering of whimsy and terror in a single scene or passage; it is quite Marvell's own technique. But he returns to the Donnean method again in setting forth an exalted panegyric of Maria as the epitome of beauty, law, and harmony, and then promptly contrasting it with corrupt womankind:

> Go now fond Sex that on your Face
> Do all your useless Study place,
> Nor once at Vice your Brows dare knit
> Lest the smooth Forehead wrinkled sit:
> Yet your own Face shall at you grin,
> Through the Black-bag of your Skin;
> When *knowledge* only could have fill'd
> And *Virtue* all those *Furrows till'd*.[50]

Again at the conclusion of the poem the disorder of the great world is satirically observed, and then, with a rapid shift to panegyric, the contrasting paradise of the Fairfax estate is recalled:

> 'Tis not, what once it was, the *World*;
> But a rude heap together hurl'd;
> All negligently overthrown,
> Gulfes, Deserts, Precipices, Stone.
> Your lesser *World* contains the same.
> But in more decent Order tame;
> *You Heaven's Center, Nature's Lap,*
> *And Paradice's only Map*.[51]

More remarkable is Marvell's use of incarnational/typological symbolism, the most striking and most often misunderstood innovation of the *Anniversary* poems. Marvell did not misunderstand it, and adapted it brilliantly to his

[50] *Ibid.*, ll. 729-736.   [51] *Ibid.*, ll. 761-768.

purposes. Donne had undertaken to incarnate or embody in a real girl (Elizabeth Drury) and a real event (her death) the human condition as it is in the realms of nature, grace, and glory: she can bear such significance by reason of her status as regenerate Christian and therefore restored image of God. This status enables her to activate a typological frame of reference also: as image of God she recapitulates the primal innocence; her untimely death recapitulates even as it stems from the death brought upon all of us by original sin; her religious death recapitulates the paradigm of our salvation through Christ, and her goodness in the state of grace is a type (foreshadowing) of the full glorification of our humanity in heaven. This typological framework made for constant ambiguities in regard to time— "Some moneths she hath beene dead (but being dead,/ Measures of times are all determined)/ But long shee'ath beene away, long, long"[52]—which arise out of the tension between the immediate, recapitulating event, and the archetype to which it relates, or the previous type which it repeats.

This, I submit, is also a controlling strategy in *Appleton House*, though Marvell develops the typological dimension much more fully, and exploits with much greater complexity the ambivalences and ambiguities of time which it permits. He has taken a particular estate (Fairfax's Nunappleton) and a real event, the retirement of Fairfax and his family to that estate from the turmoil and moral confusion of the Civil War, and he has perceived in this situation a basis for exploring the realm of nature (pristine and corrupted) and the realm of restored or regenerate nature (i.e., grace). Marvell's genre, the country-house poem, leads him to explore these matters in relation to the social order as well as the individual, so that while Donne's speaker affirms the potential of human restoration only through the repudiation of an utterly corrupt and moribund natural order (since Elizabeth Drury, who might have reordered

[52] I *Ann.* 39-41.

nature, has proved to be subject to natural death), Marvell finds a potential symbol for the reordering of nature and society in the Fairfaxes, and most notably in Maria, who yet lives and will found a family. There is something of this range of significance in Jonson's *Penshurst* but in that estate the adumbrations of the Edenic condition and of the Golden Age are seen to be in stasis, fixed and firm,[53] not located in and affected by the historical process, as they so manifestly are at Nunappleton.

As with Donne's presentation of Elizabeth Drury, Marvell makes the Fairfax estate the symbol for nature as regenerate man is able to order and restore it after the Fall. The history of the family estate and of the contemporary events impinging upon it present a paradigm of the temptation, deception, violence, wanton destruction, and chaotic disintegration which have afflicted God's people throughout history, be they Israelites or Englishmen. The estate images the social order possible for regenerate man to impose upon a fallen world. The house is "natural," designed by Humility, and its narrow door affords practice for entering into "Heavens Gate"; its "Frontispiece of Poor" and "Furniture of Friends" display the physical and spiritual support and nourishment it affords to the larger social community.[54] It is well understood, however, that the estate is not truly Eden restored, nor a stable Penshurst where the Lord "dwells,"[55] but a house of pilgrimage built here,

> Only as for *a Mark of Grace*;
> And for an *Inn*, to entertain
> Its *Lord* a while, but not remain.[56]

In its symbolic mode, *Appleton House*, like the *Anniversary* poems, incarnates universals in particular individuals

[53] See especially ll. 5-6, 25-46, "To Penshurst," *Ben Jonson*, VIII, 93-96.
[54] *Appleton House*, ll. 32, 41, 65-69.
[55] "To Penshurst," l. 102, *Jonson*, VIII, 96.
[56] *Appleton House*, ll. 70-72.

and events. This incarnation is not arbitrary but genuinely symbolic, for within God's providential order typological relationships have been established in which particular histories are seen to be figures of, recapitulations of, archetypal events. In essence, Marvell assimilates the history of the Fairfax family and the topographical features of the Fairfax estate, as well as the experiences of the speaker who is making a progress around the estate, to the course of providential history by showing both speaker and family recapitulating certain biblical situations. They are not antitypes, however, as the speaker of devotional poetry may be when he records the spiritual experiences he enjoys through the New Covenant as far surpassing those of various Old Testament figures: clearly, the personages and events in secular history cannot normally be said to present a higher order of spiritual reality than does the biblical paradigm. Yet the mode may still be termed typological, for the contemporary recapitulations Marvell treats—of the Edenic state, of the Fall, of the wilderness experience with its temptations and wanton destructions, of the Flood with its chaotic disintegration—are seen to be divinely ordered by a Providence which has designed the repetition of the historical experience of the Israelites in that of God's chosen Englishmen.[57]

In one dimension, the history of the house recapitulates the history of mankind. It begins with the tale of a fair and lovely virgin tempted by wily deceivers (the nuns), seduced by them to break faith with her intended betrothed (Fairfax) and to dwell with them in a convent characterized by perversions of nature and religion. She is rescued from captivity in this convent, which epitomizes the perversions of the orders of both nature and grace, by the

[57] This view of the typological dimension of the poem, and the basis for it, is developed in greater detail in my essay, "Typology and Poetry: A Consideration of Herbert, Vaughan, and Marvell," *Wit's Zodiac: Viewpoints for Early Seventeenth-Century Literature*, ed. Earl Miner (Berkeley and Los Angeles, 1973).

founder of the house. With him she establishes a family, which act restores the estate to the good purposes of nature and also reforms religion: it "was no *Religious House* till now."[58] This particular, true history of the Fairfax estate recapitulates and fuses, in a conflation characteristically Marvellian, the event of mankind's first fall through the seduction of Eve by the serpent and her (our) rescue by the Bridegroom, the Second Adam, and also the corruption of nature and religion in the English nation by popery, and their restoration through the Protestant Reformation.

The garden Fairfax established, with its martial formation of flowers and its gardening efforts directed to the weeding of ambition and the tilling of conscience, is the possible garden state after the Fall—which demands a constant readiness for defensive Christian warfare in relation to the five senses (if not the Cinque Ports), as well as a posture of self-defense toward proud and threatening Cawood Castles. And this poses a question: whether this kind of garden state can be maintained in the human community on a broader scale than that of the Fairfax family. There was a time when England herself was garden-like, the "*Paradise of four Seas*," and when "All the Garrisons were Flow'rs."[59] Fairfax had the ability (had conditions been propitious) to restore the nation to such a garden state of regenerate nature, but he chose to restrict his concern to the smaller family community where ambition could certainly be uprooted and conscience tilled—as they could not well be in war-torn, ravaged England where decisions must be made about overthrowing and executing monarchs. Yet it remains an open question whether Fairfax ought not to have continued his efforts in the nation at large:

> And yet their walks one on the Sod
> Who, had it pleased him and *God*,
> Might once have made our Gardens spring
> Fresh as his own and flourishing.[60]

[58] *Appleton House*, l. 280.   [59] *Ibid.*, ll. 323, 332.
[60] *Ibid.*, ll. 345-348.

The harvest scenes viewed in the meadow, "the Abbyss . . . / Of that unfathomable Grass" are emblematic of and are conflated with the bloody events of the English Civil War—the mowing of the grain (all flesh is grass); the sometimes unintentional and sometimes wanton destruction of the creatures living in the grass, high and low alike; the harvest maids (bloody *Thestylis*) turning their pitchforks on the quick rails and pillaging the grain. These scenes are further conflated with and shown to recapitulate the Exodus story, with the Israelites affording a type (recapitulated in the English Puritans and emblematized in the mowers) of the ambivalent condition of sinful man in the wilderness, pressing forward toward some version of the promised land in the wake of divine miracles and human wrongdoings. The harvest scene rings changes on all these ambiguities in the Israelites' story—their miraculous passage through the Red Sea (destroying anything in their path); their widespread slaughter and pillaging of the Pagan tribes (at the Lord's behest); their continued lusting for the flesh and the delicacies they had enjoyed in Egypt—desires which God both satisfied and punished by a rain of quails:

> But bloody *Thestylis*, that waites
> To bring the mowing Camp their Cates,
> Greedy as Kites has trust it up,
> And forthwith means on it to sup:
> And on another quick [rail] She lights,
> And cryes, he call'd us *Israelites*;
> And now, to make his saying true,
> Rails rain for Quails, for Manna Dew.[61]

The razed harvest scene recapitulates both the bare land before God began the creation of animal life, and the bullring at Madrid before the slaughter starts—reflecting at once the social state with all its ambiguities, and the reduction of the social hierarchy to the flat equality contemporary Levellers were imagined to desire. The flooded

---

[61] *Ibid.*, ll. 401-408; see Numbers 9, and discussion in Wallace, *Destiny his Choice*, pp. 246-248.

meadow with all things topsy-turvy and chaotic reflects the utter disintegration of the social and natural order produced by war (whether Israelite or English) and harks back to the chaos produced by the destruction of the whole social order in Noah's Flood. These scenes in their typological allusive character trace a steady decline from the social order possible to regenerate society after the Fall (the English Garden as Promised Land): first there was sinful and embattled Israel in the wilderness; then the levelled but stable world before the creation of any society, animal or human; then the Flood which reduced all order to a chaos reminiscent of the first Chaos which preceded all creation.

From this Chaos/Flood the speaker takes refuge in the "Sanctuary of the Wood," his "green, yet growing Ark"[62]—emblem of salvation in that it permits a vision of created nature as the Book of God, the natural order uncorrupted by man. As such it holds a mystic key to the histories and events of the speaker's experience, could he but fully understand it in the light *Mosaick*, which is both the "various light" refracted by nature and the inspired light by which Moses wrote of the first creation and the natural order before the Fall:

> Out of these scatter'd *Sibyls* Leaves
> Strange *Prophecies* my Phancy weaves:
> And in one History consumes,
> Like *Mexique Paintings*, all the *Plumes*.
> What *Rome, Greece, Palestine*, ere said
> I in this light *Mosaick* read.
> Thrice happy he who, not mistook,
> Hath read in *Natures mystick Booke*.[63]

What the speaker reads in the woods are emblems of order in nature: the stock doves as emblems of marital harmony and society; the herons that pay appropriate tribute to their Lord; the hewel (woodpecker) who fells hollow oaks but leaves sound ones untouched, and further enacts natural justice by destroying the "Traitor worm" that hollowed out

[62] *Appleton House*, ll. 482, 484.   [63] *Ibid.*, ll. 577-584.

the oak; in nature (if not in England) the royal oak itself is content to fall, as if apprehending its own hollow condition and satisfied that justice is done to the worm. The speaker attempts a complete fusion with this uncorrupted natural order, hoping to be separated wholly from the corrupt world and kept "safe." He makes himself utterly passive before nature, and gives himself over unreservedly to the knowledge of it; he supposes himself an "inverted tree," he "languishes" with ease on the velvet moss, he thinks himself safe and strong behind the trees. But he does not have the ability to sustain this state, for he is postlapsarian man, not an inhabitant of pristine nature, and nature in and of itself cannot save him. The imagery of violence, imprisonment, and crucifixion through which he urges nature to restrain him by force from the world's evils and disorders indicates that this is no solution for him, for us, for he is not pure and just as a tree or a hewel. In this context the crucifixion image itself reminds us that only through another crucifixion, above nature, not this imagined one in and by nature, is man and the human world restored to order:

> Bind me ye *Woodbines* in your 'twines,
> Curle me about ye gadding *Vines*,
> And Oh so close your Circles lace,
> That I may never leave this Place;
> But, lest your Fetters prove too weak,
> Ere I your Silken Bondage break,
> Do you, *O Brambles*, chain me too,
> And courteous *Briars* nail me through.[64]

Then, as abruptly and mysteriously as it sustained the cataclysm of the flood and the reduction to chaos, nature is righted and restored to order. The meadows are yet more fresh and green; the river, regaining its banks, orders and unifies the meadows by reflecting and therefore holding all things within itself, as in a crystal mirror. The speaker is still utterly passive in relation to this nature which manifests such overwhelming potentialities for destruction and

[64] *Ibid.*, ll. 609-616.

restoration; now he blends himself with the newly restored harmony as a compleat angler lazily fishing on the river banks in a condition of contented irresponsibility. It is upon this scene that Maria appears, providing a clarification for the speaker and "us" of the stance which man should properly take toward the natural order.

Maria is the true descendent of Elizabeth Drury. She is not Athena, Heavenly Wisdom, or Sophia, but the twelve-year-old daughter of the Fairfaxes, the pupil of Marvell who had a gift for languages and excellent matrimonial prospects. She is the culminating principle of order in the poem, and the appropriate force to resolve the issues of the poem, not a girl arbitrarily invested with abstract meanings. What she presents or incarnates within herself—as innocent young maiden, as regenerate Christian soul, as image of God restored—is what Elizabeth Drury presented: the Form of the world, which man truly is when considered as image of God.

She has therefore the power to enhance the order of nature itself, for even unfallen nature only attained an inferior version of the harmony which man—considered as image of God—displays. In these terms the hyperbolic praise of Maria is appropriate, for as regenerate Christian bearing the image of God she recapitulates that first ordering power which man in his pristine innocence had in relation to nature:

> Tis *She* that to these Gardens gave
> That wondrous Beauty which they have;
> *She* streightness on the Woods bestows;
> To *Her* the Meadow sweetness owes;
> Nothing could make the River be
> So Chrystal-pure but only *She*;
> *She* yet more Pure, Sweet, Streight, and Fair,
> Then Gardens, Woods, Meads, Rivers are.
>
> Therefore what first *She* on them spent,
> They gratefully again present.[65]

[65] *Ibid.*, ll. 689-698.

Accordingly as she walks forth, "loose" nature, responding to that principle in man which first ordered all things, "recollects" itself from its disposition to carelessness or disorder and takes on its highest perfection: the sun goes more carefully to bed, the halcyon comes forth to calm "admir'ing nature," the air and stream and fishes are charmed, indeed "vitrified" by her presence. If this response of nature in some ways recalls nature's response to the event of Christ's Incarnation as described in Milton's ode *On the Morning of Christ's Nativity*, and if the perfection of the ordering as well as the flames and the vitrification suggest the Millennium established by Christ, that is because the redemption of man and nature effected by Christ the true Image of God gives regenerate man (also an image of God) some power again to order nature. Maria's power to do so is specifically attributed to "her *Flames*, in *Heaven* try'd."[66]

In her morning walk through the garden, emblematic of her extreme youth and innocence, she had not yet assumed this role. The flowers paid the tribute of volleys of fragrance to their "Governour" and "Governess" but paid none to Maria, who "seems with the Flow'rs a Flow'r to be."[67] But in her evening walk, emblematic of a condition of mature responsibility, this has radically changed: not only the flowers but all nature recognize her as their governor and ordering principle. Her evening walk is described in imagery of surprising activity: she is as a "new-born Comet" drawing a train through the sky; she "rushes" through the evening, her effect is as flames.[68] Such force, manifesting man's proper relation to nature as its active ordering principle, makes a striking counterpoise to the speaker's passivity and brings new insight to that lazy fisherman who has hitherto attempted simply to escape from human corruption by fusing with nature as another tree or bird. Maria does not disdain the beauties of nature that urge themselves upon her; she accepts their homage, but with the clear understanding

---

[66] *Ibid.*, l. 687.   [67] *Ibid.*, ll. 297-302.   [68] *Ibid.*, ll. 682-688.

that true beauty resides in a wisdom higher than nature's. It is this regenerate wisdom in the order of grace which is the source of her power:

> For *She*, to higher Beauties rais'd,
> Disdains to be for lesser prais'd.
> *She* counts her Beauty to converse
> In all the Languages as *hers*;
> Nor yet in those *her self* imployes
> But for the *Wisdome*, not the *Noyse*;
> Nor yet that *Wisdome* would affect,
> But as tis *Heavens Dialect*.[69]

Maria not only accepts the human responsibility to enhance the order of nature, but also to order corrupt society. She deals effectively with all those wanton suitors whose "artillery" of profane love is trained against her—Cupid's whole arsenal of tears, sighs, true praises, and feigned complying innocence.[70] An antitype of the Virgin Thwaites, she is not seduced as that Eve-figure was by false or perverted views of nature and religion, but awaits instead the natural unfolding of "Destiny" which will "find a *Fairfax* for our *Thwaites*,"[71] and so entail the estate in a continuing line of goodness. Accordingly, as antitype and fulfillment of the seduced Thwaites, Maria recapitulates the role of Mary, the Virgin-Mother who was the antitype of the seduced Eve, and who was in a unique sense the bearer of the Image of God, the supreme creative and restorative force. As manifestation of such power, as Form of the world, Elizabeth Drury by dying had both revealed and caused the death of natural order. But the vibrantly alive Maria, who will marry and so provide for the continuation of the social community of the Fairfax estate (that "*Domestick Heaven*" of *Fairfax* and the starry *Vere*),[72] is a source of hope. As an active power in nature and society she may secure some extension into the public realm of the possibilities of re-

[69] *Ibid.*, ll. 705-712.   [70] *Ibid.*, ll. 713-720.   [71] *Ibid.*, ll. 744, 748.
[72] *Ibid.*, ll. 722-724.

stored and regenerate nature—in the social microcosm of the family community at least, though perhaps not in the nation as a whole: nothing further is said about that. The final contrast is between the disordered macrocosm of the world in the condition of disorder the Fall has brought it to—a "rude heap together hurl'd;/ All negligently over-thrown"—and the "Map" or reiteration of paradise which, by reason of the ordering principle in regenerate man, the Fairfax estate is. It is *"Heaven's Center, Nature's Lap./ And Paradice's only Map."*[73]

The "progress" is brought to an end by Maria's departure and the coming of evening. As the salmon fishers prepare to go home, their boats on their heads like shoes, we are invited to recall the Antipodes where conditions are the flat reverse of those we know, the paradoxical state of men as "rational *Amphibii*," and the existence of the "dark *Hemisphere*" which slowly encroaches upon and (temporarily but regularly) blots out from sight the harmony of man and nature which we have seen.[74] It is a reminder, conveyed wittily and with Marvell's vast awareness of paradox and ambiguity, of how tenuously held are all visions of human order, even that incarnated in the Fairfax estate and epitomized in Maria.

Clearly, the "Idea" of Elizabeth Drury was, in a sense not intended by the text, the "first originall" of many fair and not-so-fair copies, and Donne's praises of her did indeed raise up a numerous progeny. The line extends from Elizabeth Dutton (1613) to Eleonora (1692) and even beyond, to the "Fair Maiden" whose death Dryden celebrated in 1700. But the nearest and fairest of all the fair copies was Marvell's Maria Fairfax, for she alone inherited the metaphysical nature and the broad symbolic dimensions of that great "Idea of a Woman."

[73] *Ibid.*, ll. 761-768.   [74] *Ibid.*, ll. 774-775.

Donne's works are indexed under his name except for the *Anniversaries*, which are analyzed under that title.
Funeral sermons, letters, and elegies are indexed under author's name and subject's name.

379

Library of Congress Cataloging in Publication Data

Lewalski, Barbara Kiefer, 1931-
    Donne's Anniversaries and the poetry of praise.

    Includes bibliographical references.
    1. Donne, John, 1572-1631—Influence. 2. Donne, John,
1572-1631. An anatomy of the world. 3. Donne, John, 1572-
1631. Of the progres of the soule. 4. Elegiac poetry, English
—History and criticism.
I. Title.
PR2248.L48   821'.3   72-14027
ISBN 0-691-06258-7